DATE DUE

APR 2 0 1985 BRLS

APR 3 0 1985 BRLS   APR 0 2 1985 RET

APR 3 0 1985 RET

SEP 1 8 1986   BIRD   SEP 1 8 1986 RET

JAN 1 9 1989   DEC 1 7 1988

MAY 29 1990   JUL 11 1996

MAY 2 1990 RET

PERSONALITY MEASUREMENT
An Introduction

PERSONALITY

MEASUREMENT

An Introduction

BENJAMIN KLEINMUNTZ
Department of Psychology
Carnegie University

1967

THE DORSEY PRESS · Homewood, Illinois

First Printing, April, 1967

Library of Congress Catalog Card No. 67–18564

Printed in the United States of America

To My Parents

A college teacher usually writes a text because he believes existing ones do not serve his needs or because none exist for the area in which he is instructing. This book is no exception. At the present time there are few texts available which cover exclusively the important area of personality measurement. In view of the rapid proliferation of personality tests, and the corresponding controversies associated with their development and use, such a textbook is needed.

The main intent of this book is to fulfill that need by presenting a balanced compendium of the major personality measurement procedures. Courses for which this book could serve as a supplementary source include those that deal with the psychology of personality, tests and measurements, abnormal psychology, personality adjustment, clinical psychology, and mental hygiene as well as a variety of educational psychology and counseling courses where it is desirable to have students familiarize themselves with personality measurement approaches.

For use as a comprehensive text in an introductory personality measurement course at the undergraduate or elementary graduate level, this book should be supplemented liberally by readings of a primary source nature. The suggestions for further reading at the end of each chapter should be helpful in assisting instructors to plan such a course.

My own practice in teaching a course called "Theory and Measurement of Personality" has been to use Hall and Lindzey's *Theories of Personality* (1957) for the first portion, and to refer students to the chapters on personality measurement in the leading texts on psychological testing (Anastasi, 1961; Cronbach, 1960; Freeman, 1962; Nunnally, 1959; Thorndike & Hagen, 1961) for the second portion of the course. Although this latter practice provided students with adequate information about personality measurement, the need was nevertheless often expressed for a volume that assembles material in one place.

Consonant with my desire to keep this book brief, a number of arbitrary decisions about inclusions and exclusions had to be made.

One of these decisions was to omit discussion of the following areas, all of which can be properly considered within the domain of personality: ability, aptitude, attitude, interest, and value testing. Another decision was to refrain from oversimplifying concepts and issues merely for the sake of presenting a wide range of topics; therefore, the sampling of research studies and the selection of areas for discussion are limited. Undoubtedly the selection of topics and illustrative studies reflect my biases about the subject matter at hand. But in this regard and in my critical evaluations of techniques and approaches I have assumed throughout that readers may find it more useful to disagree with my opinions than to try to find out what my opinions are.

Serving to complicate the task of writing a book of this sort, was the fact that it has grown out of my experience in teaching this subject matter to a diverse student audience. At times my audience has consisted of sophomore, junior, or senior undergraduates with no more psychology background than an introductory course; and at other times my students have been elementary and high-school teachers, guidance counselors, social workers, or graduate students with little or no psychological sophistication. Aside from differences arising from their varied backgrounds in formal psychological instruction, their motivations for taking a personality course differ. Typically, the undergraduate is interested in the personal relevance of the subject matter. The school teacher or the professional worker, on the other hand, focuses his attention on experienced or anticipated needs to use certain skills in interpreting personality test scores or to develop competence in evaluating the usefulness of particular measurement approaches.

The attempt to meet these diverse needs in one book is difficult and it called for a decision to distinguish information valuable to the *expert* from that which is of value to the *user*. Accordingly, topics and issues essential for conducting research or constructing personality tests (e.g., the expert) have been omitted or passed over lightly in favor of information that is essential for intelligent understanding of the subject of personality measurement (e.g., user knowledge). This distinction, to be sure, has necessitated limited development of several essential concepts and approaches, but it is my hope that what has emerged is an introductory personality measurement text that serves to sensitize the student to some of the issues and debates currently taking place in the area.

Those readers who would like to go beyond the material presented, especially those who are in advanced classes and whose needs approximate closely those of the expert, are again urged to supplement this text. They may go directly to the sources mentioned in the annoted lists at the end of each chapter, or they may consult the extensive bibliography at the end of this book. The bibliography was compiled to include all the references used in the text, as well as books consulted, but not cited in the writing of the manuscript.

For any success this book may have in communicating its subject matter, I am indebted to several anonymous reviewers who expressed their opinions about earlier versions of this manuscript, and to Professors Donald W. Fiske and Alfred E. Hall who read the manuscript in its entirety and offered many incisive and valuable criticisms. A debt of gratitude is also due my former teachers at the University of Minnesota, under whose influence I have absorbed much of what I know about the subject matter at hand. Especially noteworthy among them are Professors Kenneth E. Clark, Starke R. Hathaway, James J. Jenkins, Paul E. Meehl, William Schofield, and the late Ephraim Rosen.

I should also like to acknowledge my appreciation to Mrs. Betty H. Boal, whose patience, even temper, human relations and secretarial skills contributed to the completion of this manuscript.

Finally, to my wife Dalia, and our three sons Don, Ira and Oren— the real victims of my venture into authordom—I am deeply grateful. It was not easy, I am certain, to live with a husband and father whose replies to most mundane demands consisted of such well-rehearsed prose as, "In the study of personality. . . ." "It is probably safe to assume. . . ." "The measurement point of view in the study of personality. . . ."

BENJAMIN KLEINMUNTZ

Pittsburgh, Pennsylvania
March, 1967

PART I

Introduction

CONSIDERATION

CHAPTER 1

THE MEASUREMENT OF PERSONALITY

In the study of personality, everyone is his own expert. Each of us develops skill in "sizing up" people because our whole lives are spent in contact with others. Lack of friction in our relationships with others proves our skill in sizing them up. The neighbor's ability to get along with the family next door, the parent's ease in relating to a child, the teacher's knack for motivating students, and the salesman's success with prospective buyers are proof of their skill in understanding the actions and reactions of other human beings.

However, each of these persons is a participant in a fairly complex process; and although each is cast in a different role and faces different kinds of problems as neighbor, parent, teacher, or salesman, all have at least one thing in common when they size up others—they are engaged in some sort of *personality measurement.* True, this is measurement only in the broadest sense, and it is implicit in their activities rather than intentional. Nevertheless, it is clear that the neighbor is interested in how much cooperativeness or friendliness he can expect from persons next door; the teacher makes comparisons of students' motivations; and the businessman or professional makes estimates of his associates' honesty, dependability, or needs. Just because this process is so taken for granted in everyday living, it is difficult to move forward from common-sense notions to the measurement point of view.

THE NEED FOR MEASUREMENT

The psychologist has adopted the measurement point of view in the study of personality because he has a relatively greater need to

3

express his observations in terms of quantities rather than words. Consider the difference in precision between the words the ordinary layman uses to describe fish sizes ("big," "enormous," "colossal," and so on) and the classification of these fish by scientists in terms of numerical indices of size and weight. Similarly, the psychologist who studies personality is interested in more subtle discriminations, and correspondingly in more precise descriptions, than an everyday vocabulary of personality trait sizes would permit. He would like to know, for example, how much of a trait manifests itself in an individual and how many particular traits are present. Often he is called upon to compare one person with another or to compare him with some group standard; or he may wish to compare the characteristics of a person with his characteristics at a prior time. All of these processes—i.e., determining degree, amount, and comparison—involve measurement operations. The difference, then, between the layman's approach to the study of personality and that of the psychologist is the latter's relatively greater need to express his estimates in terms of quantities rather than words. Whereas most people correct their errors in personality judgment as they go along, the psychologist is frequently called upon to base irreversible decisions about individuals on his measurements. He is not often provided the opportunity to revise his personality judgments as he goes along, and hence his need for greater precision.

Take the case, for instance, of a person who presents himself at a mental hygiene clinic and complains of dizziness and constant worry. His condition will usually be described by the layman in such vague commonsense terms as "nervous," "restless," and "having a mental breakdown." The psychologist will not find these terms adequate, for he must answer specific questions about this person: Should his condition be classified as "mental disorder" A or B? What degree of disease A or B does he display? How have persons with similar symptoms been treated? Measurement is needed to answer any of these questions, and depending on the answers to some of them, the psychologist must decide whether to recommend further tests, specific treatments, assignment to a particular psychotherapist, hospitalization, or some combination of these. Many of these decisions depend on a complex interaction of factors, but personality measurements—or more specifically, certain personality measurement techniques—are involved in making them and in answering the above questions.

THE NATURE OF MEASUREMENT

Measurement has been described as the assignment of numbers according to certain agreed-upon rules. The general formulation of different kinds of rules, and correspondingly, several *levels* of meas-

TABLE 1–1

Levels of Measurement

Level	Function	Arithmetic Operation	Example
Nominal	Numerals used to label objects, places or persons.	Can count number of cases labeled in a certain category, or the number of categories labeled, but numerals cannot be manipulated.	
Ordinal	To rank-order objects or persons.	Statements of greater than, equal to, or less than, and all operations comparing ranks.	A is greater than B, and B is greater than C, therefore A is greater than C.
Interval	To compare measures or scores of persons.	Permits comparisons about extent of differences between measures.	On test X, person P obtained a score 20 points higher than person R.
Ratio	To specify precise relationships among objects, things or persons.	It has an absolute zero point and therefore all manner of arithmetic operations are permissible.	Person P, whose height is 78 inches, is twice as tall as person R who is 39 inches tall.

urement that have been most useful to psychologists, is the system suggested by S. S. Stevens (1951).

In the Stevens system, which is illustrated in Table 1–1, measurements which follow different sets of rules are referred to as measurements on four different *scales*. Each scale represents a different level of quantification of the variable under consideration and permits different arithmetical procedures.

LEVELS OF MEASUREMENT

The first, or lowest level of quantification, the *nominal* scale, involves nothing more than the assignment of numbers as labels or tags to identify objects, entities, concepts, terms, or persons. Where this kind of scale applies, numbers are used to name the categories into which objects are classified. These categories have the relationship of being different from one another, but there is no arithmetical relationship between the numbers. Thus a person, or a group of persons, may be labeled "dependable," "punctual," "honest," or "deceitful," and these traits may be assigned the numerals[1] 1, 2, 3, or 4; but these numbers can never be added, subtracted, multiplied, or divided.

Use of the nominal scale, however, does not preclude the use of other arithmetical operations. For example, it is permissible to count the number of cases in each class and the number of classes identified by the numerals. Thus, in a study of the relationship between personality and hospitalization, it is possible to establish some criterion on the basis of which to classify people according to personality types, and then by counting, it is possible to determine whether a given type is hospitalized more frequently than other types.

The next level of measurement, the *ordinal* scale, defines the relative positions of objects or individuals with regard to the characteristic being measured. The psychologist is limited to statements of "greater than," "equal to," and "less than," and no statement is permitted about the size of the difference between positions. An ordinal scale has been aptly described (Selltiz *et al.*, 1964) as resembling an elastic yardstick which is being stretched unevenly, and the scale positions as indicated by the numbers on the stick are in a clearly defined order, but the numbers do not provide any definite indication of the distance between any two points on the stick.

The meaning of an ordinal scale can be illustrated by considering the situation in which persons are ranked with respect to the scores they received on a test measuring, let us say, "anxiety."[2] Instead of

---

[1] They need not be assigned numerals (Weyl, 1949). The important point to keep in mind is the classificatory nature of this level of measurement.

[2] Anxiety is similar in many respects to fear, except that in the latter state the feared object is identifiable, whereas in anxiety the person cannot identify such an object.

being satisfied with simply measuring persons as either "anxious" or "nonanxious"—as might be done on the nominal scale—these persons are assigned numerals representing their relative scores on the anxiety variable. The numeral 1 may be assigned to the most anxious person, 2 to the next most anxious, and so on down the line. The fact that the most anxious person may have earned a score that is considerably higher than the next two lesser anxious individuals is not taken into consideration in ordinal measurements. Accordingly, the common arithmetical operations of addition, subtraction, multiplication, and division are not appropriate. However, statistical procedures based on ranks can be used, and it is permissible to determine, for example, whether persons who rank high on anxiety also rank high on some other variable such as cooperativeness, achievement, and so forth.

At the third level of measurement—the *interval* scale—it is possible, in addition to determining relationships of greater, equal, or less, to make statements about distances between points. What distinguishes interval from ordinal measurement is that the former, by virtue of having equal units (or intervals) between points on a scale, permits comparisons about distances between two things or persons. Addition and subtraction are possible on the interval scale, but because these scales have no real zero point—that is, the zero point on such a scale is arbitrary and assigned as a matter of convention—division and multiplication are not allowable procedures.

The centigrade and Fahrenheit scales for measuring temperature are well-known examples of the use of interval scales in physical measurement. Everyone is familiar with the fact that 20° F. is warmer than 10° F.—and that 0° F. does not mean absence of warmth (or cold). Similarly, in psychological measurement, it is possible to compare two persons in terms of scores they earned on, let us say, an anxiety scale. If person A scores higher than B, it is meaningful to say how much more anxious is A than B, but it is not legitimate to express these anxiety scores in ratios. Thus if A's and B's scores are 80 and 40 respectively, it is permissible to specify that A is considerably more anxious than B, but it is not correct to state that B is only half as anxious as A. And if on some other test occasion, A scores 40 and B scores 0, it is permissible to say that A's and B's relative positions with regard to amount of anxiety have remained the same, but it is meaningless to say that B has no (or zero) anxiety. Such statements as the latter, or assertions about ratios between persons' scores, are not permissible because they presuppose an exact zero point.

The *ratio* scale is the highest level of measurement. It has an absolute zero point, and consequently, all arithmetical operations and all statistical techniques based on these scales are permissible. Ratio scales permit statements of relationships that are impossible with any of the other scales. On the ratio scale all numerical values conform to the scale of cardinal numbers—i.e., the scale used when counting such things as people, dollars, variables in an experiment, and so on. In the use of such a scale of cardinal numbers, with its zero point fixed, zero means "complete absence" of the dimension in question.

Although this level of measurement is rarely achieved in psychology, it is probably the most familiar among the previously mentioned scales. All common physical dimensions—height, weight, volume—are measured this way. It is meaningful to say that when one person weighs 250 pounds and another 125 pounds, the latter is half as heavy as the first. If a particular length, weight, or volume is given, it is only a matter of simple arithmetic to determine exactly twice, three times, or any multiple of that particular value.

In personality measurement, most numerical findings are expressed in terms of the ordinal or interval scales. What does this mean practically? It means that the limitations that accompany such measurement must be recognized and observed. The student who is familiar with the restrictions imposed, as well as the procedures permitted, by these levels of measurement should be able to obtain a better understanding of some of the problems and pitfalls of personality measurement that are discussed in subsequent chapters.

DIMENSIONS OF PERSONALITY

The description and evaluation of personality measurement techniques could probably proceed satisfactorily without defining carefully what is meant by personality. In the course of our discussion throughout this book, a tentative eclectic picture will emerge that will identify the major personality dimensions of interest to psychologists. But it may be well to consider the matter briefly

before detailed discussion of measurement techniques is undertaken.

Definitions of Personality

Generally, psychologists are agreed that the term *personality*
refers to the *unique organization of factors which characterizes an
individual and determines his pattern of interaction with the environment*. More colloquially, personality is an individual's total
makeup—the type of person that he is. To the psychologist, personality has no positive ("he's got lots of personality") or negative
connotations. It is neutral.

Psychologists are not agreed, however, on such questions as the
following: How does personality develop? What are the effects of
early experiences on personality? Is there a critical period in
personality development? How do heredity and environment affect personality? What is the influence of sensory deprivation on
personality? Nor do psychologists agree on ways of talking about
personality. Thus, Freud had one particular way of explaining personality, coined special terminology to describe it, and formulated a
particular set of principles about its organization, and other well-
known students of personality such as Adler, Rank, Horney, Reik,
Fromm, and Rogers offered alternatives to Freud's system. This
book is not the appropriate place to list the details and evaluate the
particulars of the numerous definitions and theories of personality.
That task has already been carried out in various ways (Bischof,
1964; Hall and Lindzey, 1957). All that is really required here
is an identification of the dimensions of interest to psychologists
who measure personality.

Psychopathology

Many of the theories and measurement techniques of personality
originated in actual clinical work. Freud, Adler, and Reik, to name
just a few of the aforementioned theorists, were clinicians first and
personality theorists only later. They were primarily concerned
with the causes and treatment of psychological disturbance, or

psychopathology; they considered normal behavior as a less severe manifestation of the same process that operates in mental illness.

The basic classification of psychopathology now in use divides mental disorders into three major groupings: *psychosis, psycho-neurosis* (sometimes abbreviated as "neurosis"), and *sociopathic personality disturbance.* The thought processes of individuals diagnosed as psychotic are usually sufficiently distorted and bizarre that most persons around them tend to recognize that something is wrong. More specifically, the most common psychosis, schizophrenia, is characterized by delusions (false and persistent beliefs in one's greatness or that one is being persecuted), hallucinations (hearing or seeing things that are not there), withdrawn behavior, irrational thinking, unusual gesturing, and a "flattening" of affect (inability to respond with emotion).

Psychoneurosis, the second major grouping of psychopathology, is not as debilitating as psychosis. It is characterized by symptoms of irrational fear, obsessive thoughts that recur persistently, and complaints of physical ailments that have no identifiable physiological basis (tiredness, weakness, back pains, headaches, paralysis, and even losing the use of certain organs and limbs). Although this form of personality disorder is sometimes thought too mild for hospitalization, the subjective discomfort to the person could be considerable. In sharp contrast to schizophrenic individuals, who often believe they are well, psychoneurotics are very much aware of the fact—and speak of it incessantly—that they are emotionally disturbed.

The third large grouping of psychopathology consists of the sociopathic personality disorders. Persons classified in this group are characterized by antisocial (sometimes asocial) behavior—that is, behavior that is in opposition to (or disregards) the mores of society. Among many other characteristics that have been used to describe these persons (see especially, Cleckley, 1955), are the following few: undependability, pathological lying, ability to charm, intelligence, untrustworthiness, and inability to profit from experience.

The most popular personality tests of the past 30 years grew out of the need to diagnose or detect individuals whose behavior patterns were psychopathological. Such personality tests as the Minnesota Multiphasic Personality Inventory (MMPI) and the Rorschach demonstrated their usefulness as diagnostic instruments for this purpose, and thus became increasingly popular measurement tools for the psychologist.

The Need Approach to Personality

Sigmund Freud, the founder of the psychoanalytic[3] movement, proposed a theory of unconscious motivation. In this theory, he postulated an unconscious mind as a repository for many unwanted instincts, ideas, feelings, and desires that individuals *repress* (or disavow). However, the person is not entirely free of these unacceptable thoughts because, according to Freud, the impulses that result from their repression reappear in fantasies, dreams, symptoms, and generally in many facets of that person's behavior. These reactions to repression, as a matter of fact, were considered by Freud to have particular significance in throwing light on the individual's motives and goals.

As a result of the influence of Freud, many personality theorists came to view man in terms of the motives that direct his behavior. Among the best known of the theories that stressed the need—or motivational—approach to the study of personality, is the one developed by H. A. Murray (1938). Both as founder of a personality test—the Thematic Apperception Test (TAT), to be discussed later in this book—and as an early leader in personality theory and research, H. A. Murray cataloged a list of *needs,* their definitions, and ways of assessing their strength.

These needs—some of which are presented below in Table 1–2—are still useful to psychologists and exemplify an attempt to describe behavior in terms of its direction. Murray also emphasized that the understanding of behavior must include an analysis of environmental pressures, or *press* as he calls them, exerted on the individual. These press are also presented in Table 1–2.

Normality

The psychologist has a difficult time describing the so-called "normal" person. Usually he thinks of a normal person as one who does not exhibit some of the symptoms of psychopathology, thus defining health by a process of elimination. This is not peculiar to

---

[3] *Psychoanalysis* sometimes refers both to the theory of personality and the method of psychological treatment proposed by Freud.

TABLE 1-2

Selected List of Murray's Needs and Press

Need	Brief Description
n Achievement	To strive hard for success. To get ahead in business, to persuade or lead a group, to create something.
n Aggression	To fight. To hate. To avenge an injury with excessive brutality. Sadism. To break, smash, burn, or destroy.

Press	Brief Description
p Affiliation	The hero has several friends or sociable companions. He is a member of a group.
p Dominance	Someone tries to force the hero to do something. A person tries to influence the hero.

the personality measurement area. Medicine was also founded on pathology, and if there had been no physical ills the science of medicine would probably not have developed.

Contemporary approaches to personality measurement, much like present-day medicine, have become concerned with more than just pathology. There have been serious efforts to approach normality on its own terms. Perhaps more than any psychologist, Gordon W. Allport (1953, 1961) has been responsible for the renewed interest in normality per se. He has stressed throughout the years that normality and abnormality are not on a continuum; and Allport has maintained that the proper study of normal personality should consist of observations and inquiry into the behavior, conscious motives, and purposes of normals. Tests discussed later in this book, such as the Edwards Personal Preference Schedule, Strong's Vocational Interest Blank, and the California Psychological Inventory are instruments relevant to the study of normal personality, and they were not designed to identify psychopathology.

The Self-Actualizing Personality

A direct outgrowth of the psychologist's interest in normal personality development has been the study of individuals who behave with unusual effectiveness. The best example of this approach is the work of Abraham Maslow (1954, 1962), who has criticized psychologists for accepting the notion that social motives result from conditioning in relation to drives like hunger, thirst, and sex. His focus is on "peak experiences," and he believes that the emphasis on psychopathology leads to a negative conception of man. Maslow views man as taking active steps toward *actualization,* or self-fulfillment, and he is less interested in conflict, misery, and pathology than in psychological health.

Accordingly, Maslow has urged that psychologists study unusually effective persons more extensively than other types. He notes that these exceptional people are difficult to find, but that historical and personal documents of and about them (i.e., Lincoln, Jefferson, Einstein) could help identify some of the important distinguishing personality characteristics. In his search for the healthy and self-actualizing individual, Maslow has studied some famous contemporary persons (for example, Eleanor Roosevelt) and even his own acquaintances. The characteristics of self-actualizing persons that set them apart from ordinary citizens, according to Maslow, include realistic attitude, acceptance of self and others, spontaneity, and problem-centeredness rather than false idealism, self-interest, autonomy, and independence.

Personality in Terms of Traits and Types

Finally, regardless of the particular theory of personality espoused, and independent of one's interest in psychopathology or normality and self-actualization, there is an extensive vocabulary available in the English language to describe persons. In everyday contacts with people, such words as kind, happy, resourceful, aggressive, and dependent are used to describe others. As a matter of fact, nearly 18,000 words have been found in the English language which describe human characteristics and differentiate people from one another (Allport and Odbert, 1936). The systematic use of such descriptive terms, called the *trait* approach, is one of the psychologist's most common ways of talking about personality.

Psychologists also classify persons into types on the basis of patterns of traits. Thus an introvert would be a type of person who characteristically removes himself from worldly contacts, possesses an inner-directedness, and whose intellectual manner is reflective and ruminative. An extrovert, on the other hand, is a type of person who is likely to possess a high degree of spontaneity, outgoingness, and objectivity. This dichotomous classification of persons into introverts and extroverts was first proposed by the Swiss psychiatrist, Carl Jung (1928).

It is important for the student of personality to recognize that when psychologists describe personality in terms of traits or types, they may be using identical terminology but may have completely different theories as to what traits exist and how these traits are organized within the individual. Equally important is awareness of the fact that the same trait or type names are sometimes used to describe entirely different behavior characteristics. This apparent paradox will be discussed in more detail in Chapter 3, where some technical problems in personality testing are examined.

PERSONALITY MEASUREMENT SETTINGS AND PURPOSES

Many professional psychologists in various applied and research settings are directly involved in the measurement of personality. These test situations, which are presented in Table 1–3, can be

TABLE 1–3

Personality Test Settings and Purposes

Purpose	Setting	Function
Diagnosis	Mental hygiene clinic or psychiatric hospital.	Classification of person into clinical type or treatment group.
Counseling	Clinic, hospital, or counseling center.	To obtain personality assessment before, during, and/or after counseling sessions.
Personnel selection	Industry, government, school, military, or training program.	To aid in determining suitability for proposed assignment.
Personality research	Any or all of the above settings.	Before-and-after treatment evaluations. To assess effects of experimental manipulations. To ascertain the adequacy of the measurement tool itself.

broadly described under four headings: clinical diagnosis, counseling and psychotherapy, personnel selection, and personality
research.

Clinical Diagnosis

Clinical diagnosis calls for personality measurement in the
context of a mental hygiene clinic or hospital and involves classification of patients into clinical types. The psychologist ascertains
the extent and nature of a patient's personality disorder and prescribes some form of appropriate treatment. The problems of clinical diagnosis are fundamentally the same as those of personality
measurement in general: a description of the personality structure
and organization that led up to the individual's particular set of
difficulties.

There are some psychologists who oppose classification because
they believe that pinning labels on persons (i.e., psychotic or
neurotic) does them little good, and they feel that it would probably
be more helpful to try to understand the forces and stresses that
motivate persons to act in particular ways. They point out also that
the state of the art in clinical diagnosis is not as advanced in
psychopathology as in medicine, and therefore diagnostic labeling is
little more than an academic exercise. Nevertheless, these psychologists do employ personality testing for the purpose of obtaining
information about clinic or hospital patients.

Proponents of clinical diagnosis, on the other hand, agree that
labeling per se is not particularly helpful to the patient, but that
many diagnostic classifications carry strong implications for treatment. For example, if in the past a person was diagnosed as
"depressive reaction"—that is, an individual who is inclined toward
being sad, morose, or dejected—and he was observed to benefit
from a particular treatment, then in the future, persons with the
same diagnosis become likely candidates for the same treatment.
Furthermore, labeling facilitates communication between psychologists. Once there is agreement that symptoms A, B, C, H, and R are
associated with "depressive reaction," and that treatment Z is
appropriate, then that particular classification communicates a
whole host of information about the nature of a patient's disorder
and about appropriate treatment procedures. When more is learned
about the etiology, or causes, of particular personality disorders,

and this etiologic knowledge is used in arriving at diagnostic labels, then classifications will communicate that additional information also. In the meantime, regardless of the pros and cons of the classification controversy these psychologists' interest in administering tests for classification purposes does not mean that they regard motivational forces as unimportant. On the contrary, they are working toward inclusion of these motivational factors in a classification scheme that is more comprehensive than the one currently available.

Counseling and Psychotherapy

Counseling and psychotherapy are characterized by the treatment of personality disturbance by psychological means. They consist of verbal interchange between a patient and the psychologist for the purpose of accomplishing changes in the patient that will facilitate his better adjustment. The use of personality measurement before, during, or after treatment is continuous with that of clinical diagnosis. The purpose served by such measurement is the assessment of the extent of change brought about by treatment.

Some psychologists distinguish between counseling and psychotherapy by reserving the latter for more "deep-seated" personality disorders; and they say that counseling is directed toward helping persons with superficial problems. In practice, there is much overlap between the two processes, because it is exceedingly difficult to distinguish between a deep-seated and a superficial problem. For example, does a student who is unable to concentrate on his studies qualify for counseling or psychotherapy? Under the present system, if his difficulty is a result of his hearing voices, he would probably be a candidate for psychotherapy. But if he cannot concentrate because of faulty study habits, he would be counseled. The distinction being made here seems to be in terms of the amount of alteration in personality that is judged necessary (psychotherapy) or unnecessary (counseling). Many colleges actually maintain both a mental hygiene clinic and a counseling center. When psychologists from both of these settings compare notes, they discover that the overlap is considerable in the kinds of problems they handle and the types of personality tests they administer.

The origins of counseling and clinical psychology were somewhat distinct. Counseling psychology had its origin as a separate field interested mainly in educational and vocational "guidance." In the course of assessing individuals' patterns of abilities and aptitudes, the counselor would "guide" his clients into suitable courses of study, vocations, or professions. However, it was soon recognized by counselors that individuals could not be fragmented into separate abilities, aptitudes, or interests without regard for the total personality structure, and thus they found themselves administering many personality tests in order to get this total picture.

Clinical psychology developed more directly in mental hygiene settings, and therefore techniques used by its practitioners for personality measurement were designed to diagnose more seriously disturbed persons. In the diagnostic work of the clinical psychologist—over the years—he began to recognize that patients' personalities could not be regarded simply in terms of symptoms and signs of psychopathology, and that identification of more positive components of persons was equally important.

The results of these discoveries by counseling and clinical psychologists has led to an interchangeable use of the terms counseling and psychotherapy. There are still separate training facilities for the two professions at many major universities, but it is becoming increasingly clear that no sensible distinction can be made between the two.

Personnel Selection

Personnel selection includes personality measurement for the purposes of choosing or promoting individuals for particular jobs and admission of persons in training programs designed for future nurses, doctors, pilots, salesmen, psychologists, policemen, and so on. In short, personnel selection has one specific objective: to contribute to the increasingly effective use of manpower within an organization. Technical qualifications for one of the above jobs or educational programs may be important, but these can usually be ascertained from the candidates' records. Often the most crucial issue is whether a candidate possesses a suitable combination of personality traits, and this can be decided with the aid of personality testing.

It has been pointed out by many psychologists (Guion, 1965; Thorndike, 1949; Vernon, 1964, that in admitting men and women for training in particular vocations or professions, selecting an individual with the "wrong kind" of personality may prove wasteful or even dangerous. Such errors in personnel selection are legendary among veterans who had served in the military forces. Stories abound of biochemists assigned to cleaning garbage cans, of mechanics forced to be cooks, and of unskilled and untrained people placed in teaching positions ("This here gun is not a gun, it's a rifle to you"). Aside from the irresponsible waste of trained (and untrained) manpower, it is probably also true that the personality characteristics of the biochemist, mechanic, or untrained person were unsuitable for the jobs they were assigned to perform.

Personality Research

Research using personality measurement techniques generally takes one of four forms. The most common form occurs in practical settings and involves measuring the effects on personality of a certain treatment procedure or training program. For example, in psychiatric hospitals, radical treatments such as electroshock therapy are sometimes necessary to alleviate severe disturbances of personality. Because it is important to assess the extent and nature of personality change induced, personality tests are administered before and after treatment.

In industrial settings, special management training programs are conducted with a view toward shaping aspiring managers' personalities along certain lines (i.e., to become more sensitive in interpersonal relations, have greater leadership qualities, and so forth). The effectiveness of the program in achieving its objective is sometimes measured with personality tests.

The second use of personality tests for research takes place in a more artificial setting such as a college psychological laboratory. Usually, volunteer subjects in a psychology experiment are tested, exposed to experimental manipulation, and then are tested again at the end of such exposure. For example, in one such experiment psychologists (Guetzkow and Bowman, 1946) were interested in determining the effects of prolonged food deprivation on the personalities of a group of individuals. The latter were conscientious objectors during World War II who agreed to participate in such an experiment. These men—married and respected citizens of their communities—after a period of food deprivation were caught stealing food from store counters and from one another, fought among themselves, hoarded dishes and silverware, told lies in an effort to obtain more food and generally displayed behavior that signified extensive personality changes. Other personality changes included a newly developed interest in reading recipes and cookbooks and pinning magazine pictures of lavish meals on walls. The men reported that much of their waking days were spent in daydreaming about sumptuous feasts. Many of these behavioral changes were observed in their personality test scores. On measures of ability, aptitude, and intelligence, however, their scores were essentially the same after the food deprivation as before. In other words, the only observed changes were in personality and these were reflected in numerous personality tests.

The third type of research with personality measuring devices is concerned specifically with ascertaining the adequacy of the measurement technique itself. Perhaps the reader has already noted that in the above uses of personality measures, the test users assumed that the test was adequate and appropriate for the problems under investigation. This last form of research makes no such assumptions. These investigations are designed to explore whether a particular instrument measures traits consistently and whether the traits it measures are those that the tester intended. Specific needs of a hospital or industrial organization may dictate the development of a particular type of personality test, and research would then be undertaken to determine the extent to which that test meets these needs.

Finally, the fourth form of research with personality tests is designed to contribute to the knowledge and theories about the way persons function. This is not a practical aim, and usually this form of testing does not take place in applied settings. Thus in contrast with the emphasis on decision making which is characteristic of testing in the clinical or personnel settings, greater emphasis is placed upon identifying motives, attitudes, beliefs, or defenses underlying overt and inferred behavior patterns. In short, the major purpose served by this type of personality measurement is the building of a sound theoretical system in which constructs can be measured and from which relationships between behavioral patterns can be deduced.

SOURCES OF INFORMATION ABOUT PERSONALITY

The psychologist who is interested in the study of personality collects information about the behavior and private experiences of the individual under consideration. There are three major sources of information available: observations of individual behavior, the interview, and the psychological test. These sources, and the types of information each yields about persons, are outlined in Table 1–4, and are the focal points of the remainder of this book.

The psychologist may obtain observations of individual behavior as a result of reports by others who have had contacts with the person (i.e., family, job supervisor, neighbors) ; or he can collect it by personally observing the individual's behavior in a laboratory or a number of everyday life situations.

The interview is probably the most obvious way to collect information about someone. If you want to know about a person's private experiences, perhaps the most direct method is to ask the person himself. There are, of course, difficulties with such an approach. For example, the person may elect to withhold information, or he may exaggerate, minimize, or otherwise distort what he relates to the psychologist. However, the interview, in the hands of a trained clinician, can offer considerable versatility, because it allows the interviewer to observe behavior at the same time that he collects information about the person's "mental interiors" (Cattell, 1958).

Essentially, psychological tests are situations in which the best features of observation and interview techniques are combined. The observations are taken in an artificial situation rather than in situ; and these observations often are in the form of answers to questionnaire items about the person's well-being, ideas, experiences, or habits. In that sense, tests are like interviews and experimental situations in which each person is subjected to a standard set of questions to answer and given a uniform set of tasks to perform.

There are rather specific criteria that distinguish psychological tests from more informal ways of obtaining information about persons, and these criteria are the topic of the following chapter. The special problems encountered in measuring personality and the adequacy of available personality tests are the main concern throughout the rest of this book.

TABLE 1–4

Sources of Information for Personality Study

Source	Variants	Information Yield
Observation	1. Direct observation (natural setting)	1. Reactions to everyday situations. Scars. Tattoos. Expressive behaviors. Characteristic modes of responding to specific persons. Ratings of any of these.
	2. Direct observation (laboratory)	2. Reactions to "rigged" stimuli. Information about specific behaviors under controlled conditions. Ratings of any of these.
	3. Indirect observations	3. Reports or ratings by others who remember (or do not) the subject.
Interview	1. Employment or personnel interview	1. Information for and about job candidate. Generally, the interview yields data about content of individual's thinking.
	2. Diagnostic interview	2. In medicine, the past history of the patient. In psychological assessment, the mental status of the respondent.
	3. Stress interview	3. Reactions of persons under unusual or stressful conditions.
Psychological tests.	1. Self-report inventories	1. Responses about personal habits, attitudes, beliefs, or fantasies.
	2. Projective tests	2. Responses to ambiguous or unstructured situations. These responses are assumed to reflect inner states of the person.

SUMMARY

The measurement viewpoint has replaced commonsense notions in the study of personality because of the psychologist's relatively greater need for precision. He is often interested in making more quantitative discriminations than a vocabulary of trait names permit, because he must base decisions about persons on his description.

Measurement consists of the assignment of numbers according to rules. There are four scales of measurement—nominal, ordinal, interval, and ratio—and different sets of rules correspond to the use of each of these scales. Each represents a different level of quantification and delimits the kinds of arithmetical procedures permitted.

Dimensions of personality that are of interest to the psychologist include psychopathology (psychosis, neurosis, or sociopathy), the structure of needs, normality, unusually effective behavior, and personality in terms of traits and types. The major personality test situations may be classified as clinical diagnosis, counseling and psychotherapy, personnel selection, and personality research.

There are three major sources of information about personality available to the psychologist. These are observations of individual behavior as reported by others or collected by the psychologist himself, the interview, and psychological testing. Each of these has its particular advantages and disadvantages, and the remainder of this book addresses itself specifically to the problems surrounding and an evaluation of these personality-measuring techniques.

FOR FURTHER READING

1. BAUGHMAN, E. E. & WELSH, G. S. *Personality: A behavioral science.* Englewood Cliffs, N.J.: Prentice-Hall, Inc., 1962.

   In Chapter 1, which is especially relevant to the present discussion, these authors contrast the study of personality from both the common-sense and the scientific points of view. Chapter 9, which is a succinct summary of Freud's psychoanalytic concepts, is also valuable here.

2. CATTELL, R. B. *Personality and motivation structure and measurement.* New York: World Book Co., 1957.

   This book is a survey of R. B. Cattell's and his associates' factor analytic research on basic personality dimensions. Chapter 1 is of immediate interest as supplementary reading here. "Scientific advance," R. B. Cattell asserts at the outset of Chapter 1, "hinges on the introduction of measurement to the field under investigation."

3. FARBER, I. E. A framework for the study of personality as a behavioral science. In WORCHEL, P. (Ed.), *Personality change.* New York: John Wiley & Sons, Inc., 1964. Pp. 3–37.

The importance of theory in the study of personality is emphasized in this paper. It is an interesting review of many topics relevant to the philosophy of science view of personality study, and accordingly touches on the following topics: causation, finalism, and explanatory fictions; the control of behavior; prediction versus understanding; psychological concepts; generalizing from empirical findings to real life; and the nature and function of theories.

4. GUILFORD, J. P. *Personality*. New York: McGraw-Hill Book Co., 1959.

The author's delineation of conceptions of personality (Chapter 1) and issues and approaches to personality (Chapter 2) round out some of the topics touched upon in the present chapter.

5. HOLTZMAN, W. H. Personality structure. In FARNSWORTH, P. R., MCNEMAR, OLGA, & MCNEMAR, Q. (Eds.), *Annual review of psychology*, volume 16. Palo Alto: Annual Reviews, Inc., 1965. Pp. 119–156.

This is the latest comprehensive review currently available of the state of personality structure and measurement. Always informative, this author's current review is especially notable for its handling of the basic issues presently being debated about personality measurement (e.g., test-taking attitudes, indirect approaches to measurement).

6. KAPLAN, A. *The conduct of inquiry: Methodology for behavioral science*. San Francisco: Chandler Publishing Co., 1964.

Professor Abraham Kaplan is a philosopher of science who, in this scholarly and thoroughly enjoyable book, has focused on the problems and pitfalls that await behavioral scientists interested in applying scientific methodology to their subject matter. Chapter 5 deals with the functions and structure of measurement, and includes an advanced treatment of scales of intensive and extensive measurement.

7. LAZARUS, R. S. *Adjustment and personality*. New York: McGraw-Hill Book Co., 1961.

The nature of personality is discussed in Chapter 2 (pp. 24–49). In it, Professor Lazarus presents an interesting conceptualization of the personality construct. Chapter 13 (pp. 381–425) is a tight treatment of many personality assessment techniques and problems.

8. MESSICK, S. Personality structure. In FARNSWORTH, P. R., MCNEMAR, OLGA, & MCNEMAR, Q. *Annual review of psychology*. Palo Alto: Annual Reviews, Inc., 1961. Pp. 93–128.

Most of the annual reviews on personality structure and measurement are essential reading for students in this area. But the present one is especially recommended for a survey of the following structures of personality: perceptual-cognitive; stylistic; temperament; attitudinal; motivational; defensive; and organizational constructs.

9. ROSEN, E., & GREGORY, IAN. *Abnormal psychology.* Philadelphia: W. B. Saunders Co., 1965.

For a review of or a lucid introduction to the specific syndromes of the personality disorders, Part II (Chapters 12 to 22) is unexcelled. All the psychoneurotic, psychotic and psychophysiologic disturbances are discussed as well as a number of additional problems such as alcoholism, drug addiction, brain damage, mental retardation, and childhood disorders.

10. STERN, G. G., STEIN, M. I., & BLOOM, B. S. *Methods in personality assessment.* New York: The Free Press, 1956.

Four major methodologies of personality assessment are presented in this book: the *analytical, empirical, synthetic,* and *configurational.* A series of studies provide the reader with concrete examples of each of these methods. Assessment, according to the authors, includes an understanding of the individual's environment as well as of the individual himself.

11. SUNDBERG, N. D. & TYLER, LEONA E. *Clinical psychology: An introduction to research and practice.* New York: Appleton-Century-Crofts, 1962.

Of immediate relevance to the present discussion is Chapter 4 (pp. 77–101), in which the authors trace the clinical psychologist's assessment of others. They describe assessment as a way of going about understanding others, and they trace it from a mechanistic, data processing standpoint similar to one that is adopted in Chapter 11 of this book.

12. TAFT, R. The ability to judge people. *Psychological Bulletin,* 1955, 51, 1–23.

Along with studies and papers by Bruner and Taguiri (1954) and Allport (1961), this article lists a number of qualities the good judge of personality must possess. Of some interest is Taft's refutation of the popular notion that sensitivity in judging others is highly correlated with neuroticism (cf. also Cronbach [1955] and Cline [1964]).

13. TAFT, R. Multiple methods of personality assessment. *Psychological Bulletin,* 1959, 56, 333–352. Also reprinted in SARASON, I. G. (Ed.), *Contemporary research in personality.* Princeton, N.J.: D. Van Nostrand Co., Inc., 1962.

Problems that arise in personality measurement are discussed. This is an advanced treatment of these topics and should serve to sensitize readers to issues discussed in Chapters 3 and 11 of the present book.

14. TYLER, LEONA E. *Tests and measurements.* Englewood Cliffs, N.J.: Prentice-Hall, Inc., 1963.

This book is an exceptionally lucid compendium of the large area of psychological testing. The treatment of the topic of measurement in Chapter 1 is especially interesting.

15. VERNON, P. E. *Personality assessment: A critical survey.* London:
    Methuen & Co., Ltd.; New York: John Wiley & Sons, Inc., 1964.

The author of this book presents a critical account and review of
the research evidence regarding the diagnosis and assessment of personality. For supplementary reading to the foregoing chapter, Part I
(pp. 25–71) is particularly helpful because it deals with the empirical
and theoretical evidence used in making naïve interpretations of
personality.

CHAPTER 2

ESSENTIAL ATTRIBUTES OF PSYCHOLOGICAL TESTS

It is probably safe to assume that the life of every person reading this book either has been, or will be, influenced in some way by a test score. This is inevitable because psychological testing is conducted at all levels of the school system, in large industrial organizations, in the military service, and in private and public clinics. It was estimated recently that more than four million people took tests administered by only five of the many agencies that give tests on a nationwide basis; and it has been reported that close to a million individuals are tested each year in private and public clinical services (Sundberg, 1961). Certainly when something becomes as important as this has in our society, it must be worth learning about.

The purpose of this chapter is to cover the essential characteristics and principles of psychological tests. Such coverage should provide the student with some background to help him judge the technical excellence of a number of personality-measuring tools discussed later in the book. But more important, perhaps, this chapter may equip the reader with a basic background about standards and elements of tests so that he can judge some of the crucial technical and ethical issues that are currently being debated (see Chapter 3). Further, an acquaintance with the limitations and capabilities of tests should enable the student to differentiate good and poor instruments and may dispel, at one extreme, complete faith in all tests, and at the other, utter disbelief in the usefulness of any test.

SOURCES OF INFORMATION ABOUT TESTS

Psychologists who use tests in their work must keep informed regarding new principles of testing constantly emerging from research, as well as with the development of new tests. The two most important sources for such information are the series of *Mental Measurements Yearbooks* edited by O. K. Buros (1938, 1941, 1949, 1953, 1959, 1965) and the *Technical Recommendations for Psychological Tests and Diagnostic Techniques* and *Standards for Educational and Psychological Tests and Manuals* published by the American Psychological Association (1954, 1966). The first of these consists of critical reviews of most commercially available tests; the *Technical Recommendations* and the *Standards* include a set of basic principles for the evaluation of psychological tests.

PSYCHOLOGICAL TEST DEFINED AND CRITERIA FOR JUDGING TESTS

So far in this book no distinction has been made between *measurement* and *test*. These terms were used interchangeably, but it may be useful now to distinguish between them.

Measurement, as used by psychologists, is the broader and more inclusive of the two terms, and it applies to many areas of psychological research where tests would not be appropriate. The psychologist may measure, for example, the amplitude of experimental subjects' reactions to stress. Or he may measure amount of time that intervened between the onset of a stimulus and the associated response. These measures are not tests.

Psychologists who use statistics to evaluate their findings also make extensive use of measurement. If the question under examination is, for example, "What is the probability that, in this experiment, variables x and y occurred by chance?" the answer usually includes measurement: counting, adding, or dividing, and a number of statistical procedures based on these arithmetic procedures. This type of measurement is not a test either.

A psychological test includes measurement but serves a much more restricted purpose than those described above. Most psychologists would probably agree that the following definition of a psychological test is adequate: *A psychological test is a standardized instrument or systematic procedure designed to obtain an objective measure of a sample of behavior.*

This definition is intended to be sufficiently broad to include procedures for systematic recording of behavior observations, scoring items on personality tests, and quantifying personality data culled from personal documents, case histories, and interviewing. All unsystematic, casual, spur-of-the-moment techniques for measuring personality are excluded. Moreover, no distinction is made in this book between the use of the terms *test, examination, technique, procedure,* or even *measure*—and often these words are used interchangeably—although it is recognized that such distinctions could serve a useful purpose.

The remainder of the chapter deals with a discussion of criteria essential for judging psychological tests. Evaluations of specific measurement procedures throughout the book are made in terms of these criteria. We begin our discussion by first referring the reader to the above definition of a psychological test, and taking up each of its major components—standardization, objectivity, measurement, and behavior sample.

Standardization

A standardized test is one in which test administration procedures, test apparatus or materials, instructions to subjects, and the scoring or recording operations have been precisely specified so that the test situation, insofar as feasible, is identical for all persons at all times (see Table 2–1). Under optimal conditions—hardly ever attained in practice—the test constructor controls all variation except the one that his test or procedure purports to measure.

The term standardization, as commonly used, includes the collection of test data from a comparison group which is relevant to a particular test. Here the word is not used in this sense but is intended to emphasize the standardization of procedure. Such standardization assures uniformity of test administration and scoring. Thus it is possible that a test was administered to a comparison group, even though its procedures were not uniform or clearly specified.

Standardization has a place in all research, and it refers to what is essentially "experimental control." All scientific observations should be made under controlled conditions. If the findings obtained

TABLE 2–1

Standardized and Unstandardized Test Materials

	Instructions	Items	Scoring
	Standardized		
Time.....1 Person....1 Situation..1	"Answer *each* of the following items TRUE or FALSE."	1. I feel rested most mornings. 2. People annoy me. 3. *Most* persons will cheat to get ahead.	1. TRUE 2. FALSE 3. FALSE
Time.....2 Person....2 Situation..2	"Answer *each* of the following items TRUE or FALSE."	1. I feel rested most mornings. 2. People annoy me. 3. *Most* persons will cheat to get ahead.	1. TRUE 2. FALSE 3. FALSE
	Unstandardized		
Time.....1 Person....1 Situation..1	"Answer *each* of the following items TRUE or FALSE."	1. I feel rested most mornings. 2. People annoy me. 3. *Most* persons will cheat to get ahead.	1. TRUE 2. FALSE 3. FALSE
Time.....2 Person....2 Situation..2	"Answer *any* of the following items TRUE or FALSE."	1. I feel rested most mornings. 2. People annoy me. 3. *Many* persons cheat to get ahead.	1. FALSE 2. TRUE 3. FALSE

by different experimenters are to be comparable, experimental equipment and instructions for its use must be the same for all. In psychological experiments, the Skinner box, nonsense syllables, classical conditioning, and the specification of the use of each of these materials or procedures for particular investigations, are examples of experimental controls.

A psychological test can be compared to a miniature controlled experiment in which all aspects of the situation—i.e., identical test materials, observance of strict time limits, same instructions for all respondents, absence of intruding or distracting factors in the surroundings—are controlled for all subjects. If such uniformity of conditions prevails, then the tester may conclude with some degree of confidence that the score he obtained from a person reflects the respondent's variation on the dimension being measured.

In personality testing it is especially important to control the test situation so that all respondents have similar goals and motivations in mind. If the directions to respondents differ, for example, so that one group is told that its test results are being used to determine eligibility for a training program,[1] and the other group is not so instructed, and perhaps is even assured that test scores are to be used only for research purposes, then it may be expected that each group's goals and motivations would differ considerably. It is probably also to be expected that the first group would have a greater tendency than the second to fake or distort the test. Such distortion reflects characteristics other than those the test was designed to measure.

Objectivity

Measurement is objective, broadly speaking, if the administration of the test, and the scoring and interpretation of test results, remain independent of the subjective judgment of the tester. There are degrees of objectivity that can be attained, and complete objectivity is an ideal toward which test constructors aim.

If a test is fully objective, any tester scoring the same set of responses will arrive at precisely the same score. Objectivity of a test, then, reflects the extent to which an instrument is free from the personal error or bias of the test administrator and scorer. Tests in which the person selects the best of several alternative answers (e.g., true or false, multiple choice) are objective in the sense that all scorers can apply a scoring key and agree completely on the result—i.e., arrive at identical scores. Subjective tests, on the other hand, in which scores rely on the judgment of scorers, allow for disagreement among them, and therefore do not yield identical scores. However, the amount of subjectivity can be reduced considerably—and hence objectivity enhanced—by instructing observers or scorers about procedures they are to follow in recording behavior or in scoring a test. Examples of items from objective and subjective tests are presented in Table 2–2.

Objectivity is used in an entirely different sense by some psychologists who are interested basically only in personality testing. In an article "What Is 'Objective' in 'Objective Personality Tests' " (1958,

---

[1] Of course, this information need not be conveyed to the respondent in the directions. He may infer as much from the test setting and other recent circumstances.

1964), R. B. Cattell recognizes the importance of some of the older meanings of "objective," such as were described above, but he defines an objective test as "a test in which the subject's behavior is measured, for inferring personality, without his being aware in what ways his behavior is likely to affect the interpretation" (1964, p. 264). Further, for Cattell, objectivity of a test is synonymous with its being resistant to motivated distortion, faking, and situation-sensitivity. The all-important condition, then, that he would like to have prevail in personality testing—and the one which qualifies it

TABLE 2-2

Examples of Objective and Subjective Test Items

Objective	Subjective
Strange thoughts occur to me (TRUE or FALSE).	Describe the thoughts that occur to you.
I am concerned about the opinions others hold about me (TRUE or FALSE).	Do the opinions of others concern you?
Occasionally I suspect that persons talk "behind my back" (TRUE or FALSE).	Are you a suspicious person?

as objective measurement—is that situation which keeps the person in the dark about the meaning and significance of his test responses.

Measurement

Measurement, as noted in Chapter 1, is the assignment of numerical values to objects, events, or phenomena according to a specified set of rules. All quantitative indices that result from assessment procedures are measures within the scope of this definition.

Behavior Sample

Behavior, in this context, refers to any series of responses which occur during the time that persons take a test. These responses may be observable physical acts or may be introspective statements. On personality tests, true or false answers about wishes, memories, beliefs, attitudes, or symptoms are verbal behaviors about oneself. The extent to which these behaviors reflect internal states or the personality of the subject must be determined by validity studies.

Psychologists usually must settle for obtaining a sample of an individual's behavior. A prime requisite of this sample is that it is carefully selected to represent the behavior in which the tester happens to be interested. The use of a behavior sample, rather than sampling the entire domain of relevant behaviors, is governed by many practical considerations such as time, expense, and energy expenditure. In this respect, the psychologist proceeds in much the same way as other people who must settle for samples of things. The merchant accepts a shipment of goods by examining a portion of the shipment, the consumer judges a bunch of grapes by sampling (or viewing a sample of) a few grapes, students have been known to sample an instructor's course by attending several lectures, and the chemist tests a supply of water by analyzing one or more samples of it. Similarly, on a test, the psychologist examines performance with a set of representative questions or miniature situations.

So much for the components of the definition of a psychological test. There are many more important questions about tests that remain to be answered. For example: "Is it an accurate measure of behavior?" "How relevant is the test for measuring this trait?" "Can I use the test for this group of individuals?" In psychological testing, these questions are partially answered by establishing a test's *reliability* and *validity* and by collecting *normative* data.

RELIABILITY

The concept of reliability answers the questions: "How well does the test measure the characteristic it was designed to measure?" and "Is the test a consistent and accurate measure"? Whenever measurements are made, whether in the physical or behavioral sciences, the problem arises that obtained differences between objects or between persons may be attributable to chance fluctuations. These fluctuations may be due to the nature of the thing measured, the inadequacy of the measuring instrument, the limitations of the measurer himself, or any combination of these factors.

Ideally, test scores should reflect variation between individuals that is due to actual or true differences among them rather than to chance factors.

An individual's score on a personality test is influenced by many chance factors quite apart from the personality trait the test has been designed to measure. For example, if a person lacks motivation to concentrate on the meaning of certain items, he may give answers that are casual or haphazard. The result may be a score that varies from one that may have been gotten the day before when he was in a more cooperative frame of mind. Such variation is sometimes referred to as random or chance error.

There are many sources of chance error that contribute to score variation from one measurement to the next. Such chance error, or error variance, can be due to poor test environment, fatigue, eyestrain, luck in selecting certain answers, ambiguously worded items, errors in scoring, and a host of other possible sources. Essentially, any condition that is extraneous to the purpose of the test, and influences the test score in undetermined ways, contributes to error variance.

Test constructors strive to devise tests that are impervious to factors other than the ones to be measured. Thus standardization of test materials, test conditions, instructions, and time limits can serve to reduce error variance and make tests more reliable—that is to say, control of these factors contributes to the increased accuracy of the test. But error arises nevertheless, and the tester's problem is to obtain as close an estimate as possible of the person's true score on the variable under consideration.

Generally speaking, a test with high reliability yields measurements where error variance has been reduced, and the test score accurately reflects the trait being measured. A test with low reliability means that it was extremely subject to the influence of chance circumstances. There is no such thing, however, as *the* reliability of a test. Numerous kinds of reliability can be computed and the statements, "this test is reliable," or more technically, "the reliability of this test as measured by a correlation coefficient is +.95," are meaningless unless the procedures used to arrive at these estimates are specified.

In practice, there are at least five distinct ways to compute reliability—retest, equivalent forms, split-half, internal consistency, and scorer reliability—and each of these are briefly described in the following sections. Since the first four (sometimes all five) of these reliabilities are expressed as *correlation coefficients*—called *reliability coefficients* when they are used in this way—some of their elementary characteristics are noted here.

The Correlation Coefficient

A correlation coefficient reflects the extent of relationship among variables (i.e., tests, traits, events). This is accomplished through a statistical technique yielding a value, the correlation coefficient, which expresses the degree to which standing on one trait is associated with standing on another trait. Although there are many ways of computing correlations, the one technique which is commonly used in reporting the reliability of tests is called the *product-moment* coefficient.

To compute a coefficient of correlation, one needs two sets of measures on a group of individuals. Thus if one wished to compute the degree of correlation between personality test scores and treatment success, test scores are required as well as ratings of treatment success for each person in the group. Essentially, then, each person's scores and success ratings are viewed in relation to everybody else's.

The correlation coefficient may take on any value from 0.00 (no relationship) to +1.00 (perfect positive relationship) or −1.00 (perfect negative or inverse relationship). A coefficient of +1.00 means that the person who stands highest in one trait also stands highest in the other, and that throughout the series of measures the *correspondence* is exact, or 1 : 1. A correlation of 0.00 indicates a complete absence of relationship. Negative, or inverse, correlation means that a person who ranks high in one trait ranks low in the other. Perfect correlations (i.e., +1.00 or −1.00) are never encountered in actual practice, and coefficients generally fall somewhere between these values. Commonly, correlations that hover around ±.20 (read "plus or minus"), ±.60 and ±.85 are considered to reflect mild, moderate, and substantial relationships respectively.

The meaning of a correlation coefficient can be clarified by examining a *scatter diagram*, which is a graphic plot of the relationship between two percentages of measures. In a scatter diagram each dot or point represents an individual, and the position of the dot on the grid of the graph indicates the person's scores on the two measures. The overall arrangement of the dots indicates the degree of correlation. Figure 2–1 is a scatter diagram in which the horizontal axis represents ratings of success in treatment and the vertical axis represents scores of each individual on a personality test.

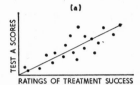 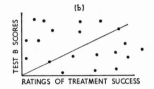 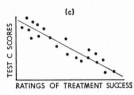

FIGURE 2–1. Scatter diagrams showing high positive (*a*), zero (*b*), and high negative (*c*) correlations. Notice that in diagram (*a*), the scores and ratings cluster around the straight line drawn from lower left to upper right. In diagram (*b*), no such clustering occurs. The straight line in diagram (*c*) can be drawn from lower right to upper left.

The success rating of each individual can be determined by noting the position of his dot above the horizontal axis, and his score on the test can be noted by recording its value from the vertical axis.

Scatter diagram 2–1*a* shows an arrangement of dots in which there is a high degree of positive correlation; 2–1*b* indicates no or very low correspondence between treatment success and test scores; and 2–1*c* is a scatter diagram with a substantial negative correlation. From such relationships among these measures, knowing nothing else about the way they were collected, and assuming that the vertical axes of diagrams *a*, *b* and *c* represent different personality tests, with treatment held constant across tests, we could assert that test A (diagram 2–1*a*) is the best predictor of success in treatment from among the tests.

A final word of caution is in order regarding the interpretation of the correlation coefficient. It expresses neither simple percentage nor causation. Thus, it is not correct to say that a correlation of +.90 predicts with twice as much certainty as a correlation of +.45, or that the proportion of the relationship in the first coefficient is 45 percent greater. Nor is it correct to suppose that a substantial relationship (i.e., ±.95) between two measures indicates that one causes, or is responsible for, the other.[2]

As an expression of test reliability, the correlation coefficient—or more properly, the reliability coefficient—reflects the degree of similarity between two sets of scores obtained by administration of the same test (on one or two occasions) or two versions of the same

---

[2] The correlation between the number of churches and alcohol consumption in a city is said to be +.90 or higher—not because one causes the other, but because the third variable, size of a city, is responsible for the presence of both.

test. The reliability coefficient is estimated by five distinct procedures—retest, equivalent forms, split-half, internal consistency, and interscorer agreement. The first three of these methods are illustrated in Figure 2–2. Usually coefficients in the high +.80's and +.90's are considered necessary to establish a test's reliability.

TEST X   CORRELATED   TEST X
ON DAY A   WITH   ON DAY B

(a)   TEST-RETEST METHOD

TEST X   CORRELATED   TEST X'
ON DAY A   WITH   ON DAY A

(b)   EQUIVALENT-FORMS METHOD

The Retest Reliability Coefficient

The reliability of a test can be estimated by administering the same test on two occasions—usually with a short interval between sessions. The reliability coefficient in this case reflects the scores obtained by the same subjects on two occasions, and is said to be an index of a test's *temporal stability*.

Temporal stability indicates the extent to which scores on a test are affected by the chance or random fluctuations in the condition of the subject or of the test surroundings; and the logic for computing this type of reliability lies in the notion that temporary factors (i.e., health, motivation, mood fluctuation) may help an individual on one occasion and lower his score on the other. Such transient factors lower the test-retest consistency and are counted as error.

$\frac{1}{2}X$

CORRELATED WITH

$\frac{1}{2}X$

(c)   SPLIT-HALF METHOD

FIGURE 2–2.   Diagrams (a), (b), and (c) illustrate the test-retest, equivalent-forms, and split-half procedures.

For personality test purposes, this form of reliability is not an entirely appropriate measure of an instrument's (or the person's) stability. Many personality traits are supposed to be of a fluctuating nature. Some personality inventories include mood scales designed specifically to reflect an individual's daily variations. On such scales it is difficult to distinguish variance which is due to random variation from that which truly reflects an individual's fluctuating moods. For instance, if an individual is depressed at the outset of psychotherapy, and a personality test reflects this depression accurately, then if the individual becomes less depressed as therapy progresses, it is expected that a sensitive measuring instrument will reflect these changes.

There are other disadvantages of reliability estimation by retests that should be highlighted here. Whereas this procedure does assure the complete equivalence of test content on two occasions, the experience of having taken the test the first time may change test taking attitudes on the second occasion. The group is now more "test-wise" and perhaps has taken the opportunity during the interval between tests to inquire about the nature of the instrument. Or some persons may have taken the trouble to read up on certain symptom-disease relationships and may utilize this information on the second test occasion. This problem is also relevant to tests that measure amount of progress in a particular course of study (or achievement tests), or to tests of potential ability (aptitude tests), because persons tend to *recall* responses they made to items on the previous occasion and sometimes actually rehearse, practice, or acquire certain skills in order to "pass" previously "missed" items. These effects—i.e., test-wiseness, recall and practice—are sources of error variance that serve to influence test scores on retests. To counteract these effects it is recommended for achievement, aptitude, or even personality testing that an interval of at least one week be allowed to intervene between the first and second test administration.

Equivalent–Forms Reliability

In order to minimize the effects of practice and eliminate the effects of recall, reliability is estimated by means of administering parallel or equivalent forms of a test. The two forms which are administered on two occasions should be closely comparable with regard to the number of items, content, and in the mechanics of administering and scoring the alternate tests. The correlation between the scores on the two forms represents the reliability coefficient. Usually the time interval between test administrations is minimal, and often the two forms are given in immediate succession.

Since it is impossible to administer two tests to the same individuals simultaneously, the error arising from temporal fluctuations is only minimized, not eliminated. Additionally, different scores on the two forms might also be obtained because the tests were not exactly equivalent—that is to say, it is possible that the items of the two forms of the test are not measuring precisely the same traits. However, since the time-to-time fluctuations are kept small, and because there are statistical procedures available for making two forms of a test equivalent, parallel-forms reliability has been useful and popular among psychologists.

Due to the expense and the difficulties inherent in constructing a truly parallel set of tests, equivalent forms for most personality measures do not exist. Intelligence and aptitude test constructors are far advanced in this regard and consider the construction of parallel tests almost from the inception of the idea of a test. Clearly, the personality test movement may be well advised to follow an important example.

Split–Half Methods

Where only one form of a test can be given, a split-half procedure is sometimes used as a substitute for parallel-forms reliability. This procedure calls for one administration of a test—hence eliminating error arising from time-to-time and test-to-test variations—and calls for scoring of two halves of the test. The most common way to accomplish this is to score a test on all of the even-numbered items and then to score separately all of the odd-numbered items. For a group of examinees, then, the two halves of the same test can be correlated to obtain an estimate of the instrument's reliability. This method essentially is the same as equivalent-forms reliability in that the correlation of the two parts of the test yields a coefficient of equivalence for the half-tests. There is a correction formula available—the Spearman-Brown formula—that is designed to help compute the probable reliability of the test if it were lengthened or shortened (Ghiselli, 1964; Guilford, 1954).

Split-half coefficients by the odd-even method are inappropriate for tests with time limits unless the test author splits the test into times rather than odd and even items. It is difficult to accomplish this in practice because it entails establishing new time limits for already existing tests. This method has been described in some detail elsewhere (Anastasi and Drake, 1954; Kleinmuntz, 1965).

Internal Consistency Reliability

Two internal consistency formulas, often employed to obtain coefficients of equivalence for a test from a single administration of that test, can be briefly mentioned here. These procedures, developed by Kuder and Richardson (1937), and appropriately named after their authors,[3] are similar to the split-half method. However, rather than requiring two half-scores, the techniques are based upon an examination of group performance on each item. Both coefficients are generally used as good approximations to an equivalent-form correlation. Because they require only a single administration of a test, they are popular formulas when more than one form of a test is not available and in instances where two administrations of a test are not feasible.

Scorer Reliability

With most standardized tests for which procedures for scoring responses have been precisely stipulated, the agreement of two or more scorers[4] (or the same scorer at different times) is used as evidence of scorer reliability. Scorer unreliability is hardly ever a problem in objective tests. In personality testing, however, particularly with such projective techniques as the Rorschach inkblots and TAT, where some degree of judgment in scoring is necessary, scorer reliability can be cause for serious concern. Both the Rorschach and the TAT are discussed in later chapters of this book, and the special reliability problems they present will be detailed there.

The problem of determining scorer reliability will crop up in most test situations where scorer subjectivity looms important. Thus, with observation methods, ratings, and interview procedures for obtaining personality measures, as well as with projective tests, determination of scorer reliability is extremely important. For example, the score on a rating form or an interview recording

---

[3] KR 20 and KR 21.

[4] R. B. Cattell (1957) has coined the term "conspect reliability" for the index that reflects the degree of correspondence between scorers.

schedule depends on the behavior of the person under study, as well as on the traits and behavior of the rater or interviewer.

Estimation of scorer reliability can be expressed by the correlation coefficient. But more often, especially with dichotomous ratings (i.e., psychotic or neurotic), estimation is accomplished by merely determining the percentage agreements among scorers, observers, raters, or interviewers.

VALIDITY

Unquestionably, the most essential characteristic of a good psychological measuring instrument is its validity, i.e., the extent to which a test actually measures what it sets out to measure. The concept of validity can best be described by contrasting it to reliability. If an instrument is not measuring accurately or consistently (i.e., reliably) whatever it is supposed to measure, then it cannot be valid for any purpose. On the other hand, it may measure something with a high degree of reliability without being at all relevant or useful (i.e., valid) for the purpose for which it is intended. For example, a test printed in the Sunday supplement with the title "Emotional Stability Index," may on numerous test occasions consistently yield similar or identical results. Therefore high reliability coefficients would be obtained on retests. However, in spite of its name, it may not be an index of emotional stability at all. In other words, it may be useless or *not valid* for its stated purpose.

A test may appear to measure a particular trait or behavior—and thus is said to have face validity—but whether or not it really measures what it is supposed to measure is not dependent on the extent to which it "looks valid." Moreover, many face-valid tests have failed as predictors of the trait or behavior they purport to measure. A certain amount of face validity is desirable in a test so that the instrument does not look inappropriate, implausible, or silly for its purpose. In personality testing, however, too much face validity may result in highly fakeable items that render the resulting test score meaningless.

Just as there is no such concept as *the* reliability of a test, there is no such thing as *the* validity of a test. A test which has high validity for one purpose may have moderate or negligible validity for another. Consider the Sunday supplement test once again. It may be that it is not valid for predicting "emotional stability," but it is likely that it is a valid index for predicting perseverance (ability to complete crossword puzzles), or perhaps the test is even a valid predictor of intelligence (or lack of it). Whether or not it predicts any of these traits, however, is a question that can be settled only by conducting some of the validity studies mentioned below.

Validity, then, refers to what the test measures and how well it predicts certain traits. Essentially, all procedures for establishing test validity are concerned with the relationships between performance on a test and other independently observable facts about the behavior characteristic in question. There are three basic types of validity relevant to personality measurement: content, empirical, and construct validity. Each type includes several procedures. Only the major points can be outlined here. More basic sources than this book should be consulted for detailed coverage (Anastasi, 1961; Campbell and Fiske, 1959; Cronbach, 1960; Guilford, 1954; Helmstadter, 1964).

Content Validity

Content validity, as the name suggests, is obtained by representative sampling of the behavior domain which the test sets out to measure. The content area to be tested is carefully analyzed so that all its major aspects are proportionately represented on the test. Thus a final test in an introductory psychology course which covered the topics of perception, learning, motivation, personality, and individual differences, should include items that sample each of these topics in approximately equal amounts.

This type of validity is most appropriate for tests of achievement, and except in the early days of personality inventory construction it is hardly ever relevant for personality testing.[5] The latter is not based on a specified course of instruction or uniform materials from which test content can be sampled.

Empirical Validity

Empirical validation provides evidence that a relationship exists between scores on the test and behavior on some extra-test crite-

---

[5] Content validity is relevant for a personality test intended to reflect a theory; then the test's content should represent theoretically relevant behaviors.

rion. For example, if a personnel selection test is to be used in choosing promising candidates for a training program, then success in that program would be the criterion. This relationship between test predictors and a criterion is expressed in terms of the correlation coefficient. And depending upon whether or not the criterion is one that exists at the time of testing or one that will become available in the future, a distinction is made between *concurrent* and *predictive* validity. Correlation coefficients are considered adequate evidence of validity when they reach about +.40.

Concurrent Validity. Concurrent validity consists of the correlation between scores and criterion when both are made at about the same time. Sometimes it is expensive, inconvenient, or in other ways difficult to wait for the accumulation of criterion data, and therefore available information (i.e., in the files) is used for purposes of validation. For example, a psychologist in a mental health clinic, who is interested in learning whether a new personality test predicts psychosis, may elect not to wait the several years it would ordinarily take to allow a sample of psychotic persons to appear at that clinic, and therefore administers his test to a group for which criterion data are already available (i.e., to psychotics and nonpsychotics currently being seen at the clinic). The correlation between the test scores and the number of persons diagnosed as psychotic provides an estimate of the predictive efficacy of the test.

Concurrent validity, then, accepts some available index of the behavior that a test purports to measure. This type of validity is also established for a test by comparing it to a criterion such as an already existing test. New scholastic aptitude batteries, for example, are usually correlated with existing tests whose validity has been studied extensively. Some personality tests were developed in this way and presently are themselves considered criteria for still newer tests. The procedure of utilizing tests as criteria is useful only if those tests indeed measure the relevant dimensions. Thus it is possible that several tests which are presumably measures of "neuroticism," let us say, actually measure intelligence, or some other trait. Such tests would not be considered adequate criteria for the neuroticism dimension.

Predictive Validity. A demonstration of a significant relationship between a test's scores and empirical evidence gathered at some subsequent period of time, establishes a test's predictive validity. For this purpose, test scores are correlated with persons' subsequent performance or diagnoses (i.e., criteria are collected at a later date). This type of validity is often determined by the "follow-up" method. For this reason, a statement of predictive validity is an "after-the-fact" assertion, a statement of a relationship that exists between a test and an earlier sample which is now the criterion.

Predictive validity is most relevant for tests used in the selection and classification of personnel, for screening persons likely to develop emotional disorders under stress, and to help identify psychiatric patients likely to benefit from treatment. However, in all these instances it is only assumed that because a correlation exists between a test and an earlier sample, such a relationship still holds. If circumstances of the test's future use change considerably, such an assumption is unjustified. For example, if predictive validity studies suggest that a test is an adequate predictor of success on a particular job, but the conditions of work change (change of supervisor, longer hours, lower morale), then the use of that test is no longer justified. Similarly, conditions and circumstances are constantly in a state of flux in schools, mental health clinics, and other settings where tests are used as predictors, and therefore the psychologist must constantly be alert to these changes.

Another problem encountered in establishing predictive validity centers around the question of the amount of time that should be allowed to intervene between test administration and collection of criterion data. The question boils down to, "When does a criterion measure 'settle down' enough to be called a criterion?" Thus a test may be a valid predictor of short-term behavior, but may be invalid for longer term predictions. For example, a personality test that predicts persons' initial emotional adjustment to stress could be a poor predictor of continual adjustment to stress situations. Perhaps if the tester had allowed a longer period to intervene between test administration and collection of criterion data, he would have discovered that the initial adjustment he had observed disappeared over a somewhat longer period of exposure to stress.

Reliability of the Criterion. It is frequently assumed that the criteria against which tests are validated are perfectly reliable measures of the behaviors in question. However, a perfect criterion is just as improbable as a perfectly reliable test. Criterion measures are obtained by interviews, observations, and ratings, and as we noted earlier, are established by correlations with substitute psychological measuring instruments. It is therefore important to emphasize that all of these criteria—as will be demonstrated throughout this book—are fallible tools that are subject to many errors.

Ideally each test constructor seeks to validate his test against the "perfect criterion." But since perfect criteria are as rare as perfect tests, a statistical procedure is available that helps the psychologist correct for this imperfection. When the reliability of the criterion is known, a validity coefficient is evaluated in terms of its magnitude relative to the ceiling imposed by the unreliability of the criterion. This is called *correction for attenuation in the criterion variable* (see Ghiselli, 1964; Guion, 1965).

There is a special variety of criterion unreliability—called *criterion contamination*—that merits mention here because of its relevance to the collection of criterion data in clinical settings. Criterion contamination occurs when test scorers themselves influence an individual's criterion status. For example, when a clinician or a psychiatric nurse is assigned to observe and rate a particular patient, and that patient's scores on a personality test are known by these raters, then such knowledge may influence the ratings given to the patient. These ratings are then said to be contaminated by the rater's knowledge of test scores. This type of criterion contamination is common in clinical settings, because it is often difficult, for practical reasons, to withhold psychometric information from persons involved in providing ratings. Careful prior planning on the part of the research investigator is required to preclude such contamination.

Construct Validity

The construct validation of a test, as has been clarified and elaborated by Cronbach and Meehl (1955), involves no correlation with a criterion, but arises whenever a test's psychological meaning is systematically investigated. In studies of construct validity, the test and the theory (or "theoretical construct") underlying the test are simultaneously validated. The validation procedure involves two steps: (1) the inquiry by an investigator, "From this theory, what predictions can be made regarding the variation of scores from person to person or occasion to occasion?" and (2) the gathering of data to confirm these predictions (American Psychological Association, 1966).

Typical theoretical constructs of interest to the psychologist designing a personality test are neuroticism, psychoticism, anxiety, and introversion. Validation of these constructs requires the gradual accumulation of supporting information from a variety of sources. Any data that throw light on the nature of the theoretical construct under consideration, and help explain the conditions affecting its behavior and manifestations, contribute to the construct validity of a test.

Construct validity is distinguished from the other types of validation in that no definitive criterion measure is used by the tester, nor does he sample a content domain. Instead he uses indirect measures to validate his theory; and the trait or quality underlying the test takes on major importance.

There are various specific procedures for gathering construct validity data, and these are discussed below. The opinion has been expressed by some psychologists that construct validity merely serves as an honorific label for evidence falling far short of the standards set up by procedures for criterion validation (Loevinger, 1959). However, this criticism is unjustified because the procedures of construct validation demand more kinds of evidence than are required for criterion validation and therefore they eliminate the approach to test validity that depends so heavily on the single criterion and the unreplicated study.

Group Differentiation. Many traits are presumed to exist in various amounts in different groups. Thus "intelligence" is supposed to increase with age (until maturity), and therefore on an intelligence test one should expect children of different age groups to exhibit more or less "mental age" as a function of their chronological age differences. Likewise, one might expect that male college students as a group, because of their relatively greater interest in books, fine arts, music, flowers, and so on, would score higher than construction workers on a femininity interest scale. If scores on an intelligence or interest test do not reflect some of these differences between well-defined groups, then these tests may very likely not be valid measures of the dimensions under study.

Factor Analysis. A second way of organizing data about construct validity is factor analysis—a technique based on rather complex statistical procedures that need not concern us in detail here (see Cattell, 1946; Fruchter, 1954). Essentially, factor analysis is a systematic technique used to examine the meaning of a test by studying its correlations with many other variables. The factors derived from such an analysis are constructs (or variables presumed to exist) and reference to a table of factor loadings discloses the number of constructs a test measures.

Effect of Experimental Variables on Test Scores. A third convincing source of evidence for construct validity is the demonstration that manipulation of specific experimental variables results in predictable test score changes. A test designed to measure, for instance, reaction to stress should yield different scores depending on whether or not a stress situation is introduced. Similarly, if it is supposed that a particular test score indicates probable ability to resist stress, this supposition may be validated by placing individuals in an experimental stress situation and noting whether the behavior corresponds to that prediction.

Convergent and Discriminant Validation. Finally, a recently proposed method for inferring construct validity (Campbell and Fiske, 1959) consists of a systematic way to study correlational evidence from a table of intercorrelations. This method is based on a convergent and discriminant procedure which emphasizes the importance of establishing both what a test measures and what it does not. The convergent principle suggests that two measures of the same trait correlate highly with one another. The discriminant notion designates that two measures should not correlate highly with one another if they measure different traits.

The utilization of evidence for convergence between independent measures of the same trait (or construct) is a trial of that trait's fitness to survive the onslaught of a series of measures. The verification of distinctions between the trait in question and other traits is an important part of the definition of that trait. Therefore, once a trait has been confirmed by two or more independent measurement processes, and has been distinguished from other dimensions, the uncertainty of its meaning is reduced considerably.

Cross–Validation

Neither factor analysis, construct validation, nor any of the criterion-oriented techniques for obtaining validity coefficients can serve as a substitute for the method of cross-validation. The latter calls for conducting a second study, or administering the test items to a second sample in the same, or similar, setting as the one in which the test was developed. It is advisable to replicate the study in a setting in which the sample subjects are totally new, although perhaps similar to the original ones. This procedure has also been called *validity generalization* (Cronbach, 1960).

All too often, test constructors obtain satisfactory validity coefficients and then fail to obtain further validity information regarding their tests. This practice is questionable because high validity coefficients can be obtained as a result of random fluctuations of a number of variables. A validity coefficient computed on the same sample that was used for the development of the test maximizes chance errors within that particular sample and therefore will be spuriously high. Cross-validation studies serve to point out the extent of "shrinkage" in the size of the validity coefficient that may be expected when a test is applied to a new sample.

Cross-validation is especially important in studies which attempt to develop *signs* to predict, for example, adjustment, maladjustment, certain specific personality disturbances, or other criteria. In all studies where these signs (indices such as elevations on special scales or a combination of test score characteristics) have been applied to a new group of individuals for the purpose of distinguishing them along a relevant dimension, considerable shrinkage in cross-validation coefficients are usually observed. Again, it is essential to determine the extent of this shrinkage.

NORMS

Psychological tests have no absolute standards of "pass" or "fail." All meaning for a given score of a person derives from comparing his score with those of other persons. Norms provide such points of comparison, and as its name implies, a norm represents "normal" or average performance.

Although it is suggested by the American Psychological Association (1954, 1966) that norms be published at the time of a test's release for operational use, and that these norms refer to defined and clearly described populations, it is recognized in practice that the test publisher cannot anticipate the multitude of groups for which his test will be used. Therefore, it is advisable that a test interpreter, whenever he has the opportunity to accumulate local norms, prepare such data for the groups with which he deals directly. In this regard, one test publisher had the following to say (Seashore and Ricks, 1950, p. 19) :

Local norms should be constructed by the user for appropriate groupings of cases. This is of great importance, both for personnel selection tests used by a firm and for tests used in educational and vocational counseling. It may be necessary to begin by using reasonably appropriate norms published in the test manual, but local norms should be prepared as soon as a hundred or more cases have been accumulated and should be revised from time to time as the testing program continues and additional data become available. While published percentile or standard score norms[6] may provide a temporary starting point, cut-off scores for hiring purposes would be established *only* on the basis of specific local experience and not merely taken from published reports.

In summary, then, test scores are meaningless unless they can be evaluated in terms of normative data. Moreover, normative populations should be clearly defined, and for many purposes it is advisable that local norms be developed for specific samples and occasions. For a fuller analysis than is possible here of standard scores, cutoff points, stens, stanines, T-scores, and percentile ranks —all relevant for the interpretation of norms—more basic sources should be consulted (Ghiselli, 1964; Helmstadter, 1964; Lyman, 1963).

Most of the test characteristics described in this chapter apply equally to ability, achievement, aptitude, attitude, interest, and personality testing (many authors do not distinguish between the latter three), but there are some special problems that arise, particularly in personality measurement. These problems are mentioned and discussed in the next chapter and, in their turn, also in sections where specific techniques are described.

SUMMARY

A psychological test is a systematic procedure for obtaining an objective and standardized measure of a sample of behavior. Conventionally, objective measurement refers to a set of operations performed in scoring and interpreting test results that render test scores independent of the subjective judgment of the tester;

---

[6] Percentile scores or ranks are expressed in terms of the percentage of persons in the normative sample who fall below a particular score. Standard scores express the individual's distance from the arithmetic mean or average of a distribution.

and more recently it refers to a test's imperviousness to distortion. Behavior, in the personality test sphere, includes wishes, memories, beliefs, attitudes, response tendencies, and projected needs. Standardization insures uniformity of test materials, administration, conditions, and scoring.

The concepts of test reliability and validity are as important for personality measurement as for other forms of psychological testing. Reliability studies reflect the precision of a measuring instrument, and they are indices used to estimate the effects of extraneous variables on test results. Validity refers to the extent to which a test actually measures what it purports to measure; and it is estimated by criterion-oriented comparisons and by certain special noncorrelational or construct validation procedures. Construct validity is a procedure especially relevant in the clinical field, since there are no identifiable performance criteria for many of the personality constructs measured.

An additional validation procedure, all too often overlooked by test constructors in a hurry to publish their instruments, consists of cross-validation studies. These usually involve a replication study in the same setting as the one in which the test was developed but with a totally new sample of subjects. Validity coefficients often undergo "shrinkage" in the second study, and such shrinkage serves to dampen a test constructor's initial—and perhaps, unwarranted— enthusiasm for his instrument.

Finally, the importance of collecting relevant normative or comparison group data cannot be overemphasized. Norms must be based on persons with whom it is relevant to compare a given set of new individuals, and no meaningful interpretation of test scores is possible without orientation to some reference group.

FOR FURTHER READING

1. ANASTASI, ANNE. *Psychological testing.* (2d ed.) New York: Macmillan Co., 1961.

    Along with texts by Cronbach (1960), Freeman (1962), Nunnally (1959), and Thorndike and Hagen (1961), this is one of the most widely read books on the subject matter of psychological testing. The first portion of the book presents an excellent account of the basic principles of psychological testing, and covers the following topics: the functions, origins, characteristics, and use of tests as well as a discussion of norms, reliability, and validity.

2. CAMPBELL, D. T. & FISKE, D. W. Convergent and discriminant validation by the multitrait-multimethod matrix. *Psychological Bulletin,* 1959, 56, 81–105.

In this article, which has become required reading in all graduate courses on psychological testing, the authors draw attention to the importance of the method used in testing. They point out the need to tackle the same construct by different methods.

3. CATTELL, R. B. What is "objective" in "objective personality tests"? *Journal of Counseling Psychology,* 1958, 5, 285–289. Also in BARNETTE, W. L. (Ed.), *Readings in psychological tests and measurements.* Homewood, Ill.: The Dorsey Press, 1964. Pp. 260–265.

This paper presents a clear statement of Cattell's notions of L-data, Q'-data, Q-data, and T-data and carefully defines the essential meaning of "objective" testing as applied to personality data.

4. CRONBACH, L. J. *Essentials of psychological testing.* (2d ed.) New York: Harper & Row, 1960.

The first portion of this book contains the information important for a basic comprehension of psychological testing. Although the topic headings overlap with those of Anastasi (see above), Cronbach's treatment is an entirely different one. The facts are identical, of course, but the approaches are divergent and serve to complement each other. For a special treatment of one form of internal validation (e.g., coefficient alpha) see Cronbach (1951).

5. CRONBACH, L. J. & MEEHL, P. E. Construct validity in psychological tests. *Psychological Bulletin,* 1955, 52, 281–302.

The fundamental principles of construct validation are laid down in this important article.

6. GHISELLI, E. E. *Theory of psychological measurement.* New York: McGraw-Hill Book Co., 1964.

Somewhat less demanding than Gulliksen's text (see below), and aimed at presenting an elementary discussion of the basic problems of psychological measurement, many chapters of this fine book will serve to introduce students to several important topics on testing.

7. GOLDMAN, L. *Using tests in counseling.* New York: Appleton-Century-Crofts, 1961.

Chapters 2 and 3 (pp. 11–63) of this useful and practical book deal with the purposes and selection of tests.

8. GUILFORD, J. P. *Psychometric methods.* (2d ed.) New York: McGraw-Hill Book Co., 1954.

This book, now in its second edition, has been the handbook of psychological testing since 1936.

9. GUION, R. M. *Personnel testing.* New York: McGraw-Hill Book Co., 1965.

By way of introducing personnel psychologists to the foundations of mental measurements, Guion presents a somewhat advanced, but highly readable discussion of reliability (Chapter 2), prediction (Chapter 3), and the elements of test construction (Chapter 7).

10. GULLIKSEN, H. *Theory of mental tests.* New York: John Wiley & Sons, Inc., 1950.

    After 17 years on the book shelves, this advanced text on the theory of testing is still recommended reading. However, much has happened in the intervening years and consequently the advanced student is advised to consult Horst (1966), and Rozeboom (1966).

11. HELMSTADTER, G. C. *Principles of psychological measurement.* New York: Appleton-Century-Crofts, 1964.

    A considerably easier book to read than Gulliksen's (or Horst's and Rozeboom's), this text is a relatively less quantitative summary of the logic and major principles of measurement. Chapters 2, 3, 5, 6, and 9 are especially recommended and deal with standardization (this topic includes normatization, according to Helmstadter), reliability, empirical and construct validity, and multiple measurement. The illustrations of major concepts should be especially helpful to the less quantitatively oriented student.

12. LaFORGE, R. Components of reliability. *Psychometrika,* 1965, 30, 187–195.

    The traditional conceptualization of reliability lies within the analysis of variance framework. In this article, the author examines the concept of reliability from a multiple-factor analysis approach (see also Cronbach, *et al.,* 1963; Rajaratnam, *et al.,* 1965; Gleser, *et al.,* 1965).

13. LORD, F. M. A strong true-score theory, with applications. *Psychometrika,* 1965, 30, 239–270.

    Only for the quantitatively sophisticated, this article presents a mathematical model for the relation between observed and true scores. Students without adequate training in the calculus and differential equations will not follow the arguments presented.

14. LYMAN, H. B. *Test scores and what they mean.* Englewood Cliffs, N.J.: Prentice-Hall, Inc., 1963.

    This paperback should be an invaluable aid to those persons who must use test results, but have little or no training in testing.

15. NUNNALLY, J. C. *Tests and measurements: Assessment and prediction.* New York: McGraw-Hill Book Co., 1959.

    All the basic topics of psychological testing are discussed succinctly in the first 8 chapters (out of 18). Nunnally's style of writing in this text is somewhat less wordy than that of either Anastasi (1961) or Cronbach (1960) and therefore might be a useful supplement to either of them.

16. SINES, J. O.   Actuarial methods as appropriate strategy for the validation of diagnostic tests. *Psychological Review*, 1964, 71, 517–523.

   In this paper, Sines argues for using psychological test dimensions
as the initial bases on which to classify persons. Of course, he is not
alone in advocating this approach. The logic of his argument has
recently been criticized (see Lieberman, 1966).

CHAPTER 3

SOME TECHNICAL AND ETHICAL PROBLEMS OF PERSONALITY MEASUREMENT

Suppose you are instructed to indicate whether you agree or disagree with each of these statements:

—I am inclined to be tense or high-strung.
—Despite obstacles, I tend to see a job through.
—Often I am in low spirits.
—I am worried about sex matters.
—I wish I had more "pep."
—Dirty stories do not upset me.
—Once in a while I believe people are out to get me.
—Criticism of my work does not upset me.
—I am lonesome much of the time.
—Sometimes I am troubled by bothersome thoughts.

What is your reaction to the task? Are you inclined to be candid or resistant? Would your responses to the items differ depending on the conditions under which they are administered? That is to say, would you tend to answer one way if they were given you as part of a routine examination that you requested, and another way if they were part of an employment interview? What about these items as clues to the type of person you are? Do they seem relevant? And, finally, how did you feel about their personal and probing nature?

Imagine now a situation in which you are presented with a set of abstract drawings such as are shown in Figure 3–1, and asked to produce stories in association to each of them. What is your reac-

53

tion to this assignment? Would your stories vary under different circumstances? Suppose you had requested psychiatric aid for a particular problem. Does it seem likely that these abstract drawings and your associations to them would help the psychologist reconstruct the type of person you are? Certainly you would not object to the personal nature of the drawings. They are amorphous, abstract,

(a)   (b)

(c)   (d)

(e)

FIGURE 3–1.   Five ambiguous test stimuli similar to projective devices used by psychologists. Diagram (e) is very similar to a test item on the Rorschach inkblot technique.

nonrepresentational forms. But perhaps the very ambiguity of such a test situation—fraught as it may be with camouflaged bait—is an even more frightening experience than responding to written statements?

Personality measurement today uses tests that are made up of such items and drawings as were illustrated in the foregoing examples. The use of these tests to measure personality has occasioned reactions and questions similar to the ones you may have raised. Some of these questions are related to technical problems of personality measurement and concern the adequacy of the instruments used, and others raise ethical issues about the morality of using personality tests under various circumstances. In the discussion which follows several of the preceding and some other important technical and ethical problems of personality measurement are considered. An overview of the technical and ethical issues, and suggestions for their possible resolutions, are presented in Table 3–1.

TABLE 3–1

Technical and Ethical Problems of Personality Testing

	Problem	*Suggested Resolution*
Technical	1. Too many personality definitions.	1. Closer collaboration between theorist and psychometrician.
	2. A multitude of uses.	2. Careful validation of the test prior to its publication.
	3. The goals of the tester and respondent are disharmonious.	3. Construct "maximum performance" type tests rather than question-and-answer procedures.
	4. Personality sampling is difficult.	4. Devise more "real-life" test situations. Sample intensively. Tester must become as unobtrusive as feasible.
Ethical	1. Invasion of privacy.	1. Safeguard respondent's privileged communication. Inform respondent of the nature and purpose of the inquiry and the uses to which tests are put.
	2. Immorality.	2. Explain reason for personal probing (e.g., personality disorders are personal).
	3. Personality tests tend to dehumanize.	3. Remind oneself that more than just test results are involved in the test situation.
	4. Tests encourage cheating.	4. This is not a valid ethical problem. However, test critics' advice to cheat seems tantamount to instructing patients to "heat" their thermometers or "raise" their blood pressure.

TECHNICAL PROBLEMS

Problem 1: Descriptive versus Dynamic Conceptualizations of Personality

Earlier in this book it was noted that there is general disagreement among psychologists on a definition of personality and that there is a wide difference in the way various theorists conceptualize the structure of personality components. This difference creates many problems for personality measurement because it leads to the use of dissimilar organizing principles to add meaning to personality dimensions. Thus one investigator focuses on traits, and he chooses the method of factor analysis to arrive at personality variables; another is interested in physique and its relation to temperament, and he elects to measure body build of numerous personality types; and a third psychologist believes that early experiences are the key to personality development, and he focuses on the early recollections of individuals.

With a few exceptions, the formulations reflected in current personality measurement efforts tend to be of two kinds: the descriptive and dynamic approaches. Generally, descriptive approaches focus on the "what" or *surface* facets of behavior, and dynamic formulations probe into the "why" or *depth* aspects. Without detailing the specific definitions and theories that have been proposed by either side, it is sufficient to outline these broadly and to mention merely that the measurement goals of investigators within and between both sides of the descriptive-dynamic fence have been radically different.

Description of Personality. Descriptive formulations assert that personality is a composite of traits, habits, or specific response tendencies. The challenge that this approach presents to psychological measurement is expressed by Cronbach (1960, p. 500) in this way:

Therefore traits are sought which describe consistent behavior in a wide range of situations. The trait approach to personality hopes to describe economically the significant variations of behavior, neglecting unduly specific habits. Since the English dictionary offers no less than 17,953 adjectives describing traits, the problem of economy is a serious one.

The major proponents of description in personality have been G. W. Allport, H. J. Eysenck, R. B. Cattell, and J. P. Guilford. Each of these psychologists has a different mode of attack in the measurement of personality—and tends to define type, trait, and response tendencies differently—but all agree on the need for a quantitative approach to personality description.

Allport favors inference of traits from behavior observation, from case-study material, and through content analysis of personal documents (see especially Allport, 1942, 1965, 1966) rather than through psychological tests. His approach is more "idiographic" than those of most other descriptivists. Thus he would assert, for example, that persons are "honest" or "meticulous" in some situations but not in others. Consequently his idiographic analysis would define new traits as needed to fit each individual for a class of specific situations. The measurement difficulties of this approach are immense because of the large number of possible situations.

Eysenck, Cattell, and Guilford, on the other hand, who prefer to extract their traits by the method of factor analysis and the use of factor-pure tests, tend to think of traits as if they were general over a large class of situations. Thus Eysenck and Rachman (1965, p. 19) refer to dimensions as "stable" components of personality; and Cattell and Scheier (1961, p. 500) define a trait as a "characterological or relatively permanent feature." Guilford (1959, pp. 69–70) treats trait variability over time and situations as a problem of measurement reliability, and he attributes to errors of measurement any fluctuations from "true" trait positions.

There are personality measurement techniques in the descriptive tradition that fit into none of the above approaches, and have been constructed according to the "sign" principle of psychiatric classification. The Minnesota Multiphasic Personality Inventory (MMPI) is the outstanding example of this approach. It groups persons into psychiatric types on the basis of self-reported signs or symptoms, deviant response tendencies, and habits. It is a personality measuring instrument that not only lacks theory but is in fact intentionally atheoretic. The main guiding principle that governed this test's construction (Hathaway and McKinley, 1943) was the idea that any item is a good one if, and only if, it differentiates statistically between one group of persons and another. For example, if significantly more neurotic than normal persons respond "true" to the item, "The top of my head sometimes feels tender," then that item was considered an appropriate one to be placed on one of the test's "neurotic" scales.

The major difficulty that the descriptive approaches have presented for personality measurement has been the confusion created by the almost arbitrary coining of trait names. Consequently, the following questions are sometimes raised: What is the relationship between Eysenck's factor of Neuroticism and Bernreuter's Neurotic Tendency? Is Guilford's Introversion similar to the MMPI's Social Introversion (Si scale), or is it intended to measure something akin to Eysenck's Extroversion-Introversion dimensions? What about Cattell's Psychoticism—is that similar to Eysenck's use of the term? That some progress has been made in reaching a closer agreement between investigators in the field has been recently emphasized by Cattell (1957, 1961) and Eysenck (1965, p. 18), but there is much need for yet greater improvement.

Dynamics of Behavior. The descriptive tradition proceeds by isolating separate dimensions of personality and assigning scores to those dimensions. Individuals are then compared along a continuum of the trait under consideration. Dynamic dimensions, on the other hand, are difficult to measure, and investigators who advocate dynamic formulations generally tend to eschew quantitative efforts at anchoring their depth constructs. The depth theorists are interested in total personality patterns and integrating processes, rather than in discrete physical measures, habits, or particular object preferences. They rely principally on the interview and use ambiguous test stimuli (see Figure 3–1) as measurement techniques. Although the interview may yield valuable qualitative judgments about personality concepts, as it is commonly used it yields little more than subjective impressions of personality phenomena. Baughman and Welsh (1962, p. 282) aptly summarize the situation by drawing an analogy between a psychoanalyst who relies on the interview technique and a "chemist who, given an unknown substance to analyze, can report only what elements are present, not their amounts." The use of a series of drawings, symmetrical inkblots, or photographs to elicit personality components, although possibly productive from the point of view of the volume of verbal associations secured, is itself accompanied by a set of difficult measurement problems. By far the most recalcitrant of these problems is the depth theorist's reluctance to quantify these verbal productions.

Furthermore, psychologists who are interested in the dynamics of behavior use terms such as "ego-strength," "anality," or "super-ego,"[1] and they take their observations of these phenomena in clinical settings. Aside from the problem of recognizing such

---

[1] Common synonyms for these terms are willpower, stinginess, and conscience, respectively, but their technical meanings are embedded in Freudian Psychoanalytic theory and refer to a lifetime of developmental patterns.

personality dispositions or tendencies in persons, the question of validating these states arises. What, for example, shall the clinician use as a criterion of "ego strength" or "anality"? Moreover, how much of the quality must be observable before it merits one of these labels?

Therefore, dynamic constructs abound and it is difficult to connect theories of personality and its measurement. Depth-oriented psychologists who sense a need to introduce measurement to their conceptualizations simply have their personality constructs forced into the mold of available measuring devices. A notable exception to this is H. A. Murray's (1938) motivational or need theory of personality and his development of the *Thematic Apperception Test* (TAT) to measure the constructs of that theory. The TAT consists of cards showing pictures of people, and the respondent's task is to make up a story for each picture. Interpretation of these stories consists of analyses of the needs, feelings, and attitudes of the storyteller. Most psychologists use this information as a basis for verbal descriptions of the respondent, rather than a quantitative index of his personality dimensions; but the theory and the instrument used to measure its constructs are amenable to quantification.

There are disagreements within the descriptive and within the dynamic schools on what constitutes personality structure; but these disagreements are on a greater order of magnitude between schools. The major difference between the two seems to be in the extent to which the descriptivists are heavily committed to measurement, almost to the exclusion of theorizing about their measurement goals, and the extent to which the proponents of depth approaches overemphasize theory and ignore measurement. Part of the problem, to be sure, is due to the fact that dynamic personality constructs do not easily lend themselves to measurement and that descriptive approaches tend to defy theorization. In large part, however, there has been a lack of understanding and only a minimum of communication between psychologists interested in the measurement of personality and those interested in studying personality in depth. And this has led one psychologist (Fiske, 1963) to advise that if the study of personality is to progress as a science, a closer collaboration than exists now must be forged between psychometrician[2] and theorist.

---

[2] Psychologists interested in the theory and application of psychological tests.

Problem 2: The Many Uses of Personality Measurement

Personality measurement techniques are used for diverse purposes and have come to include many aspects of behavior variation. In Chapter 1 a number of these uses were noted, and they included such varied purposes as clinical diagnosis, counseling, personnel selection, and research. Maller (1944, p. 168) has presented a list of terms which these tests presumably measure, and it sounds like a free-association exercise to the word personality. The list includes mental health, personality adjustment, emotional adjustment, self-control, self-esteem, ascendance-submission, introversion-extroversion, neurotic tendency, personal inferiority, happiness, anxiety, fears, frustrations, and so on. The confusion for measurement arises when the test maker does not communicate to the user the purpose and appropriate use of his personality measuring technique. Added to this confusion is the fact that many investigators of different theoretical orientations borrow each other's techniques to measure their own favorite concepts—or, even more confusing, they use each other's techniques and apply different methods of scoring and interpretation.

The situation in achievement or ability testing is less complex. A test constructor interested in ascertaining the extent to which persons have benefited from a course of instruction or possess abilities in certain areas, proceeds in a straightforward manner to construct such a measure. Then test users interested in measuring similar areas can consult Buros' *Sixth Mental Measurements Yearbook* (1965) for the test most appropriate to their needs. A glance at the table of contents of the *Yearbook* will illustrate the point being made here. Achievement Batteries, for example, are divided into those that test business education, English, fine arts, foreign languages, and mathematics; and these sections are further subdivided into more specific subcategories (i.e., English is subdivided into composition, literature, speech, spelling, and vocabulary). The same specificity of purposes can be observed in the "Ability" and "Aptitude" test sections of the *Yearbook*.

The "Character and Personality" section, however, is divided only into the "nonprojective" and "projective" areas. Buros' table of contents, which is reproduced in Figure 3–2, reflects a real difference in specificity of aims between achievement and ability testing on the one hand, and personality measurements on the other. This difference in the main is due to the confusion that exists among personality test constructors about the purpose for which they design and intend to use their instruments. We do not mean to imply that a test constructed for one purpose is necessarily unsuitable for another. But unless much evidence—preferably in the form of empirical or construct-validity studies—is brought to bear on the

Table of Contents

* * * * *

<table>
<tr><td></td><td>PAGE</td><td></td><td>PAGE</td></tr>
<tr><td>CONTRIBUTING TEST REVIEWERS . . .</td><td>xi</td><td>Russian . . . .</td><td>670</td></tr>
<tr><td>PREFACE . . . .</td><td>xxiii</td><td>Spanish . . . .</td><td>672</td></tr>
<tr><td>INTRODUCTION . . . .</td><td>xxvii</td><td>INTELLIGENCE . . . .</td><td>680</td></tr>
<tr><td>TESTS AND REVIEWS . . . . . .</td><td>1</td><td>Group . . . .</td><td>680</td></tr>
<tr><td>ACHIEVEMENT BATTERIES . . . .</td><td>1</td><td>Individual . . . .</td><td>795</td></tr>
<tr><td>BUSINESS EDUCATION . . . . .</td><td>128</td><td>Specific . . . .</td><td>846</td></tr>
<tr><td>Bookkeeping . . . .</td><td>131</td><td>MATHEMATICS . . . .</td><td>862</td></tr>
<tr><td>Miscellaneous . . . .</td><td>132</td><td>Algebra . . . .</td><td>884</td></tr>
<tr><td>Shorthand . . . .</td><td>132</td><td>Arithmetic . . . .</td><td>895</td></tr>
<tr><td>Typewriting . . . .</td><td>136</td><td>Geometry . . . .</td><td>916</td></tr>
<tr><td>CHARACTER AND PERSONALITY . . .</td><td>141</td><td>Miscellaneous . . . .</td><td>920</td></tr>
<tr><td>Nonprojective . . . . . .</td><td>141</td><td>Trigonometry . . . .</td><td>921</td></tr>
<tr><td>Projective . . . .</td><td>409</td><td>MISCELLANEOUS . . . .</td><td>921</td></tr>
<tr><td>ENGLISH . . . .</td><td>540</td><td>Agriculture . . . .</td><td>921</td></tr>
<tr><td>Composition . . . .</td><td>586</td><td>Computational and Scoring Devices</td><td>921</td></tr>
<tr><td>Literature . . . .</td><td>599</td><td>Courtship and Marriage . . . .</td><td>924</td></tr>
<tr><td>Speech . . . .</td><td>602</td><td>Driving and Safety Education . .</td><td>936</td></tr>
<tr><td>Spelling . . . .</td><td>605</td><td>Education . . . .</td><td>938</td></tr>
<tr><td>Vocabulary . . . .</td><td>610</td><td>Etiquette . . . .</td><td>953</td></tr>
<tr><td>FINE ARTS . . . .</td><td>616</td><td>Handwriting . . . .</td><td>953</td></tr>
<tr><td>Art . . . .</td><td>616</td><td>Health and Physical Education . .</td><td>955</td></tr>
<tr><td>Music . . . .</td><td>619</td><td>Home Economics . . . . . .</td><td>967</td></tr>
<tr><td>FOREIGN LANGUAGES . . . . .</td><td>632</td><td>Industrial Arts . . . . . .</td><td>967</td></tr>
<tr><td>English . . . .</td><td>638</td><td>Listening Comprehension . . .</td><td>968</td></tr>
<tr><td>French . . . .</td><td>641</td><td>Philosophy . . . .</td><td>968</td></tr>
<tr><td>German . . . .</td><td>656</td><td>Psychology . . . .</td><td>969</td></tr>
<tr><td>Greek . . . .</td><td>667</td><td>Record and Report Forms . . .</td><td>969</td></tr>
<tr><td>Hebrew . . . .</td><td>667</td><td>Religious Education . . . . .</td><td>969</td></tr>
<tr><td>Italian . . . .</td><td>667</td><td>Socioeconomic Status . . . .</td><td>972</td></tr>
<tr><td>Latin . . . .</td><td>668</td><td>Test Programs . . . . . .</td><td>972</td></tr>
</table>

ix

FIGURE 3–2.   Reproduction of a portion of the Table of Contents of Buros' *Sixth Mental Measurements Yearbook* (1965). Notice that with the exception of the "Character and Personality" and the "Fine Arts" sections, all other test categories are further subdivided into three or more headings.

test's relevance for a variety of purposes, its use and interpretation should be restricted to the purpose and setting for which it is appropriate.

Problem 3: The Special Test Conditions of Personality Measurement

The usual instructions for a test of ability go something like this: "In this test you are to try to do your best, but do not expect to be able to answer all questions. If you do not know the answer to a question, you are encouraged (or not encouraged) to guess about the right one." These instructions are intended to motivate respondents to put forth a maximum effort. And if all other components of the test have been standardized, thus holding all conditions constant in this experimental setting for all respondents, then the test scores are presumed to be the dependent variables[3] which reflect true differences in ability.

However, the experimental operations for measuring personality are different from the foregoing. Personality testers cannot specify that personality is being measured because such information would modify the variables of greatest interest to them. Thus they resort to a deception when they instruct examinees that "there are no right or wrong answers"; certainly they cannot say, "try to do your best," because a personality test is a measure of what Cronbach (1960) calls typical rather than maximum performance, and instructions that encourage the respondent to maximize his efforts are irrelevant. The purpose of the examiner and the examined are not as harmonious, therefore, in personality testing as they are in other forms of psychological measurement because the examiner does not tell the respondent about the variable being measured. In other words, in personality measurement the goals of the investigator and subject are not shared; the former is interested in obtaining a sample of typical performance, and the latter may or may not be able to interpret his role accordingly. The way the respondent interprets the purpose of the test situation may have a number of unforeseen effects on the test scores, not the least of which includes intentional and unintentional test distortion.

---

[3] In every test situation, which essentially is a miniature experimental setting, there are independent and dependent variables. The former are the respondent and the information or disposition he brings to the test; and the dependent variable is the test outcome, or the score he earns.

As a partial solution to the uniqueness of the personality measuring situation, Fiske and Butler (1963, pp. 260–263) suggest that new types of instructions and new kinds of item materials be developed in an effort to make the testing conditions more comparable among respondents. They consider the MMPI correction scale K, which reflects intentional as well as unintentional test faking, to be a development in the right direction. The K scale consists of items that were included on the MMPI because they detect "fake good" and "fake bad" tendencies.

A more direct attack, they feel, might be to arrange test conditions and procedures in a way that would elicit or arouse the relevant personality dispositions to the greatest degree, without disclosing the nature of the variable being measured. Such procedures would set a reasonable task that the person would readily undertake, and would elicit responses that differentiate individuals on relevant personality dimensions. Essentially aptitude tests meet these requirements. Following the instructions, the respondent manipulates a set of dials and makes perceptual judgments of movement, color, apparent size, or binocular resolution. In short, when applied to personality measurement such procedures would resemble maximum performance tests, but would correlate with relevant personality dimensions.

Problem 4: Difficulties in Obtaining Representative Samples of Personality

The attempt to measure personality has run into another special kind of difficulty that does not exist in achievement or ability testing. The method of placing an examinee in a standard situation and obtaining a representative sample of what he has learned, or of his skills in performing certain tasks, generally is not applicable here. How would one go about setting up a situation to sample honesty, thrift, generosity, laziness, or cantankerousness? Many of the most important personality traits occur in social contexts and are elicited under a special set of circumstances.

It has been suggested (Cronbach, 1960) that the logical way to sample representative behavior would be to observe the individual repeatedly in situations likely to reveal the aspect of personality under investigation. To study honesty, therefore, one would observe what the individual does when tempted to cheat. To measure a professor's generosity one would note his grading of papers, his reactions to students' pleas for mercy, and his dealings with those around him.

Assuming that it is possible to obtain numerous observations of the respondent in a series of representative situations, problems arise nevertheless. The act of observing itself may alter or distort the behavior observed. The mere thought of the presence of a state highway patrolman, for example, has been known to alter the behavior of drivers. It is no wonder, then, that on most holiday weekends, police patrol cars (usually unoccupied) are placed at strategic and visible points on major highways.

One method psychologists have used to correct for such distortion as arises in observational settings has been to substitute reported for observed behavior. Instead of trying to reproduce an artificial social setting, or attempting to take observations of representative behaviors *in situ,* the psychologist may ask others to report the subject's behavior. Or the person himself may be asked to relate what are his typical patterns of reactions in a number of situations. Of course, these substitute methods themselves are fraught with pitfalls. Persons reporting others' behavior may be motivated to elaborate, embellish, withhold, or distort whatever information they possess. Similarly, self-reports are subject to numerous falsifications that invalidate the information being sought.

Another method that has been used to get around the difficulty of measuring typical or representative performance has been to set up a series of laboratory conditions likely to elicit certain kinds of specific behaviors. Thus a psychologist interested in observing persons under stress may arrange a set of stress conditions designed to evoke the desired reactions. But the artificial laboratory setting is so atypical for most persons, and the special tasks they are asked to perform are so unfamiliar to them (e.g., push levers, react to flashing lights, or arrange materials according to some specified order) that the elicited responses may not generalize to real-life situations. Moreover, the fact that in a laboratory stress situation a person "froze" and was unable to manipulate a certain series of dials properly may not carry over to stressful circumstances in real life where he may be called upon to perform a series of familiar or well-rehearsed responses.

The test-room setting, where the respondent is asked to indicate whether he agrees or disagrees with certain statements, or where he is instructed to tell stories about drawings, also suffers from a similar unrepresentativeness. When, for instance, in everyday life, is a person asked about his reactions to criticism or about his worries concerning sexual matters? And how often is the average person asked to make up stories about a series of abstract drawings or photographs? These are all unfamiliar experiences and require, for most people, an entirely new set of responses. And these responses may or may not reflect dimensions relevant to personality.

Problem 5: The Probabilistic Nature of Personality Indices

Finally, in personality measurement, the psychologist is interested in studying characteristics or indices of personality dimensions that appear sometimes, but may be nonexistent at other times. That is to say, personality measurement is concerned with moods, dispositions, propensities, and with response tendencies that are probabilistic rather than all-or-none, present-or-absent phenomena. For example, in an achievement test, a respondent either is or is not able to solve a problem, define a concept, cite a date or complete a series of questions about a subject matter. In personality testing, however, moods vary from one time to another, dispositions change, and responses can be elicited at certain times but not at others.

Personality measurement in clinical settings, where the psychologist may be interested in diagnostic classification, is beset by similar difficulties. Thus, a patient may be brought to a hospital by members of his family who report that he was abusive and assaultive. The psychologist then interviews the patient—perhaps several hours or a day or two after the patient's hospitalization; and he observes none of the characteristics that fit the description of the patient given by his family. As a matter of fact, the psychologist's impression is that the patient is a meek, humble, nonviolent person who is probably incapable of the acts ascribed to him by his family.

What has happened? Any one of a number of things. Possibly, the patient's anger or whatever led him to violence subsided by the time he was seen by the psychologist. Maybe the patient's awareness of the measurement situation altered his characteristic response tendencies. Or perhaps the patient's assaultiveness is only evoked by a particular set of circumstances, and by the presence of certain family members.

Many other instances illustrate the probabilistic nature of similar response tendencies in diagnostic work. For example, symptoms and signs of psychosis or neurosis are present in certain degrees and with specifiable probabilities. Thus not every psychotic person necessarily manifests bizarre behavior; or if such behavior is present, it is not evident at all times. The situation is no different in medicine, where the appearance of certain physical symptoms or signs (such as skin rash, swelling, or the presence of certain significant reflexes) is a probabilistic matter. Occasionally a case of mumps occurs with no evident glandular swellings; or a case of measles turns up without the typical accompanying rash or elevated body temperature. Thus it is apparent that in both medical diagnosis and personality measurement, certain symptoms, responses, and manifest behaviors have only a *tendency* to appear.

In personality measurement, these tendencies must be studied carefully; if their appearance is computed over a large number of persons and situations, then determinations can be made of their probable occurrence in given instances. Such computations require optimally reliable personality measuring tools and call for standardized test and laboratory conditions.

ETHICAL AND MORAL CONSIDERATIONS

The use of personality tests has been criticized on moral as well as on technical grounds, and most recently the ethical and moral issue climaxed in congressional investigations by Senate and House committees. A complete edition of the American Psychological Association's major professional journal of communication to its members, the *American Psychologist* (November, 1965) is devoted to a discussion and full coverage of the latest public airings of the ethical issues in psychological testing. The following discussion of these issues and others regarding the ethics of personality measurement, draws heavily on the material published in that edition.

Some Quasi–Technical Objections

Professor Smith's Argument. Perhaps the most discomforting experience for psychologists interested in maintaining the highest standards of scientific and professional integrity was the appearance at the congressional hearings of Karl U. Smith, the University of Wisconsin professor of industrial psychology. Aside from the irony of having a psychologist testify against the usefulness of tests, Professor Smith, in his testimony, portrayed the psychological tester as a sinister clod with "prescientific views of mental life." And, referring to personality measurement, Professor Smith asserted that there are "three types of 'character-reading' systems which persist in modern times: phrenology, body reading, and graphology." His testimony continues, ". . . although graphology and the reading of body types have been converted into quantitative procedures which are said to provide detailed descriptions of character, the evidence is that neither can specify personality characteristics with any validity."

Then in referring to the MMPI, which is a questionnaire type of test constructed to measure tendencies toward various kinds of psychiatric difficulties, Professor Smith commented[4]:

I would not make any recommendations for any department of the Federal Government in regard to its personnel programs, but I would say that any department of the Government which uses such a hodgepodge, claptrap series of questions ought to have its whole personnel operation carefully investigated from top to bottom.

Karl U. Smith's major quarrels with the technical aspects of the MMPI are (1) "the test has no theory"; and (2) it has "no relationship whatsoever to medically significant abnormality except in extreme cases."

Even Smith does not take his own first criticism seriously, because he states: "I look upon the work of Strong as possibly one of the few really good efforts in this whole field of inventory construction." As a matter of fact, Strong's Vocational Interest Blank (SVIB) and the MMPI were constructed by the same method —*empirical keying* (see Chapter 7)—and have "no theory" in the strict sense of the word. That is to say, both the SVIB and the

---

[4] Professor Smith's testimony came as no surprise to psychologists because he had expressed his dissatisfactions with tests on numerous occasions. However, his emotional outbursts about the "pseudo-quantitative mental-medical mumbo-jumbo of the psychiatrist and clinical psychologist, and the misleading propaganda of organized psychology" were unexpected. Equally surprising, but perhaps significant, was his testimonial for a personality assessment procedure of his own which he calls "a human quality control program."

MMPI were intentionally constructed by considering the experience with the items (i.e., do the items discriminate between different diagnostic groups?) rather than by using theory or common sense in deciding how items should be scored.

His second criticism suggests either that abnormality is not an extreme case or that the MMPI is valid in extreme cases but not valid for medical diagnosis. There is, of course, voluminous documented evidence to indicate that the MMPI is a valid instrument for screening maladjustment and for some psychiatric classification assignments (see Chapter 8); and by definition, maladjustments and psychiatric group membership are statistically infrequent occurrences or "extreme cases."

William H. Whyte's Argument.   The argument of William H. Whyte, Jr., author of the *The Organization Man* (1956) and assistant editor of *Fortune* magazine, was that personality tests are inaccurate because they are fakeable. Whyte's major criticism of personality tests is not focused on their inaccuracy but rather on their particular use in industry. In presenting his case, however, he does highlight their vulnerability to dissimulation. With a word of caution about cheating on the MMPI, "which is not a test for the amateur to trifle with" (p. 452), Whyte gives the following advice on how to cheat on personality tests (p. 450):

To settle on the most beneficial answer to any question, repeat to yourself . . .

   a) I loved my father and my mother, but my father a little bit more.
   b) I like things pretty well the way they are.
   c) I never worry much about anything.
   d) I don't care for books or music much.
   e) I love my wife and children.
   f) I don't let them get in the way of company work.

Actually these rules do not work in practice. One psychologist (Shaw, 1962) tested them in a study in which he administered the Bernreuter Personality Inventory—a relatively easy test to distort—to 51 respondents, once under ordinary job applicant conditions and then again following Whyte's rules. He did not find any statistically significant differences in test scores under the two conditions. However, *response set*—that is, the characteristics people consciously or unconsciously express in their answers to test items—and its possible effects on accuracy of test scores is a real concern to personality testers. Much has been done and written about this problem (see Chapter 8), and if it can be assumed for the moment that there are occasions when it is important to measure personality—and to measure it well—then William Whyte's aforementioned solutions are inadequate.

The Argument of Martin Gross. Martin Gross (1962), a former newspaper reporter and editor, who appeared at the Senate and House committee investigations, objects to personality tests on two grounds: "their inaccuracy and their immorality." The first of these criticisms is of immediate interest here. His technical arguments are somewhat less knowledgeable than those of Professor Smith, and seem to rest heavily on evidence that he borrowed from a superficial reading of the *Fifth Mental Measurements Yearbook* (Buros, 1959) and on vague reference to studies that failed to predict success on performance criteria. His major argument, simply stated is: "We have almost no information on how mental health relates to personality test scores." The overwhelming evidence indicates that this argument generally is not valid, and in this book an attempt is made to show that there are such relationships. That further studies are necessary to strengthen these relationships and the predictive power of personality tests cannot be denied. But to dismiss them on these grounds is unreasonable.

Invasion of Privacy

The most basic criticism of personality measurement—and a theme that came up recurrently at the congressional hearings—suggested that the use of these tests is an invasion of personal privacy. Aside from the issue that personality inventory questions about sex and religion are personal and should only be asked in privileged communication relationships, larger issues are raised by the invasion-of-privacy objection. These deserve the serious attention of psychologists.

Senator Sam J. Ervin, Jr., under whose chairmanship the Senate hearings were conducted, is concerned with the power over individuals that such tests give government administrators, and the employee's possible loss of due process.[5] Thus he writes in the *American Psychologist* (1965, p. 880) that he is concerned about

---

[5] In August 1966, Senator Ervin introduced a bill to the senate which, if passed, would outlaw "any psychological or polygraph tests" that would probe into private or personal matters.

"the procedural and due process issues involved in the administration of tests, including the employee's right to confront his accusers when his emotional stability and mental competency are questioned."

Congressman C. E. Gallagher, writing on the same topic in the *American Psychologist* (1965, pp. 881–882) states,

Remember there is nothing voluntary about these tests . . . persons could not select their own private psychologists and doctors to conduct and evaluate the tests. . . . I am sure that in some cases the tests are a useful tool in psychiatric evaluation when they are used in a clinical situation where there is a doctor-patient relationship. . . . What bothers me is that personnel people often are interpreting these tests, and the answers are reposing in some Government file somewhere, all set to follow the person throughout his career or non-career.

These are reasonable charges, brought against some uses of personality tests with which responsible psychologists have been

| Civil Service Bans Use Of Personality Testing | FIGURE 3–3. Headline in the *Washington Post*, Friday, June 4, 1965. |

CALIPERS ON THE HUMAN MIND

Why we misbehave like human beings was the question, and behaviorism was the answer – or was it?

By JOSEPH WOOD KRUTCH

FIGURE 3–4.   Headline in the *Saturday Review*, June 19, 1965.

Pupils Given 'Offensive' Personality Test

FIGURE 3–5.   Headline in the *Washington Post*, Friday, June 11, 1965.

concerned over the years. Unfortunately, in the past, uninformed and unreasonable critics such as Gross (1962) and Professor Smith, with their melodramatic displays of emotion and curious rhetoric, have managed to camouflage effectively similar objections. These are charges that should, and have, motivated psychologists to reexamine carefully their current test practices. It is precisely for these reasons that a leading advocate of personnel testing in industry, Professor Guion (1965, p. 379), has underscored the care that must be exercised in personality testing. He has advised that it is not enough, from an ethical viewpoint, to measure well. The measurement is justified only if it is related intrinsically or has demonstrated validity for performance on jobs, and if it is administered with the applicant's full realization of the purpose of the assessment.

There are occasions when personality tests are administered for screening purposes (such as in military settings, police work, or in the Peace Corps) where it is essential to know whether a person is unsuited for a particular assignment because of a potentially serious personality disorder. Tests such as the MMPI are administered in those instances not for their contribution toward making distinctions, for example, regarding a person's potential as sales manager or stock room clerk, but rather to help identify persons who could do serious harm to themselves and others, and who might even benefit from professional psychological counseling. It seems that such testing cannot be put on a voluntary basis because of the very nature of the situation. To ask candidates for critical job assignments to volunteer for personality tests might eliminate selectively the very persons on whom it is most important to obtain such test scores. However, the tester's twofold responsibility in these instances is, clearly: to safeguard the test results so that examinees' responses to items are kept in complete confidence; and to impart to respondents—insofar as possible and before test administration—the purpose of the inquiry and the uses of the test results.

Religious Prejudice and Immorality

The charge has been made that such MMPI items as "religion gives me no worry," and "I am very religious (more than most people)," violate the American tradition and the constitutional rights of a man to worship in any religion of his choosing. Moreover, the implication of critics has been that incorrect responses to these items could cost a person his job on grounds of religious discrimination. However, these items must be considered within the context of other questions that probe into a person's private affairs. For example, there are items on body functions, on

PSYCHING OUT

You Can't Flunk This Test But It Tattles On Your Id

By ART BUCHWALD

FIGURE 3–6.

Headline in the *Washington Post*, Sunday, June 20, 1965.

FIGURE 3–7.

Headline in the *Washington Post*, Sunday, July 4, 1965.

Personality X-Rays or Peeping Toms

By WILLARD CLOPTON
Washington Post
Staff Writer

Shriver Defends Personality Tests For Peace Corps

FIGURE 3–8.

Headline in the *Washington Post*, Thursday, June 10, 1965.

private thoughts, family matters, sex, and in short there are items relevant to most aspects of psychological life that may be symptomatic of maladjustment and emotional disorder.

This is a delicate issue, one that Professor Hathaway, coauthor of the MMPI, discussed recently; and one that requires some technical understanding of the MMPI's rationale. Hathaway (1964, pp. 206–207) draws the following analogy which makes the point aptly:

If the psychologist cannot use these personal items to aid in the assessment of people, he suffers as did the Victorian physician who had to examine his female patients by feeling the pulse in the delicate hand thrust from behind a screen . . . it is obvious that if we were making a new MMPI, we would again be faced either with being offensive to subgroupings of people by personal items they object to or, if we did not include personal items and were inoffensive, we would have lost the aim of the instrument.

To interpret the MMPI or any other personality test as an immoral instrument intended for uses of religious discrimination is a favorite tactic and the creation of such alarmists as Gross (1962). Their solution is the abolishment of these evil instruments, and their appeal is pitched at the level of the anxious test victims that they helped create. For them the individual

. . . victim is projected into a frightening situation where his livelihood depends on the whims of some shadowy institutional decision-maker poring over his test protocols, while his children, under the watchful eyes of school teachers, are recording his intimate family habits on test blanks. (Forehand, 1964, pp. 853–854).

In a singularly inelegant appeal to the power of the state, Gross (1965) makes the following charge of immorality (p. 959) :

Personality tests, in my opinion, are the newest pseudoscientific form of prejudice. With the enactment of legislation and the increasing awareness of the community, many of our older racial and religious prejudices are dying. However, the false discipline of personality testing is attempting to bring it back by stating—through unreliable test scores rather than proven behavior—that someone is "neurotic," or "potentially schizophrenic," or "maladjusted," or "introverted". . . I would think that potential victims of this new discrimination need equal protection under our FEPC laws.

This is a curious statement indeed in our time when preventive medicine is being practiced and everyone is urged to get chest X rays ("RADIATION!!" cry the alarmists), to obtain immunizing shots, and even to drink fluoridated water. The basic justification for personality tests is the same. It is no more prejudicial or immoral to be called "tubercular," "allergic," or "cardiac" than it is to be called "maladjusted." All of these conditions are amenable to treatment—and that is all that really matters, alarmists' objections to the contrary notwithstanding.

Personality Tests Encourage Conformity and Safe Attitudes

The notion that personality tests entrench the mundane and the prosaic by encouraging conformity and "safe" attitudes has been offered by both Whyte (1956) and Gross (1962). Whyte cautions the aspiring organization man to recognize that you do not win a good score on a personality test, "you avoid a bad one" (p. 449). Play it "safe," he advises, and "give the most conventional, run-of-the-mill, pedestrian answer possible."

Similarly, Gross refers to personality tests being used to find the "Square American." Respondents who confess an interest in art, music, literature, or culture are too well-rounded to be accepted. To be "well adjusted" is to be unimaginative, docile, safe, and dull—and these are the men hired and promoted to positions of power in industry—while the imaginative, intense, risk-taking men are rejected as potential rabble-rousers.

Perhaps this is all true—although again we find the popularizers overstating their case—but what has this to do with personality tests? The problem of conformity is a real one. There are pressures in our society that dictate undue attention to fads, customs, and conformity. There are also pressures among certain groups to oppose conformity at any cost. Possibly the public at large is long overdue for reeducation on this matter. To conform or not to conform is not the basic question here; rather, the issue seems to be that certain uses of personality tests by hiring employers and agencies have been in the direction of seeking persons with safe attitudes. Neither blame for conformity nor credit for individuality can be attributed to testing. If it is argued that personality tests are the tools of persons who will misuse them, and therefore we should abolish these tools—then equally convincing arguments could be mustered for the abolition of other man-made evils such as electricity and automobiles. Hathaway (1964), in this regard, rather than trying to defend every use or misuse of personality tests, sums the situation up as follows (p. 204):

To attack tests is, to a certain extent, comparable to an attack upon knives. Both good and bad use of knives occurs because they are sharp instruments. To eliminate knives would, of course, have a limiting effect upon the occurrence of certain hostile acts, but it would also greatly limit the activities of surgeons.

Personality Tests Encourage Lying and Cheating

The notion that personality tests encourage cheating is closely related to the suggestion that tests are responsible for conformity. Insistence on the prosaic and the mundane—the argument goes—creates a situation in which applicants who prize their individuality are morally obligated to cheat. And to dispense their own moral obligation to those who would like to cheat, Gross and Whyte even offer sets of rules on "how to cheat in personality tests" to guide the imaginative but inept faker.

Professor Smith (1965), in his testimony before the Senate, has the following to say about lying on tests (p. 911):

. . . a test like the MMPI probably most effectively picks out people who either know how to, or are willing to, carry on superficial lying in a situation when it is more or less socially approved. The application of such a test to the Peace Corps means that you probably have in the Peace Corps a great number of people whose prime trait is the ability to lie in a minor way in situations where it is socially approved. These results are not our own results, but the results of some of the best studies which have ever been done on the MMPI.

Faking or lying is a real problem on personality tests, but for different reasons than Professor Smith suggests. We touch upon some of the "best studies" referred to in Smith's testimony in Chapter 8, and even a casual perusal of the findings of these studies indicates that it takes more than just a willingness to "carry on superficial lying" to succeed in this enterprise. As a matter of fact, the L, F, and K scales of the MMPI—designed specifically to detect faking—perform surprisingly well in picking up such tendencies. Perhaps it is incumbent upon the psychologist, in order to discourage lying and cheating on personality tests, to publicize the difficulty that a prospective dissimulator may encounter.

Dehumanizing Aspects of Personality Tests

Willard Clopton (1965), a feature writer for the *Washington Post,* calls attention to a problem with which every testing psychologist ought to familiarize himself (p. 875):

Because I respect psychology as a profession and have liked or admired most of its practitioners that I have met, I am inclined to give it the benefit of any doubt. Still, in psychology, I have run across a few human data processors. I think we need to be aware of those who are so uneasy in their dealings with people that, rather than treat with them in their infinite complexity, they much prefer converting them to a set of coded traits in a card index.

And again in the special edition of the *American Psychologist* (1965), Monroe Freedman, an attorney and a person keenly aware of the potential harm that lies in the misuse of tests, has this to say (p. 878):

. . . modern computer technology makes it possible to analyze, sort and retrieve quantities of data that would have been impossible to use on a comprehensive basis formerly. Thus, a central law enforcement agency can today compile dossiers of the most extensive and intensive type. The ready availability of psychological tests of tens of thousands of our citizens is not the least frightening aspect of the impact of modern technology on the relationship between state and citizen.

These thoughtful and provocative reminders to the practicing psychologist of his special responsibility to his fellow human beings set important goals for the psychologist and serve a valuable function. It is possible to become so deeply involved in the technical details of one's craft that perspectives about the objects of that craft are lost. This must not be allowed to happen.

Ethical Standards of Psychologists

To the charges made against the technical excellence of personality tests—wherever relevant and informed—the psychologist can only reply with further research efforts designed to sharpen his measurement tools. For this purpose he must be well trained in his craft and he must use—among other sources of information—the two standard guidelines which reflect the most critical thinking on this matter: *Standards for Educational and Psychological Tests and Manuals* (American Psychological Association, 1966) and the *Sixth Mental Measurements Yearbook* (Buros, 1965).

The accusations regarding the misuse of tests must be heeded rather than defended against, because undoubtedly there are instances of abuse. As a professional group, psychologists are probably the most self-critical of all practitioners, and if they are not the first to detect unethical practice or incompetence, they are certainly not slow in recognizing it when it is revealed by others.

Here too, as in the instance of technical guidelines, the psychologist's conduct is directed by a code of *Ethical Standards of Psychologists* (American Psychological Association, 1953, 1959, 1963). In view of the charges recently made, it is relevant to reproduce here the preamble to the statement of *Ethical Standards* (American Psychological Association, 1959, p. 279):

The psychologist is committed to a belief in the dignity and worth of the individual human being. While demanding for himself the rights of freedom of inquiry and freedom of communications, he accepts the responsibilities that these freedoms imply. He maintains integrity with respect to the facts of his science and in his relationships with other psychologists and with the public. He does not use his psychological knowledge or insights to secure personal advantage, nor does he knowingly permit his services to be used by others for purposes inconsistent with his own ethical standards.

Specific violations of ethical standards with regard to personality measurement are carefully spelled out and include: selling personality tests to unqualified persons, and making unwarranted claims for a clinical instrument's ability to predict job-relevant behavior. Violators of these standards are often admonished to "cease and desist" their activities. Failure to comply with such admonishment has in numerous instances resulted in expulsion from the American Psychological Association.

SUMMARY

The many conceptualizations of personality, the varied uses of personality tests, and the lack of agreement about the behavior domain to be sampled and predicted have made personality measurement a particularly difficult enterprise. Formulations of personality structure generally fall into two broad classes: the descriptive and the dynamic. Descriptive or surface explanations assert that personality is a composite of traits, habits, or response tendencies, and accordingly measurement efforts are concentrated on quantifying these attributes. The major contributors to this approach have been G. W. Allport, H. J. Eysenck, R. B. Cattell, and J. P. Guilford.

Theorists who are interested in dynamic personality formulations, because of their search for the "why" of behavior, have tended to regard description as static and sterile. Their method of choice for studying personality has been the interview; and when they turn to psychological tests, they tend to prefer less structured test stimuli than the descriptivists' personality questionnaires.

The major difference between the two approaches is that the proponents of personality description have a strong psychometric tradition—sometimes to such an extent that they lack understanding of the problems of the personologist; and individuals who favor the dynamic approach tend to ignore measurement problems and concentrate their efforts on theorizing. There is an urgent need for closer collaboration between psychometrician and theoretician.

Additionally, the unique relationship that exists in personality testing between examiner and examinee is not duplicated in any other form of psychological testing, and this creates a special type of measurement problem. Because of the nature of the information the personality tester attempts to obtain, his goals are not harmonious with those of the respondent. The tester cannot say "try your best" or "there is only one right answer," but must resort, instead, to such instructions as "be as honest as possible in your self-descriptions," or, "there are no right or wrong answers."

The problems of personality testing include ethical and moral considerations as well as technical ones. Criticism has been launched with increasing frequency against testing in general, and personality test practices in particular. Not all the criticism reflects rational and careful consideration, and some of it is blatantly misinformed. All varieties of points of view on the ethics of personality testing were recently represented at Senate and congressional committee hearings.

Some of the objections to testing were couched in quasi-technical jargon and claimed that personality tests are inaccurate tools and are outgrowths of phrenology, body reading and graphology; but the major objection raised recurrently at the hearings concerned invasion of privacy. Related considerations were, that tests may be used in a manner that denies persons due process, and the power that tests give government administrators. Some specific personality test items came under attack at the hearings because they probe into an individual's religious beliefs, and thus seem to violate the traditional American regard for freedom of worship. Moreover, critics pointed out that the frank sexual nature of personality test items are immoral and constitute intrusions into the citizen's private life. Many of these objections point to shortcomings of personality tests that psychologists have been trying to correct for years; others are directed at the very aims of personality testing, which must deal with extremely personal and sometimes deeply embarrassing topics. The inconvenience caused some persons in answering such items is one of the unfortunate by-products that deserves the attention of testing psychologists.

Most interested and informed psychologists are concerned about, and have always been responsive to, the public's reactions to their practices. Accusations made regarding the misuse of tests have been heeded rather than defended against in the past, and there is little question that forthcoming editions of the American Psychological Association's *Ethical Standards of Psychologists* will reflect, as in the past, some of the thoughtful objections that were raised at the recent hearings.

FOR FURTHER READING

1. ALLPORT, G. W. *Pattern and growth in personality*. New York: Holt, Rinehart & Winston, 1961.

Professor Allport's book is the revised and up-to-date version of his well known *Personality: A Psychological Interpretation* (1937). Of special pertinence here is the author's section on "Assessment of Personality" (pp. 395–494) which consists of a survey of methods used to study personality. It is a knowledgeable analysis of the area by one of its foremost contributors.

2. AMRINE, M. The 1965 Congressional inquiry into testing: A commentary. *American Psychologist*, 1965, 20, 859–870.

Traditionally, the cover of the psychologists' trade journal has been blue. This edition, November, 1965, is green, possibly designed to reflect the profession's mood regarding the Hearings on tests. The Congressional Hearings are adeptly summarized by Amrine.

3. CRONBACH, L. J. The two disciplines of scientific psychology. *American Psychologist*, 1957, 12, 671–684. Also reprinted in MEDNICK, MARTHA & MEDNICK, S. A. (Eds.), *Research in personality*. New York: Holt, Rinehart & Winston, 1963. Pp. 3–22.

In his APA presidential address, Cronbach spoke of two mainstreams in the history of psychology: experimental and correlational psychology. He reviewed the contributions of each of these disciplines and emphasized the need to study phenomena experimentally without losing sight of individual differences (e.g., correlational psychology).

4. FISKE, D. W. Problems in measuring personality. In WEPMAN, J. M. & HEINE, R. W. (Eds.), *Concepts of personality*. Chicago: Aldine Publishing Co., 1963. Pp. 449–473.

Always lucid in his analyses of measurement problems, Fiske provides a cogent argument in this chapter for the rapprochement of theory and measurement in the study of personality.

5. FOREHAND, G. A.　Comments on comments on testing. *Educational and Psychological Measurement*, 1964, 24, 853–859.

At a conference held at the Pennsylvania Psychological Association in 1963, which included among its participants Martin Gross, alarmist and author of *The Brain Watchers*, Professor Forehand presented this sane analysis of the testing scene. The conference topic was "The Use and Misuse of Tests."

6. FULKERSON, S. C. & BARRY, J. R.　Methodology and research on the prognostic use of psychological tests. *Psychological Bulletin*, 1961, 58, 177–204.

Prognostic studies are beset with difficulties. Some of these difficulties, and a number of possible resolutions, are detailed in this tightly packed review.

7. HOLT, R. R.　Experimental methods in clinical psychology. In WOLMAN, B. (Ed.), *Handbook of clinical psychology*. New York: McGraw-Hill Book Co., 1965. Pp. 40–77.

Recognizing the limited scope of one chapter in a Handbook for tackling large problems, Holt sets out nevertheless to sketch the many problems that beset the clinician who aspires to introduce experimental methodology in the applied setting. His outline, which includes a listing of technical as well as ethical problems, will undoubtedly become required reading for all students of personality.

8. LOEVINGER, JANE.　Person and population as psychometric concepts. *Psychological Review*, 1965, 72, 143–155.

In her presidential address to the APA Division of Evaluation and Measurement (Division 5), Dr. Loevinger examined the logic of measurement in psychology. She concluded that many psychometric methods rest on the tenuous assumption of random sampling in realms where such sampling does not occur.

9. WHYTE, W. H.　*The organization man*. Garden City, N.Y.: Doubleday-Anchor Books, 1956.

Although highly critical of the use of tests in personnel selection on ethical and technical grounds, Whyte instructs the inept faker on how to cheat on personality tests.

PART II

Personality Testing Approaches

CHAPTER 4

OBSERVATIONAL METHODS

Basic to all scientific study—physical, biological, or psychological—is direct *observation* of the subject matter under investigation. In sharp contrast to the layman's everyday casual, haphazard, or unsystematic perceptions, the psychologist's observation of persons and events consists of deliberate and systematic *search*, carried out with planning and forethought. Scientific observation does not differ from everyday perception by being infallible; rather, it differs in that it is more accurate. The trained psychologist, being familiar with the limitations of his senses and with his previous errors of observation, strives in future observations to take into account his errors and he tends to correct them.

Direct observation is a useful way to obtain information about the way persons behave in various situations, but it is not the only way. There are *indirect* observational[1] procedures for collecting behavioral data—i.e., interviews,[2] self-report tests, questionnaires, available records, and personal documents are used as substitutes for direct observation. The real advantage, however, of direct viewing of behavior over its substitutes is that it permits the noting of behavior simultaneously with its spontaneous occurrence. Moreover, direct observation is independent of the subject's ability or willingness to report.

In this chapter, the first of two on observational procedures, numerous techniques of, and data collected by, direct observation

[1] The term "indirect observation" is used by some authors (Kaplan, 1964) to denote inferences based on observations. In this book, indirect observation refers only to the collection of data that does not consist of direct viewing of behavior.

[2] Direct observation does occur, of course, during the interview.

83

are considered, as well as some of the advantages and disadvantages of available methods. The emphasis will be on *naturalistic* rather than *controlled* observation. The next chapter focuses on methods in which the observer exercises certain controls over the situation, as well as consideration of a number of hardware and record-keeping aids he uses to sharpen his observations.

NATURAL AND CONTROLLED OBSERVATION

The psychologist can obtain his raw data by direct observation of persons in a natural or in a controlled setting. The former is an attempt to view behavior of organisms in their familiar, indigenous or native surroundings, and is an especially useful technique when one wants to interfere as little as possible with the unfolding of behavior in all its complexity. The clinician who visits the home of clients to observe family patterns (e.g., at dinner or at play), the anthropologist who lives among aborigines, the zoologist who views gorillas in their natural habitat, and the parent who visits his child's classroom, all exemplify the method of taking observations in natural, living environments. Although their presence may modify the objects under study, they nevertheless obtain firsthand impressions of their subjects' behavior and surroundings. Thus they need not rely on reports or hearsay of, for example, the squalor, splendor, peculiarities, or any other characteristics or conditions possibly significant in their influence on the subjects under study.

In the controlled observation, which usually occurs in the laboratory, the observer modifies the surroundings according to his research needs. The major distinction between the two conditions of observation, although not always a sharp one, is that in the natural situation the psychologist must wait for behavior to unfold; whereas in the controlled arrangement he can create circumstances and systematically introduce variables that elicit certain responses. The controls may consist of special arrangements of furniture and toys in a playroom, or they may be more rigid and be characterized by the systematic introduction of a number of variables into the observed situation (i.e., amount of stress, noise level, number of persons). In controlled observations, the investigator strives to set up a situation in which conditions are standard and replicable and where similar behavior dimensions may be observed repeatedly.[3] Illustrations of both natural and controlled observational settings, and some behavior patterns typically viewed under each of these conditions, are presented in Figure 4–1.

(a)

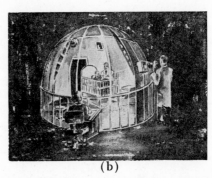
(b)

FIGURE 4–1. Children at play in (a) natural and (b) controlled settings.

OBSERVER PARTICIPATION

As a personality measurement technique, direct observations of behavior in natural or controlled situations can proceed in any one of four possible ways: (1) the observer is present in the setting, and the subject is aware of the fact that he is being studied; (2) the observer is present but blends into the setting, and the subject does not know he is being observed; (3) the observer does not participate, but the subject knows he is being observed; (4) the observer does not participate and subject is unaware of being studied. These forms of observation, and examples of each, are present in Table 4–1.

The first situation—in which the subject knows he is studied and the investigator is present—is perhaps best exemplified by the *clinical* method. This method is so called because data are collected in the clinic from observations made by a diagnostician or therapist in the course of interviewing and treating his patients for psychological problems. During the interview, observations are made of the respondent's appearance, mode of dress, attitudes, and general behavior, as well as the quality and quantity of his speech (e.g.,

---

[3] When the observer has control over all the variables that influence the subject under consideration—except, of course, that he cannot control the outcome—then he has conducted an "experiment." An experiment, psychological or otherwise, is nothing more than "controlled observation."

TABLE 4-1

Observer and Subject Participation in Direct Observations

Observer	Subject	Example
Visible	Aware	Clinical interview
Visible	Unaware	In the study of infants or very young children; or with some deception, adults can be studied by this method also.
Not visible	Aware	Usually the subject being observed in a training setting (e.g., learning to interview) knows he is being watched or recorded.
Not visible	Unaware	Observer may conceal himself behind screen or viewing mirror.

what he talks about, the level of his vocabulary, how much he says, and how quickly he speaks). While these data are being collected and verified, the clinician forms hypotheses regarding the relationship among the various social, economic, parental, educational, and other factors responsible for the respondent's behavior. He enter-

Photo: Bill Witte

FIGURE 4-2. Although the interviewee is aware of being studied, the skilled clinician can often succeed in making himself as unobtrusive as possible.

tains a number of hypotheses, and rejects or accepts them as further observations and his own experience may indicate. To be sure, there are a host of variables operating in such a situation that may serve to distort his observations, but the method can be extremely useful in the hands of a clinician who recognizes the limitations of his presence in the situation and interprets the findings accordingly.

The second condition for observation, where the observer is visible and the subject is unaware of being studied, is appropriate either in instances where very young children are subjects or when the observer assumes an incognito role.

In the study of children, the observer is usually an interested parent or relative who studies and records the behavior of a single child. This approach is best suited to the study of child development from infancy onward and has been called the *longitudinal* method. Longitudinal study furnishes information about the patterns and processes of change over the long run. Of course, this method of

FIGURE 4–3. Photograph of an infant under observation. (From "The visual cliff," E. S. Gibson and Donald Walk, *Scientific American*, April, 1960. Photo © William Vandivert.)

observation is subject to errors due to the biases of the interested observer. For example, parents who are eager to have their children walk, talk, or use certain skills "on time," may record the occurrence of such behavior prematurely or they may train their children selectively for those behaviors that will be recorded.

When an observer assumes an incognito role, either he or a confederate chosen by him attempts to blend into the setting with his subjects. This calls for considerable planning, and often necessitates deception in order to achieve unobtrusiveness. Allen Funt, of the television show "Candid Camera," who has been called "the most visible of the hidden observers" (Webb *et al.*, 1966, p. 156), is noted for particularly skillful ways of disguising his or one of his staff member's identity. In one sequence of film, for example, he prepared a comparison situation of how men and women react to viewing a woman driver maneuvering an automobile out of a tight parking space. The woman driver managed in each of the episodes to convince either a male or a female "victim" that she needed assistance in getting out of her space. The critical materials are the facial expressions, the conversation, and the bodily gestures of the men and women onlookers, as they watched her systematically wreck first the automobile behind her, then the automobile parked in front of her. The men typically winced, shouted, pleaded for her to stop, volunteered to do it for her, and seemed generally to react in utter despair. The women onlookers, on the other hand, showed little emotion, kept up a constant chatter with the driver ("no, honey, that's not quite it"), and generally reacted as if wrecking two automobiles were just one of the hazards to be expected under the given circumstances.

In the third observer-to-subject relationship, where the subject knows he is being observed but the investigator is not visible, the arrangement calls for placing the observer behind a screen, or could consist of placing tape recorders or movie cameras within settings where subjects are observed. Typically, this procedure is used in training programs where it is important to study the reactions of trainees in certain situations. For example, in teaching students to interview clients, it is helpful both to the student and the client if such an interview is monitored by an observer. Although the observer is usually behind a two-way viewing mirror, and not visible to either the client or the interviewer, the latter is very much aware of being studied, and his interview behavior is influenced by such awareness.

Finally, the optimal method of study is one in which the observer does not participate and the subject is unaware of being observed. It is optimal because it is the situation least likely to modify the behavior under consideration. This arrangement is most easily accomplished when studying young children. Thus in child guidance clinics, play sessions are often observed when toys and equipment of a playroom have been especially contrived to elicit reactions to some of the problems that arise in the child's interaction with parents or peers. It is useful also at times to bring several adult members of the family into the playroom in order to note the ensuing interaction patterns. Generally, it is exceedingly difficult, for practical reasons, to study adults without their knowledge and consent, and therefore the behavior observed when they are introduced into a setting is altered considerably.

SPECIAL TYPES OF OBSERVATION: IN NATURAL SETTINGS

Regardless of the extent of observer participation, the types of observations taken in a natural setting play a major role in determining the amount of information obtained. There are two major special types of observations that are common—time sampling and incident sampling—each with advantages for particular purposes, and each with its own set of problems.

Time Sampling

Time sampling is one of the best approaches to precise observation. Arrington (1943) has defined time sampling in natural settings as a method of observing behavior "under the ordinary conditions of everyday life in which observations are made in a series of short time periods so distributed as to afford a representative sampling of the behavior under observation." This technique was designed to overcome many of the disadvantages encountered in anecdotal descriptions of children's behavior. Originally used by Willard Olson (1929) to record the incidence of "nervous habits" in school children, the method has undergone many changes over the years.

In time sampling, a schedule of observations is determined in advance and the objective of such a schedule is to obtain short, well-distributed time samples. The advantage of such sampling is that it allows for variation of situations; and the cumulative picture which is obtained over many short periods is more likely to be typical of the subject's behavior than one obtained in less frequent, but longer, periods.

Most time sampling studies have been conducted with children, and among the specific behaviors studied have been language usage, level of vocabulary, physical contacts, quarrels, friendship patterns, and aggression. A set of thorough procedural rules for obtaining time samples has been proposed by Barker and Wright (1955). They emphasize the importance of training observers to function as objective recording instruments and call for standardization of the observational routine.

Standardization of this procedure should include, among other things, complying with observational periods that do not exceed 30 minutes; taking verbatim recordings; timing the duration of certain observed episodes; and subsequent to the observation, a careful dictation of notes. The latter should be followed by several interrogation periods in which the observer clarifies to a nonparticipating judge certain ambiguities that may exist in the dictation.

More specific "content rules" are also recommended for observers. These consist of reminders to focus on the behavior and the context within which it occurs, and to record behavior positively —i.e., to record what the subject did and not what he omitted to do. Finally, and most important for time sampling, Barker and Wright suggest continuous, minute-by-minute notations, and they caution the observer not to delimit his observations within time intervals. Thus it is incorrect to record that between 3:15 and 3:20 the subject sat quietly; rather the correct procedure is to note that at 3:15 "S is sitting quietly"; 3:16, "S is sitting quietly"; 3:17, "S got up to get a drink of water," and so on. This method of continuous recording avoids the problem of obtaining selected behavior over time. Thus rather than *sampling* behavior, they *census* it. In one of their studies (Barker, 1963), observations were made of a child during a morning "break" at school. Excerpts of these notations are presented in Table 4–2. A sample of the investigator's classification of behavior units is presented also. In the stream of behavior presented in Table 4–2, the units occurring during one minute are classified within a larger category and then within a small subcategory, representing less and more fragmentary behavior segments, respectively.

TABLE 4-2

Excerpt of Behavior of Brett Butley During Morning "Break"

Eating orange	Noting hurt child	10:39—Miss Graves (Brett's teacher) came through the yard leading a loudly crying little girl, and turned her over to Miss Rutherford (the teacher of the lower Infants), who was near the canteen building.
		Brett glanced at this.
	Watching Cricket	He stood watching the cricket game.
		He stuffed the last piece of orange into his mouth.
Noting hurt child		Miss Rutherford came by with the girl who now had a large discolored bump on her forehead.
		Brett glanced at this girl with mild interest.
Playing cricket		10:40—Brett walked over to the boy who had been batting.
		He took the bat. . . .

SOURCE: Adapted from Barker, 1963.

An example of a study in which many of the procedures suggested by Barker and Wright were followed is one which studied the interpersonal behavior of six children in a residential treatment center (Raush et al., 1959). The boys were observed during breakfast, when taking snacks before bedtime, during structured game activities, while busy at unstructured group activities, and during an arts and crafts period. The investigators dictated their observations and refrained as much as possible from interpreting their data. In the later analysis, they coded their data according to love-hate and dominant-submissive bipolarizations. Their results indicated that over an 18-month observation period, the interpersonal behavior of the children shifted mainly in their relationships to adults. All the changes were in the direction aimed at by the treatment program. However, it has been pointed out (Sundberg and Tyler, 1962, p. 403) that it is not clear from these observations to what extent the changes can be attributed to treatment and to what extent they resulted from the natural development of children over an 18-month period.

Some researchers (Johnson and Medinnus, 1965) have correctly noted that time sampling will not work when the behavior under study is either covert or not readily observable. The technique is particularly unsuitable for observing behavior which is infrequent or rare. For example, such infrequent occurrences as the development of attachments, compliance, undependability, or fire-setting could not be readily observed by this method.

Incident Sampling

In incident sampling, certain occurrences of selected behavior, rather than behavior during selected periods of time, are observed and recorded. For example, the clinician who is interested in obtaining observations of a patient each time the latter converses with his imaginary persecutor, or the clinician who wants information about the circumstances surrounding a patient's tremor, must either know when the incidents are going to occur and be present when they do, or he must wait until they occur. Because of this feature, and because it is difficult to predict the occurrence of certain incidents such as quarrels, emotional outbursts, or even repetitively occurring rituals, this method probably is better suited for the observation of planned incidents rather than behavior which unfolds slowly and in natural settings. Such planned incidents could consist of problem-solving situations, or a "rigged" playroom in which a child is required to cope with a certain incident. The time sampling technique, as we noted earlier, would ordinarily miss such infrequent and variable behaviors.

The *critical incident technique*, devised by Flanagan (1954), requires that instances of behavior be recorded that are especially favorable or unfavorable for a given purpose. Thus, during a two- or three-week period, a teacher or a parent may be instructed to keep a record of all instances of specific actions of a child; or a mother may be asked to record, in detail, every instance of aggression observed in her child. Similarly, in industry, a supervisor may be instructed to keep a record of all instances of specific actions that are characteristic of good and poor workers on his staff.

TYPES OF DATA OBTAINED IN NATURAL SETTINGS

Exterior Physical Signs and Cues

What are some of the cues that influence people's judgments of others? Generally, facial appearance, physique, such modes of adornment as clothes, jewelry, and personal possessions have been used as indices of personality traits. That these cues are often mistakenly perceived as present when they are not, and that they are often interpreted incorrectly as significant indices of personality traits, have been repeatedly demonstrated in a miniature classroom experiment.

Typically, in such an experiment, an instructor invites a student (who is an accomplice in the experiment) to come into the room and join him in conversation. After an exchange of some pleasantries about the weather and similar topics, the eyewitnesses are instructed to write for three minutes their impressions of the visitor. Invariably, students who witness such demonstrations report widely separate impressions regarding the visitor's physical characteristics (weight, height, clothing) and his conversation and behavior in the classroom. These disparate descriptions have been shown frequently to be due to divergent past experience, different expectancies, and varying attitudes among observers. Even under conditions where the untrained observers know they will be questioned about the scene they are going to witness, such distortions occur.

The personality descriptions of these observers tend to be widely separate also, and suggest that most observers go beyond the facts as presented. Moreover, viewers tend to make all they can of such facts as they obtain. Some of the cues that contribute to distortions in person perceptions have been isolated in a number of ways outside of the classroom experimental situations.

In an early study, one psychologist (Thornton, 1943; cited in Smith, 1961) took two photographs of each of four men and four women. In one photo they wore glasses; in the other they did not. He then asked groups of observers to rate the persons on a series of personality traits. He found that the eight persons were judged as intelligent, dependable, and honest more often when they wore glasses than when they did not. Using the same procedure, he found that persons were more often judged as honest, kind, and humorous when they were smiling than when they were not (see Figure 4-4).

Another psychologist (McKeachie, 1952) studied the influence of lipstick on observations of personality. Six men rated six women on 22 different personality traits. Each man interviewed three girls with lipstick and three without it; each girl appeared in three interviews with lipstick and in three without it. The men had been told that the purpose of their repeated interviews was to determine

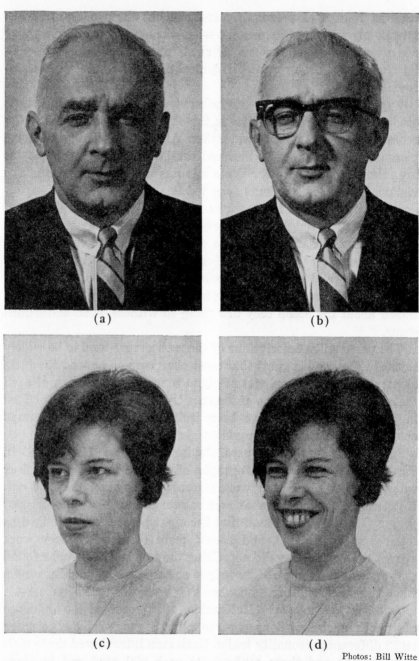

(a)   (b)

(c)   (d)

Photos: Bill Witte

FIGURE 4–4.   Observers who rate photographs tend to attribute intelligence, honesty, and dependability more often to persons with (b) than without (a) glasses; and tend to judge smiling photographs of persons (d) as more honest, kind, and humorous than serious portraits (c).

the reliability of personality ratings based on 10-minute interviews. The results of this study—not unexpectedly—indicated that a girl without lipstick was more often judged as being conscientious, serious, talkative, placid, and not interested in men. With lipstick, a girl was judged as more frivolous, anxious, and silent, but much interested in men.

One psychologist (Secord, 1958) noted the tendency of persons to ascribe friendliness, humor, and easygoingness to photographs of faces that show wrinkles at the eye corners. In the same study, he found that persons ascribe to dark-skinned people attributes of unfriendliness, hostility, and lack of humor; blondes and fair-skinned persons were perceived to have favorable qualities.

Most generalizations based on observations of exterior cues are the product of easy associations between the cue and some presumed quality. Thus older women are perceived as motherly, because most older women happen also to be mothers. A person with eyeglasses may have strained his eyes through study and, of course, people who study are intelligent. Some of the exterior physical signs that have some basis in fact follow (cited in Webb *et al.*, 1966). It has been found that

1. Tattoos are associated with delinquency and antisocial behavior (Burma, 1959).
2. College fraternity men dress differently from nonaffiliated college males; and that within fraternities, better grades are made by the more neatly dressed (Sechrest, 1965).
3. Shoe styles correspond with certain patterns of living, with the flashier shoe belonging to the more culture-bound persons (Gearing, 1952).
4. Preference for certain patterns, colors, and texture of clothing are related to various moods, traits, and personality changes (Kane, 1958, 1959, 1962).
5. Social status of some persons is related to the houses they occupy (MacRae and MacRae, 1961).

There are numerous other possible exterior signs that may be significant, but little controlled work has been conducted to associate the observation of these signs with personality characteristics. Some of these observable indicators include jewelry (type, quality, design, amount), automobile (sports v. sedan, color, length, adornment), sport preference (participator v. nonparticipator, golf, boxing, football, tennis), cigarette brand (filter v. nonfilter, king-size v. regular length), food preference (gourmet, exotic, European, Oriental), as well as such readily observable clues of body usage and care as scars, calluses, missing fingers, sunburn, and grooming. A number of psychologists (Phillips, 1962; Webb et al., 1966) suggest that with any of these measures used alone, the validity of the inference drawn is tenuous. However, the use of multiple indicators of observational data probably would improve the effectiveness of their use as cues about personality.

As an illustration of the way certain cue words influence impressions of persons, a study may be cited in which a group of researchers (Bruner, Shapiro and Taguiri, 1958) have shown how one bit of information—i.e., that Sam is intelligent, leads most people to observe that Sam is also clever, deliberate, energetic, cheerful, neat and imaginative.

Generally, distortions in observations of persons can be traced to the sets of stereotypes or theories that individuals build up over the years, in terms of which they sort others and make judgments about them (Vernon, 1964). Although these stereotypes account for a fair amount of consensus among observers who share common cultural values and folklore, they also lead to wide divergencies attributable to differences in attitudes, needs, education, social class, interests, and age.

Observation of Expressive Behavior

Psychologists have been less fascinated than either the layman or literary authors with the possible significance of expressive behavior as clues to personality. That feelings, emotions, and personality traits are revealed by expressive movements is known by most writers of fiction, and they make ample use in their description of personalities of expressive cues such as posture, gesturing, and manner of speech. Such idioms as a "truculent shuffle," "sly squint," and "self-righteous stance" are commonly used and therefore tend to suppose some evidence of their significance for personality. Often a person's gait or posture is so unmistakably unique that it can be recognized immediately as characterizing only him.

A survey of the sections on "personality" in the first 15 volumes of the Annual Review of Psychology reveals that only one paragraph of eight lines by McClelland (1956) is devoted to the subject.

One psychologist (Bonner, 1961) attributes this neglect in part to the facts that the study of expressive behavior is out of fashion and that the topic has been a favored target of charlatans, "character analysts," and other questionable pseudoscientific groups. But to abandon the study of expressive movements as irrelevant to personality assessment because of the paucity of validating evidence is as unreasonable as rejecting certain drugs whose side-effects are unknown. And to neglect it because charlatans favor it only makes it a more attractive pseudoscientific enterprise for exploitation by frauds.

The Nature of Expressive Behavior

The most systematic statements on the subject of expressive behavior have been made by Allport and Vernon (1933), and more recently by Allport (1961), Bonner (1961), Guilford (1959), Maslow (1954), McClelland (1951), Vernon (1964), and Webb *et al.* (1966). Allport and Vernon especially have maintained that there is considerable reliability, generality, and clustering in expressive movements. This discussion leans heavily on these sources.

Allport (1961, p. 445) distinguishes between expressive and coping behavior. Expressive behavior is freely and spontaneously emitted by the person (walking, talking, writing, posturing, gesturing, shaking hands), whereas coping behavior is purposive, controlled, and consciously performed. Thus, within the scope of these definitions, expressive behavior is uncontrolled and unconscious (i.e., below the threshold of awareness), and can be observed in a person's handwriting, gait, posture, and gestures; and coping behavior can be observed in more self-conscious activities such as throwing a ball or bicycling. These latter activities require skill, judgment, and knowledge, but nevertheless do reflect unique styles that are related to the more fundamental characteristics of persons. When expressive behavior must be modified in order to cope with situations, much of its spontaneity and uniqueness are destroyed. Hence, there is less individuality in the handwriting of an architect, engineer, or calligrapher than in most persons' scripts; and there is less expressive uniqueness in a newscaster's voice because he uses it as an instrument of coping.

Expressive behavior, then, is spontaneous and unlearned. Accordingly, training, conditioning, and social influence play a negligible role in its origin but may modify its form. Moreover, expressive behavior is unmotivated and is little subject to direction and control. Unlike much of our adjustive behavior, which is triggered by our awareness of environmental stimuli, expressive acts are below our threshold of awareness and thus not easily controlled. Finally, expressive acts find their most characteristic outlets in unstructured situations and are strongly associated with the personality of their expresser.

A Survey of Expressive Behaviors

Movements, Gesture, Posture, and Gait. Some persons' *movements* are expansive, vigorous, crude, dainty, lethargic, phlegmatic, or lively. These movements are often highly correlated with an individual's overall performance. The vigorous person has been observed to go about his business rapidly and strenuously, and the lethargic one tends to linger and dawdle. Allport and Vernon (1933) demonstrated that an individual's style of movements is consistent. In three experimental sessions, separated by several weeks, they instructed 25 subjects to perform a number of simple tasks such as copying prose passages, drawing rectangles, walking, talking, shaking hands with a dynamometer, drawing in a sandbox (with a toe), and arranging cubes in order of weight. Measures on these tasks correlated about .75 within the same session, and about .63 between sessions. The substantial correlations indicate generality or clustering in such movements within individuals, and they suggest the reliability of this behavior over time.

Freud (1904) observed that *gestures* and mannerisms are cues to mental and emotional dispositions and are symbolic of unconscious attitudes or repressed impulses. In this regard, one psychologist (Krout, 1935; 1954) collected empirical evidence that certain gestures have deeper inner meaning than is sometimes evident. Under laboratory conditions,[4] certain gestures were elicited through creating verbal-conflict situations in subjects. During the interval of conflict induced by having his subjects contemplate an undesirable thought (e.g., "Did you ever wish that one of your relatives was

---

[4] Webb *et al.* (1966) point out that there is also a good possibility of eliciting and observing such gestures in natural settings.

dead? I want you to think"), observations were taken of the movements of their hands.

The movements observed and their meanings included open hands dangling between legs to signify frustration, placing the hand to the nose to express an attitude of fear, and gesturing with the fist to characterize aggression. Such movements have been called autistic gestures (Krout, 1935). They have only unconscious meaning for the subject, and no meaning at all for the casual observer. It has been suggested by some investigators (Krout, 1935; Birdwhistell, 1960, 1963) that certain expressions that have been suppressed effectively by most persons for social reasons (e.g. yawning when bored, baring teeth when angry) occasionally turn up in psychotic persons and have a deeper meaning than is sometimes evident.

That gestures are highly influenced by cultural factors was also demonstrated in an interesting report by two researchers (Efron and Foley, 1937, 1947). These investigators compared gestural behavior patterns in Italian and Jewish groups living under different as well as similar environmental conditions. They concluded that the gesture patterns of traditional Italians and Jews could be unmistakably distinguished in terms of such characteristics as the part of the body utilized to form the movement and the laterality, symmetry, radius, rhythm, and tempo of the movement itself. The traditional gesture patterns tended to be absent in the assimilated groups. The gesticulations of the assimilated groups as a whole were less frequent than in the traditional nationality groups. Their gestures resembled more closely those typical of American groups (see Figure 4-5).

There is some evidence to indicate that *posture* is related to stable personal characteristics. From among more than a thousand different "steady"[5] postures that the human body is capable of assuming (Hewes, 1955), preferred postural positions seem to characterize individuals. As with gestures, there are cultural determinants that shape posture (e.g., customary manner of carrying heavy loads; whether or not shoes are worn), but to a large extent the posture that one chooses probably reflects personality characteristics. Most of the evidence is anecdotal and is based on casual observations of correlations between posture and certain personal-

---

[5] "Steady" indicates a static position that a person can maintain comfortably for some time (Allport, 1961).

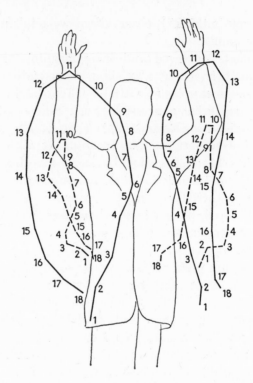

FIGURE 4–5. An illustration of the
graphic technique used to analyze the gestural behavior of different cultural groups
(Efron and Foley, 1937, 1947).

ity traits. Thus psychoanalysts report that the postures of patients
upon the couch reflect moods, that "pessimists" stand crouched, and
that euphoria is accompanied by a boldly upright stance. Careful
investigations to corroborate these relationships are needed.

Gait is closely related to the diffuse psychomotor state that tends
to determine posture. Certain aspects of gait that are being studied
are speed, length of stride, balance, and rhythm. Since disturbance
of gait is an important topic in neuropathological diagnosis,
considerable progress in instrumentation has been made for the
precise study of leg motions in walking, and in establishing norms
for cadence, stride length, and speed (Drillis, 1958). Perhaps basic
research in the biomechanics of gait will serve as a springboard
for psychologists who are interested in establishing the personality
correlations of certain characteristic types of gait.

The importance of posture and gait as expressions of psychological traits is widely acclaimed by teachers and students of physical education. Rathbone (1959, pp. 84–85), for example, in her book *Corrective Physical Education* mentions that good posture in sitting and standing has its psychological correlates. "The habitual postures each assumes," she states, "are aspects of . . . a general state of mind. If he is buoyant and happy, his usual postures will be erect and extended; if he is ill or depressed, his body will tend to be slumped, because the extensor muscles will not have sufficient tone." Again, data are urgently needed to support these popular notions.

Graphology. We have noted that movements, gestures, posture, and gait are highly consistent within individuals and that they tend to be highly characteristic of the person who is responsible for them. Expressive consistency and stability can also be demonstrated in a person's script. The analysis of handwriting, or graphology, as it is sometimes called, has become of increasingly greater interest to psychologists.

A number of schemes have been devised for measuring handwriting style: vertical length, width, and pressure (Luthe, 1953; Tripp, Fluckiger and Weinberg, 1957). An electronic device for the "motion study" of writing has been invented (Smith and Bloom, 1956) ; and even the electronic digital computer has been called into service in the study of handwriting. *Pandemonium,* a computer program devised by Selfridge (1959) to study sloppy hand-lettered characters, was used (Doyle, 1960) to match handwritings with persons to whom they belong. Although the program is more relevant to problems in pattern recognition and artificial intelligence than to personality assessment, the fact that the computer could recognize 87 percent of the characters correctly (humans can recognize 97 percent) carries with it the implication that there exist a large number of attributes that can be isolated in the study of handwriting characteristics. Selfridge and Dinneen (1955) list some 30 attributes, such as number of intersections of vertical and horizontal lines and the number of cavities facing left, up, down, and right. The implication for the study of personality rests in the fact that both humans and a properly programmed computer can "recognize" and match correctly handwritings associated with particular individuals. Thus there is little doubt about the existence of unique styles or patterns of handwriting, but the precise relationships between style and personality still remain a mystery, and await further study.

ADVANTAGES AND DISADVANTAGES OF NATURALISTIC
OBSERVATION

Direct natural or uncontrolled observations of behavior have much to recommend them. Such observations yield data at first hand, and therefore produce a picture of what an individual does, not what he says he does. The behavior of persons communicates a great deal about them, and when such behavior is viewed directly, and with minimum constraints placed on its occurrence, then the observer need not deal with their rationalizations or their reactions to a set of laboratory artifacts.

As a personality measurement procedure, naturalistic observation is more closely related to the phase of collecting ideas than with interpreting or evaluating them, and as such it serves as a basis for formulating hypotheses about the probable meaning of the viewed behavior as it is unfolding. Subsequent information may dictate that the observer revise his initial hypotheses, but at least he has had the advantage of observing the behavior firsthand.

Naturalistic observation need not occur in the subject's habitat. Thus, in the early phases of clinical diagnosis, direct observation of the client's behavior and general appearance are naturalistic within the scope of our definition. These observations provide valuable clues about personality that can be confirmed or discredited by subsequent inquiry, psychological testing, or counseling. The chief advantages of naturalistic observation are that the individual is unaware of being observed and it avoids placing constraints on its subject matter.

Some of these gains are counterbalanced by disadvantages. Because naturalistic methods avoid placing constraints on what they observe, they produce data that are difficult to reproduce and that violate one of the basic tenets of good psychological test situations—the standardization of conditions, materials, and procedures. Furthermore, heavy reliance is placed on the ingenuity of the human observer. Some observers will have better success than others in noting certain behaviors because there are large individual differences in skills among observers.

The human observer, moreover, is variable over the course of his observations. He may become bored and less conscientious as time passes, or he may become more interested as the observed subject matter becomes more meaningful to him. These sources of variability serve to decrease agreement among observers who view the same behavior (e.g., they attend to dissimilar aspects of a situation). Contributing further to the problems of disagreement among observers, and the inaccuracy of observations, is the fact that the observed person's behavior will fluctuate. Since personality is made up of response tendencies, moods, and dispositions that are of a highly probabilistic, rather than all-or-none, nature, it may be expected that the behavior under consideration will change over time.

Generally, the reliability of observations is established by having several persons simultaneously observe the same behavior situation; and reliability (agreement among observers) is highest when observers have been trained in reporting the behavior under study (Landreth, 1940; Barker and Wright, 1955). Typical agreement between observers who have undergone training and who are familiar with their subject matter has been well above 90 percent.

The amount of inference required of an observer also influences the reliability of observations. Generally speaking, molecular observations—observations where the focus is on small units of behavior—require relatively less inference than molar (large unit) ones and therefore yield higher interobserver reliabilities. In molecular observation, the observer may simply note that an individual does or says something. For example, the assignment may require the observer to note each interaction unit, which may be defined as any physical or verbal contact between a set of individuals. If contact occurs, it is reported; if it does not occur, it is not reported. No inferences—or very low level inferences (e.g., physical contact, verbal contact)—are made in such systems, and interobserver agreement is usually high. However, most observational tasks require higher degrees of inference. This is especially true when the observational assignment calls for viewing larger behavioral units, where complete interactional systems are to be reported. Thus observations that require labels such as authoritarianism, impulsivity, rigidity, and dominance require a high level of inference and therefore yield low interobserver reliabilities.

If there are so many disadvantages to the procedure of naturalistic observation, why does the psychologist persist in using it? He is aware of the fact, undoubtedly, that without such observations of behavior he loses important data about events and persons that are not otherwise accessible to him. Further, he has developed a number of procedures and conditions of observation designed to minimize as much as possible the human element that contributes to errors. These procedures sometimes take the form of such special conditions and planning of observations as the time and incident sampling techniques noted earlier in this chapter; at other times they consist of the introduction of special contrivances, rating forms, and hardware instrumentation (e.g., tape recorders, cameras) which serve as aids in the observational process. The next chapter considers some of these procedures.

(Summary appears at end of Chapter 5.)

FOR FURTHER READING

1. BARKER, R. G. (Ed.)   *The stream of behavior.* New York: Appleton-Century-Crofts, 1963.

   There are many excellent chapters, by different researchers, in this book. Among the most relevant for this discussion are the first two: "The Stream of Behavior as an Empirical Problem" (Barker), and "The Perception of Behavioral Units" (H. R. Dickman). Barker addresses himself mainly to a taxonomy of behavior units, and Dickman is concerned with the question: "To what extent does the human 'stream of behavior' attain structure and orderliness in the eyes of other human beings?"

2. BARRON, F.   The psychology of creativity. In OLDS, J. & OLDS, MARIANNE (Eds.), *New directions in psychology II.* New York: Holt, Rinehart & Winston, Inc., 1965. Pp. 3–134.

   Relevant supplementary reading to most portions of the present book, Barron's chapter discusses the problems encountered in measuring creativity. Also, he reviews the history of assessment methods. Generally, he discusses his considerable contribution to the study of creativity made at the Institute of Personality Assessment and Research (IPAR), and describes the way psychometric information was utilized and the manner in which it can be combined with nonpsychometric data.

3. BERELSON, B. & STEINER, G. A.   *Human behavior: An inventory of scientific findings.* New York: Harcourt, Brace & World, Inc., 1964.

   Chapter 2, "Methods of Inquiry" (pp. 15–36), is particularly relevant to the preceding discussion. Topics covered include experimental design, the sample survey, the case study, the interview, and direct observation of behavior.

4. FISKE, D. W.   The inherent variability of behavior. In FISKE, D. W. & MADDI, S. K., *Functions of varied experience.* Homewood, Ill.: The Dorsey Press, 1961. Pp. 326–354.

Some problems that arise when behavior is observed over two occasions are discussed. Response variability in coping behavior, expressive tendencies, and personality are examined and interpreted in terms of their functions for the organism.

5. FLANAGAN, J. C. The critical incident technique. *Psychological Bulletin*, 1954, 51, 327–358.

The critical incident technique, a method that uses detailed descriptions of behavior favorable and unfavorable to an individual, is presented in the article. Suggestions are made for its applicability in measurement and training settings.

6. HYMAN, R. *The nature of psychological inquiry.* Englewood Cliffs, N.J.: Prentice-Hall, Inc., 1964.

This is a compact and closely organized book. It covers considerable ground regarding methods of collecting, processing, and interpreting psychological data. Chapter 4, on "Getting the Facts," is especially important. Here Hyman discusses the differences between scientific and nonscientific observations, and distinguishes between naturalistic, differential, and experimental methods of data collection.

7. SELFRIDGE, O. G. Pandemonium: A paradigm for learning. *Proceedings of the Symposium on Mechanisation of Thought Processes,* 1959, H. M. Stationery Office, London.

Pandemonium is a computer program designed for pattern recognition. Doyle (1960) used this program as a model for his computer program which was designed to recognize sloppy hand-lettered characters.

8. SELLTIZ, CLAIRE, JAHODA, MARIE, DEUTSCH, M., & COOK S. *Research methods in social relations.* New York: Holt, Rinehart & Winston, 1964.

Chapter 6 (pp. 200–234), one out of two on data collection procedures, focuses on observational methods in the social sciences, and provides an excellent discussion of these procedures.

9. SHONTZ, F. C. *Research methods in personality.* New York: Appleton-Century-Crofts, 1965.

The author describes a method, called by him "natural process research," which he believes has the advantage over other procedures in that it interferes minimally with natural processes.

10. SHRAUGER, S. & ALTROCCHI, J. The personality of the perceiver as a factor in person perception. *Psychological Bulletin,* 1964, 62, 289–308.

Some of the difficulties inherent in person perception are reviewed, and the authors offer a framework for future research which delineates phases of the judgment process.

11. THOMAS, H. Problems of character change. In DAVID, H. P. & VON BRACKEN, H. (Eds.), *Perspectives in personality theory.* New York: Basic Books, 1961.

The importance of a longitudinal approach to personality study is stressed. Several relevant studies are reviewed in their proper perspective of throwing some light on the importance of life histories.

12. WEBB, E. J., CAMPBELL, D. T., SCHWARTZ, R. D., & SECHREST, L. *Unobtrusive measures: Nonreactive research in the social sciences.* Chicago: Rand McNally & Co., 1966.

This book was almost called *The Bullfighter's Beard* because of the authors' observation that toreros' beards are longer on the day of the fight than on any other day. Written in a free-wheeling style, this scholarly production is chock-full of information on methods of obtaining research data *not* secured by interviews or tests. Chapter 5, "Simple Observation," is most relevant to the present discussion; and Chapter 6, "Contrived Observation; Hidden Hardware and Control," is applicable to our own discussion in the next chapter.

OBSERVATIONAL METHODS (Continued): HARDWARE, RATING SCALES, AND CONTRIVED OBSERVATIONS

The subjects in the study of personality are people; and people are difficult to observe. Aside from the limitations set by nature on the human observer's perceptual ability, the fact is that when one person attempts to study another they both are influenced by what has been aptly called "shared humanity" (Kaplan, 1964, p. 136). For example, during the process of observation, the psychologist imbues his subject matter with his own feelings, needs, and wishes as well as his own characteristic ways of behaving, and these factors serve to distort the results he obtains. From the point of view of the observed, the awareness[1] of being studied may have a "guinea pig" effect in which the subject feels called upon to behave in prescribed ways.[2]

This complex interaction of observer and subject matter, which does not exist in the other sciences, creates problems for the psychologist that serve to complicate the process of observation. In other respects the psychologist's observational problems are no different from those of other scientists; like them, he deals with these by using techniques to make his observations precise and by

---

[1] Of course, he is not always aware of being studied.

[2] Webb et al. (1966, p. 16) call one form of this awareness "role selection." The subject asks himself the question, "What kind of a person should I be as I do these tasks?"

imposing controls on himself and the conditions of observation, as well as on the subject matter under study.

CONTROLLED OBSERVATIONS

The concept of control in scientific observation carries several connotations. In the preceding chapter the term was used in its most restricted sense to denote only forms of observation in which the investigator "rigs" the situation to induce a number of sought-after responses. But another way of thinking about controls is in terms of the constraints that are built into observational procedures. These constraints, present in all forms of observation, vary in terms of the extent to which they restrict the observer, the ways in which the observational environment is manipulated, and the methods used to elicit the responses of subjects under study.

In all psychological inquiry, the observer is constrained in the sense that he makes his observations in terms of a hunch or hypothesis he is checking, or an idea he would like to investigate. These determine his "conceptual focus" (Hyman, 1964, p. 42 ff.) and influence the way he collects his observations. The psychologist's conceptual focus helps him gather data that are pertinent to a restricted set of dimensions and enables him to select from among numerous ongoing behaviors just those aspects that seem to convey relevant information.

Hardware aids to observation, which are the topic of the next section, place minimal constraints on the observer, and need not affect the conditions of observation or the subjects under study. Rating scales, which are discussed in the section following the next, impose more controls on the observer than hardware because they restrict sharply the range of behaviors to be viewed by him. Special observational conditions that are contrived to induce specific subject responses, which are discussed in the concluding section of this chapter, place maximal constraints on the observer and his subject matter.

HARDWARE FOR LIMITING HUMAN OBSERVER ERROR

Historically, scientific progress has been proportional to the development of techniques for making observations precise. Originally man viewed the galaxies with his naked eye. Since the invention and use of the telescope in about 1609, astronomy has progressed in almost direct proportion to the sensitivity of the lens fitted to that instrument. More recently, with the invention and widespread installation of radar observation stations, meteorological forecasting has gained considerably in precision.[3] Psychology is no exception in this regard, and precision in observations of human behavior will undoubtedly progress in direct proportion to the use of existing and yet-to-be-developed instrumentation.

No matter how carefully an observer arranges the observational setting, and regardless of the pains he takes to record his subject matter, it is nevertheless difficult to obtain an accurate picture of behavior as it emerges. An observer can take in only so much at a glance, he can listen only to one conversation at a time, and human behavior usually requires simultaneous attention to a number of different facets of a situation. For example, even in a relatively uncomplicated one-person setting, while the observer is listening to the person, he may miss entirely the fact that this subject is simultaneously tapping the floor with his foot, chewing gum, not exhaling the cigarette smoke that he inhaled, and scratching himself with his free hand. If the observer does notice all of these behaviors, he may not have the opportunity to record them on paper. And if he does not record them immediately, he may try to reconstruct the behaviors afterwards. Such reconstructions are subject to numerous distortions and omissions that are dependent on the observer's ability to remember details. If we now add to the setting another one, two, or three persons, the observational burden is increased by an order of magnitude.

The recognition of the complexity of the observational task has in recent years led to the ever increasing use of a variety of hardware recording devices. The major gains realized from the use of hardware are accuracy, completeness of behavior notating, and permanence of record. In some instances, hardware implementation has facilitated the removal of the observer as a "third party" in the setting, and thus an additional gain is realized.

The most popular hardware device for notating verbal behavior has been the audiotape recorder. Clinicians who formerly spent

---

[3] The number of tornadoes sighted in the United States increased by more than 100 percent between 1952 and 1954; and 1957 was a bumper year for twisters with a reported increase of 300 percent over 1952 (*World Almanac*, 1966). This clearly reflects better and greater use of detection devices rather than changes in weather conditions.

much of their interview time writing with pencil and paper have been quick to adopt tape recorders as substitutes. Tape recordings of verbal interchanges that occurred during a session are high-fidelity reproductions of that behavior and leave little doubt about the precise nature of what was said and by whom. Moreover, such recordings are permanent, and therefore allow the verbal behavior in question to be heard over and over again, and by many different observers.

In a fascinating study of "spontaneous talk," two investigators (Soskin and John, 1963) mounted miniature radio transmitters on subjects under observation. The observers explain the use of these transmitting and recording devices as follows; and their explanation with slight modifications serves as an adequate rationale for the value of all audio or visual aids to observation:

. . . it is physically impossible to write verbatim records of many inter-actions between adults as they occur. The rate of interaction is too rapid, especially in a small group situation, and there is a tendency for observer recorders to condense some utterances, completely miss others, overlook inconsistencies, neglect to record grammatical errors, etc. Moreover it is physically impossible for an observer to record a conversation while the participants are on the move . . . just as it would be physically impos-sible for a single individual to sustain the set of an observer-recorder continuously over a 16-hour day without relaxation and at the same time attend to his own needs.

The subjects, two married couples, as an inducement to volun-teering for such lengthy recording sessions, were offered an expense-free vacation at a large summer resort—where their verbal behavior was continuously transmitted and recorded! The research-ers found it difficult to ascertain how much and under what circum-stances the behavior of the subjects was influenced by consciousness of the transmitter, but both couples reported that they were more aware of its presence at some times than at others, and that their self-consciousness diminished with the passage of time. An excerpt from one couple's "spontaneous talk" is reproduced in Table 5–1. This excerpt illustrates both the spontaneity and the self-consciousness of the subjects' verbalizations.

A somewhat different use of the tape recorder was made in the work of one psychologist (Patterson, 1966) who remains present in the setting while viewing family interaction patterns and narrates his observations into a soundproofed microphone device attached to his chin. He explains to the family, in advance of the recording

TABLE 5–1

Excerpts from "Spontaneous Talk" Protocol

<table>
<tr><td colspan="3" align="right">She splashes a little.</td></tr>
<tr><td>262.</td><td>Jock</td><td>(Laughs softly.)</td></tr>
<tr><td>263.</td><td>Roz</td><td>Honey, I promise I won't splash you again while you read.</td></tr>
<tr><td>264.</td><td>Jock</td><td>If you hold your oar up like that it's going to drip.</td></tr>
<tr><td>265.</td><td>Roz</td><td>Not on you.</td></tr>
<tr><td>266.</td><td>Jock</td><td>Hey. That way.</td></tr>
<tr><td colspan="3" align="right">(Several minutes later.)</td></tr>
<tr><td>271.</td><td>Roz</td><td>You mean I'm going to row all the way over to that point?</td></tr>
<tr><td>272.</td><td>Jock</td><td>No. (imploringly) This way. Will you please go this way? I've asked you five times.</td></tr>
<tr><td>273.</td><td>Roz</td><td>Oh, you mean. . . .</td></tr>
<tr><td>274.</td><td>Jock</td><td>I'm going to shove you in.</td></tr>
<tr><td>275.</td><td>Roz</td><td>No, you're not going to shove me in. Besides if you shove me in, they'll have it on tape, and they can get you in court for that. . . .</td></tr>
</table>

SOURCE: Soskin and John, 1963.

session, that he is not to be considered one of the participants in their conversations. When conditions permit, the observer views and comments on his subjects' interactions from behind a screen or from a corner of the room. The procedure of narrating during the unfolding of behavior allows the psychologist to code his observations into various categories as they occur, while at the same time he obtains a parallel and permanent recording of the actual verbal interchanges. The importance of immediate coding and the benefit of some on-the-scene comment are easily appreciated when one considers the fact that all observations are subjected to subsequent careful analyses.

A special device for observing and analyzing verbal interchanges, developed by an anthropologist sometime ago (Chapple, 1940, 1949) and only recently introduced into psychological studies of personality (Saslow *et al.*, 1955; Matarazzo *et al.*, 1956; Matarazzo, 1965), is called the Interaction Chronograph. This device, which is nothing more than an elaborate electrical stopwatch, allows the observer to keep a record of the action (e.g., gesturing or nodding in an effort to communicate) and with the aid of the observer (e.g., pushing in the right buttons), records the vocal contributions of numerous subjects under observation. It also performs computations of the durations of action, and the frequency and duration of interruptions. The relevance of these records for personality study rests on the assumption that the *way* people talk to one another (e.g., versus the content of their speech) provides a measure of their interpersonal adjustment patterns.

The Interaction Chronograph has been used mostly to analyze audiotaped speech durations between an interviewer and interviewee and has treated interview speech and silence as significant variables for study.[4] An especially intriguing finding (Matarazzo *et al.*, 1963) has been that the interviewer "controls" the speech duration of the interviewee. "Thus as the interviewer doubled or halved his own speech durations, he controlled in like manner the speech durations of the interviewee" (Matarazzo, 1965, p. 442). This finding was subsequently supported in an analysis of the audiotapes of conversations between astronauts in orbit and ground communicators (Matarazzo *et al.*, 1964), and more recently (Ray and Webb, 1966), in examinations of numerous transcripts of the late President Kennedy's news conferences. These analyses are interesting extensions of interview and laboratory findings to a "real life" setting. It is apparent that these findings could hardly be attributed to the astronauts' or Kennedy's awareness of the psychologists' hypothesis that speech durations are under the control of interrogators or interviewers.

The use of videotape recording, which recently has been made widely available for commercial purposes (Consumer Reports, 1966), has been reported (Webb *et al.*, 1966) in research designed to validate paper-and-pencil tests. In one such study, with implications for research in personality measurement, effectiveness of television advertising was examined by observing a person in a reception room which contained newspapers, magazines, and a turned-on television set. A hidden television camera monitored the subject's behavior in the room. Subsequent interviews were designed to determine the effects of being exposed to the television commercials and magazines and newspapers.

A variation of this study, with relevance for checking the validity of self-report personality data, might consist of affording an unsuspecting individual the opportunity to select participation from among a number of alternative activities. After a period of observation, an inquiry session could be conducted and a standard self-

---

[4] This technique could easily be discussed in the next chapter, the topic of which is "The Interview," but it is more appropriate here because it analyzes the form rather than content of speech.

report questionnaire administered, each of which is designed to compare the subject's verbal behavior about his preferences and his actual selection of specific activities. However, the use of deception in such procedures is questionable unless such research is conducted in clinical settings where findings are clearly relevant for psychodiagnosis and treatment. The use of nonvolunteer subjects outside the clinic raises a number of ethical issues that must be carefully weighed. The possible embarrassment to the subject or the invasion of his privacy must be counterbalanced by identifiable and substantial gains to be realized by the use of such deception.

Occasionally, due to the expense and inconvenience of maintaining a human observer on the scene, or because of the privacy of the behavior being observed, hardware has been used to supplant the observer entirely. Much of the work on behavior development in children at the Yale Photographic Observation Unit (see Figure 5–1) is based on lengthy sound filming of large segments of behavior. Many of the observations taken at the observatory (Gesell and Amatruda, 1947; Gesell and Ilg, 1949) are meaningful only if taken over long intervals of time—i.e., usually over periods of several months or even years—and therefore hardware recording eliminates the unreliability that results from using many different observers. Moreover, in the process of observing infants and nursery-school-age children there are usually no specifiable units of behavior to be viewed; rather, there are various possible behaviors that are notable because of their incipient or recent emergence. Therefore, it is not important, for instance, to look for the number

FIGURE 5–1. Reproduction of Dr. Gesell's cinemaphotographic observation unit at Yale University.

of times a child does something or behaves in a certain way during a given session; rather it is important to note that the child's walking has improved, or that his speech has developed since the last observation session.

The observer is sometimes entirely concealed or supplanted, also, because of the extreme privacy of the behavior being studied. Certainly the use of radio transmitters in the aforementioned study on spontaneous talk (Soskin and John, 1963) qualifies for inclusion in this category. More recently, there has been an upsurge of studies in which the sexual responsiveness of females, in particular (Kronhausen and Kronhausen, 1964), and of humans in general (Masters and Johnson, 1966) have been closely investigated before whirring movie cameras. Unfortunately, conclusions based on these studies have not taken into consideration the guinea pig effect that such procedures create in subjects. Furthermore, extrapolations made from data collected in these studies of sexual behavior are especially suspect because they did not take into account the personality and motivating factors that lead persons to volunteer (or to accept money to volunteer) for these studies, and they have tended to ignore the fact that sexual responsiveness and personality are highly intertwined.

RATING SCALES FOR LIMITING HUMAN ERROR

A *rating scale* is a device by means of which an observer can record his judgments about the behavior of another person according to the traits defined by the scale. Ratings can be made during the process of direct observation or subsequently; and most often when hardware devices are used to aid or supplant the observer, ratings are made after the observational process has been completed. Essentially, rating scales serve to *quantify* observations, and such quantification improves the observational process because it permits comparisons of persons according to specific traits. Moreover, rating scales, because they are easily *standardized*, permit the collection of information by using the same scales for a wide variety of persons, and in numerous observational settings.

Scoring and Ranking Methods

The two most common forms of rating scales are the *scoring* and *ranking* types. In the use of scoring scales, the rater assigns each person a numerical value for each trait. The numerical scores may be defined in verbal terms or they may not. An example of the type in which the scores are defined would be:

5 extremely underactive
4 somewhat underactive
3 neither over- nor underactive
2 somewhat overactive
1 extremely overactive

A common variant of the scoring method is the *graphic* rating scale. The judgment is made by making a mark on a line rather than by stating a number. Quantitative meaning is given to each point on the line by assigning numerals to both ends of the scale and to points in between. A five-point scale with verbal definitions is illustrated in Figure 5–2.

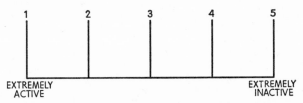

FIGURE 5–2. A graphic rating scale. The rater checks the point on the dimension of activity which best describes the behavior of the person being judged.

A ranking scale is used to rate traits relatively within an individual or to rate individuals with respect to given traits. Either the traits or the individuals are placed in size order. Thus a set of descriptive traits can be sorted according to their comparative relevance for an individual. For example, consider the adjectives penurious, honest, prodigal, fiery, indulgent, impatient, disagreeable, and unpleasant. In ranking these traits according to their relevance for an individual who happens to be parsimonious and inoffensive, the highest numeral might be assigned to the term "penurious," the next highest to "pleasant," and so on until all adjectives are placed in size order. Among these adjectives, the lowest numerals would probably be assigned to "prodigal" and "unpleasant." The extent to which this ranking system reflects accurately the description of an individual depends on the adequacy of the adjectives used and the familiarity of the rater with his subject.

The ranking method is also suitable and appropriate for making intragroup comparisons with respect to a particular trait. Thus to compare individuals with one another in regard to sloppiness of dress, the numeral 5 is assigned to the sloppiest, 4 to the next sloppiest, 3, 2, and 1 to the least sloppy persons. Numerals used in this fashion constitute an *ordinal scale* because the ranks indicate the order of the variable within the set of observations at hand.[5] These numerals, however, suggest nothing about how much of the variable is present, nor do they indicate anything about the difference between variables. Statements can be made only that the individual with rank 5 has a greater degree of sloppiness than any of the others, but not about the difference in sloppiness between persons assigned the various ranks.

The ranking method also allows division of a group into subgroups such as the top 3%, the next 10%, a middle 74%, next 10%, and then a bottom 3%. The precise percentages, of course, can be shifted to suit the occasion. The chief limitation of the ranking method is that groups are rarely comparable, and therefore a top man in one group might rank in the middle of another group.

Some Examples of Scoring Scales

Increasingly, scoring scales are being used as quantitative indices of patients' symptoms in clinical settings. These indices, when used for research in clinical settings, serve as criteria of change or improvement in before-and-after studies, or in observing the effects of tranquilizer drugs, electroshock treatment or psychotherapy. Even in its nonresearch or practical uses, symptom description often provides the only information about the severity of a patient's personality disorder; and such information serves as a basis for many important decisions about patients. For example, the kind and amount of specific treatments administered, ward assignment, and fitness for hospital discharge depend on severity of symptomatology. Furthermore, accurate knowledge about symptoms, according to some psychologists (Lorr *et al.*, 1962), would improve the current, somewhat unsatisfactory, patient classification schemes.

Wittenborn Psychiatric Rating Scales. Several scoring scales specifically designed for rating patient behavior in hospitals have been developed. The most elaborately researched tool has been the

---

[5] For a review of the characteristics of ordinal scales, and what arithmetic computations are permissible, the student is referred to Chapter 1.

Wittenborn Psychiatric Rating Scale (1955). It presents 52 scales organized into 9 scores representing different types of symptoms. Each of the 52 symptoms is rated, given a weighted score from 0 to 3, and then totaled into scores on each of the following 9 psychiatric categories: acute anxiety, conversion hysteria, manic state, depressed state, schizophrenic excitement, paranoid condition, paranoid schizophrenic, hebephrenic schizophrenic, and phobia compulsive. These nine dimensions, expressed as clusters I to IX, were defined through factor analysis. Although psychiatric terminology is used, the rating scale yields a description of the patient's condition rather than just a statement about his diagnostic cate-

Scale		I	II	III	IV	V	VI	VII	VIII	IX
6. Not conspicuously lacking in self-assertiveness.	0								*2*	
General manner and verbal expressions mild.										
Desires and opinions can be overridden by a dominant personality.	②									
Appears to give in easily to the desires and opinions of others.	3								*2*	
7. Is not particularly overactive.	⓪									
Moderately overactive, e.g., toys with objects, frequently changes his sitting position.	1									
Noticeably restless, but able to stay quiet upon request.	2									
In almost constant movement—uncomfortable if required to remain still.	3									
8. Appears to be reasonably appreciative of the feelings of others.	⓪									
Indicates that he is aware of the moods or feelings of others, but shows little personal concern; behavior is not influenced in any discernible, helpful, or sympathetic way.	1									
Apparently unaware of the feelings of others.	2									
9. No discernible psychological use made of physical disease symptoms.	0		*1*							
Use is made of physical disease symptoms to gain attention or to dramatize self.	①									
Use is made of physical disease symptoms for evading responsibilities, justifying failures, etc.	2		*1*							
10. Eats adequate serving.	0									
Eats indifferently and may leave food unless urged to finish.	1									
Voluntarily eats very little and may require coaxing or spoon-feeding.	2						*3*			
Refuses to eat.	③									
11. Does not appear to be impudent or cocky.	⓪									
Noticeably impudent.	1									
Aggressively impudent—almost invariably impolite.	2									
Deliberately disrupts routines, demoralizes situations.	3									
12. Confesses no particular irritability.	⓪									
Does not voluntarily express irritation, but admits it if asked.	1									
Readily expresses his irritation and dissatisfaction.	2									
Temper tantrums, gross rage reactions.	3									
13. No evidence of social withdrawal.	⓪									
Does not appear to seek out the company of other people.	1									
Definitely avoids people.	2									
14. No evidence of a particular loudness of voice or noisiness of manner.	0			*1*						
Manner of speech has an insistent quality. (Voice seems to carry particularly well.)	①									
Raises voice as if he desired that all in his vicinity should hear him.	2					*1*				
Shouts, sings and talks loudly as if he were addressing the whole world.	3									
Subtotals (p. 2)			*2*	*2*	*4*	*4*				

FIGURE 5-3. A page from the Wittenborn Psychiatric Rating Scales showing items 6 to 14. This particular patient's ratings earn him 2 points on factor II (conversion hysteria), 2 points on factor III (manic state), and 4 points each on factors IV (depressed state) and V (schizophrenic excitement). Of course, these subtotal scores represent only one sixth of the total scale scores. Tallying of the remainder of the ratings presents a more accurate picture. (Reproduced by permission.)

gory, and the ratings can be made by anyone familiar with the patient. Several representative items are shown in Figure 5-3. A revised version of these scales (Wittenborn, 1964) is now available and presents 72 scales organized into 12 scores.

Generally the correlations between scales are low, which means that there is a tendency for each of the nine scales to measure a dimension which is independent of the other eight scales. The median split-half reliability coefficient of .82 suggests substantial reliability. In order to obtain corroborative descriptions of a patient two or more independent ratings are usually made. This procedure is necessary because ratings are frequently made by nonprofessional psychiatric aides, who have not been carefully trained in rating procedures, and because a patient may shift through different patterns of behavior from day to day. The Wittenborn rating scale's greatest usefulness is in recording such behavioral changes as may take place as a function of hospital stay, drugs, psychotherapy, or even of changing conditions outside of any treatment.

The Hospital Adjustment Scale.   Another scoring scheme constructed for evaluating patients' behavior is the *Hospital Adjustment Scale* (McReynolds et al., 1952). It consists of 91 statements descriptive of psychiatric patients, and is also suitably worded for use by psychiatric aides and nurses. Such statements as "the patient ignores the activities around him" and "the patient's talk is mostly not sensible" are marked as "true," "not true," or "does not apply." For a given patient, the scoring key is constructed in a manner that permits computation of a total score which presumably is indicative of his general level of hospital adjustment. The scale can be filled out in 10 minutes by an aide or nurse most familiar with the day-to-day behavior of the patient over an extended period of time.

The Inpatient Multidimensional Psychiatric Scale.   A scale used by clinicians rather than lay raters[6] for making ratings of symptoms during interviews with psychotic patients has been developed by a group of psychologists (Lorr et al., 1962). This procedure, called the Inpatient Multidimensional Psychiatric Scale (IMPS; see Figure 5-4) was used in a study to collect ratings on 296 patients in each of about 50 hospitals. A team consisting of an interviewer and a silent

---

[6] The distinction is only important insofar as scales designed for clinicians consist of adjectives that convey meaning only to persons familiar with the terminology in the field.

COMPARED TO THE NORMAL PERSON
TO WHAT DEGREE DOES HE...

*   1. MANIFEST SPEECH THAT IS SLOWED, DELIBERATE, OR LABORED?

*   2. GIVE ANSWERS THAT ARE IRRELEVANT OR UNRELATED IN ANY IMMEDIATELY
        CONCEIVABLE WAY TO THE QUESTION ASKED OR TOPIC DISCUSSED?

        CUES: DO NOT RATE HERE WANDERING OR RAMBLING CONVERSATION WHICH
        VEERS AWAY FROM THE TOPIC AT ISSUE (SEE ITEM 4). ALSO, DO NOT
        RATE THE COHERENCE OF THE ANSWER.

*   3. GIVE ANSWERS THAT ARE GRAMMATICALLY DISCONNECTED, INCOHERENT, OR
        SCATTERED, I. E., NOT SENSIBLE OR NOT UNDERSTANDABLE?

        CUES: JUDGE THE GRAMMATICAL STRUCTURE OF HIS SPEECH, NOT THE
        CONTENT WHICH MAY OR MAY NOT BE BIZARRE.

     4. TEND TO RAMBLE, WANDER, OR DRIFT OFF THE SUBJECT OR AWAY FROM THE
        POINT AT ISSUE IN RESPONDING TO QUESTIONS OR TOPICS DISCUSSED?

        CUES: DO NOT RATE HERE RESPONSES THAT ARE OBVIOUSLY UNRELATED
        TO THE QUESTION ASKED (SEE ITEM 2).

*   5. VERBALLY EXPRESS FEELINGS OF HOSTILITY, ILL WILL, OR DISLIKE OF OTHERS?

        CUES: MAKES HOSTILE COMMENTS REGARDING OTHERS SUCH AS ATTENDANTS,
        OTHER PATIENTS, HIS FAMILY, OR PERSONS IN AUTHORITY. REPORTS CON-
        FLICTS ON THE WARD.

*   6. EXHIBIT POSTURES THAT ARE PECULIAR, UNNATURAL, RIGID, OR BIZARRE?

        CUES: HEAD TWISTED TO ONE SIDE; OR ARM AND HAND HELD ODDLY. JUDGE
        THE DEGREE OF PECULIARITY OF THE POSTURE.

FIGURE 5–4. A Portion of a page reproduced by special permission from Inpatient Multidimensional Psychiatric Scale by Lorr, Klett, McNair & Lasky. Copyright 1962. Published by Consulting Psychologists Press.

observer independently rated each patient. By this procedure and the use of the IMPS, substantiating evidence was obtained for the existence of a number of psychotic symptom syndromes previously identified by other psychologists. Such verification studies are important in that they provide sounder bases for the use of these syndrome descriptions in future research.

Fels Parent Behavior Scales. The *Fels Parent Behavior Scales* (Baldwin, Kalhorn and Breese, 1945) were developed to study the preschool child's family. Thirty rating scales are available for assessing parental behavior toward their children in home situations. The scales, designed for use only by qualified professional observers, require interpretation of substantial amounts of the recorded behavior. The 30 scales include ratings in the areas of emotional relationships, disciplinary methods, values of the home, discords in the home, sociability of the family, rapport with the child, and readiness for criticism. Ratings obtained with the Fels Scales are considered highly reliable because each of the scales contains examples of concrete behavior illustrative of the dimension to be rated (Holt, 1965). Reliability coefficients in the .90's have been obtained. An example of items adapted from these scales is presented in Figure 5–5.

THE SOCIAL WEATHER RATING SCALES

I. WARMTH COMPONENT: emotional tone expressing acceptance, affection and approval of the child.

     1. Acceptance: receiving the child into the emotional warmth of intimacy.

—*Avid Acceptance:*	constantly, eagerly, warmly reaches out to include the child in intimate association.
—*Accepting:*	the child warmly accepted but sometimes with reservations and exclusions.
—*Noncommittal:*	the child neither accepted or rejected; involvement only potential.
—*Resentful:*	some resentful and avoidance responses, but the child not openly rejected.
—*Rejecting:*	the child openly repulsed and rejected.

FIGURE 5–5. A portion of the Social Weather Rating Scales (Simpson, 1963) was constructed by adapting numerous items from the Fels Behavior Rating Scales. In measuring the social weather of a particular child, the rater makes himself as nearly as possible a recording instrument to report the characteristics of the behavior pattern directed toward the child by others.

Some Examples of Ranking Scales

Peer Ratings. Obtaining peer ratings is a ranking technique used to assess personality, and generally is the method whereby a person's associates rate him. In a group of 40 persons, for example, each member rates every other member in the group on a number of traits. As a consequence of the fact that persons within some of these groups know each other well (e.g., in dormitories, fraternities, flight squadrons, and so forth) and because many ratings are collected on a particular individual, temporal reliabilities generally have been found to be high, with coefficients in the neighborhood of .90.

There are many different types of peer ratings, and only some of the more common methods will be mentioned here. These include the *nomination* and the *sociometric* techniques. It is important to note that these procedures are used mainly in instances where raters were brought together with their subjects fortuitously rather than for the express purpose of rating them.

In the nomination technique each person of a group is asked to nominate a given number of persons within that group as possessing "the most" and "the least" of a particular trait. For example, in a study with college fraternity and sorority members, individuals in each of these groups were asked to name or nominate the three most and the three least "adjusted" persons in their respective groups (Kleinmuntz, 1963b). To ensure that irrelevant or extraneous variables were not used in the ratings of "adjustment," the subjects were instructed to attend only to specific traits, descriptions of which were stipulated for them: thus, raters were told that a "maladjusted" person was one who is supicious, difficult to get along with, chronically complains of aches and pains, gets into frequent trouble with people in authority, and is generally unpleasant. The opposites of these traits were to be considered as descriptive of the most adjusted in the group. Persons were considered either adjusted or maladjusted if at least 75% of their peers nominated them as such. Often this technique is used in the initial stages of research to identify certain types of persons. Subsequent research may be designed to validate or invalidate the nominations of the group members. In the study just cited (Kleinmuntz, 1963b), the "most" and "least" adjusted students served as subjects in paper-and-pencil personality testing (e.g., MMPI) designed to develop a set of decision rules to aid in the interpretation of those tests (see Chapter 11).

The technique known as sociometric ratings was developed by Moreno (1934), and is ordinarily used with a group of persons who know each other well due to long acquaintanceship in a class, institution, agency, faculty, or military division. Each person is asked to choose one or more group members with whom he would like to study, work, play, or whom he would choose as neighbors. After the choices are obtained, they are plotted in a sociogram.

A person's place within the sociogram is determined by the number or percentage of mentions he received from others in the group. For example, in the hypothetical sociogram plotted in Figure 5-6, where each of 13 persons have a first and second choice, a situation is depicted in which persons *a, b, f, g,* and *j* form a group, or clique. All of the first choices and all but one of the second choices stay within the group. Person *g* is the most popular individual in

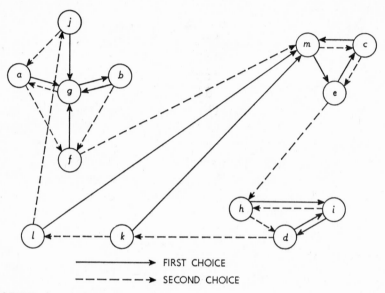

—————————▶ FIRST CHOICE

— — — — — ▶ SECOND CHOICE

FIGURE 5-6.   Sociogram depicting the selection of friends in a group of 13 persons. Three cliques are evident: *a, b, f, g,* and *j; c, e,* and *m;* and *d, h,* and *i.* Persons *k* and *l* are "isolates."

the group because he received the first-choice nominations of all other members of that group. Persons *c, e,* and *m* form another group, and persons *h, i,* and *d* form yet a third group. In the jargon of sociometry, persons *k* and *l* are both "isolates." The main difference between sociometric ratings and the nomination technique is that in the latter a group member is mentioned only if he is nominated, whereas in sociometric ratings each person is accounted for in the final analysis.

The Q-Sort.   The Q-sort technique developed by Stephenson (1953) is yet another variant of the ranking method. The judge presented with the Q-sort task is asked to sort a set of cards, each of which contains a descriptive statement. The Q-sort is considerably different from the other ranking methods in that the judge's task is to rank-order a large number of items, and hence he is required to compare these items with one another. A typical Q-sort distribution for one hundred cards is shown in Figure 5–7.

In the distribution illustrated in Figure 5–7, the judge is first required to select the two statements he believes are most "true" or most descriptive of the person he is rating and place them in pile 10. Then he chooses 4 statements that are more descriptive than the remaining 94 (and "less" descriptive than those in pile 10) and

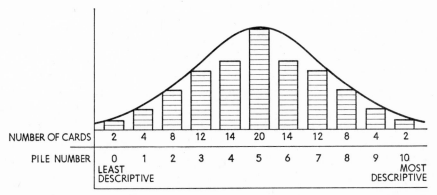

NUMBER OF CARDS	2	4	8	12	14	20	14	12	8	4	2
PILE NUMBER	0	1	2	3	4	5	6	7	8	9	10
	LEAST DESCRIPTIVE										MOST DESCRIPTIVE

FIGURE 5–7. A Q-sort distribution for 100 cards is shown here. The pile numbers are "nominal" and serve to label specific points on the scale. The number of items to be placed under each category fan out symmetrically from the center pile, and these items form the forced normal distribution. The comparisons made in ranking the item from the "least" to the "most" descriptive categories constitute judgments on an "ordinal" scale.

places them in pile 9. The judge continues in this manner until he places the remaining two "least true" statements in pile 0. There are several instructions that judges may follow in order to facilitate ranking, but the one most widely used is to have the Q-sorter start by making two piles, and then have him fan out to both extremes. Referring to Figure 5–7, this means that the rater divides his 100 statements into two stacks of 50 cards each, and then builds onto pile numbers 4 and 6, and from these he continues to fan out to pile numbers 3 and 7, and so on down the line until piles 0 and 10 each have 2 cards on them. The original two stacks then would have 20 cards and these are consolidated to form pile number 5.

In an exceptionally skillful use of Q-sorts in personality research, one psychologist (Marks, 1961) investigated the validity of diagnostic procedures in a child guidance clinic. Therapists who had treated 48 cases of mothers and their children performed Q-sorts after 10 hours of therapy. Using these sorts as criterion descriptions of the clinical cases, the MMPI was then administered to both parents and was used as the predictor of these descriptions. The most striking finding was that the parents' MMPIs, interpreted blindly (without the psychologist viewing the patients), were as predictive of the criterion as were more elaborate personality evaluations based on a battery of tests and interviews. In other words, the blind MMPI interpretations correlated more highly with the criterion Q-sorts than did a number of other personality assessment procedures that were used routinely in that clinic.[7]

Q-sort data can be analyzed in several ways. The Pearson product-moment correlation coefficient is the statistic most often used. By this method, a deck of numbered Q-sort cards sorted on two occasions or by different judges can be correlated. Correlations among sorts are often factor analyzed. One may also compute the median position of a set of descriptive statements representing a single trait of personality, or one could compare the relative positions of several different traits in the same person.

EVALUATION OF RATING METHODS

Reliability of Ratings

In clinical research, a frequently encountered phrase is, "for lack of a better criterion, ratings were used." The extent to which ratings are used as criteria in personality research and measurement probably exceeds 80 percent. Ratings are particularly suited as criteria for personality tests since objective criteria are much more difficult to find in this area than in achievement and aptitude testing. Nevertheless, rating procedures are subject to numerous types of errors that deserve attention.

There are many sources of error in obtaining ratings, and some of these were already highlighted in the discussion of observational methods in the preceding chapter. Certainly all the sources of error and all the precautions already mentioned apply here also.

---

[7] This led Marks (1961) to the interesting conclusion that present diagnostic practices may be "an extravagant waste of time" (p. 35).

Generally, the level of inference required in making ratings is higher than in most other observational tasks because ratings demand interpretation and quantification of the variables under consideration; and hence there are additional and new sources of error variance that affect the reliability of the rating method. Removal of these sources of error will improve the reliability of ratings.

Leniency Error. A type of error in which a judge tends to give favorable ratings to others is called leniency error. Frequently when raters know that their reports will be used to determine the status or possible promotion of others, they tend to err on the favorable side. The rater may be motivated by notions of being "a nice guy," and therefore refuse to shatter that image; or he may simply be the type of person who is incapable of judging others harshly.

There are also errors in the opposite direction which are made by the "hard" raters. Both the easy and the hard raters are consistent in the direction of their bias and therefore add systematic error variance to their ratings. The leniency error in either direction (easy or hard) is not of any great concern as long as the same rater or raters judge individuals on the same traits and the direction of their bias is known. However, when ratings are made by different judges and these ratings are compared with one another, then the effects of the biases must be known in order to be taken into account.

An innovation introduced to counteract the leniency bias has been the *forced choice* technique. In this type of rating, the judge is required to consider not just one attribute, but several attributes at the same time. Typically, the rater is presented with two favorable items (one of which is a valid predictor) and two unfavorable items (one of which is also a valid predictor) and he is asked to select the one statement that best describes the ratee and the one which least describes him. Thus the judge is forced to make one unfavorable and one favorable statement about the person. Some typical item choices are presented in Figure 5–8. The response is scored by assigning a plus credit for each favorable-valid item, and a minus credit for each unfavorable-valid choice.

The forced choice method is based on the assumption that the rater cannot distinguish between an item that is valid—that is, one that predicts the variable in question—and one which is not. It turns out, however, that some raters are sufficiently informed or knowledgeable to enable them to distinguish between valid and non-valid items (Highland and Berkshire, 1951). But despite the ability to distort intentionally among sophisticated raters, it has been found that in comparison with graphic rating scale procedures, the highest validity coefficients (.53 to .62) can be secured with the forced choice technique. Numerous studies suggest that the best forced choice alternatives were ones that presented four favorable traits, two relevant to the criterion and two irrelevant, with the

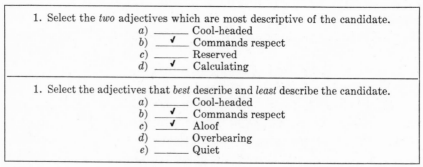

FIGURE 5–8. Items illustrative of a forced-choice rating scale. The adjectives in the upper frame present the rater with four favorable traits, two relevant to the criterion (check marked) and two irrelevant. The adjectives of the lower frame are favorable (*a* and *b*) and unfavorable (*c* and *d*), and each pair contains one criterion relevant choice. Occasionally a neutral item (*e*) is used also.

rater instructed to check the two most descriptive items. Thus, according to this system, the alternatives in the top portion of Figure 5–8 are preferred over those illustrated in the bottom portion.

Halo Effect.   A type of error sometimes referred to as the halo effect, comes about when a rater's overall impression of a person influences his ratings on many traits. For example, when the rater has a generally favorable impression, he judges the person high on most traits; and if he has an unfavorable impression, he judges him low on most traits. One consequence of this type of error is spuriously high correlation coefficients between seemingly unrelated traits. The halo effect was demonstrated in one study (cited in Cronbach, 1960) in which residents of the same women's dormitory rated one another for popularity and for personal adjustment. Since the two traits are often confounded, a correlation coefficient of .85 was obtained between their ratings on one trait and the other. This substantial correlation, however, merely reflected the degree to which the raters confused these traits with one another.

Another consequence of halo error is seen in connection with the reliability of ratings. In determining inter-rater reliability (same trait, same ratees), if the raters share similar halo biases (e.g., girls are obedient, industrious, and intelligent; boys are mischievous, lazy, and unintelligent) then the intercorrelations of their ratings would be artificially high. Moreover, ratings influenced by halo error obscure important individual differences because they pile up at the favorable, or at the unfavorable, end of the scale. Hence such ratings may be invalid because the judge has placed undue weight upon the unimportant characteristics of the ratee.

Ambiguity Error. Yet another source of unreliability, referred to as the ambiguity error, occurs when traits to be rated are not defined carefully. Such terms as "maladjustment," "leadership," and "cooperativeness" may be variously interpreted by different judges. To one judge, for example, a maladjusted person can be one whose style of clothing or automobile model may be out of date. This judge may overlook some rather blatantly neurotic traits.

Ambiguity error may result when verbal descriptions of scale positions are unclear. For example, is "substantial" more or less of something than "moderate"? What about "large"; is that more than "big" or less? Ambiguity often also arises because of poorly constructed scales in which items are included about which the rater has no information. For example, a judge who on his first rating of a group is given the adjectives "absent," "decreased," and "increased," and is required to judge the level of anxiety of each subject, may be expected to be confused by assignment. His ratings, if obtained, obviously are meaningless. Errors arising from inclusion of such ambiguous or irrelevant terms are random ones and influence ratings in unknown ways.

Central Tendency. One additional type of error, called central tendency, is also important for the effect it has on the reliability of ratings. Regardless of the nature of verbal descriptions used to define points along a rating scale, raters have been known to stay close to the center of a scale and avoid using the extreme positions.

The overall effect of this error is to decrease the reliability coefficient by minimizing individual differences among ratees.[8]

Validity of Ratings

It is quite possible to obtain rather impressive reliability coefficients and yet not get a valid assessment of the trait or traits in question. Unfortunately, all too often the validity of a rating scale is assumed by its users because agreement among judges is high. Perhaps one of the most common instances in which inter-judge reliability is high, but where validity is almost nonexistent, occurs when several judges share the same prejudices and biases. In other words, they may all agree in their ratings, but these ratings are unrelated to external criteria. For example, if they share and respond to similar and irrelevant cues about peoples' characteristics (e.g., spectacles and intelligence, smiling face associated with honesty) then their agreement will be high, but the validity of their agreements is low because it is based on false and invalid cues.

A common source of invalid ratings is lack of familiarity with information about the subject. College professors are especially vulnerable to being asked to render judgments about persons with whom they are not adequately acquainted, or about former students they have not seen for years. Nevertheless they feel obligated, both to colleagues and students, to complete the many rating forms they receive in the mail each year. After all, the colleague at University X, to which a student applied for graduate work, expects his letters answered (he would do the same); and the student's application would be incomplete without the required remarks and ratings. The ratings which result, of course, are absurd. One way to avoid obtaining such ratings is to supply the judge ample opportunity to state the extent of his familiarity with the ratee.

No general statement about the validity of rating scales is possible, because empirical evidence reported in the literature refers to specific scales used under a rather unique set of circumstances. Moreover, ratings are often collected in those situations where other measurement approaches are not feasible, and therefore

---

[8] A correlation coefficient, of which the reliability coefficient is a special case, is decreased when the variance of a distribution is restricted. The student interested in the relationships between variance and correlation is referred to two excellent texts by Guilford (1954) and McNemar (1962) on the use of statistics in psychological testing.

criterion data are not available. The consensus among test critics (Cronbach, 1960; Loevinger, 1965; Taft, 1955; Vernon, 1964) seems to be that one ought to be suspicious of the validity of ratings.

IMPROVEMENT OF RATING METHODS

It is generally agreed that a number of precautions can be observed in the construction and use of ratings which would contribute to their greater reliability and validity. Some of the specific principles that have been recommended (Thorndike and Hagen, 1961) to improve ratings can be stated as follows:

1. Rating scales should be used only to measure those traits for which more rigorous forms of testing are not available.
2. Careful attention to the structure of the rating format is necessary to ensure unambiguous items.
3. Raters should be qualified to rate. This can be accomplished by familiarization with the subjects in question, by training raters in the techniques required to perform their tasks, and by clarifying the terminology used on the rating format.
4. It is essential, also, that raters be motivated to participate and that they possess a minimal amount of intelligence to accomplish the rating task. Although it is difficult to specify an arbitrary cutoff point of "minimal" measured intelligence, there is some evidence (Dunnette, 1966) to suggest that the rater's intelligence influences the quality of rating obtained in various settings.

CONTRIVED OBSERVATIONS

The emphasis so far in this chapter has been on techniques designed to limit human observer error. Thus far the observations have required relatively few constraints on the setting, and the observer has remained more or less passive—i.e., he has not, typically, manipulated the conditions of his subjects or altered the cues in the environment to which his subjects were responding.

There are several losses associated with such passivity. In the first place, the behavior that is of greatest interest may occur so rarely that an inordinate amount of time and effort is spent in gathering large masses of data of which only a limited segment is relevant to the question at hand. Or, in the second place, the naturally occurring behavior is often elicited by stimulus events that are not identifiable to the observer; and if he wants to view several degrees or levels of intensity of that behavior, he has no control over the events that elicited the desired responses. For example, an investigator interested in learning the relative efficacy of a variety of environmental stressors on his subject, should be free to vary the introduction of these stressors into the observational setting according to some preconceived plan. Naturalistic observations do not permit this freedom.

The greatest loss incurred when the observer is cast in a passive role is that the results of his observations are not replicable and therefore not subject to confirmation or disconfirmation by the scientific community. Basic to all scientific inquiry is the require- ment that all aspects of that inquiry be precisely specifiable so that any number of persons, either out of curiosity, skepticism, or belief, can repeat the same steps taken by the original investigator. The remainder of this chapter considers several procedures which re- quire the observer's more active participation either in the planning stage or in the observational setting itself.

Manipulation of Subjects

Treatment Studies.   The most common forms of constraint im- posed on subjects in personality research has taken place in clinical settings where the effects of certain treatments are explored. Essentially, treatment constitutes a direct manipulation of sub- jects. One such study (Helper *et al.*, 1963), on the effects of a tran- quilizing drug (chlorpromazine) on learning, memory, and motor performance in emotionally disturbed children, was conducted as follows: 19 of 39 children admitted to a psychiatric institute were assigned to a drug group and the remainder to a placebo group—i.e., a group given a prescription indistinguishable from the drug but lacking the active, and presumably therapeutic, substance. Neither the individuals receiving the drug nor those administering it and testing its effects knew who was receiving the active or the placebo substance.[9] The observed findings were that as a result of the drugs, performance was markedly decreased on such tasks as stylus tapping, number of O's dotted on a mimeographed page in one minute, and maneuvering a pencil through a maze (Porteus Maze).

---

[9] This method of drug administration is sometimes called the "double-blind" procedure.

Another treatment study (Murray, 1954; cited in Shontz, 1965), where subject manipulation was in the form of psychotherapy, used verbal statements produced by the patient as the variable under observation. Judges listening to taped recordings were instructed to draw inferences about the degree to which the subject's verbalizations reflected hostility or defense. With the progression of therapy, hostile statements were observed to increase gradually, while defensive statements showed a proportionate decrease. Hostility toward particular persons was also noted; and specific patterns of hostility toward one family member and then another were observed from one session to the next. The variables of hostility and defense were selected because the particular motivational theory of conflict which governed the study predicted that the process of therapy would decrease defensiveness, which in turn would result in greater expression of hostility.

Drive States. The relationship between an individual's hunger drive and his ability to learn and perform certain tasks is a popular topic of study among psychologists. Earlier in this book the Minnesota semistarvation studies (Guetzkow and Bowman, 1946) were noted, in which volunteers were subjected to prolonged periods of food deprivation and their extreme personality changes were observed. In another investigation (Epstein and Levitt, 1962), where the controls were considerably tighter than in the Minnesota studies, hungry subjects were obtained by testing college students at 5 P.M. and at 6:30 P.M., before and after the regular evening meal. Their learning tasks consisted of food-related (e.g., cheese-cracker) and nonfood-related words (e.g., stair-ceiling). Generally, hunger was found to favor more rapid learning; and under some conditions, memory for food words was facilitated in hungry subjects.

Control of the Environment

Objects in the Environment. A number of studies at McGill University were conducted under what the investigators called "decreased variation in the sensory environment" (Heron *et al.*, 1953, 1956, 1957). These are commonly known as "sensory deprivation" studies and are extreme examples of the control of objects in observational settings. In these studies, significant decrements in performance are usually observed on a variety of perceptual and cognitive tasks.

In one such study (Wexler *et al.*, 1958; cited in Fiske and Maddi, 1961) volunteer subjects were placed in a tank-type respirator. Their movements and tactual contacts were restricted by cylinders on arms and legs, and they could see only a small area of screen and ceiling. To furnish repetitious auditory stimulation, the motor of the respirator was run. The results obtained indicated that only 6 of the original 17 subjects could tolerate these conditions long enough to complete the entire 36-hour observational period. Eight of the subjects reported hearing and seeing things that were not real (hallucinations); and most of the subjects' judgments of the time spent in the respirator were in error by as much as 50 percent.

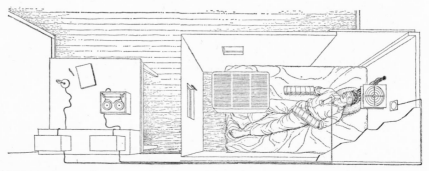

FIGURE 5–9.   The sensory deprivation experiment in which the subject lies on a bed 24 hours a day, with time out for meals and going to the bathroom. (From Heron, "The Pathology of Boredom," *Scientific American*, January, 1957. Copyright © 1957 by Scientific American, Inc. All rights reserved.)

Working in more naturalistic settings, a number of investigators experimented with sign violation (Freed *et al.*, 1955). They addressed themselves to the question, "To what extent will students violate a sign urging the use of an inconvenient side door rather than the customary and more conveniently placed main door?" The degree of prohibition was varied on the sign from high to medium or low (see Figure 5–10) and the results indicated that the least violation occurred with the lowest prohibition. In an extension of these findings another investigator (Sechrest, 1965) found a similar effect: a politely worded sign (e.g., "Please Do Not Use This

Door"), elicited fewer violations than a more prohibitively worded sign (e.g., "Use Other Door").

Group Pressure. In an investigation designed to study the effect of majority opinion, even when it is contrary to fact, on perceptual judgments, one psychologist (Asch, 1955, 1956) contrived the following situation: using a common perceptual task, he asked subjects to compare three straight lines with a previously observed standard line. He presented this task to a subject in the presence of other members of a small group. All members of the group except the subject had been instructed to agree upon a wrong answer for a majority of the trials. Thus, the observed person was subjected to group pressure by being pitted against majority opinion. Many subjects in this situation refused to agree with the majority (who were wrong), but a substantial number yielded under pressure from the others' judgments. Generally, the amount of yielding depended upon (1) the unambiguity of the conditions of the study (i.e., ambiguity of instruction and lack of clarity led to conform-

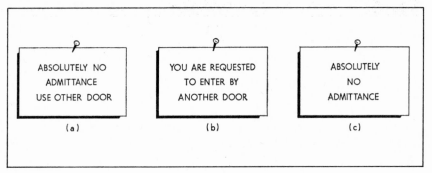

FIGURE 5–10. Which of these signs would you obey? Of the three signs, (*a*) is the strongest, (*b*) is next, and (*c*) is the weakest. The highest conformity was found with the strongest sign when an accomplice complied with its instruction. The lowest conformity (greatest violation of the prohibition) occurred with the weakest sign and the example of a nonconforming accomplice. Generally, however, when accomplices are not used the greatest conformity occurs with a politely worded sign.

ity), (2) individual difference in personality makeup, and (3) the size and the unanimity of the opposition group. With the opposition of only one other person there was very little yielding; with two against one, the amount of yielding was increased; and with three

(a)

(b)

FIGURE 5–11. (a) Six of seven subjects have been asked by the experimenter (right) to give uniformly wrong answers on 12 of 18 pairs of line-matching tasks; the seventh, who was instructed that he is participating in an experiment on visual judgment, is then exposed to the pressure exerted by the remainder of the group. In frames (b) and (c), the subject leans

against one, the effects were about as pronounced as with larger majorities.

Situational Tests and Entrapment

Essentially a situational test is one that places a subject in a complex standard setting, resembling a "real-life" situation, where his performance can be observed under various (usually stressful) conditions. Occasionally these settings are contrived to "trap" subjects into responding in specific ways. In contrast to naturalistic settings, the situational test, because it provides everyone with uniform tasks under standardized conditions, permits a sounder basis for comparisons. Some of the better known tests are discussed below.

(c)

(d)

forward and looks perplexed. In frame (*d*), although apparently puzzled by the others' choices, he makes the correct selection. (From Asch, "Opinions and Social Pressure," *Scientific American*, November, 1955. Photos © William Vandivert.)

Character Educational Inquiry. Among the first situational tests used were those of Hartshorne and May (1930) for the Character Education Inquiry (CEI). They set out to measure traits in school children such as honesty, truthfulness, cooperativeness, and self-control. The CEI techniques made use of the familiar, natural situation within the school child's daily routine. The tests were administered in the form of regular classroom examinations and the children were not aware of being tested except in that ordinary way. For example, one of the measures of cheating was obtained by allowing students to grade their own papers and then noting the number of alterations of answers. The examiners accomplished this by administering a vocabulary and an arithmetic test to the children; then, after collecting the test papers and making duplicates of each child's responses, they returned the original unscored papers. The children were given a list of the correct answers and were asked to score their own papers. Scores reported by the children, with their alterations, if any, were then compared with the scores actually obtained as measured by their duplicate test copies. The number of discrepancies between the two scores provided a measure of cheating.

Honesty was measured by means of several tests to detect stealing and lying behavior (Hartshorne and May, 1928). Children were given the opportunity not to return all the coins distributed for arithmetic "exercises," to peek during "eyes-closed" tests, and to exaggerate the number of chin-ups when allowed to make their own records "unobserved." Lying was tested by questions that were designed to "trap" the student into answering in a socially desirable way. If the student answered 24 or more of the 36 items in a socially approved direction he was considered to be lying.

More recently (Merritt and Fowler, 1948), in a study of honesty appropriately entitled "the pecuniary honesty of the public at large," two psychologists "lost" two kinds of stamped and addressed envelopes. One kind contained an ordinary message of no consequence, the other a lead slug of the dimensions and weight of a large coin. They "dropped" the letters over an extended period of time and in numerous cities to ensure representative sampling of the "public at large." The results: 95 percent of the ordinary letters (control letters) were returned and so were 54 percent of the slug letters (test letters). However, some 13 percent of the latter had been opened.

Resembling more closely the Hartshorne and May entrapment strategies, a recent study (Brock and Guidice, 1963) used second-to sixth-grade elementary school children. These children were individually asked to go to another room to participate in an experiment. At the experimental room, the child found the experimenter on the floor and on all fours searching for money that had "spilled" from her purse. The experimenter then acted as though she had to keep an urgent appointment, and, leaving the room, asked the subject to pick up the contents of her purse before she returned. The measure of dishonesty used was the amount of money stolen by the subject. A question raised by this study, with implications for similar deception studies, is to what extent some of the children, having been instructed that they were to serve as subjects in an experiment, may have become suspicious. Perhaps perspicacity rather than honesty may account for the return of the money by some subjects.

Stress Situation. A method of observing subjects under standardized stress conditions was used in a screening program developed by the Office of Strategic Services (OSS) during World War II. The purpose of this program was to select men for military intelligence work. In addition to the ordinary tests for intelligence, memory, and other abilities, each candidate was given a series of real-life problems or situational tests.

One example of the type of stress introduced into these situations is provided by a description of the Construction Test (OSS, 1948). In this situation the candidate had to assemble a 5-foot cube from wooden poles, pegs and blocks. The candidate was promised two helpers in order to complete the task within the 10-minute allotted time period. It turned out that the helpers were psychologists whose purpose it was to obstruct, criticize, harrass, ridicule, and do anything else that would interfere with the completion of the task. Actually the obstructionist strategy worked so well that no one ever completed the task during the allotted period. In the meantime, the candidate's behavior was observed in a stressful, tense, and frustrating situation. His reactions were noted and rated by observers.

Clinical Psychology Trainee Studies. Although available validity data of the OSS studies were discouragingly low, the circumstances and the time pressures that existed dictated that these tests continue to be used because they seemed the best techniques available to accomplish the necessary ends.

Since World War II, however, a number of attempts have been made to use situational tests, and the best known and most carefully devised of these is an outgrowth of the OSS work. A five-year project (Kelly and Fiske, 1951), the purpose of which was to select student trainees in clinical psychology, consisted of assembling at the University of Michigan a group of VA clinical psychology trainees from 30 universities during a testing period of several days. In addition to tests of aptitude, ability, and personality, a number of situational tests were used. One of these tests consisted of a social situation in which the candidate had to improvise responses. A second test consisted of a discussion situation in which the candidates were told to act as a citizens' committee called together to discuss the use of a large monetary endowment. A third test required that the subject demonstrate the emotions expressed in poetry with gestures and facial expressions. The fourth test consisted of a group of problem-solving tasks.

Four years later, criterion ratings were obtained from university teachers and clinical supervisors who were closely acquainted with the trainees. These ratings reflected the judges' opinions of the trainees' clinical competence, research competence, and preference for hiring. The correlations between these ratings and the situational tests were generally low, rarely exceeding +.20. It has been pointed out (Cronbach, 1960) that the correlations may well have been reduced by the restricted range of ability (all were of high ability) within the group, and because of the unreliability of ratings by clinical supervisors. Overall, the obtained correlations between ratings and clinical competence were much too meager to be of value in selection of future clinical psychology trainees.

In sharp contrast to the low correlations in the prediction of later success, predictions of academic success in graduate school were impressively high and ranged from .35 to .60. These predictions, however, were based almost entirely on two objective tests, the Miller Analogies (widely used as test of verbal ability) and the Strong Vocational Interest Blank, rather than on ratings.

Leaderless Group Discussion.   Situational tests similar to those used in the Michigan studies were the Leaderless Group Discussion (LGD). These tests originated in German and British military psychology. The LGD was designed to appraise such characteristics as cooperativeness, team work, initiative, ingenuity, and leadership. In one type of test situation (Bion, 1946), for example, a group of persons, perhaps applying for similar jobs, are instructed to discuss a certain problem (e.g., the unsatisfactory performance of junior executives in the accounting department) while observers rate predetermined and presumably job-related aspects of each member's performance.

In another study (OSS, 1948), in which candidates are instructed to solve a "wall problem," a team of subjects under observation approach a wall 10 feet high and 15 feet long. They are instructed that it is an impassable barrier, several miles long, and that between this wall and one beyond it is a canyon. Lying nearby are a heavy log, an old board slightly longer than the log, and some short 2 by 4's. The object is to get across the canyon. During the solution of the problem, observers note how the men organize themselves, who takes leadership, and who tends to discourage the others or shows signs of despair.

One investigator (Bass, 1954) has worked out objective indices by means of which each individual's leadership potential can be

FIGURE 5-12. In this situational test, known as the "wall problem," a group of men is given the task of climbing and crossing the "canyon," taking their "bazooka" (log) with them. They have only the materials shown and are not allowed to look around the wall. Courtesy: Donald W. MacKinnon, Institute of Personality Assessment and Research, University of California, Berkeley.

scored in terms of his effectiveness in changing group opinion. Other variables commonly rated relate to prominence, goal-facilitation, forcefulness, and sociability. The reliability of the LGD is fairly high. Correlations within the range of .75 to .90 have been found when the interval between tests has been one week. Correlations dropped to about .50 when longer time intervals were used.

Validity studies that use concurrent ratings of successful performance in military, industrial, and social settings (Bass, 1954; Guilford, 1959) suggest that LGD techniques are highly predictive. When LGD scores were compared with ratings by supervisors as much as nine months later, correlations were still as high as .40 to .45 (Bass and Coates, 1952).

CRITICAL COMMENT AND SUMMARY

As the discussion and illustrations of observational techniques progressed throughout the last two chapters, the emphasis shifted from procedures with minimal constraints on the observer, subject, and setting to those involving ever increasing controls. On this continuum, the least control is exercised in those situations where the observer merely views behavior with his naked eye and notates, usually with pencil and paper, the actions and reactions of the subjects in question. For the most part he remains passive and lets the data happen. In addition to the amount of time and energy wasted in waiting for relevant behavior to occur, this form of observation presents numerous problems arising from the fallible observer's perceptual and cognitive limitations.

The introduction of instrumentation into or at the periphery of the observational setting does not eliminate the observer's waiting game, but does serve to add precision to such observations as he takes. There is little question that audiotapes and movies can take in more of a given scene than the human observer; and at the same time these hardware aids provide faithful and permanent records of behavior that allow subsequent viewing and analyses. Yet the activation of hardware devices is completely under control of the human observer—unless, of course, a setting is saturated with constant hardware vigil—and the problem of viewing relevant behavior still remains.

Rating scale procedures, with the increased constraints they impose on the observer, partially solve the problem of viewing relevant behaviors because they prescribe specifically, and hopefully unambiguously, the behaviors to be noted. Further, rating scale procedures, because they yield quantitative values and can be standardized, have the advantage that they allow comparisons to be made of individuals (or the same individual) viewed by the same, or different, observers. However, rating scales are beset with a number of problems of their own that require careful attention for their resolution.

In contrived observations, the investigators are highly constrained and in turn place considerable controls on their subject matter and environment. By forcing data to emerge, contrived observations yield highly pertinent information. Such data allow comparisons with observations taken under similar conditions; and permit the observer to introduce fine gradations of stimuli, which in turn may yield subtle discriminations in relevant behaviors. However, as the observer becomes more actively involved in the observational procedure, he loses some of the naturalness of *in situ* observations, and the really unsettling question becomes, "To what extent are these observations relevant to real life?" He also runs the risk—as he moves to more contrived observations—that his subjects will detect his hardware or his contrivances, and thus his intentions and objectives.

Finally, all observations of human behavior deal only with the manifest form of behavior and neglect completely the content of that behavior. Thus, for example, no information is obtained about a person's beliefs, perceptions, feelings, and attitudes, or about his past behavior and future plans. Yet this knowledge is indispensable in the study of personality. To obtain this information, such techniques as the interview, self-report inventories, and projective testing are used extensively. The first of these methods, the interview, is the topic of the next chapter.

FOR FURTHER READING

1. FISKE, D. W. Effects of monotonous and restricted stimulation. In FISKE, D. W. & MADDI, S. R., *Functions of varied experience.* Homewood, Ill.: The Dorsey Press, 1961. Pp. 106–144.

   Effects associated with prolonged tasks involving monotonous stimulation are examined, and some of the problems arising in the conduct of such studies are discussed.

2. KELLY, E. L. & FISKE, D. W. *The prediction of performance in clinical psychology.* Ann Arbor: University of Michigan Press, 1951.

   This article reports a five-year research project which had as its purpose the prediction of later success in clinical psychology. Follow-up data to and a summary of this project are reported in a monograph by Kelly and Goldberg (1959).

3. LORR, M. Classification of the behavior disorders. In FARNSWORTH, P. R., MCNEMAR, OLGA, & MCNEMAR, Q. (Eds.), *Annual review of psychology.* Palo Alto: Annual Reviews, Inc. 1961. Pp. 195–216.

   Together with Messick's chapter cited earlier (see P. 23), Dr. Lorr's review of studies of the personality disorders comprises a complete survey of the field to that date.

4. LORR, M., MCNAIR, D. M., KLETT, C. J., & LASKY, J. J. Evidence of ten psychotic syndromes. *Journal of consulting Psychology,* 1962, 26, 185–189.

   This article serves as a research demonstration of the way observational data are taken and then quantified into factors that are comparable to psychotic syndromes (see also Eysenck's criticism [1963] and these authors' reply [1963]).

5. MASLING, J.   The influence of situational and interpersonal variables in projective testing. *Psychological Bulletin,* 1960, 57, 65–85.

The implications of this review article extend beyond the projective test situation. Among the topics examined are the influences examiner and subject have upon one another.

6. RAY, M. L. & WEBB, E. J.   Speech duration effects in the Kennedy news conferences. *Science,* 1966, 153, 899–901.

Transcripts of 61 regular Kennedy news conferences were examined in an effort to replicate the "speech duration effect" reported by Matarazzo *et al.* (1964).

7. ROSENTHAL, R.   The effect of the experimenter on the results of psychological research. In MAHER, B. A.   (Ed.), *Progress in experimental personality research.* Vol. I. New York: Academic Press, 1964. Pp. 80–114.

In this fascinating paper, the author presents a cogent case for the conclusion that human beings can engage in highly effective *unintentional* communication with one another. The subtlety of this communication is such that casual observation does not reveal its presence.

8. STARKWEATHER, J. A.   Content-free speech as a source of information about the speaker. *Journal of abnormal and social Psychology,* 1956, 52, 394–402.

A distinction is made in this study between vocal (e.g., content-free) and verbal (e.g., with content) aspects of speech (cf. Dittmann & Wynne, 1961).

9. SWENTZELL, R. & ROBERTS, A. H.   On the interaction of the subject and the experiment in the matching model. *Psychometrika,* 1964, 29, 87–101.

These psychologists demonstrate that there is an interaction between the tactics, strategies, and actual knowledge of human subjects and the type of design used. When the subject's knowledge is held constant, different results are obtained than when it is not.

10. THORNDIKE, R. L. & HAGEN, ELIZABETH.   *Measurement and evaluation in psychology and education.* New York: John Wiley & Sons, Inc., 1961.

An excellent outline on rating scales and problems associated with their use can be found in this volume (see pp. 351–387).

THE INTERVIEW

Language most shows a man; speak that I may see thee!
Ben Jonson

The personality assessment interview is a face-to-face verbal communication between two people, initiated for the specific purpose of allowing the interviewer to learn about the respondent's personality characteristics. Historically, interviewing is closely associated with psychotherapy. The medium for most forms of psychological treatment is a two-person verbal interaction. Interviewing is distinguished from everyday, ordinary acts of communication—in which one person requests information and another supplies it—by its purposive and probing nature.

Strictly speaking, the interview is not a measuring device, because ordinarily it does not yield quantitative information. However, the interview as conducted by a trained psychologist or psychiatrist produces more valuable information than, for example, ratings by untrained observers or well-meaning acquaintances. Further, since the interview presents a relatively uniform situation to many respondents, it has potential as a scientifically valid method for personality study. Moreover, the interview easily lends itself to quantification. Just as it was possible to summarize direct observations in terms of scores or scale positions, responses to carefully standardized interview questions can be treated similarly.

In contrast to observational methods, the interview provides information about an individual's perceptions, beliefs, past behavior, and future plans. Commenting on this valuable source of information, Gordon W. Allport (1937) put the matter succinctly, "If we want to know how people feel: what they experience and what they remember, what their emotions and motives are like, and the reasons for acting as they do—why not ask them?" By their very nature these "personal" or "private" bits of information are difficult, if not impossible, to elicit by direct observational methods.

In the course of the interview, observation is used in several ways. If the interview is conducted in the respondent's home, for example, the psychologist can observe the interviewee's taste in home furnishings, his interaction with his children or spouse, and any number of other aspects of his style of living. Such observations provide the interviewer with clues about socioeconomic status and generally are more valuable in painting the respondent's background than are answers to questions by themselves. Careful observation of the respondent's nonverbal responses, regardless of where the interview is conducted, yields valuable clues about his personality characteristics. Thus, observations are made of his general appearance (slovenly, unkempt, neat), attitude (cooperative, hostile), manner of speech (tone of voice, level of vocabulary, speed of verbal productions) and his facial expressions (mobile, masked, contorted).

STRUCTURED AND UNSTRUCTURED INTERVIEWS

Interviews vary from the highly structured types to the totally unstructured and random forms. Often the kind of interview conducted will depend upon its purpose and the idiosyncracies and preferences of the interviewer. The amount of structure in an interview can vary from one extreme, where questions are asked by the interviewer from a fixed list, through the less extreme case where a basic set of questions are asked but many others may be brought in, to the other extreme where no plan is followed. The interviewer may, for example, stick to a rigid form of questions that will provide basic information about the person's age, nationality, social background, degree and type of education, occupational history, and plans; or in the process of inquiring about these matters he may ask questions about the person's ambitions, fears, worries, marked aversions, sex experience, philosophy of life, and numerous other topics; or he may allow the respondent to lead the direction of the interview.

The Unstructured Interview

The unstructured interview takes various forms and goes under various names that reveal its close relationship to psychotherapeutic interviewing, such as the "focused," "clinical," "nondirective," or "depth" interview. Its distinguishing feature is that it places minimum constraints on the interviewer or his subject in terms of the nature of the topics covered or the types of questions asked. The flexibility of this type of interview, if used properly by a trained psychologist, may help bring out the emotion-laden implications of a respondent's communications and therefore disclose the personal significance of his various responses.

For the interviewer, the unstructured interview offers tremendous versatility because he is free to roam over a wide variety of topics. This freedom is at once the major advantage and major disadvantage of this type of interview. The flexibility frequently results in lack of comparability of one interview with another. Therefore, this type of interview is used when little would be gained by asking each respondent for the same information because each may have a different contribution to make, depending on his relationship to the person under study—whether, for example, in the personality study of a hospital patient, he is a relative, a friend, a neighbor, or the patient himself.

The unstructured interview is also used to identify general problem areas that can subsequently be explored by means of the structured interview, or as a source of hypotheses that can later be submitted to systematic tests.

Even within the unstructured interview situation, there are degrees of unstructuredness. Thus at the most unstructured end of the continuum, in the so-called *nondirective* interview, the initiative is largely in the hands of the respondent. The term "nondirective" became popular as a method of counseling in college settings as a result of the work of Carl Rogers and his associates. During the nondirective counseling interview, the client—as he is called by Rogers' followers—is encouraged to express his feelings without suggestions or questions from the counselor. The latter's function is simply to encourage the client to talk, with a minimum of direct questioning or guidance. Examples of some typical statements made by the interviewer during the nondirective situation include, "You seem to feel that . . . ," "Can you repeat that . . . ?" "Isn't that interesting," or "Tell me more."

Somewhat more structured than the nondirective interview is one that was employed by a group of behavioral scientists (Adorno *et al.*, 1950) in the study of *The Authoritarian Personality*. The interview schedule used in that study is presented in Table 6–1. It may be noted that although the interviewer has a framework of questions he wants answered, he has nevertheless some freedom to explore reasons and motives, and he is given latitude to probe further in numerous directions within some of the categories. In contrast to the nondirective interview, however, the direction of this interview is clearly in the hands of the interviewer.

TABLE 6–1

Excerpt of Interview Schedule Used by Adorno *et al.*, (1950)

FAMILY BACKGROUND: SOCIOLOGICAL ASPECTS

Underlying Questions:

   a) *National origins* of father and mother (not just racial; e.g. third generation Polish, German immigrant, etc.).
   b) *Important ingroup memberships* of father mother (e.g., unions, Masons, etc.).
   c) Picture of *socioeconomic status* of parents and grandparents (as reflected in occupation, education, way of life, etc.), with special attention to social nobility.

Suggested Direct Questions:

Background

   a) Father's and mother's national antecedents, occupation, education, politics, religion.

Economic

   b) Actual standard of living of father and mother (ask specific questions to get clear: cars, servants, housing, entertaining, etc.; enough to eat, on relief, have to work as child, etc.).

Ingroups

   c) Who were your father's (mother's) friends mostly: What organizations did your father (or mother) belong to? How did your father (mother) spend his (her) spare time?

The Structured Interview

The structured interview or, as it has sometimes been called, the standardized interview, attempts to use the same form of questioning and collect the same information from each respondent. In personality assessment this amount of structuredness is desirable in situations where quantification of data is necessary for subsequent intra- or interrespondent comparisons. Thus in one study (Wittson and Hunt, 1951), the results of which are presented in Table 6–2, in which 944 seamen were interviewed briefly, the severity of symptomatology of these seamen was expressed in terms of a very crude three-category quantitative scheme: mild, moderate, and severe symptoms. A follow-up study, as illustrated in the second and third columns of Table 6–2 (Subsequent Neuropsychiatric Discharge), permitted comparisons of psychiatric discharge rates between persons diagnosed mild, moderate, and severe. The results indicated a remarkable relationship between this crude quantitative diagnosis and the discharge rate. This illustration is intended to point out that without such quantification, even as simple as it was, the obtained comparisons would not have been possible.

TABLE 6–2

Incidence of Subsequent Neuropsychiatric Discharges
among Men Interviewed and Diagnosed in Terms of the Severity
of Their Symptoms.

Severity of Symptoms	Number of Cases	Subsequent NP Number	Discharges Percent
Mild.............527	34	6.5
Moderate.........367	74	20.2
Severe........... 38	34	89.7

Source: Adapted from Wittson and Hunt, 1951.

In the most common form of standardized interview, also called the *schedule* interview, the wording and sequence of questions are determined in advance, and the questions of the schedule are asked of all respondents in exactly the same way. The alternative approach, somewhat less structured, is the *nonschedule standardized* interview (Richardson *et al.*, 1965), so called because it attempts standardization without the use of a prepared schedule of interview items. Instead, the interviewer is taught thoroughly and exactly what information is required of each respondent. If precise standardization is to be attained, the sequence of the interviewer's questioning should not vary from one respondent to the next. A hypothetical illustration of a schedule interview is presented below. The items are varied somewhat in their coverage and format, in order to exemplify different types of scoring schemes. Items numbered one through four permit the interviewer freedom to phrase his own questions, and the remainder of the items are cast in question form:

1.   *Orientation to Interview*
     0 Seems to understand purpose of interview.
     1 Shows some insight as to purpose.

    2 Accepts stated explanation of purpose.

    3 Completely misinterprets purpose.

2. *Attention*

    0 Completely attentive to flow of conversation.

    1 Relatively undisturbed by extraneous stimuli.

    2 Easily distracted by extraneous stimuli.

    3 Impossible to get and hold attention.

3. *Amount of Speech*

    0 Underproduction.

    1 Moderate.

    2 Substantial.

    3 Abnormal overproduction.

4. *Expressive Ability*

    +2 Excellent.

    0 Adequate.

    +1 Good.

    −1 Inadequate.

    −2 Very inadequate.

5. *Are you bothered by ill health?*

    0 Never.

    1 Hardly ever.

    2 Sometimes.

    3 Often.

6. *Do you experience dizzy spells?*

    0 Never.

    2 Often.

    1 Sometimes.

7. *How often are you troubled by stomach upset?*

    3 Often.

    2 Sometimes.

    1 Hardly ever.

    0 Never.

Critical Comment

In general the advantage of the more structured interview is that it guarantees that important information is obtained concerning various aspects of the person. The structured interview provides standardization which is designed to guarantee that all interviewees are asked the same questions and are provided with similar situations. An especially important advantage for the beginning interviewer is that the structured situation requires less psychological acumen and experience than the unstructured one. Another advantage of considerable importance is that the structured interview, because of its amenability to quantification, permits interobserver, intrarespondent, and interrespondent comparisons.

There are, however, several important disadvantages that are encountered as we move toward greater structuredness. A formal list of questions and topics necessitates a rigid procedure which often interferes with a facile communication process. The interview can assume the aura of an inquisition and consequently may yield little more than answers to questions. If just enough time is allowed for asking the prescribed questions, opportunities for ferreting out some interesting bits of information are missed.

The free or unstructured interview, in contrast to the structured one, permits expression of the desired information and at the same time allows the conversation to find its own path with a minimum of direction. In many respects the unstructured interview resembles an ordinary conversation between two persons. Being more free and casual, it is often more natural, and consequently the respondent may be more at ease. Further, since there are no time limits or topic pressures, the interviewer has a chance to follow up promising leads that arise. If the interview is conducted skillfully, the necessary information is obtained casually, and possibly without awareness by the respondent of the kind and amount of data that are being elicited.

On the debit side, the disadvantage of the free interview is that each respondent faces a different situation and therefore it becomes more difficult to compare results on an equitable basis. Such a situation, as Guilford (1959) points out, biases the sampling of traits that will be brought out and the ones that will be concealed, because these variables are left under the control of the respondent, who may direct the conversation toward his stronger points and away from his weaker ones.

In summary, the advantages and disadvantages for each form of interview, as is shown in Table 6–3, are about equal. The question of how much structure to incorporate in any one interview is governed by the aims and goals for which the interview is intended. Generally speaking, it is probably correct to say that if the interview's purposes are to develop rapport, to provide an opportunity to orient the respondent to a new setting, or to introduce testing procedures, then the more unstructured format is suitable. If, however, the interview is intended as a measuring device by means of which research and practical decisions and predictions are to be made, then the structured and standardized framework is to be preferred.

TABLE 6–3

The Structured v. Unstructured Interview

Type of Interview	Advantage	Disadvantage
Structured	Standardized. High information yield. Requires less experience. Permits quantification. Permits comparisons.	Rigid procedure. Interrogation atmosphere. Encourages check marking.
Unstructured	Permits free expression. Is more natural. Free reign of questions. No time limits.	Encourages rambling. Resembles conversation. Unstandardized. Respondent conceals information.

TYPES OF INTERVIEWS

Cutting across the structured-unstructuredness dimension guiding the conduct of interviews, there are numerous types of interviews. They differ in terms of their purposes and goals rather than in the amount of structure. The various type of interviews and their aims and characteristic problems are summarized in Table 6–4.

The Employment or Personnel Interview

The interview is an important and integral part of the employment process. This type of interview, variously called an employment or personnel interview, is usually conducted in one of a number of cubicles in the personnel department of the hiring corporation or may take place in the office of a consulting psychology firm especially retained by the corporation for evaluating candidates. The purpose of the interview may be to help in a decision about the interviewee's qualifications for a particular unfilled position or for promotion within the corporation to a new position. In either case, the interviewer performs both an information-getting and an information-giving function.

To the employer, the personnel interview provides information regarding the candidate's past work experience, personal characteristics, interests, and abilities. This information serves as a basis

TABLE 6–4
Types of Interviews and Their Settings, Aims and Problems

Type of Interview	Setting	Purpose	Problem
Personnel	Industry	To assess candidate's qualifications	Interviewer's dual role
Troubleshooting	Industry	To determine cause of interpersonal difficulties.	Interviewer's dual role
Poll	Door-to-door	Assess attitudes, opinions, beliefs	Rigid structure and leading questions
Stress	Military or training programs	Assess reactions to unusual circumstances	Generalizability
Medical diagnostic	Clinic or hospital	Diagnosis	Accuracy of reporting
Psychiatric intake	Mental hygiene clinic or hospital	Gather preliminary information about patient and establish relationships	Patient's anxiety
Mental status	Mental hygiene clinic or hospital	Ascertain patient's mental state	Overprobing and pathological bias
Case history	Clinic, hospital, or home	Background information	Selectivity of information
Pre- and post-test	Psychiatric	Before-and-after test decision making	Amount of test information to impart
Termination	Psychiatric	Set patient free	Premature timing

for an initial recommendation as to whether further tests should be conducted, the candidate's probable qualifications for the position, and the sort of position he may be qualified to occupy. The obviously unsuited candidate should not be encouraged to continue his application procedures. During the course of the employment interview, this information, along with helpful suggestions about his suitability for certain other positions (if such information is available to the interviewer), should be conveyed to the candidate.

For the job applicant, the employment interview consists mostly of information giving and can be a frightening experience. Depending on the skills of the interviewer, the prospective employee may overcome his initial apprehension about the interview and settle back and be relaxed and at ease, or he may become even more tense and frightened. The conduct of the interview, and the information the candidate obtained and was asked to provide during its course, may motivate him to accept the position (if offered), or may lead him to the conclusion that he really doesn't care for the job anyhow.

The function of a final or follow-up interview with a job applicant, after all information about him from interviews, tests, application forms, and references have been gathered and integrated, is to communicate to the candidate the favorable and unfavorable aspects of his qualifications and to convey to him the company's decision about his suitability for the position. During the course of that final interview, the employer (or his representative) may ask certain last-minute questions to help him in his final decision to hire or to reject, and he may once again convey to the job applicant some of the characteristics of the position for which the candidate has applied. If the decision not to hire (or not to promote) is made, either before or during the follow-up interview, the reason for this decision should be communicated to the candidate so that he too may have benefited somewhat from the interview experience.

The Troubleshooting Interview

In industrial settings, situations arise where a supervisor may find occasion to interview a subordinate employee about a number of difficulties between that employee and other workers. This is troubleshooting in the sense that the interview provides the supervisor with information about the nature of the difficulties or disagreements, and any solutions the employee may have for their remedy; and such an interview may pave the way for arbitration of disagreements, or it may serve to convince the supervisor that attempts at arbitration are premature or likely to be unsuccessful. The troubleshooting interview demands considerable skill in understanding interpersonal relationships, and only recently, in recognition of this fact, have psychologists been used as interviewers or advisory consultants to supervisors or employers.

The special difficulties of this type of interview are well documented (Kahn and Cannell, 1957) and center around the dual role of the interviewer (or his representative) as supervisor and interviewer. This duality also exists, of course, in the interviewee's role as respondent and subordinate. It is as difficult for the supervisor to shed completely his supervisory position as it is for the respondent to ignore the status and power differences that exist between them. The result is the tendency for the employee to become defensive and to withhold or distort information. For his part, the interviewer's task is to correct for such distortions, and this can best be accomplished by emphasizing the information-getting function of the interview. He must learn, therefore, like all interviewers in other settings, that he must be permissive, accepting and nonjudgmental.

The Poll-Type Interview

Generally, the poll-type interview consists of a prepared list of questions which limit the respondent to stated alternatives. Frequently the questions deal with various aspects of one topic; and they may or may not be set up in such a way that they form a rating scale. Poll-type interviews are essentially the same as poll-type questionnaires, and the reason for not using the latter is to reach persons who are either unable or unwilling to fill out questionnaires. Sample items, in rating- and nonrating-scale format, are presented in Table 6–5.

Poll-type interview items, because of their quantifiability, are used when distinctions of degree rather than of quality are desired. The clinical psychologist would like to assert, for example, that patient X is more anxious than patient Y, rather than to be limited to the qualitative statement that their anxiety levels are different.

This type of interview, with its rigid structure and easily quantifiable alternative responses, has the advantage of being standardized, simple to administer, quick to analyze, and relatively inexpensive. But its disadvantages for personality measurement far outweigh the advantages.

Fixed alternative responses may force an individual to adopt a trait or express an attitude which he does not possess. Many questions are of the "Why do you beat your wife? Yes or No" type; and the tendency of poll-type interviewers is to press for a definite response. An "I don't know" or "insufficient information" response is usually accepted only as a last resort. The effects of such pressure on respondents has been cleverly demonstrated in a sequence of film

TABLE 6–5

The Poll-Type Interview

Interview Questions	Fixed Alternative Responses
How long have you been hospitalized?	Less than 1 week ____; 1 week ____; 2 weeks ____; 3 weeks ____; etc.
Have you found your stay a pleasant one?	Yes ____; No ____.
Describe the nature of your illness within the framework of one of these categories.	I have been feeling dejected and unhappy ____. Nothing seems to work out well for me ____. I have been disturbed by unpleasant thoughts ——. A long rest will benefit me____.
Rate your present mental state in comparison to what it was on prior hospitalizations (check mark the correct choice).	Much worse | Worse | No change | Better | Much better
Has your family been visiting you regularly?	Yes ____; No ____.
Do you expect your family to visit you?	Yes ____; No ____; Cannot predict ____; They may or may not, depending on their whims ____.

obtained by the "Candid Camera" crew. In that film, a bogus pollster conducts door-to-door and street interviews in which he asks persons about products or topics about which they hold no opinions. The critical material in the film occurs when the interviewer pleads that they express a positive (or negative) opinion, and the respondents graciously comply with his requests.

Even when no pressure is exerted in these fixed alternative interviews, the answer chosen by a respondent often reflects an uncrystallized attitude or opinion, and may reflect an artifact of the wording or phrasing of the question, or of the stated alternative responses. One of the subjects of Kinsey's study of sexual behavior is said to have expressed his frustration with the poll-type interview by complaining that, "No matter what I told him, he just looked me straight in the eye and asked, 'How many times?' "

The Stress Interview

Another type of interview, the stress interview, was developed during World War II for selection and assignment of men by the Office of Strategic Services (OSS). This type of interview, as noted in Chapter 5, was used to determine how well an individual can keep command of his resources under extreme emotional stress.

Typically, such an interview starts with a conversation, in a relaxed and friendly manner, between the subject and a panel of about three to five interviewers. The conversation may gradually change from a relaxed one to a more probing type, and an occasional hint may be dropped that the interviewee will be eliminated from competition. The whole atmosphere may change from a congenial one to one in which cool disdain for the subject is expressed. Often the candidate is instructed to answer factual questions or to participate in a performance test. The questions and performance tasks are intentionally made complicated or difficult and are often impossible to complete. The interviewee, however, is led to believe that there are correct replies and solutions to these problems.

At the completion of the questions or tests the respondent is told that he performed extremely poorly and that there is very little hope of his "making it." The atmosphere can be changed and varied according to the requirements of the situation, and often it is one of relaxation and then pressure, and then relaxation again, in order to assess the candidate's ability to recover after the pressure is off.

A variant of the stress interview, occasionally used to screen candidates for clinical psychology training programs, is designed to assess the emotional reactions of subjects to unusual interview situations. There is one well-known psychologist at a large midwestern university who has built a considerable reputation for conducting this type of interview. In one such situation, where the candidate had never previously met the interviewer, the latter sat opposite the subject in the waiting room as he waited an inordinate amount of time past the appointment hour. The psychologist engaged the candidate in casual conversation, and after a short observational period introduced himself as Dr. X, the man responsible for inconveniencing the candidate. Of course, the prospective trainee is then left with the question, "I wonder what I said about Dr. X?" at the same time he is trying to maintain his interview composure and presence of mind.

Another form of this psychologist's interview technique, used either in conjunction with the preceding treatment or, if the candidate is acquainted with him, used by itself, is the following situation: The psychologist invites his subject into the office, and after they settle into their respective chairs, the interviewer dozes off. Upon awakening, perhaps after several minutes of feigned sleep, the interviewer glances at the candidate's record folder, shakes his head from side to side, and inquires: "What are you doing here?" This question, or some variation of it, is left sufficiently ambiguous to elicit the subject's defenses. After replying that he is there to be interviewed, the candidate is again unsettled by the matter-of-fact observation: "I know that (as well as you); I mean your record indicates that you're from New York, but this is Ann Arbor."

The Medical Diagnostic Interview

Physicians conduct interviews at various stages of their diagnostic and therapeutic processes. The medical diagnostic interview is used in order to obtain information as a basis for an initial diagnosis; its purpose is to ascertain the extent and nature of the patient's complaints and to allow the physician to formulate working hypotheses regarding the possible causes of those complaints. The interview also furnishes information that may enable the physician to reject some hypotheses and to retain others.

Essentially, the medical diagnostic interview is terminated at the point where the physician thinks he has obtained as much information as the patient is able to communicate. The diagnostic interview is followed by a thorough physical examination and laboratory tests during which the physician narrows down the possible sources responsible for the patient's symptoms.

Of the many forms of interviewing, the medical diagnostic interview, according to some authorities in the field (Kahn and Cannell, 1957), is one of the most complex and demanding of skilled communication techniques. The physician must obtain sufficient information from the patient to permit him to formulate hypotheses, while at the same time he must frame additional questions to test those hypotheses. And since the hypothesis and question formulation processes are active ones, the physician must constantly reject some of his possible explanations in the light of new information. Thus the physician, if skilled and properly trained, becomes the theorist, interviewer, analyst, and experimenter combined.

From the point of view of its personality assessment function, the medical diagnostic interview demands that the physician be thoroughly familiar with some of the personality characteristics and anxieties that accompany various physical diseases; and that he recognize that there are numerous imagined ills, which by their very nature have no physical basis. In either case—whether or not physically identifiable sources caused the complaint—the patient's emotional involvement in the interview is considerable. As far as he is concerned, what he tells the physician influences the latter's verdict as to whether the patient is to be hospitalized or not; or whether he is essentially healthy or suffering from an incurable ailment. With such emotions close to the surface, the patient is likely to withhold information, or exaggerate irrelevant symptoms, or generally distort the picture he presents. Additionally, because of these emotional forces, the patient tends to imbue the doctor's questions with medical significance, and may frame his replies partly in terms of his symptoms and partly in terms of what he believes to be the significance of the physician's query. Because of all these factors, it is the rare physician indeed who is skilled in both personality assessment interviewing and in medical diagnostic problem solving.

The Psychiatric Intake Interview

The psychiatric intake interview, as the name suggests, is the initial contact between interviewer and respondent and is usually conducted in a mental health setting. For the interviewee the intake is often an ordeal; and it may be assumed that his feelings are apt to be near the surface and ready to operate. More often than not the decision to seek help for an emotional problem—or being forced to seek it—is likely to make him ill at ease, self-conscious, and defensive. Perhaps he now has some misgivings about his decision to seek help, and possibly he entertains several of the common misconceptions about the interview process. His awkwardness and discomfort may be intensified if he has been coerced into coming. For most persons the interview is an unfamiliar experience, and since the intake is an initial session, the interviewer is an unfamiliar other person. The interviewer must make some sort of adjustment to all of these factors, and it is clearly his responsibility to carry the bulk of the burden of this initial session.

Beyond the first goal of the psychiatric intake interview, which is to establish relationship with the patient, the clinician must understand the latter's expectations. He learns and makes inferences about these attitudes by observing the patient's initial behavior. The respondent may be eager and interested, he may be unmotivated and sluggish, or his attitudes may fall somewhere in between these extremes. Since the groundwork must be laid for possible further contact, the interviewer usually imparts preliminary information about the nature of the institution or operation that he represents, fees to be charged, and the extent to which the patient's expectations can be met by the agency or hospital.

The intake interview may also include the gathering of preliminary information about the patient's identification (e.g., name, age, education), the nature of his problems, and other relevant matters that are explored more thoroughly in the mental status and case history interviews, which are the topics of the next two sections. Frequently the initial interview serves to clarify to both participants whether the particular agency to which the patient has come is appropriate for handling his problem. If the agency is inappropriate, other community facilities could be discussed and recommended. In spite of the superficiality of coverage of some areas, the first contact with an interviewer can be a very important one. It sets the tone for all future contacts.

The Mental Status Interview

Another type of interview, sometimes considered a part of the intake, is the mental status examination. A mental status interview is essentially a cross-sectional study taken at the earliest possible time after the person has presented himself at a clinic or hospital. Its purpose is to ascertain what abnormalities or pathologies of behavior are present in the patient. Under each of the six areas presented in Table 6–6 and discussed below, the interviewer attempts to collect observations without interpreting such observations. It is often recommended (Wells and Reusch, 1945; Menninger, 1952) that the interviewer collect as many direct quotes as possible, and that he refrain—at least at this stage of the diagnostic process—from making inferences based on his observations.

TABLE 6–6

Excerpts from a Mental Status Interview of
a 29-Year-Old Male

Category	Example of Report
General appearance, attitude, and behavior	He is friendly and cooperative. Has made no complaints about ward restrictions. He smiles in a somewhat exaggerated and grotesque manner.
Discourse	He answers in a deep, loud voice, speaking in a slow, precise, and somewhat condescending manner. His responses are relevant but vague.
Mood and affective fluctuations	His facial expressions, although not totally inappropriate, are poorly correlated with subject of discourse or events in his environment.
Sensorium and intellect	The patient's orientation for place, person, and time is normal. His remote and recent memory also are normal. Two brief intelligence measures indicate about average intelligence.
Mental content and specific preoccupations	He readily discusses what he calls his "nervous trouble." He complains of "bad thoughts" and a "conspiracy." He reports hearing voices saying, "Hello, Bill, you're a dirty dog."
Insight	The patient readily accepts the idea that he should be in the hospital. He feels that hospitalization will help him get rid of these "bad" thoughts. He is not in the least defensive about admitting to auditory and visual hallucinations or to the idea that everyone on earth is his enemy.

The six areas of interest during the mental status interview are: (1) *attitude, appearance,* and *behavior,* under which heading are included a résumé of the patient's demeanor during the most recent period; (2) *mental content,* during which the interviewer probes for evidence and traces of such symptoms as delusions, hallucinations,[1] repetitive rituals, mental preoccupations and phobias; (3) *emotional tone,* when the patient's subjective reports are elicited about his feelings. Notations are made by the interviewer of overt and covert signs of affect or emotion; (4) *sensorium* and *intellect,* when the person's orientation to time, place, and person is examined, and brief tests of arithmetic or reasoning are administered as evidence is sought of his level of intellectual functioning; (5) *stream* of *speech* or *discourse,* which includes observations on slips

[1] See p. 10, Chapter 1 for definitions of these terms.

of the tongue, and the rapidity, coherence, organization, and peculiarities of speech;[2] and (6) *insight*, during which time the patient's appreciation of the extent to which he is ill is assessed.

Case History Interview

The purpose of the case history interview is to gather as much background information as possible about a particular person. This interview can be conducted at the time of the original contact or, more appropriately, any time after the intake interview has been conducted. The case history interview has its roots in the field of social work. Its prominence came about when social work joined forces with the psychoanalytic movement. Early in the history of social work, case studies were made in order to determine an individual's eligibility for public assistance. During the 1920's and 1930's it became firmly linked to the mental hygiene movement (Taft, 1923, 1937) ; and it was then that its major purpose became the study and description of the person and the family group.

When psychiatry, psychology, and social work joined forces in the mental hygiene setting, the social worker's unique contribution to the mental health team was in the form of case histories. This procedure of personality assessment also was readily accepted and adopted by psychologists, who were accustomed to explaining behavior in terms of a subject's past experience.

There are three primary sources of information for the case history which a clinician must consider: interviews, formal records, and agency reports. The interview is the most common source of information, and will be the only one discussed here.

Case history interviews are conducted with the client or patient, as well as with members of his family, neighbors, friends, teachers, employers, and others. These interviews cover, among other areas, such basic topics as history of the complaint, hereditary background, childhood development, and medical history. Information gathered in these interviews must be checked and cross-checked, because in all likelihood it will be colored by the biases and opinions of the individuals being interviewed.

---

[2] The use of speech peculiarities as cues about persons is as old as the history of man. In a biblical account, the Gileadites made Ephraimites pronounce "shibboleth," the Hebrew word for ear of corn or stream. As the Ephraimites could not say *sh* but only *s* ("sibboleth") this was regarded as a test of an Ephraimite (of which 42,000 were thus detected).

The object of collecting case history data is almost never for the purpose of writing a complete biography, but rather to answer particular questions such as, "Should the patient be committed to a state institution?", or more usually, "What are the history and background of his presenting complaints?" Kinds of information sometimes collected are (Sundberg and Tyler, 1962, pp. 508–510) : (1) Identifying data (e.g., name, age, sex) ; (2) reason for coming; (3) description of work and status on the job; (4) family constellation; (5) early recollections; (6) birth and development; (7) history of physical and psychological health; (8) education and training; (9) work record, (10) recreational activities and interests; (11) sexual development; (12) marital and family data; (13) self-description; (14) significant or turning points in life; and (15) other information voluntarily supplied by the patient.

The fundamental assumption underlying the collection of case history data is that a person's present personality is part of a continuous process of development. The importance of this longitudinal and continuity approach has been especially emphasized by the proponents of the psychoanalytic school of psychiatry. Presumably a patient's behavior in the past indicates more or less clearly what may, in all probability, be expected of him in similar situations in the future.

Some writers have proposed that the case history should be the primary tool of personality assessment (Dailey, 1960). This view extends beyond merely the interview portion of data collection and holds that the life history, gathered from interviews as well as from secondary sources, reveals personality most thoroughly and accurately. There is some evidence indicating the superiority of life history data in understanding people. In one study (Horn, 1943), biographic data were found to have more value than other types of information available about his subjects. In another study (Kostlan, 1954), in which various types of data (Rorschach, MMPI, and case history) were selectively eliminated, the superiority of the case history as a source of cues was demonstrated. More recently, Soskin (1959), Sines (1959), and Golden (1964) have reported similar findings.

However, assessment of personality by the case history alone presents numerous problems that arise because of the unreliability of information obtained from the individual or his acquaintances. The data, insofar as they depend on the person's memory or the

memory of those who knew him, are extremely fallible. As an example of this, Lazarus (1961) reports an early study made by Doering and Raymond (1935) on the reliability of information given by
mothers of 60 patients of the Boston Psychopathic Hospital. Even
factual items (e.g., date of birth, high school grades) were incorrectly reported by 11 percent of the mothers. Twenty-six percent of
these mothers gave incorrect information about such threatening
items as the incidence of mental disease in the family. Thus the
sources of case history information must be checked, wherever feasible or possible, against baby books, school records, and other informal and formal records.

Moreover, inferences based on reported events in a person's life
are often unwarranted. One psychologist (Hovey, 1959) conducted
research in which he demonstrated the discrepancy between clinicians' interpretations and the actual facts of the case. In that study,
six psychologists and psychiatrists were asked to check a long list
of history items of psychiatric patients with whom they were well
acquainted. These workers were instructed to check items they
believed to be significantly related to the patients' conditions. The
results, when compared with a list derived from actual case histories of these patients, indicated that clinicians were right in the
predictive value of about 73 percent of the items but that many
errors were made in which items were incorrectly predicted to have
significance for mental illness.

In a comparative study of the personal histories of schizophrenic[3]
and nonpsychiatric patients, the findings of Schofield and Balian
(1959) discredit the popular view that the origins of mental illness
are readily found in life experiences. In a survey of over 300 studies
of life histories of psychiatric patients, they found very few with
"traumatic histories" and did find "traumas" in the life histories of
one fourth of "normal" persons! The most stunning finding of their
statistical analysis was the substantial overlap of the normal and
schizophrenic samples on distributions for personal history variables. Schofield and Balian caution against retaining the popular
notion that any single set of events or circumstances leads toward
schizophrenia, and they suggest that the study of patterns and
configurations of life events may be more valid predictors than
isolated events.

---

[3] See p. 10, Chapter 1 for definition.

Pre- and Post-Test Interviews

At some point during the psychiatric diagnostic procedure, patients are administered questionaire-type self-report tests, as well as a number of tests that consist of abstract drawings, photographs, or inkblots. These tests usually follow the intake interview, and are themselves followed by further interviewing. Pre-test interviews are used to estimate the patient's condition and to aid in the decision about what tests are to be used; and post-test interviews, usually conducted after the tests have been scored and briefly studied, are used to communicate recommendations to the patient and to help clarify a number of issues that may be raised by the test findings.

Further, in the post-testing interview, the clinician examines hypotheses formulated as a result of observations made during the pre-testing period and throughout the process of clinical evaluation. In some instances, when test results are incongruent with nontest observations and clinical impressions, these incongruencies can be examined during the post-test session. For example, a test score or an answer to an item may suggest that a patient's thinking pattern is rather bizarre, but nothing that transpired during the initial interview pointed in that direction. The interviewer now has the opportunity to pursue this lead and can question the patient rather probingly about that particular test response. Stories abound in psychiatric clinical circles of instances where test responses provided valuable leads about patients' symptoms or signs that were missed during the initial phases of personality evaluation.

The Termination Interview

Either during the post-test interview in the employment or clinical setting—if no further contacts are indicated—or at the close of treatment with patients, there is customarily a final or termination interview. In the industrial setting such an interview is the occasion to transmit to the candidate information regarding the likelihood of his being hired or promoted.

For the psychiatric patient—either seen on an inpatient or outpatient basis—the final interview serves as a sort of punctuation mark to what may have been a lengthy and intense relationship. If the person was an inpatient and is about to be discharged from the hospital, he must be prepared to make a major transition; a number of problems he may encounter on the "outside" can be anticipated and discussed. This is also a good opportunity for the psychologist to assess the nature and extent of personality change if, indeed, such change has been induced.

The nonhospitalized patient, or outpatient, may profit from a similar interview and must be encouraged to cope singlehandedly with his problems. At the same time that he is being thus encouraged, he must be assured that should he need additional assistance he can still rely on the therapist.

THEORETICAL ORIENTATION OF THE INTERVIEWER

The theoretical orientation of the interviewer cuts across the structured versus unstructured, as well as across the types of interviews conducted, and adds other dimensions to the interview situation that determine the manner and framework within which it will proceed. As noted at the outset of this chapter, the history of the interview as a method for personality assessment is closely tied up with the history of the psychotherapeutic movement, and therefore the contributions to its theory and technique of such reputed psychotherapists as Freud, Adler, Sullivan, and Rogers have been extensive. Depending on whether the interviewer is from the psychoanalytic school of Sigmund Freud, for example, or from the client-centered orientation of Carl Rogers, he will vary in his formulation of objectives, the interpretation of his role, and his notions about interviewer-to-interviewee relationships. These several orientations toward interviewing are briefly sketched here, and the interested reader may consult more basic sources for detailed information about the various personality theories underlying them (Bischof, 1964; Hall and Lindzey, 1957; Munroe, 1955).

The Psychoanalytic Technique of Freud

Freud's interview technique was designed to help the patient explore his unconscious and conscious personality. As a result of the insights that Freud derived from listening to his patients' free associations and dreams, he believed he was gaining glimpses of the formation of personality structure. Freud's major interview objective was to help the patient reconstruct his basic personality, and in the process of attaining this goal, he devised the technique of free association and dream analysis.

Essentially free association is an interview technique in which the respondent is required to say anything and everything that comes to mind, regardless of how trivial, inappropriate, or ludicrous he thinks it may sound. In the course of this, the patient must also report all his dreams and fantasies. This interview technique puts a heavy burden on the patient to produce verbalizations. The interviewer, after initially and briefly instructing the patient what his role is in the interview situation, withdraws from the interaction and plays largely a passive role. Occasionally he prods the patient by asking probing questions.

The duration of these interviews may be from two to five years, and their frequency per week may be as high as four to five times. During this time, Freudian psychoanalysts attempt to learn about the personality of the individual by penetrating into his most inaccessible regions and piecing together in some meaningful way all of the patient's verbalizations. The process of diagnosis and therapy are carried out simultaneously.

Alfred Adler's Directive Technique

As with Freud, Alfred Adler's empirical observations were gleaned from the interview setting. Adler's goals in therapy were different from those of Freud. His interview techniques were more directive than Freud's, and his objectives were to (1) help the patient understand his life style (e.g., gain insight into his characteristic coping patterns) ; (2) encourage the patient to try new ways of solving everyday problems; and (3) help the patient reorient himself toward greater social interest.

In studying the personality structure of the individual, Adler placed prime emphasis on discovering and understanding a person's life story, and the attitudes adopted by that person toward it. Thus, during the interview, the areas that are stressed most heavily are: the nature of his vocation, history of his illnesses, his attitudes and moods, his relations with his family and friends, and his love affairs. Furthermore, art productions, early memories, and dreams all represent important information for the interviewer.

Adlerian interviewers routinely ask the patient to report the "first memory." Presumably the first memory is not fortuitously selected but is revealing of the person's life style. Contrasted to Freud's interview system, Adler interpreted the role of interviewer as a much more active one, and he often put the patient to work on finding the reason for his problems. Typically, as the interviews progress, the patient is required to assume ever increasing responsibility for his actions.

Harry Stack Sullivan

Harry Stack Sullivan's theory about individuals stresses personality as a purely hypothetical entity that can best be observed or studied from interpersonal situations. Accordingly he was interested, during the interview situation, in learning about the sequence of interpersonal situations to which an individual was exposed in passing from infancy to adulthood.

Again, in common with the approaches of Freud and Adler, Sullivan acquired his information on personality structure in the clinical setting. Sullivan's patients, however, were not mainly psychoneurotic, as were those of Freud and Adler; rather, he treated schizophrenics and severe obsessional[4] cases. The interview techniques, as set forth in his books, *The Interpersonal Theory of Psychiatry* (1953) and *The Psychiatric Interview* (1954), were much influenced by these types of patients. Sullivan is the only one among the psychiatrists discussed so far whose books are specifically addressed to an exposition of the interview technique itself.

The psychiatric interview, which may be a one-shot affair, or may extend over a long period of time, was divided by Sullivan into four stages: (1) the formal inception, (2) reconnaissance, (3) detailed inquiry, and (4) the termination (Sullivan, 1954). During the first stage, the interviewer formulates working hypotheses about the other person; during the reconnaissance period, he is expected to define clearly any major problem of the patient. The detailed inquiry is the major portion of the interview, and Sullivan prescribes a list of diagnostic signs and symptoms for which the interviewer should be on the alert. These include apathy, sadness, elation, overdramatic extravagance, tenseness, bizarre thinking, and peculiar mannerisms. Finally, the termination of the interview

---

[4] An obsessional patient has repetitive and unpleasant thoughts occurring to him. It is difficult for him to put these thoughts out of his mind, and often they become occasions for repetitive rituals (compulsions).

consists of a *final statement, prescription of action, final assessment,* and a *formal leave taking.* Again, each of these stages is carefully spelled out.

Of the three interview approaches discussed so far, Sullivan's technique unquestionably lends itself most readily to standardization and subsequent quantification. This is due to his careful specification of stages and procedures, as well as his suggestions for overall interview strategies and his prescription of particular interview tactics to be used for various contingencies.

The Nondirective Techniques of Rogers

Carl Rogers' interview procedures and goals—like those of Freud, Adler, and Sullivan—were formulated in the clinic and are closely related to his theory of personality. His belief in each person's ability to solve his own problems, together with his therapeutic goal of helping an individual toward self-actualization are probably most responsible for the nondirective interview approach that he has chosen.

Much of his interview technique is described in his book, *Counseling and Psychotherapy* (Rogers, 1942) and elaborated in his 1951 book, *Client-Centered Therapy,* as well as in recent publications (Rogers, 1961). In these writings he advises the interviewer to avoid giving advice, to refrain from asking highly specific questions, and to go to great lengths to avoid criticizing the client. Recognition and clarification of feelings, on the other hand, are encouraged, along with nonjudgmental acceptance of the interviewee's statements. In addition to specifying carefully the manner in which interviews are to be conducted, Rogers published extensive verbatim transcripts of interview sessions (see pp. 261–437, Rogers, 1942). According to one psychologist (Matarazzo, 1965), much of the popularity of the nondirective interview is due to these publications.

From the standpoint of standardization of interview procedures, and possible subsequent quantification of interview variables, Rogers' technique seems to lend itself least well for these purposes. Such constructs as *empathy, congruence,* and *positive regard* seem to be elusive and difficult to identify. Certainly many of Sullivan's interview procedures seem more amenable to such analysis. It is therefore surprising to note that the groundwork for much research with interview techniques and for content analysis[5] of counseling interviews was laid by students of Rogers (Covner, 1942; Lipkin, 1948; Porter, 1943; Raimy, 1948; Seeman, 1949; Snyder, 1945).

EVALUATION OF THE INTERVIEW

Reliability

Generally, the nature of the dimensions on which interviewers (and judges listening to tapes of interviews) are expected to agree affects the overall reliability of the interview. For example, a high degree of agreement between interviewers can be achieved when they are required to classify a group of patients into such distinct categories as paranoid schizophrenia, mongoloid, imbecile, or obsessive-compulsive neurotic.[6] However, agreement becomes less accessible when the descriptive classifications sought are more similar. Likewise, if there is disagreement among interviewers about the classification system—and this is rather common in the area of personality measurement—then reliability is affected in a downward direction.

Sources of Error

There are three major sources of error in the interview situation, as shown in Table 6–7, that contribute to its unreliability. These are errors due to the *interview process,* and errors that are *interviewee* and *interviewer* based. Before tracing some of these sources, it might be well to clarify the concept of error in the interview. The reader also is referred to Chapter 2, where the relationships between reliability and error variance are discussed.

In the assessment of personality—as in other assessment

---

[5] Content analysis of interview information consists mainly of formulating a series of categories by means of which the verbalizations of an interviewee can be coded, counted, and classified; and in the use of the interview as a personality assessment tool, it is one method of scoring the assessment outcomes.

[6] It is important to note that percentage of agreement among judges about a category is meaningless without information about the base rate (the rate with which a disease category occurs in the population under study): thus if 95 percent of a group belongs to category X, and the judge has knowledge of that, he will achieve over 90 percent correct classifications by chance, and 95 percent if he guesses all to be in category X (Fiske, 1966).

TABLE 6–7

Sources of Error in the Interview

Error Source	Description	Resolution
Interview process	Error resulting from the complex inter-action of inter-viewer, interviewee, and the setting. Usually this results in random rather than directional error.	Conducting as many interviews as feasible with the same re-spondents.
Interviewee	Fears and anxieties. Role expectations.	Careful structuring of the interview situa-tion and anticipa-tion of expectations.
Interviewer	Idiosyncracies of vari-ous interviewers. Recording errors. Making inferences beyond obtained data. Poor training. Theoretical biases.	Standardization of interviewer strate-gies and intensive training within a uni-form system of inter-viewer data collec-tion.

areas—the goal of using the interview as a method of measurement is to obtain accurate descriptions that reflect the true values of certain symptoms, signs, habits, response tendencies, and attitudes. The true value can be said to represent the parameter or the ideal that we want to estimate. An observed value, which represents the measurement that is actually obtained during the interview, differs from true value to the extent that measurement error is introduced by the interview procedure. Errors of measurement can be random, and vary from one interview to the next, or from one interviewer to another, and cause deviations in fortuitous ways; or errors can be systematic and cause deviations from the true value only in one direction (e.g., high or low; over- or underestimates). The difference between random and nonrandom error should become apparent from our discussion of the various sources of error.

Interview Process Error. The complex nature of the interview situation—with the interaction of its two participants and the effects of the setting itself—can contribute in unknown amounts to the inaccuracy of the interview measurement process. Such errors are random, in the sense that they are chance variations, and do not produce inaccuracies in one particular direction.[7] Thus, an interviewee may happen not to be feeling up to par on a particular day and therefore may present an atypical sample of his behavior. If he had been interviewed a day later—perhaps shortly after receiving some good news—his interview behavior would have been considerably different. In the first instance, the respondent may present an exceedingly depressed picture; in the next, he may be overly elated. The point is that neither behavior is particularly representative of his day-to-day mood level. Likewise, the interviewer may just not be able to achieve a good interview on a particular day. Possibly a little of each of these influences is operating, and this impedes (or facilitates) easy communication between the two participants and contributes further to random errors of measurement.

In principle, if a large number of interviews are conducted with one person, such chance variations should "cancel out." However, this averaging out process is not feasible with the interview, because measures are never obtained under similar circumstances and because the interview situation—which usually is a one-shot affair—makes the collection of many measures highly impractical. Therefore the presence of chance variations must be recognized, and their influence on the dimensions measured must be attenuated.

Interviewee Error. The earlier discussion of the intake interview mentioned that the interviewee's anxieties and misgivings, especially those that are operative during his first contact, exert an influence on his verbalizations. These fears and anxieties affect the character of the interaction and the content of the interview. They may be put to advantage, in that a skillful interviewer can use them to enlist the respondent's cooperation; or if neglected, they may handicap the interview process by being so disruptive that they do not permit the respondent to express himself readily.

Moreover, every interview puts some pressure on a respondent that leads him to wonder about the roles he is expected to fill. Suppose, for example, a person who has read about free association and has heard of the importance of dreams in revealing personality finds himself in a situation where he is expected to produce associa-

---

[7] Many sources of inaccuracy that contribute to errors of measurement, if they can be explicitly identified, thus enabling a guess about the direction of their influence, should not be properly classified as "random errors" (Fiske, 1966).

tions and dreams—or so he thinks. This constitutes pressure, and he will probably *adapt* to this form of interview pressure in a manner characteristic of his behavior in similar situations. He may withdraw, or he may become overtalkative; perhaps he will giggle and relate trivial stories; or he may lose his voice entirely. If he has been interviewed before—especially if he has had many contacts with one particular interviewer—he may have certain expectations that are not met. His *adaptive techniques* in that situation, as Sundberg and Tyler (1962) refer to them, may be to become hostile and defensive. In short, he may perform in any of a number of ways that are not characteristic of his noninterview behavior. His coping tactics—giggling, verbosity, nervousness, or withdrawal—constitute error variance.

In order to understand and perhaps control the effects of the patient's *role expectation* and his concomitant adaptive techniques, the interviewer must at the outset assess the nature of those expectations. Certain generalizations can probably be made with some degree of assurance on the basis of knowing something about the characteristics of the group of which he is a member; but more specific information would be helpful. As a matter of course, the interviewer should actively form hypotheses about the patient's motivations and expectations during the process of "structuring" the interview situation, and the interviewer should then strive to "work through" or reduce the effects of these attitudes. In this regard, one psychologist (Bordin, 1955) identified what he called *interview ambiguity,* and stated that an interviewer who provides few cues for a respondent—that is, one who provides ambiguity—tends to increase the interviewee's level of anxiety, which in turn is a source of error variance that distorts self-reporting.

Interviewer Error. Broadly speaking, there are three possible sources of interviewer error. The first source arises from the particular techniques of interviewing employed by various interviewers. Thus, although interviewers may be highly trained to conduct identical interviews, errors due to their unique techniques or styles of interviewing will nevertheless come about.

Second, errors in data recording serve to affect the reliability of interviews. Such recording errors may be simple notating mistakes or they may be due to the interviewer's expectancies and mental set. As a consequence of the latter sources of error, the interviewer may amplify, minimize, complete, roundout, or omit responses. These recording errors may occur either during the interview or after its completion.

The third source of interviewer error may arise because of his extrapolations or inferences beyond the data he has observed. For example, during the course of an interview, one psychologist may observe a respondent's rapid speech production and label it "anxious" or "nervous" speech. Another interviewer, listening to the identical speech pattern, may label it as "manic" speech. All of these terms—anxious, nervous, and manic—are interpretations and inferences rather than observations.

More specifically, numerous other errors arise that are not easily subsumed under the preceding three categories. Thus untrained and inexperienced interviewers, who have not mastered the techniques of motivating respondents to talk freely about a large number of topics pertinent to the task of personality assessment, are responsible for a variety of errors. One common type of error of this sort comes about when interviewers allow the interview situation to deteriorate to a "palsy-walsy," "hail-fellow" relationship. Such an atmosphere does not encourage the respondent to divulge his most private thoughts, nor to unload his problems. After all, why should he bother his newly found friend with his troubles? In this regard it has been recommended (Sundberg, and Tyler, 1962) that the interviewer maintain an attitude of "deeply interested detachment." Such an attitude, which is free of the interviewer's emotional involvement, allows him to elicit information that covers a wide range of emotion-laden areas. Likewise it serves to standardize the interviewer variable of the interactive process.

Inexperienced and poorly trained interviewers are not the only ones who commit errors. One particular error, called the probing error, is made by some highly experienced interviewers. A comment such as, "Well, I guess we beat that subject to death," can close the door to any further probing in that area. Or conversely, the interviewer may be morbidly interested in particular areas, and thus may probe into them prematurely, relentlessly, and irrelevantly. For example, the interviewer who himself is close to retirement age may, during the course of a mental status interview with an insurance representative, collect information that is relevant mainly to his own interests. Or still worse, an interviewer may probe mercilessly into sensitive areas. Professor Roy Schafer (1954, p. 21), in an excellent chapter on the dynamics of an interpersonal assessment situation, analyzes the "peeping Tom" or voyeuristic aspects of this type of probing error.

Interviewer error can also arise because of the vagueness of the concepts to be questioned, observed, and recorded. This point is well illustrated in the following example (Kahn and Cannell, 1957): Suppose the objective of an interview is to ascertain a respondent's age. There should be little difficulty in determining the true value of this measurement objective. He was born on a certain day in a certain year, and there is only one response that can be correct. Error may, of course, arise due to a respondent's unwillingness to reveal his exact age—and this can be due to any number of factors ranging from vanity to a desire to conceal this information for employment purposes—but in principle at least, it is possible to establish definitively this person's age. But what is the true value of an emotion? Is the interviewee crying because he is happy or sad? Can we trust his report that he feels "down in the dumps"? How does he really feel, and how may this be ascertained? Perhaps the tough and "couldn't care less" attitude of the hardened criminal is just a coverup of other emotions. The level of inference that the interviewer must make when observing such elusive concepts as anxiety and emotion is much higher than that required in questioning about age or education. Besides, the latter are easier to substantiate. Unless interviewers are carefully trained in using and recording agreed-upon terminology, such errors are commonly made.

Thus far, interviewer errors discussed have included only those that are mostly of the random variety, or those in which guesses about directionality can sometimes be made. A number of systematic or nonrandom factors are equally important for their role in affecting the accuracy of this measurement technique. One common source of these errors, aptly called the pathologic bias (Dailey, 1960), characterizes the tendency that some interviewers have to see symptoms and defense mechanisms in everyone. In this regard, one psychologist (Shoben, 1957, p. 183) has said, ". . . there is abundant empirical knowledge concerning the . . . anxious and the neurotic . . . there is little information and even less conceptual clarity about the nature of psychological normality." The pathologic bias, in addition to making it difficult to think accurately about normal people, systematically ascribes an overabundance of symptoms to emotionally ill persons.

The interviewer's theoretical as well as cultural background is the source of many of his attitudes, perceptions, expectations, and motivations. Thus the interviewer's theory of personality may systematically affect the ways he elicits and interprets information. Certain cultural background characteristics, such as education, socioeconomic status, religion, and race, may dictate an interviewer's perceptions and expectations, or they may affect the respondent's interview behavior. Cultural divergencies that exist between interviewer and interviewee also may affect the latter's interview behavior. There is one particularly interesting study (Canady, 1936) in which it was demonstrated that Negroes' attitudes in the interview and psychological test situation are affected by the race of the examiner. Negro and white examiners administered the Stanford-Binet intelligence test to white and Negro children. The average I.Q. of both groups rose by six points when tested by an examiner of their own race. A similar effect was reported in another study (Pasamanick and Knobloch, 1955), in which it was noted that the presence of a white examiner served to inhibit Negro childrens' responses in a test situation. These effects, although not always in the predicted direction, can add systematic error variance to a particular interviewer's perception of either Negroes or whites with regard to his observation of specific personality traits.

Finally, two other sources of interviewer inaccuracy, which may or may not influence his measurements systematically are the loaded question and the anticipatory bias errors. A question may be worded in such a way as to lead the respondent toward an answer. Such loaded questions betray the interviewer's opinion of what constitutes an appropriate answer; and not surprisingly, many respondents are eager to please their inquisitors. Thus when the interviewer asks, "I take it you are eager to accept this job if offered?" he leaves the respondent little room to express his real attitudes and feelings. Related to the loaded question is the anticipatory bias, in which questions are introduced with such phrases as: "I guess a person of your stature would think . . . ," or "A good looking chap like you must have. . . ." Not many persons are likely to contradict an interviewer who entertains such high opinions (or low opinions) of them.

Validity

The aim of every personality assessment interview—regardless of whether it takes place in the clinical-counseling setting or in an employment context—is the measurement of specific traits or dimensions. Information resulting from an interview, then, contains predictors that can be subjected to the same kind of statistical analysis that is used on tests; and, along with other information about a person, it can be weighed for its relative contribution to accuracy of predictions. A reasonable analogy has been drawn (Guion, 1965, p. 396) between the interview and a test battery: the interview can be thought of as a multivariate technique, yielding a number of predictors which, when combined, are like a set of scores on the dimensions under investigation.

In many validity studies with the interview, it is difficult to determine how much predictive value to attribute to the interview alone and how much to other sources of information. Some evidence of the predictive value of the interview in personality assessment comes from incremental validity studies, in which the relative contribution of each bit of information is systematically determined. In one study (Winch and More, 1956), comparisons were made between ratings obtained by judges using only interview information, ratings obtained from judges using only case histories, and ratings secured from judges using only the TAT. These ratings were compared with criterion judgments derived from a panel of five judges using all three kinds of information. The findings suggested that the TAT made no statistically significant contribution beyond that which was provided by the interview and case history data. Similar results were reported by Sines (1959), who found that when the interview comes early in the assessment series it contributes considerably to the prediction of certain personality variables.

Unfortunately, results of the largest bulk of studies conducted on the validity of the interview are not encouraging. In an early study by one psychologist (Sarbin, 1943), in which academic success in college was predicted for 162 freshmen on the basis of tests and interviews, the validity coefficients without the interview information added were .57 for men and .73 for women. With the results of the interview added, they were .56 and .73 respectively. The investigator correctly concluded that the interview added nothing to the information obtained from tests in predicting college achievement.

Interview methods have been used to select successful clinical psychology students. The ratings made from interviews in one of these studies (Kelly and Fiske, 1951) yielded small correlations with criterion measures but not enough to be of practical import; and therefore these authors also were forced to suggest that nothing was gained by conducting the interviews. Similar results were obtained in a study (Holt and Luborsky, 1958) where interview-based ratings were obtained on candidates for psychiatric training. Using supervisors' ratings as criteria of success in the training program, this study obtained validity coefficients that ranged from −.17 to .62, with a median correlation coefficient of .05.

Generally, it is true that the validity of the interview varies considerably with the purposes for which it is used, and with the way the interviewer's information is recorded. The less clear the structure of the interview, the less reliability and validity it is likely to have. When Adorno, Frenkel-Brunswik *et al.* (1950), in their studies on the *Authoritarian Personality,* used the interview as criterion information for high and low scorers on certain personality scales, they recognized the difficulties in evaluating such material. Therefore, they structured carefully, insofar as possible, the general plan for the interview. They standardized the role of the interviewer and developed an extensive set of scoring categories. The list of 62 main categories they developed was accompanied by explanations and definitions. A *Scoring Manual* was provided which could be consulted for scoring directions. With such careful quantification and planning, they were able to zero in on the parts of the interview that were valid predictors of the variables under consideration. Their example may be well worth emulating by investigators concerned with oft-reported low-validity findings.

In spite of the generally discouraging evidence for the reliability and validity of the interview, it will probably continue to be used as a prime personality assessment technique. There is little question that in most situations, such as in the clinic or the counselor's office, it serves purposes other than those of personality evaluation. In the clinic, the interviewer is given firsthand evidence about the appearance, voice, mannerisms, and such other impressions and cues as can be gotten only from an interview contact. Also, the interviewer conveys to the patient the fact that there is interest in him as a human being rather than just another hospital or clinical record. In the employment setting, the interview may also serve a valuable public relations function in that it permits a corporation to introduce its functions and purposes to many persons. Finally, although there is considerable evidence in the psychological literature to suggest that interviews may lower the accuracy of predictions, most clinicians and some amateur practitioners feel confident that they can secure valid information from the interview.

SUMMARY AND CONCLUSIONS

A personality assessment interview is any prolonged contact between two persons in which a face-to-face communication is initiated for the specific purpose of allowing the interviewer to learn about an individual's personality characteristics. Interviews vary from the highly structured to the less structured; and in general, the advantage to be gained as one moves from the less to the more structured interview is in the increasing breadth of topic coverage. Structured interviews have the advantage of providing some semblance of standardized conditions. However, the major disadvantage of structure results from the inquisitorial atmosphere that may be created by a crisp question-answer interview session.

The unstructured interview has the advantage of creating conditions that are conducive to free expression, which permits the interviewer greater latitude in exploring promising leads. Often the theoretical orientation of the interviewer dictates the type of interview he conducts; and depending on, for instance, whether he is oriented to the theory of Freud, Adler, Sullivan, or Rogers, his interview goals and techniques will vary accordingly.

Cutting across the structured versus unstructured dichotomy and across the particular theoretical orientation of the interviewer, there are numerous types of personality assessment interviews: the employment, troubleshooting, poll-type, stress, and medical diagnostic interviews, as well as the following types conducted in psychiatric settings: intake, mental status, case history, pre- and post-test, and the termination interview. Each of these serves a different purpose, and its structure and problems reflect these differences.

Generally, reliability and validity indices are low when the interview is not structured. In most studies of the predictive value of the interview, it is difficult to know how much validity to attribute to the interview alone and how much is due to other sources available to the interviewer. Incremental validity studies—in which increasing amounts of evidence are systematically made available to the interviewer—have tended to show that the interview does not add much to the size of the validity coefficient nor to information obtained by more formal psychometric techniques.

However, in spite of some discouraging reliability and validity evidence, the interview serves a valuable function in the clinical and employment setting. There seem to be more important considerations than just the consistency and accuracy of a procedure, and foremost among these considerations is the fact that the interview imparts qualities of interest and warmth from one human to another.

FOR FURTHER READING

1. BERG, I. A.   The clinical interview and the case record. In BERG, I. A. & PENNINGTON, L. A. (Eds.), *An introduction to clinical psychology*. New York: Ronald Press Co., 1966. Pp. 27–66.

   This 40-page review provides an adequate introduction to the interview and case record as clinical diagnostic and therapeutic tools. For a more detailed review of the research literature on interviewing, the reader is referred to the chapter by Matarazzo (see below).

2. BINGHAM, W. V. D., MOORE, B. V., & GUSTAD, J. W.   *How to interview.* (4th ed.) New York: Harper & Row, 1959.

   Most portions of this book pertain to screening and selection. This has been the interviewer's handbook for more than 30 years.

3. DOHRENWEND, BARBARA SNELL & RICHARDSON, S. A.   Directiveness and non-directiveness in research interviewing: A reformulation of the problem. *Psychological Bulletin*, 1963, 60, 475–485.

   A framework for the design of research interviews is outlined in this review. Three kinds of research interviews are examined by the authors and they call attention to the importance of the interviewer's "prescriptions" (e.g., he prescribes length, topic, and function of interviews).

4. KAHN, R. L. & CANNELL, C. F.   *The dynamics of interviewing.* New York: John Wiley & Sons, Inc., 1957.

   These authors set before themselves the task of describing the dynamics (e.g., the psychological forces at work) of interviewing, and the result is a skillfully written book which interrelates the theory and technique of interviewing.

5. MARSDEN, G.   Content-analysis studies of therapeutic interviews: 1954 to 1964. *Psychological Bulletin,* 1965, 63, 298–321.

Three models of content analysis are presented, and the rationale for two of these are examined. The author calls for a greater coordination of research efforts.

6. MATARAZZO, J. D.   The interview. In WOLMAN, B. B. (Ed.), *Handbook of clinical psychology.* New York: McGraw-Hill Book Co., 1965. Pp. 403–430.

A thorough review of the recent literature on interviewing is presented. Of special interest also are the sections on the reliability of the interview in psychiatric diagnosis and the research on the "anatomy of the interview." The latter section is largely a review of Matarazzo's and his associates' work on content-free speech durations.

7. MEEHL, P. E.   Some ruminations on the validation of clinical procedures. *Canadian Journal of Psychology,* 1959, 13, 102–108.

Unfortunately this article has not had the circulation or visibility it deserves, and consequently has not stirred the psychological community as it should have. In it, Professor Meehl expresses his views on the importance of psychiatric diagnosis, and he raises a number of questions regarding the validation of such diagnosis.

8. RICHARDSON, S. A., DOHRENWEND, BARBARA SNELL, & KLEIN, D.   *Interviewing: Its forms and functions.* New York: Basic Books, Inc., 1965.

In this book, the authors discuss the interview as a research instrument designed for data collection. The techniques of interviewing are described and the research literature reviewed.

9. SCHOFIELD, W., & BALIAN, LUCY.   A comparative study of the personal histories of schizophrenic and nonpsychiatric patients. *Journal of abnormal and social Psychology,* 1959, 59, 216–225.

From a study comparing the life histories of "normals" and psychiatric patients, the authors concluded that there is *no* simple one-to-one relationship between illness and "traumatic" histories.

10. STRUPP, H. H. & WALLACH, M. S.   A further study of psychiatrists' responses in quasi-therapy situations. *Behavioral Science,* 1965, 10, 113–134.

One of many reports that the senior author has written about his experiments in interviewing, this article describes the latest efforts. Mainly, his technique consists of vicarious interviewing by means of films, and he inserts "What would you do?" questions at selected intervals in the film sequence. Numerous interview variables have been investigated in this manner: emotional reaction to patient, training, skill, and level of experience.

11. ULRICH, L., & TRUMBO, D.   The selection interview since 1949. *Psychological Bulletin*, 1965, 63, 100–116.

Unquestionably, this is the most comprehensive review of the uses and research of that special interview technique.

12. ZIGLER, E., & PHILLIPS, L.   Psychiatric diagnosis: a critique. *Journal of abnormal and social Psychology*, 1961, 3, 607–618.

These authors present a critical reappraisal of the value of psychiatric diagnosis and conclude that a taxonomic system may serve a number of psychiatrically significant selection and prediction functions.

PART III

Specially Derived Personality Tests

CHAPTER 7

THE SELF-REPORT INVENTORY

The self-report inventory essentially is a standardized interview composed of items such as these:

—Are your feelings easily hurt?
—Do your interests change quickly?
—Do you tend to get angry with people rather easily?
—I daydream very little.
—I enjoy detective or mystery stories.

Instead of interviewing each person individually, the questions or statements of an inventory are printed in a booklet and administered to a group of subjects simultaneously. For any particular personality questionnaire, the items given each respondent are identical. This equivalence of items for all subjects, and the fact that administration and scoring procedures are uniform and standard, are the distinguishing features of the self-report inventory. These features serve to render the scores obtained by any individual comparable to scores obtained by others, provided, of course, that norms are available.

Because of the nature of mass test administration procedures, subjects' answers on inventories are limited to fixed alternative response categories (e.g., "yes," "no," or "cannot say"). The disadvantage of these limited alternatives is that subjects are severely restricted in the freedom of their responding. The advantages of fixed response categories, however, are that they eliminate judgmental factors in scoring these tests and obviate the necessity of relying on memory to reconstruct a subject's responses.

Just as the type and content of interviews are varied to suit their different purposes, so the item content of self-report inventories is modified to reflect their distinct uses. Therefore, if the purpose served in a particular test situation, let us say, is to assess respondents' attitudes toward authoritarian persons,[1] then an inventory composed of one set of items might be used. If the intent, to take a second instance, of the test is the diagnosis of personality disorders, then an entirely different questionnaire containing altogether different items is more appropriate. In the first instance, items might probe into subjects' feelings about prejudice, minority groups, democracy, and attitudes toward being ruled by others. Items designed for psychiatric diagnosis might concentrate more heavily on respondents' views about themselves, their ability to get on with others, and their attitudes toward their own habits and past experiences.

THE FIRST ADJUSTMENT INVENTORY

Historically, the first self-report inventory was developed during World War I, when the U.S. Army commander in chief, General Pershing, sent the message from France that the "prevalence of mental disorders" suggested that screening methods should be utilized to eliminate unfit draftees.[2] Two psychologists who at the time were researching into the problems of emotional fitness for warfare, Woodworth and Poffenberger, responded with the development of the pioneer Woodworth Personal Data Sheet (Woodworth, 1920).

The Woodworth Personal Data Sheet was designed to identify soldiers emotionally unsuited for combat. Prior to this time, the selection procedure consisted mainly of brief psychiatric interviews. However, since hundreds of thousands of military recruits had to be processed and only limited numbers of skilled interviewers were available for the job, a paper and pencil version of the psychiatric interview was a natural development. In this way, each

---

[1] The authoritarian personality (Adorno *et al.*, 1950) is said to be characterized by highly conventional behavior, cynicism, and prejudice. Accordingly he finds security in a social hierarchy in which every individual knows and keeps his appropriate place.

[2] One psychologist (Hathaway, 1965, p. 457) traces the development of personality inventories to biblical times: "For example, Gideon had collected too large an army . . . the Lord suggested two screening items for Gideon. The first of these items had face validity: Gideon proclaimed that all who were afraid could go home. More than two of every three did so. The second was subtle: those who fought the Midianites were the few who drank from their cupped hands instead of lying down to drink. . . ."

person could be given an interview by asking him such standard questions as: "Do you make friends easily?" "Do you often feel miserable and blue?" and similar other probing items, some of which are presented in Table 7–1.

The personal data sheet was developed by collecting seemingly symptomatic items from the available psychiatric literature. Psychiatric texts were thoroughly scoured by Woodworth for every symptom of psychological disturbance he could find. To this list he added symptoms gleaned from case histories compiled by psychiatrists. The final set of items included most of the common symptoms

TABLE 7–1

Sample Items from the Woodworth Personal Data Sheet

Have you failed to get a square deal in life?
Is your speech free from stutter or stammer?
Does the sight of blood make you sick or dizzy?
Do you sometimes wish that you had never been born?
Are you happy most of the time?
Do you find that people understand and sympathize with you?
Do people find fault with you much?
Do you suffer from headaches or dizziness?

SOURCE: Woodworth, 1920.

associated with mental disorders. They were listed in the data sheet in the form of 116 "yes" or "no" items, and a respondent's score consisted of the number of symptoms, out of a possible 116, that he claimed to have. Recruits who reported many symptoms were detained for further questioning and the personal data sheet, by that criterion, seemed an impressive predictor of maladjustment. This type of inventory came to be considered a time-saving form of group interview in which many individuals respond to personal questions about themselves.

The success of personality testing during World War I encouraged mass development of these tests and the Woodworth Personal Data Sheet is forerunner of some one hundred such personality inventories (Buros, 1965). The self-report tests chosen for discussion in this chapter and the next—obviously only a small proportion of those available—are arranged according to the approach used in developing, formulating, and grouping inventory items, and are intended as illustrations of those approaches. Basically there are four major procedures used to develop personality test items.

These are: (1) content validation, (2) criterion, or empirical keying, (3) factor analysis, and (4) forced choice techniques.

CONTENT VALIDATION

The method of inventory constructing by content validation was borrowed from proficiency and ability testing. When seeking to measure a student's proficiency in a particular subject domain, the test constructor looks for items that adequately sample the relevant domain. The items are selected to be typical of the universe of possible items that represent the subject matter, or the kind of skill, the test is designed to measure. Thus for constructing such tests, Cronbach (1960, p. 364) suggests that the test author define a universe to be measured and then select a representative sample of items from that content universe.[3]

In personality test construction, it is difficult to determine what content domain should be sampled because of the elusive nature of personality dimensions. The content of personality study consists of response tendencies, attitudes, symptoms, coping strategies, and other difficult-to-sample aspects of behavior. But even if it were possible to sample this domain adequately, there is the problem that such sampling would result in the construction of a test that is too obvious and lacks subtlety. Nevertheless, item selection for personality inventories must come from some source and, as in the instance of the personal data sheet, this source sometimes consists of observations of signs and symptoms, or textbook descriptions of a psychiatric population.

The problem of test subtlety—which has received increasing attention in recent years—was of no great concern to the early personality test makers. "If it's going to be a personality test," they reasoned, "then by all means let us have it look like one." The Woodworth Personal Data Sheet was developed by the content sampling method, and with its many items about psychoneurotic, psychosomatic, and psychotic symptoms, it really looked like a personality test (see Table 7–1). Because the items on the data sheet were selected on the basis of judgmental procedures rather

---

[3] It is important to note that although the term "validation" is used to designate this particular technique of item sampling, tests derived by this method nevertheless must be subjected to empirical or construct validation studies.

than on careful statistical sampling techniques, such sampling is sometimes called a priori, or rational item selection—i.e., the item is included in the inventory because it seems on a priori or logical grounds to be a measure of the relevant personality dimension.

The Mooney Problem Checklist

A more recent example of content validation than Woodworth's data sheet is the Mooney Problem Checklist (1950). Its items also

TABLE 7–2

Instructions and Items of the Mooney Problem Checklist

Instructions	Sample Items on the Checklist
"Read the list slowly and as you come to a problem which is troubling you, draw a line under it. For example, if you are often bothered by headaches, you would draw a line under the first item like this: '1. Often have headaches.' "	1. Often have headaches. 2. Often get sick. 3. Too crowded at home. 4. Slow in getting acquainted with people. 5. Too few dates. 6. Unpopular. 7. Too easily discouraged. 8. Drinking. 9. Dislike church service. 10. Family quarrels. 11. Getting low grades. 12. Tests unfair. 13. Need to decide upon a vocation. 14. Want to leave home.

SOURCE: Mooney, 1950.

were selected on an a priori basis and were designed to cover a wide range of problems. The items were gleaned from case records, counseling interviews, and a list of problems specifically elicited through interviews with 4,000 high school students. The Mooney Problem Checklist is available in junior high school, high school, college, and adult forms. The examinee is instructed to check items appropriate to his problems (see Table 7–2). The problem areas include: morals and religion, finances and living conditions, adjustment to school work, and social relations. The checklist is not so much a personality measuring device as it is a preliminary interview designed to direct the professional counselor's attention to several of his client's salient problems. In this sense, it relies almost completely on the examinee's motivation and willingness to cooperate in a forthright manner. No score, in the usual sense of an additive numerical value, is computed.

The Bell Adjustment Inventory

Another example of content validation is illustrated by the Bell Adjustment Inventory (Bell, 1934 to 1963). Bell's strategies of item selection consisted of a three-stage sequence: (1) items are written that in the test constructor's judgment seem appropriate, (2) items are eliminated if they fail to correlate with the scale as a whole, and (3) the surviving scale is validated against external

TABLE 7-3

Items from Bell's Adjustment Inventory (Student Form)

Alternatives	Item
Yes No ?	Do you find it easy to ask others for help?
Yes No ?	Are you frightened by lightning?
Yes No ?	Do you have many colds?
Yes No ?	Are you considerably underweight?
Yes No ?	Do you get upset easily?

SOURCE: Bell, 1934

criteria. The last stage—which is accomplished by correlation studies that use expert ratings and similar adjustment scales as well as life history data as criteria—is a recent innovation and improvement which indicates that Bell no longer relies exclusively on content sampling.

The Bell Adjustment Inventory is still quite popular, although it has been around since about 1934. It consists of questions (see Table 7-3) designed to supply information about a student's adjustment in six areas: home, health, submissiveness, emotionality, hostility, and masculinity. There are two forms of the test: one for high school and college students and another for adults. The Bell Adjustment Inventory was an innovation in that it provided information regarding the specific kind of maladjustment from among five or six areas. Up to the point of its introduction, maladjustment was reported by a single score. Some astonishingly high reliability and validity coefficients have been reported for most of the scales (Vance, 1965).

CRITERION KEYING

In sharp contrast to a priori or rational sampling approaches, criterion keying is a technique which makes few theoretical assumptions about an item included on a personality test. After an item has been selected from a pool of self-descriptive statements, it is retained solely on the basis of observed correlations between it and a number of external criteria. This empirical method of test construction, therefore, may begin by choosing its statements from psychiatric experience and textbooks but will retain items and develop scoring keys only in terms of demonstrated relationships between these items and real-life dimensions.

The Strong Vocational Interest Blank

The Strong Vocational Interest Blank (SVIB) was among the first tests to be developed by means of a criterion keying procedure. Soon after World War I, Edward K. Strong and some other psychologists observed, in their study of various occupational groups, that persons of separate vocations and professions were consistently different in their avocational interests and in what they said they liked and disliked. Some of these differences are readily apparent from casual observations of persons belonging to these groups. Thus it is not surprising to learn that office workers prefer the indoors and that forest rangers like the outdoors; but significant differences were found also in preferences that have no apparent connection with jobs. It turned out, for example, that artists, lawyers, and engineers differed in their answers to items concerning preferred hobbies, books, amusements, and many other aspects of leisure living. Such findings suggested that professional interests may represent a way of life as well as a way of earning a living.

E. K. Strong recognized the implications that such differences between, and similarities within, occupational groups held for the prediction of professional careers. In an extended program of research, he worked with persons from one occupation after another, comparing the responses they gave to test items with the responses given by persons in general (Strong, 1943, 1951, 1955, 1963).

In constructing a scoring key for the engineering scale, for example, he instructed several thousand practicing engineers to take the test. Item by item, he tabulated their answers to find out which ones they answered "like" (L), which "indifferent" (I), and which "dislike" (D). Any item for which the difference in answers between engineers and men in general was overwhelmingly large[4] was retained for the engineer scoring key. Overall, a high score on the engineer scale permits the prediction, "This person is more likely to be successful in engineering than persons with lower scores."

In a sense, this empirical approach to testing is "actuarial" (Cronbach, 1960), because in the interpretation of test scores it asserts, as would an insurance actuary, that "persons who share this combination of test responses with one another are likely to be members of the same group." The insurance actuary might say, "Individuals with this history and combination of signs and symptoms probably do not live much beyond the age of 75."

Responses to SVIB items (see Table 7–4) are scored in terms of their relevance to responses made by successful persons in each of several occupational groups. The scoring key is devised in such a way as to differentiate the people in a particular profession from people in general. Accordingly, each key consists of a set of weights that range from +4 to −4. A positive weight means that people in a particular profession mark a certain set of items "L" more frequently than people in general. The greater the difference between the profession and people in general, the larger is the weight.

Several years after the construction of the basic set of scales, Strong devised a special form of the test for women, and developed scales along similar lines. Normative data were provided for all the occupational groups included on the SVIB; and the author and his associates have, over the years, been active in research designed to explore the relationship of test scores to other personality factors, special abilities, and many other human characteristics.

The SVIB for men consists of 400 items; the blank for women contains some of the same items, along with others that are more typical of women's avocational and recreational activities. In all, the tests for men and women consist of 45 and 26 occupational keys

---

[4] These answers were tested for *statistical significance*. Two measures are significantly different, from a statistical standpoint, if it is unlikely (improbable) that the difference in question would occur by chance factors alone.

TABLE 7–4

Items from the Strong Vocational Interest Blank (for Men)

Alternatives	Area	Item
L I D L I D L I D	Occupations	Auto salesman Editor Computer operator
L I D L I D L I D	School subjects	Algebra Botany Dramatics
L I D L I D L I D	Amusements	Golf Chess Poker
L I D L I D L I D	Types of people	Beachcombers Optimists Emotional people
Mark *three* you would like most; also the *three* you would like least. Mark the remaining *four* occupations in the *middle* row.	Occupations	Plant scientist Opera singer Inventor Manufacturer Nationally known artist General of the Army Member of the Supreme Court Author of best seller Manager of large department store

Source: Form 399TM, Testscor, Minneapolis, Minn.

respectively. Along with the test profile, which depicts the respondent's scores on all scales and allows him to compare his relative standing on all scales, the person who takes one of these tests receives interpretive information. A portion of such a profile, and the accompanying interpretations are presented in Figure 7–1.

The Humm-Wadsworth Temperament Scale

In personality inventory construction, the Humm-Wadsworth scale (1935) was the first to use empirical methods of scale derivation (Hathaway, 1965). Humm and Wadsworth set out to develop a test which consisted of items which discriminate between members of one or more pathological groups from a nonpathological population. For all six categories of pathology (schizoid-autistic, schizoid paranoic, schizoid mania, schizoid depressed, hysteroid, and epilep-

PROFILE – STRONG VOCATIONAL INTEREST BLANK FOR MEN

Here is an example of some profile scores; an explanation is given below.

Group	Scale	Plus Score	Minus Score	Raw Score	Std. Score	C	C+	B–	B	B+	A
								LETTER RATINGS AND STANDARD SCORES			
I	DENTIST	45	14	31	55						
	OSTEOPATH	29	28	1	35						
	VETERINARIAN	33	61	-28	10						

A Guide to Understanding Your Scores

On the other side of this sheet are your scores. The columns headed "Plus Score," "Minus Score," and "Raw Score" are used by the test scorer to determine your standard score; you should be concerned only with your standard scores, the ones marked somewhere along the 0-to-65 range at the right. For each occupation, your standard score shows how your likes and dislikes compare with the characteristic likes and dislikes of men in that occupation. More than two-thirds of the men successfully engaged in any of these occupations score in the A range on their own scale; less than 2 per cent of them score in the C range on their own scale.

The profile also permits you to compare your scores with men-in-general. The shaded area for each occupational scale shows the average range of scores made on that scale by a group of men-in-general—a large number of men drawn from a variety of occupations. As the profile shows, the men-in-general score in the C's or low B's on all the scales.

These results will not tell you anything about your abilities, nor about how hard you are willing to work, nor about how successful you might be. They simply give you some idea of how your interests compare with men successfully engaged in these occupations. With this information it is possible to predict, with a fair degree of accuracy, what types of work you will find interesting.

The example above shows a high score (or A rating) on the DENTIST scale, a medium score (B rating) on the OSTEOPATH scale, and a low score (C rating) on the VETERINARIAN scale. The higher the score, the more certain we can be that the person has interests in common with men in that occupation. These scores indicate that this person:

1. Has many interests similar to those of dentists and would probably enjoy that type of work.

2. Has some interests like those of osteopaths but we cannot tell whether or not he would enjoy that occupation.

3. Dislikes many things that veterinarians enjoy, likes many things that they dislike, and probably would not be satisfied as a veterinarian.

Many years of research with this inventory have established the following conclusion, "A person should consider seriously those occupations in which he receives high scores (A ratings) before entering some unrelated occupation. On the other hand, he should study very critically any occupation in which he receives a low score (C rating) before accepting it as a final career choice."

Occupational Groups. The occupations are arranged in groups along the left side of the sheet. The occupations in each group have roughly similar interests. For example, the first group contains occupations from the biological sciences, and the second group is composed of occupations mainly from the physical sciences. It is often more helpful to look at the overall level of the scores in each group than to look at each score separately.

If you have high scores for most of the occupational scales in one group, you should definitely consider the occupations in that group. Of course there are many occupations related to each group that are not listed here, and you should explore those also.

Supplementary Scales. These scales, listed near the bottom of the profile, are recently developed ones that have not yet been combined with the scale groupings of the profile.

Nonoccupational Scales. These are the four scales listed across the bottom of the profile. They have to do with the overall pattern of your scores, and are sometimes useful to counselors in interpreting unusual profiles.

Will your interests change? After about 25, most men's interests remain stable over long periods of time, as long as thirty years. There is generally not much change between the ages of 20 and 25, either, though a few people show some shifts during these years. But between the ages of 15 and 20, many people do show changes in interests; for the young man in this age range, the scores can be a great help in planning the general direction of his career, but no specific decisions should be made until he has had more experience. It is not unusual, with young men and women, to find profiles with no high scores at all, simply because their occupational likes and dislikes have not yet become well established.

Your ratings on this inventory must be used with caution. Many other factors should be considered in planning your career, especially your abilities and past experiences. It is very helpful to discuss these points with a skilled counselor; he is especially trained to help you make careful use of this information about yourself.

David P. Campbell, Ph.D., Director
Center for Interest Measurement Research
University of Minnesota

FIGURE 7–1.   Sample of Strong Vocational Interest Blank profile. For each occupation, the standard score shows how the respondent's likes and dislikes compare with the likes and dislikes of men in that occupation. The shaded area allows comparison of scores between the respondent and men in general. Some typical score interpretations are also illustrated. (Reproduced by permission of the copyright holders and the publishers, Stanford University Press.)

toid), each item response was weighted according to its discriminatory power.

The Humm-Wadsworth Temperament Scale (1934 to 1960) also represents one of the first attempts to cope with the problem of test-taking attitudes. Most personality inventories up to that time assumed that respondents are cooperative and forthright. Humm and Wadsworth proposed a check on that assumption by the introduction of their "no-count" score. Since the response "yes" for most of the items on the Humm-Wadsworth scale is a pathological one, a respondent who piles up an unusually large number of "no" responses is suspected of trying to fake the test in a normal direction. An un-

TABLE 7–5

Items from the Humm-Wadsworth Temperament Scale

Alternatives		Item
Yes	No	Are you a good mixer?
Yes	No	Have people ever stolen your good ideas?
Yes	No	Are you easily embarrassed?
Yes	No	Do heights make you nervous?
Yes	No	Do you dislike to concern yourself with details?

SOURCE: Humm and Wadsworth, 1934

usually low "no-count" score would also be suspect because a person who is trying to fake pathology would tend to respond "yes" more often than is statistically expected.

Unfortunately, for many years the use of the Humm-Wadsworth Temperament Scale was restricted to persons who were specially trained in D. G. Humms' method, and therefore very little research information about the test has been reported in the literature. The research that has been conducted with the Humm-Wadsworth is not encouraging in terms of the test's promise as a personality assessment device (Ruch, 1965).

Minnesota Multiphasic Personality Inventory (MMPI)

In sharp contrast to the Humm-Wadsworth Temperament Scale, at least in terms of the amount of research it has stimulated since its publication, is Hathaway and McKinley's (1942) Minnesota Multiphasic Personality Inventory (MMPI). The MMPI was developed along the same lines as the Humm-Wadsworth and is another example of a test constructed by criterion keying of its items. Its appearance at an opportune time, during wartime and postwar expansion of clinical psychology, and its authors' exceptionally thorough research, are responsible for the fact that the MMPI has been studied more extensively and more adequately than any other personality test. Because of its popularity, importance, and extensive research literature, a large portion of the next chapter is set aside for its detailed discussion. Only a brief description of the test is given here.

Discouragement with the a priori or "rational" approach to test construction led Hathaway and McKinley to the development of the MMPI. The earlier tests, with the exception of Strong's interest inventory and the Humm-Wadsworth, consisted mostly of items scored according to some test author's theory about personality structure. This rational approach assumed that test respondents were giving honest self-reports. In contrast, the MMPI was developed empirically (v. rationally) by selecting items which differentiated statistically between normal and abnormal groups, and it made no assumptions about honest self-reporting. Professor Paul E. Meehl (1945, p. 9), one of the earliest contributors to the construction of this inventory, clarified the rationale of self-reporting when he stated that the MMPI scales consider a "response to a test item . . . as an intrinsically interesting segment of verbal behavior . . . which may be of more value than any knowledge of the 'factual' material about which the item superficially purports to inquire. Thus if a hypochondriac says that he has 'many headaches' the fact of interest is that he *says* this."

The MMPI consists of 550 affirmative statements (e.g., "everything tastes the same"), printed on separate cards and sorted into three categories: "true," "false," or "cannot say." A group form of the inventory was prepared later, and in this version 566 statements (550 separate items with 16 items repeated) are printed in a test booklet and the responses are recorded by the subject on an answer sheet. The statements cover a wide range of personal topics, including general health, religious attitude, gastrointestinal complaints, family and marital attitudes, mood, delusions, hallucinations, phobias, masculinity-feminity, and social interest (see Chapter 8).

FACTOR ANALYTIC APPROACHES

Factor analysis is a method used by psychologists to simplify large arrays of variables. The simplification is achieved by correlating each variable with every other variable under consideration.[5] From an inspection of the resulting correlation matrix, certain clusters among the variables may suggest an underlying factor common to all of them. If many test items have been administered to several hundred persons, for example, the first step is to compute the correlations of each response with every other; and the next step is to inspect the matrix of these correlations. Thus, if the responses to items, let us say, about defensiveness, suspicion, guardedness, and distrust have high correlations with each other and low correlations with other item responses, an inference is tentatively made that a paranoid[6] factor is present.

In practice, the data matrices are too large to permit judgmental inferences. Therefore, the more precise statistical technique of factor analysis has been developed to locate factors. The statistical technique begins with a table of correlations such as described above and ends with a factor matrix. This matrix is a simplified and much reduced version of the intercorrelations and is arrived at by computing geometric distances along reference axes. It is at this step in the procedure that some of the mathematical rigor gives way to judgmental processes, because there is no general agreement among psychologists where reference axes should be placed with respect to the points that represent the variables in question. Inferences are also required when the factor matrix is inspected and the process of trait naming is underway.

The personality test constructor who develops his inventory by the method of factor analysis does not begin with preconceptions about the particular traits he wants to measure. He usually starts with a large pool of items selected with a minimum of theoretical justification, and then intercorrelates the responses to these items

---

[5] The details of this mathematical method are beyond the scope of this book, and the reader is referred to more basic sources such as the texts by Cronbach (1960), Fruchter (1954), and Helmstadter (1964), and to descriptions of the uses of this technique by Schutz (1958) and Vernon (1950).

[6] A paranoid personality is characterized by distrust and suspicion of others. Often persons so described manifest delusions (false but persistent beliefs) that others are trying to harm them.

until all possible pairs of items have been treated. The resulting correlation coefficients are then factor analyzed to determine which items cluster together sufficiently closely to constitute a factor. An examination of the apparent characteristics that seem to be involved in the structure of these item clusters determines the name that is to be assigned to that cluster of items. He then attaches a label to these items. The latter constitute a scale for the evaluation of that personality trait.

J. P. Guilford, R. B. Cattell, and H. J. Eysenck are the leading proponents of personality inventory construction by the method of factor analysis. As should be apparent from the discussion which follows, each of these psychologists differs somewhat in his inventory construction procedures. It is important to bear in mind throughout this discussion that the grouping of items according to factor analytic procedures does not ensure the validity of an inventory so devised. Separate demonstrations of validity for various uses of these tests are always necessary. Such validity evidence can consist of correlations with real-life criteria (e.g., empirical validity) or, as in the case of factorial validity (which is considered by some a form of construct validity), the test scores can be correlated and factored with other test and nontest data to define more completely the traits it measures.

Guilford–Zimmerman Temperament Survey

Guilford and his associates developed tests along factorial lines. They computed the intercorrelations among individual items from many existing personality inventories; and as a result of these computations they emerged with three inventories of their own. By combining the highly correlated factors from these inventories, Guilford and his associates constructed the new and now popular Guilford-Zimmerman Temperament Survey (1949, 1956). The GZTS, as it is called, was designed to cover in a single test 10 of the 13 traits that were represented in the three original inventories.

The test consists of 300 items, with 30 items to represent each of the 10 traits. Each item is expressed in the form of an affirmative statement which the respondent is invited to mark "yes" or "no" (e.g., "You can think of a good excuse when you need one"). Guilford designed his inventory statements in an affirmative mode because he believed that the first person pronoun and the question form invite the examinee's resistance. He states that "on a priori grounds it would seem that the succession of statements of the form I—becomes a series of confessions" (Guilford and Zimmerman, 1949, p. 4).

Three scoring keys are available, which were designed to be indices of respondents' tendencies to distort their responses on the GZTS (Jacobs and Schlaff, 1955); but further research to substantiate their value is urgently needed. The three scores are intended to detect gross falsification in the "good" direction (intentional test faking), subtle falsification in the "good" direction (unconscious faking), and carelessness or deviancy of subjects who respond in a random or erratic manner by giving an unusually large number of infrequent responses.

The GZTS is composed of the following 10 scales. Clinical interpretations of each of these and a number of representative items found in the GZTS *Manual* (1949 to 1955), are also presented here:

G–General Activity: Some of the adjectives associated with high scores on this scale are strong drive, energy, and activity. A very high G score may indicate overactivity. A very low G score may indicate the presence of some physical cause for inactivity. (Sample item scored +: You are the kind of person who is "on the go" all of the time.)

R–Restraint: High scores may indicate serious-mindedness, persistence, and self-control. Low scores on this scale tend to suggest that the respondent is a happy-go-lucky, carefree, and impulsive person. (Item, +: You sometimes find yourself "crossing bridges before you come to them.")

A–Ascendence: Some of the traits associated with high scores on this scale are self-defensiveness, persuasiveness, and conspicuousness. Low scores connote their opposites. (Item, +: You can think of a good excuse when you need one.)

S–Sociability: The high and low scores represent the contrast between persons who are at ease with others, have many friends, like social activities, seek the limelight, and those who are withdrawn, refrain from conversation, and avoid the limelight. (Item, −: Shyness keeps you from being as popular as you should be.)

E–Emotional Stability: High scores on this scale tend to indicate evenness of mood, optimism, and composure; low scores suggest frustration of moods, dreaminess, gloominess, and excitability. (Item, +: You seldom give your past mistakes a "second thought.")

O–Objectivity: Presumably, a very high score on this scale may mean extreme unsensitivity, versus the hypersensitivity of the low scores. (Item, +: You nearly always receive all the credit that is coming to you for things you do.)

F–Friendliness: Descriptions associated with high versus low scores respectively are dislike of hostile action versus belligerence, acceptance of domination versus resistance to domination, and respect for other versus contempt for others. (Item, —: You would like to tell certain people a thing or two.)

T–Thoughtfulness: Reflective, meditative, observant of self and others, characterize persons with elevated thoughtfulness scale scores; their polarities describe the low scorers. (Item, +: You are frequently lost in thought.)

P–Personal Relations: High scores mean tolerance and understanding of other people; low scores suggest fault-finding and hypercriticalness. Guilford refers to this scale as the one which consistently correlated highest with all criteria involving human relations. (Item, +: Nearly all people try to do the right thing when given a chance.)

M–Masculinity: High scores indicate interest in masculine activities, resistance to fear, and inhibition of emotional expression. An extremely elevated score suggests that the person is somewhat unsympathetic and calloused. (Item, +: You can look at snakes without shuddering.)

Reliability estimates of the scales, as determined by the split-half method, range from .75 to .87. These reliabilities are about as high as can be reasonably expected for temperament scales. Evidence of validity was obtained from correlations computed between ratings by psychologists of workers' attributes and scores of traits *G, A, S,* and *P.* These coefficients approach adequacy and fall within the range .30 to .50. There is some information on the predictive validity of scales *R, T,* and *F.* Coefficients of .42, .34, and .25 were reported when these scales were correlated with college grade-point averages (Goedinghaus, 1954).

Generally, the GZTS has been found most valid and useful with normal people (versus psychiatric patients) in industry and schools (Jackson, 1961; Khan, 1962; Watley and Martin, 1962). Distinct patterns of scores have been found that characterize male and female librarians (Bryan, 1952), nurses in training (Beaver, 1955), engineers (Kirkpatrick, 1956), and teachers (Leeds, 1956). Evidence for its usefulness in clinical installations is nonexistent, possibly because clinicians working in these settings have not availed themselves of its potentialities. It is interesting to note, in this regard, that in a survey of tests used in hospitals, mental hygiene clinics, state institutions, and counseling centers (Sundberg, 1961), none of the Guilford temperament inventories are included in the list of 62 tests used by 10 percent or more of the sample agencies (Dreger, 1966). It seems curious indeed that a test that has had much success in a large variety of settings should not be popular among psychologists in clinical and counseling centers.

Sixteen Personality Factor Questionnaire

R. B. Cattell, who has also used the factor analytic approach to personality test development, utilized an approach somewhat different from that of Guilford in that he assembled personality trait names rather than inventory items. Cattell's source of trait names was a dictionary of some 18,000 adjectives describing personality characteristics (Allport and Odbert, 1936). He supplemented these trait names with terms he found in psychiatric and psychological texts. By a process of editing and combining synonyms, this extensive list was reduced to 171 traits. For each of these traits he obtained ratings on 100 subjects of both sexes, all of whom were rated by a person of close acquaintance. Then these ratings were correlated, and all traits that correlated over .45 with each other were combined to form, at first 67, and then through further combination, 35 clusters; and a factor analysis reduced the number of traits to 12.

On the basis of these factorial results, Cattell (1949 to 1963) prepared the Sixteen Personality Questionnaire (16PF), which includes the original 12 traits and 4 factors identified in subsequent factorial analyses of questionnaires. What this test purports to measure may be judged from the list of traits presented in Table 7–6.

The 16PF Questionnaire consists of equivalent Forms A and B, each with 187 items (10 to 13 items for each factor), and is intended for use with adults. It is an easily administered test, and most subjects find its items interesting. Although the development of the 16PF reflects a high order of technical skill, and the test has had substantial acceptance and considerable impact on self-report personality measurement, it has been strongly criticized for a number of its flaws.

In two separate critiques of Cattell's work, one psychologist (Becker, 1960, 1961; see also Cattell's reply, 1961) raises doubts concerning the value of the data used in the construction of the 16PF test, and questions the independence of the 16 factor scales from one another (Becker, 1961). Along similar lines, the test may be criticized for some of its low split-half reliabilities (co-

TABLE 7-6

Descriptions of Traits Measured by the Sixteen Personality Factor Questionnaire

Factor	Description
A	*Reserved*, detached, critical, cool, versus *Outgoing*, warmhearted, easy-going, participating.
B	*Less intelligent*, concrete-thinking, versus *More intelligent*, abstract-thinking, bright.
C	*Affected by feelings*, emotionally less stable, easily upset, versus *Emotionally stable*, faces reality, calm, mature.
E	*Humble*, mild, accommodating, conforming, versus *Assertive*, independent, aggressive, stubborn.
F	*Sober*, prudent, serious, taciturn, versus *Happy-go-lucky*, impulsively lively, gay, enthusiastic.
G	*Expedient*, evades rules, feels few obligations, versus *Conscientious*, persevering, staid, rule-bound.
H	*Shy*, restrained, diffident, timid, versus *Venturesome*, socially-bold, uninhibited, spontaneous.
I	*Tough-Minded*, self-reliant, realistic, no-nonsense, versus *Tender-Minded*, dependent, overprotected, sensitive.
L	*Trusting*, adaptable, free of jealousy, easy to get on with, versus *Suspicious*, self-opinionated, hard to fool.
M	*Practical*, careful, conventional, proper, versus *Imaginative*, wrapped up in inner urgencies, careless of practical matters, bohemian.
N	*Forthright*, natural, artless, sentimental, versus *Shrewd*, calculating, worldly, penetrating.
O	*Placid*, self-assured, confident, serene, versus *Apprehensive*, worrying, depressive, troubled.
Q_1	*Conservative*, respecting established ideas, versus *Experimenting*, critical, liberal, analytical, free thinking.
Q_2	*Group-Dependent*, a "joiner," and sound follower, versus *Self-Sufficient*, prefers own decisions, resourceful.
Q_3	*Undisciplined Self-Conflict*, careless of protocol, versus *Controlled*, socially precise, following self-image.
Q_4	*Relaxed*, tranquil, torpid, unfrustrated, versus *Tense*, frustrated, driven, overwrought.

SOURCE: Cattell and Eber, 1962.

efficients of .54 to .93), which make it unsatisfactory for individual use; and for the lack of evidence presented for its retest and equivalent forms reliabilities. The validity data provided for use of the test suggests ways in which the test may be useful in industry, college, or the clinic, but offers incomplete statistical data on how well the 16PF scores actually predict the behavior the test is intended to measure.

Not many tests, however, have escaped similar criticism at one time or another. Generally speaking, the consensus among test reviewers (Adcock, 1959; Lorr, 1965) seems to be that the 16PF shares certain shortcomings with other nonfactored devices but that it has potential for practical application and is worthy of serious further attention and research. Considering the skill and almost boundless energy of R. B. Cattell and his associates at the laboratories of the Institute for Personality and Ability Testing (IPAT), such research will certainly be forthcoming in the near future.

Maudsley Personality Inventory (MPI)

Out of many years of intensive research on the quantitative and experimental analysis of personality, Eysenck (1959a) identified two independent factors—neuroticism and extroversion-introversion—which he claims represent most of the variance of personality measurement. Eysenck developed the Maudsley Personality Inventory (1959 to 1962) to measure neuroticism (N) and extroversion (E). The first of these factors refers to general emotional instability, emotional overactiveness, and the predisposition to neurotic breakdown under stress. Extroversion, as the name connotes, refers to uninhibited, outgoing, and sociable characteristics. Sample items used to measure these factors are presented in Table 7–7.

The MPI and its American version, the Eysenck Personality Inventory (EPI, 1963), consist of 48 items, of which 24 are keyed to each of its two factors. The test is easily administered, is short (requires about 10 to 15 minutes to complete), and the items are written at levels appropriate for adolescents and adults. Normative data on comparison groups are adequate, and reliability reports (split-half: .75 to .90; test-retest: .70 to .90) are about as promising as could be expected of a personality test.

Validity data collected over the years—and still being collected by the Maudsley group—are mostly of the construct validity type.

The N and E dimensions have shown significant and replicable correlations with perceptual motor learning and other experimentally manipulated variables. The MPI is solidly anchored in a measurement theory of personality and is sensitive to the experimental findings of that theory. The test is continually undergoing modification as a consequence of the laboratory findings of Eysenck and his followers.

TABLE 7-7

Items Similar to Those Appearing on the Maudsley
Personality Inventory

Alternatives		Item
Yes	No	Do you have dizzy turns?
Yes	No	Do you find it difficult to get into conversation with strangers?
Yes	No	Are your feelings easily hurt?
Yes	No	Are you rather shy?
Yes	No	Have you sometimes walked in your sleep?
Yes	No	Do you often feel disgruntled?
Yes	No	Do you suffer from sleeplessness?
Yes	No	Are you troubled by aches and pains?
Yes	No	Do you lack self-confidence?
Yes	No	Are you touchy on various subjects?

SOURCE: Maudsley Medical Questionnaire (Eysenck, 1952).

The MPI's paucity of items is its weakest characteristic. Forty-eight items, no matter how carefully chosen, and regardless of factorial purity, hardly could be considered an adequate sampling of such a complex construct as personality. The test's current lack of popularity, however, has been attributed to the fact that clinicians generally need more detailed information about persons than is provided by the respondent's scores on just two broad dimensions of personality. Furthermore, N and E do not correspond to the presently used diagnostic nomenclature, and this may also help to account for the test's not winning currency among most practitioners (Jensen, 1965).

FORCED CHOICE KEYING

An entirely different approach to personality test construction is the method of forced choice keying. This method had its origins in the observation that answers to personality inventories such as the MMPI reflect the tendency of persons to present themselves in a favorable light. On an item (e.g., "Do you tend to get angry with people rather easily?") where only one response is socially desirable, persons tend to select that response rather than answer the question truthfully in terms of the content of the item. Professor Allen L. Edwards (1957) has called this tendency the *social desirability* variable and, using subjects' answers to the MMPI as data, demonstrated the distorting influences of this variable on the accuracy of personality test scores. By counting the number of agreements with answers that the majority of a general population give, Edwards constructed a 39-item social desirability scale (SD). He found substantial correlations between SD and many MMPI scales which reflect respondents' tendencies to conform to social expectations. For example, correlations were found of +.61 between SD and a status scale (Gough, 1948), +.52 with a responsibility scale (Gough *et al.*, 1952), and a correlation of −.90 between SD and a social introversion scale (Drake, 1946). This tendency to answer items in a socially acceptable direction—sometimes also called the "facade" effect (Cronbach, 1960)—is a feature that Edwards attempted to correct in his Personal Preference Schedule, by forcing choices between items rated equal in social desirability.

Edwards Personal Preference Schedule (EPPS)

In the Edwards Personal Preference Schedule (1953 to 1959), items are paired on the basis of their similar social desirability scale values. The EPPS consists of 210 pairs of items, in which the item response choices are equally attractive and similarly socially acceptable to the examinee. Starting with items whose content seemed to reflect 15 of the personality *needs* postulated by Henry A. Murray (1938) in *Explorations in Personality* (e.g., needs for achievement, affiliation, order), Edwards built his test by representing each need by nine items. The items for each need were paired with items from the other needs that had similar average social desirability ratings. Each pair of needs is compared twice in this way, and this results in 210 pairs of items. Some of these item pairs are presented in Table 7–8.

Three kinds of scores are provided by the EPPS: scores for each need (the number of times the need was endorsed as being more descriptive than the other needs) ; a consistency score (agreement in responses on 15 pairs of items that are identical) ; and a profile stability score (the correlation between the score profiles for the two halves of the inventory).

As is apparent from the names of the traits or needs measured by the EPPS (e.g., achievement, deference, order, autonomy, dominance, aggression), this test is not intended for use in psychiatric settings, as is the MMPI, but rather is designed for use in counseling with normal persons and for research in personality theory.

TABLE 7-8

Items from the Edwards Personal Preference Schedule

Alternatives	Items
A B	A: I like to tell amusing stories and jokes at parties. B: I would like to write a great novel or play.
A B	A: I like to say what I think about things. B: I like to forgive my friends who may sometimes hurt me.
A B	A: I like to go out with attractive persons of the opposite sex. B: I like to make as many friends as I can.

SOURCE: Edwards, 1959a.

Accordingly, its normative data are based on college men ($N = 749$) and college women ($N = 760$). Additional norms are provided for a general adult sample of nearly 10,000 men and women.

The retest reliabilities of the 15 scales are moderate (.74 to .88), and split-half coefficients of .60 to .87 are reported. No evidence for the validity of the EPPS was presented in the test manual (Edwards, 1959a), and although the test has stimulated vigorous research since its inception, critics (Bordin, 1959; Radcliffe, 1965; Stricker, 1965) are essentially in agreement that Edwards and his test publisher have been negligent in collating this information, and seem to have been unresponsive to much of the criticism made of their test. In its present form, although the EPPS urgently needs further work, it nevertheless holds promise for use among nonpsychiatric groups.

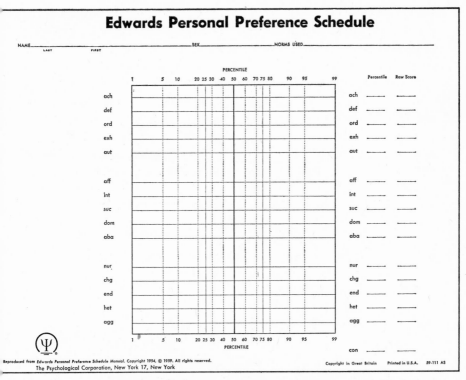

FIGURE 7–2. Sample profile sheet of the Edwards Personal Preference Schedule. (Reproduced by permission. Copyright 1954, 1959, The Psychological Corporation, New York, N.Y. All rights reserved.)

SELF-RATING TECHNIQUES

In addition to personality inventories, other methods are available for the study of self-perception. Like personality inventories, these methods depend on statements that persons endorse as applicable to themselves; but there the similarity ends. Each of these techniques, three of which are discussed here (Q-sort, Semantic Differential and the *Rep* Test), confronts the subject with tasks considerably different from those required in self-report inventories.

Q-Sort

In Chapter 5, the Q-sort was briefly described as an illustration of a rating scale procedure. The Q-sort is also valuable as an instrument for self-rating. In the use of the technique to collect data about self-perceptions, the respondent is given a set of cards on which are printed statements or adjectives which he is instructed to sort into piles ranging from, let us say, "most characteristic" to "least characteristic" of himself. The number of categories or piles varies from one study to another in accordance with the number of Q-cards.

Carl Rogers and his associates (1954) have adopted the Q-sort as the *sine qua non* for research on the effectiveness of psychotherapy. These researchers assert that unfavorable self-evaluations of persons who come for counseling are reflected in a discrepancy between their actual and their ideal personalities. In order to test this proposition, and further, so that they may validate the notion that clients benefit from their psychotherapeutic contact, the Rogerians instruct clients to perform a "self-sort" and an "ideal-sort" prior to therapy. After the completion of treatment, the client again is asked to perform the two Q-sorts. Statements typically used for this purpose are similar to those of self-report inventories.

A successful therapy case, in Q-sort terms, would be one in which there is a greater confluence after therapy than before, in the way the client sees himself and the way he would like to be. That is to say, Rogers' theory predicts that there is less discrepancy between self- and ideal-sorts after therapy than there was before treatment began. Further, as a check on the persistence of the benefits derived from psychotherapy, the client is followed up within six months to one year after the termination of treatment.

As a self-rating technique, the Q-sort has been subjected to some of the same criticism as other personality inventories. Several authors (Edwards and Horst, 1953; Edwards, 1957) indicate that interpretation of subjects' Q-sort responses require the same corrections for the influence of the social desirability response tendency as do answers to inventory items. In this regard, Edwards (1957) cites as evidence a study (Kogan *et al.*, 1957) in which Q-sort statements, presumably related to 25 personality variables, correlated +.89 with the social desirability dimension. As a result of such findings, which indicate that social desirability rather than personality is being rated, Edwards suggested that the Q-sort include only those statements that have comparable or equivalent social desirability scale values.

The criticism most often leveled against the Q-sort is that the ratings are *ipsative* (Cattell, 1944). This means that each person's scores are distributed around his own average, and therefore the analysis of his scores or ratings is meaningful only when interpreted in terms of his own performance on previous Q-sorts. Ratings of the more usual type give trait positions for individuals that are *normative*—that is, trait positions that are distributed about the general population average for each trait. In normative measurement, which is the type used in most psychological tests, scores are interpreted in terms of the performance of other individuals on the same trait or in the same situation.

A consequence of using ipsative ratings is that the averages of

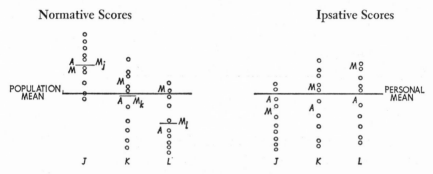

FIGURE 7–3.   Hypothetical distribution of the Kuder Preference Record (Vocational) of three individuals, J, K, and L, as they would be obtained in ipsative form at the right and their corresponding normative scores at the left. Mechanical and Artistic scores are indicated by M and A. The normative means for the three persons are indicated by M_j, M_k, and M_l, respectively. Adapted by permission Guilford, 1959.

scores among persons tend to be about the same; and this does not represent the true state of affairs. Guilford (1959, p. 215), in the context of a discussion of ipsative versus normative ratings on forced choice items, cogently illustrates the point being made. Figure 7–3 presents a hypothetical distribution of scores of three individuals, J, K, and L, on a vocational interest test, the Kuder Preference Record, as they would be obtained in ipsative form and in normative form.

For each of the three persons in Figure 7–3, ten "true" scores for various interest variables are assumed, all on the same measurement scale. A comparison of the relative ranking of the obtained scores on the mechanical (M) and artistic (A) scales in the two scoring schemes discloses what can happen when means of all individuals are arbitrarily equated. For example, on the normative scale for mechanical interest, J ranks highest, K is next, and L is lowest. On the ipsative scale the order is reversed and the differences are larger.

Self-ratings such as those obtained with Q-sorts also tend to present difficulties for the subject in terms of the introspective attitude he is required to assume. For example, when he is instructed to compare himself with others, he is likely to shift in his introspective attitudes: he may rate himself normatively on some items (e.g., "How do I feel compared to others?") and ipsatively (e.g., "Is this statement more true about me than the previous one?") on certain others. These shifts, which are not possible on self-report inventories because of the specificity of the wording of items and their forced alternative responses, may result in changes in the subject's frames of reference during any single sorting session. The obtained sortings, consequently, do not always reflect the personality characteristic they are designed to measure.

Semantic Differential

The semantic differential was developed by Osgood (1952) and his associates (Osgood *et al.*, 1957) as a tool for the measurement of meaning. Its possibilities as a method for personality assessment were recognized early by the authors; and their assertion was that differences in meaning can be expected from individuals with differing *personality dynamisms*. Strictly speaking, the semantic differential is not a personality measuring instrument, nor do its authors publicize it for any use but personality research or as a clinical aid to psychotherapists. Its potential, however, for routine personality measurement should become apparent from the ensuing discussion.

The logic of the semantic differential method is summarized by Osgood somewhat as follows: (1) the process of description or judgment can be conceived as the allocation of a concept to an experimental continuum definable by a pair of polar terms; (2) many different experimental continua, or ways in which meaning can vary, are essentially equivalent and hence may be represented by a single dimension; (3) a limited number of such continua can be used to find a semantic space within which the meaning of a concept can be specified.

The semantic differential consists of a group of seven point scales, each defined by a pair of polar terms (e.g., excitable-calm,

---

DIRECTIONS

On the following pages there is either a word or a sentence in capitalized letters at the *top* of the page. You will also notice that there are 17 pairs of opposite words underneath the capitalized word or sentence. Between each of the pairs of opposites there are 7 dashes. You are to place a check mark on one of the 7 lines that are between the two opposite words and the check mark should indicate what the word or sentence at the *top* of the page means to you. Look at the examples below:

EXAMPLE 1:   MAN

Line 1:   Good __✔_:___:___:___:___:___:___ Bad
Line 2:   Slow ___:_✔_:___:___:___:___:___ Fast
Line 3:   Cruel ___:___:_✔_:___:___:___:___ Kind

In this example MAN is the word at the top of the page and the pairs of opposites are Good-Bad, Slow-Fast, and Cruel-Kind. If MAN seemed to you to mean something very Good, you would make a check as in Line 1. If MAN seemed to you to mean something quite SLOW, then you would place your check mark as in Line 2. And if you feel that MAN means something which is a little Cruel, then you would put your check mark as in Line 3.

In the following example a check has been placed to illustrate how someone would place his check marks if he thought that TIGER was something very Bad, very Fast, and very Cruel:

EXAMPLE 2:   TIGER

Line 1:   Good ___:___:___:___:___:___:_✔_ Bad
Line 2:   Slow ___:___:___:___:___:___:_✔_ Fast
Line 3:   Cruel _✔_:___:___:___:___:___:___ Kind

Sometimes you will feel that the word or sentence at the *top* of the page is neither Good nor Bad, neither Slow nor Fast and neither Cruel nor Kind. On the Sample below, using the word TREE, place your check marks to indicate how you would show this feeling.

SAMPLE   TREE

Line 1:   Good ___:___:___:___:___:___:___ Bad
Line 2:   Slow ___:___:___:___:___:___:___ Fast
Line 3:   Cruel ___:___:___:___:___:___:___ Kind

On the following pages, place your check marks rapidly. What is wanted is your first impression. There are no "right" or "wrong" answers. Be sure to make only one check mark for each pair of words. Do not skip any pairs of words or pages.

FIGURE 7–4. Directions and samples for administering the Semantic Differential.

strong-weak) in terms of which words or concepts are to be rated (see Figure 7–4). The scales were chosen by having subjects write down descriptive adjectives for 40 nouns. The adjectives used most often were then converted into 50 bipolar scales, and 100 students rated 20 concepts on these scales. Factor analysis of the results indicated that three factors accounted for most of the variance. These were the *evaluative* (good-bad), *activity* (fast-slow), and *potency* (strong-weak) factors.

The raw data obtained from the semantic differential ratings are a collection of check marks on such bipolar scales as are illustrated in Figure 7–4. A digit is arbitrarily assigned to each of the seven positions on the scale. These may be in the form 1, 2, 3, 4, 5, 6, 7, or may be $+3$, $+2$, $+1$, 0, -1, -2, -3. A rater's score on a scale is the digit corresponding to the scale position he checks. For k scales and m concepts, each respondent yields a $k \times m$ matrix. If there is a group of n respondents, the matrix obtained is $k \times m \times n$ scores. Occasionally, a respondent's ratings are plotted in three-dimensional space, in which each one of his ratings on certain constructs are illustrated as semantic structures (see Figure 7–5).

The use of the semantic differential for personality study is illustrated here by citing two studies. Reeves (1954), as part of her doctoral dissertation, undertook the quantification of TAT[7] protocols by means of the semantic differential. Undergraduates were shown 10 TAT pictures, one at a time, via a slide projector. Next they rated each of these pictures against a 20-scale form of the semantic differential. These pictures were then presented to them in the same order and they were asked to write a brief statement consisting of the plot of the story that might be told about each of the pictures. The stories for all pictures were classified according to major themes, and each of these themes was judged on a positive-negative continuum by a set of 20 TAT experts. The two groups of subjects who yielded the most extreme themes were then compared on the basis of the sum of their own ratings over five evaluative scales on the semantic differential. In all cases, the direction of the difference in the evaluative ratings corresponded to the ratings of the experts, and on 7 of the 10 pictures the difference was sufficiently large to be statistically significant. In other words, the semantic differential ratings made by subjects of a set of TAT pictures corresponded closely to stories written by them to represent these same pictures. Such correspondence suggests that the semantic differential might be used as a substitute for storytelling. The advantage to be realized by this substitution rests in the greater quantification of TAT responses that could be achieved by scoring semantic differential responses rather than TAT themes.

The second study (Kleinmuntz, 1958, 1960c) was designed to investigate psychiatric patients' attitudes toward certain MMPI items, and the semantic differential ratings of two groups of psy-

---

[7] The Thematic Apperception Test (TAT) is a personality measuring procedure (see Chapter 10) in which the subject is presented with a set of picture cards and is instructed to respond to these by creating stories.

chotic patients were compared. A group of general hospital "normals" was also used for comparison. The psychotic individuals—that is, the "abnormals"—were similar to one another with respect to the severity of their symptoms (e.g., delusions, hallucinations, length of hospitalization), but were divided into two groups on the basis of an important difference between them. This clinically similar group of patients (rated for similarity by five staff psychologists and psychiatrists) was separated on the basis of their MMPI Pa scale[8] scores: one half of them had evaded detection on the Pa scale (i.e., were "test misses"), and the remaining half was identified as paranoid on this MMPI scale ("test hits"). The main question of the study was: "How do some of the psychotics evade detection?"

The semantic differential was used to compare these psychotic subgroups with themselves and with a normal group. Concepts rated by members of these groups included "me," "they," "people," "friends," "poison," and "the mind." These concepts were selected because they represent ideas and objects that tend to preoccupy paranoid psychotic persons, and ratings on these concepts were expected to differentiate between paranoid and normal respondents. It was further postulated that psychotic persons not detected on the MMPI would be differentiated from their clinical counterparts on the basis of the former's greater ability to "see through" obvious Pa scale items (Wiener, 1948). Therefore the following MMPI items, converted into rateable form, were used as concepts: "a person who is sure he gets a raw deal from life" and "a person who believes he is condemned." Two subtle Pa scale (Wiener, 1948) items were converted and used: "people who would like to get ahead" and "people who tell lies to keep out of trouble." The bipolar scales used to rate these items were mentally healthy–mentally ill, strong-weak, and calm-excitable. The semantic structures of the three groups were then plotted in three dimensional space. These structures are illustrated in Figure 7–5. The spatial orientation for the structures is that mentally healthy is down and mentally ill is up; weak is to the left, and strong to the right; excitable is away from the viewer, and calm is toward the viewer.

From an observation of the structures plotted in Figure 7–5, and from statistical analyses of the mean differences between these

---

[8] The MMPI Paranoia scale (see Chapter 8) was designed to detect the presence of paranoid tendencies.

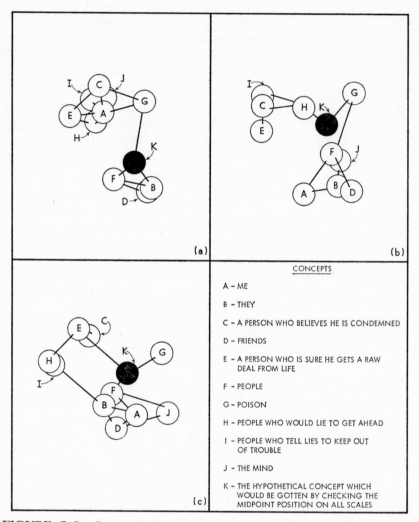

FIGURE 7–5. Semantic structures of (*a*) normals, (*b*) test hits, and (*c*) test misses. Note especially, in (*c*) that test misses describe themselves and the MIND as mentally healthy, strong, and calm.

groups, the question posed at the outset of this study can be answered in the following way: Persons of the paranoid schizophrenic groups who were not detected by the MMPI consider themselves normal—supernormal, as a matter of fact—and persons in the other clinical group consider themselves mentally ill. Results of this study further indicated that both the test misses and test hits recognized Pa scale items as descriptive of mentally ill persons! Therefore, it is not recognition per se which accounts for the MMPI differentiations; rather the differences are due to test taking attitudes in which test hits choose, for one reason or another, to admit their illness, and test misses tend vehemently to deny their illness.

Generally, the test-retest reliabilities found in studies of the semantic differential are adequate when the method is used with groups. But its use for individual assessment purposes is not recommended (Norman, 1959). Since criteria of meaning are exceedingly difficult to obtain, the problem of validation becomes one of conducting studies designed to demonstrate the technique's construct validity.

Role Construct Repertory Test (Rep)

A procedure which is quite similar to Osgood's semantic differential is George Kelly's Role Construct Repertory Test or *Rep* Test (1955). Again, as with Osgood's technique, the *Rep* test is not a recognized personality measuring instrument because no data for its reliability, validity, or standardization are in a form that enables a potential user to apply the test routinely. The *Rep* test is an outgrowth of Kelly's theory of social behavior. Professor Kelly proposes that understanding another person ("enter his labyrinth") requires a conceptualization of his construct system. To enable the therapist to obtain some glimpse of a person's construct system—in other words, to enable him to assume the client's attitudes toward himself and others—Kelly gives the examinee a list of about 20 roles and asks him to name significant persons who fill these roles for him. Some of the roles that appear on a "Role Title List" are:

—A teacher you liked.
—The girl you did not like when you were in high school.
—Your father.
—Your wife or present girl friend.
—A person with whom you have been closely associated recently.
—A person who appears to dislike you.
—Your mother.

The respondent is then offered the names of three significant persons whom he mentioned as filling these roles, and he is asked: "In what important way are two of them alike but different from the third?" This procedure is repeated with many other sets of three names, and the aim is to see how the examinee classifies these persons and how he differentiates them. This procedure is often continued until many scales are elicited and applied to the significant role fillers. A matrix of similarities and differences between these persons is then made up. By factorial analysis, the structure of the examinee's constructs is obtained. The personality picture obtained by this method is not in terms of factor scores or profile configurations, but rather in terms of a structure of constructs. In this way, constructs important for a particular individual can be identified; and similarities between this individual and other similar persons can be extracted.

Rep test results are also subjected to a "clinical" analysis. Kelly suggests that the examiner count the number of constructs elicited. He believes that the number of constructs may be an indicator either of "compulsivity" or of excessive striving for a definition of role. He also suggests that the clinician tally the extent to which constructs are repeated about different significant persons. Such a tally becomes an index of the construct's "permeability." That is to say, if a particular construct seems to permeate or pervade through varied situations in life, and if the range of the construct's permeability is wide, then this is considered evidence of a person's characteristic coping mechanisms in varied circumstances. Viewed in terms of the ingenuity that has gone into its construction and its amenability to quantification, it is surprising that the *Rep* Test has not gained the popularity among clinicians that it deserves.

(Summary appears at end of Chapter 8.)

FOR FURTHER READING

1. COMREY, A. L.　Factored homogeneous item dimensions: A strategy for personality research. In MESSICK, S. & ROSS, J. (Eds.), *Measurement in personality and cognition*. New York: John Wiley & Sons, Inc.. 1962. Pp. 11–26.

   A somewhat technical article, in which the authors assume the reader's familiarity with factor analysis, describing preliminary research designed to identify personality test items by factorial methods.

2. CROWNE, D. P. & STEPHENS, M. W.　Self-acceptance and self-evaluative behavior. *Psychological Bulletin*, 1961, 58, 104–121.

   This article provides a review of self-acceptance research, and asserts that to date very little is understood about its relationships to other personality variables. Some of the difficulties to be encountered in forthcoming work on the self-acceptance dimension are anticipated and outlined.

3. DREGER, R. M.　Objective personality tests and computer processing of personality test data. In BERG, I. A. & PENNINGTON, L. A. (Eds.), *An introduction to clinical psychology*. New York: Ronald Press Co., 1966. Pp. 154–190.

The major objective tests (e.g., self-report inventories) and psychophysiological, psychomotor, and psychophysical measures are described in this chapter. Additionally, computer processing techniques (cf. Chapter 11 of this book) are discussed.

4. HATHAWAY, S. R. Personality inventories. In WOLMAN, B. B. (Ed.), *Handbook of clinical psychology.* New York: McGraw-Hill Book Co., 1965. Pp. 451–476.

   A thoroughly readable and scholarly review of personality tests by the man most responsible for their popularity.

5. HEILBRUN, A. B., JR. Evidence regarding the equivalence of ipsative and normative personality scales. *Journal of consulting Psychology,* 1963, 27, 152–156.

   This author has garnered some evidence supporting the use of ipsative measures for normative predictions. The reader may also want to consult Cattell's (1944) original article on this topic.

6. LOEHLIN, J. C. Word meanings and self-descriptions. *Journal of abnormal and social Psychology,* 1961, 62, 28–34.

   In this study of the semantic differential, using college students to apply adjectives to themselves, Loehlin has found evidence of individual differences in ascribing meanings to self-descriptive adjectives.

7. LOEVINGER, JANE. Some principles of personality measurement. *Educational and psychological Measurement,* 1955, 15, 3–17.

   Five principles for the measurement of personality are proposed in this excellent paper, and their application to some contemporary testing trends is examined.

8. MEEHL, P. E. The dynamics of "structured" personality tests. *Journal of clinical Psychology,* 1945, 1, 296–303.

   Written more than 20 years ago by a then unknown graduate student at the University of Minnesota (long since graduated), this paper remains the classic statement on the logic of personality testing.

9. SARASON, I. G. *Personality: An objective approach.* New York: John Wiley & Sons, Inc., 1966.

   Part II of this book (pp. 123–242) is a survey of most existing personality measurement procedures.

10. SEEMAN, W. Subtlety in structured personality tests. *Journal of consulting Psychology,* 1952, 16, 278–283.

    Professor Seeman reviewed the evidence supporting the concept that subtlety in structured tests can be given experimental meaning. This article should be contrasted with Frank's (1939) statement on projective testing.

CHAPTER 8

THE SELF-REPORT INVENTORY
(Continued): THE MMPI AND SOME
PROBLEMS OF SELF-REPORTING

The Minnesota Multiphasic Personality Inventory (Hathaway and McKinley, 1942, 1951), sometimes called the Mult or the MMPI, is indisputably the most popular self-report test currently on the market (Sundberg, 1961). Serving as partial evidence of its popularity and wide acceptance among psychologists are the central place it occupied in the 1965 congressional investigations (see Chapter 3) and the numerous attacks it has occasioned in newspapers and books.

Paradoxically, the same critics who sometimes consider it vague and ineffectual criticize it at other times for being too "pruriently snooping." Likewise, the same writers who question its accuracy and morality offer elaborate instructions on how to cheat on the MMPI. It has also been the object of humorous criticism. One newspaper reporter (Dixon, 1965) wrote: "The questions are the kind you would ask the girl next door—if you wanted her to move. Just impersonal over-the-fence chitchat, like how she stands on sex, Westerns on television, church-going and stealing." And Art Buchwald, in his syndicated column, gave a list of 36 items which he intended as caricatures of the MMPI statements. Some of these—because they are humorous and do serve to point out that the MMPI may be in for some copy editing—are repeated here (American Psychological Association, 1965, pp. 989–990) :

—My eyes are always cold.
—A wide necktie is a sign of disease.

216

—When I was younger, I used to tease vegetables.
—I use shoe polish to excess.

Any test that has received so much attention, attained so much notoriety, and caused so much controversy as the MMPI deserves special mention in this book. Accordingly, considerable space is set aside in this chapter for its detailed discussion.

CONSTRUCTION AND DESCRIPTION OF THE MMPI

The MMPI, which was constructed by the method of criterion or empirical keying (see Chapter 7), received its impetus because Hathaway, a clinical psychologist, and McKinley, a neuropsychiatrist, recognized the need for a practical and valid test to use for routine clinical applications in a psychiatric service setting. Accordingly, test responses obtained from the MMPI were scored in terms of the psychiatric taxonomy of mental disorders that was current at the time of test construction and which, with minor modifications, is still in use today.

The construction of the MMPI did not proceed along the lines of any theories about the structure of personality. As a matter of fact, the MMPI is intentionally atheoretic, and its development is firmly based in a thoroughly empirical methodology. At the outset of its development, an original pool of 1,000 items was selected from psychiatric examination forms, textbooks of psychiatry, descriptions of psychiatric and neurological examination procedures, and from earlier published scales of personal and social attitudes. These items were administered to about 200 clinically diagnosed neuropsychiatric patients in the University of Minnesota hospitals, to more than 1,000 normal persons obtained from among those who were visiting relatives in these hospitals, to several hundred students seeking admission to the University of Minnesota, and to a sample of residents of the city of Minneapolis. The 550 items that were retained for further study, and subsequently for inclusion in the MMPI, were those which on the basis of frequency of endorsement differentiated between neuropsychiatric patients and groups of normal people. In other words, only those items were retained which empirically discriminated between patients and normal persons.

More specifically, the neuropsychiatric patients were divided into clear-cut diagnostic groups on the basis of clinical judgments and conferences about them. The answers each group gave to each of the 550 items were tabulated, and an item that differentiated clearly and statistically in the frequency of responses between members of one of these psychiatric groups and the several normal groups was then scored as an indicator of that psychiatric trend. For example, an item was retained on the scale for hypochondriasis[1] only if hypochondriacal patients endorsed it more often than normal persons. In this way, approximately one half of the original pool of 1,000 items was selected.

The MMPI currently in use is composed of 550 items, printed in a test booklet. The examinee is asked to respond "true," "false," or "cannot say" to such statements as "Someone has it in for me," "I certainly feel useless at times," and "Everything tastes the same." The subject records his responses on an answer sheet. The items cover a range of personality-relevant areas that include: general health, specific physical ailments, attitudes toward family and community, religious beliefs, mood fluctuations, delusions, hallucinations, and other areas of importance for diagnosing psychological disturbance. Item responses are tallied according to 10 clinical and 4 validity scales or keys, and these are plotted on a profile sheet (see Figure 8–1). Raw scores on each of these scales are expressed as T-scores.[2]

CLINICAL AND VALIDITY SCALES OF THE MMPI

The scoring for the MMPI, as noted above, is done in terms of 10 clinical scales—one for each of 9 recognized psychiatric classifications, and one additional key—and 4 validity scales. The latter consist of items designed to detect test taking attitudes as well as attempts to distort test responses in favorable or unfavorable directions. The clinical scales, conventionally called by their scale

---

[1] The first clinical scale on the MMPI profile sheet is one which measures Hs or hypochondriasis (see pp. 221–222). A person who is diagnosed as a hypochondriac is one who displays an overconcern about his physical well-being.

[2] Every distribution of scores can be expressed in terms of its arithmetic mean and standard deviation (the spread or variability of the scores). The status of an individual score can then be understood in terms of the mean and standard deviation of that distribution—i.e., how far it deviates from the mean compared to others' score deviations. The conversion of raw scores to a distribution of scores with a mean and a standard deviation results in their expression as standard scores. The T-score is a standard score derived from raw scores by reducing measurements to a common scale of units where the mean $= 50$ and the standard deviaton $= 10$. Thus a raw score which is two standard deviations above the mean is equivalent to a T-score of 70. Similarly, raw scores at one standard deviation above, at the mean, and at one and two standard deviations below the mean, are equivalent to T-scores of 60, 50, 40, and 30 respectively.

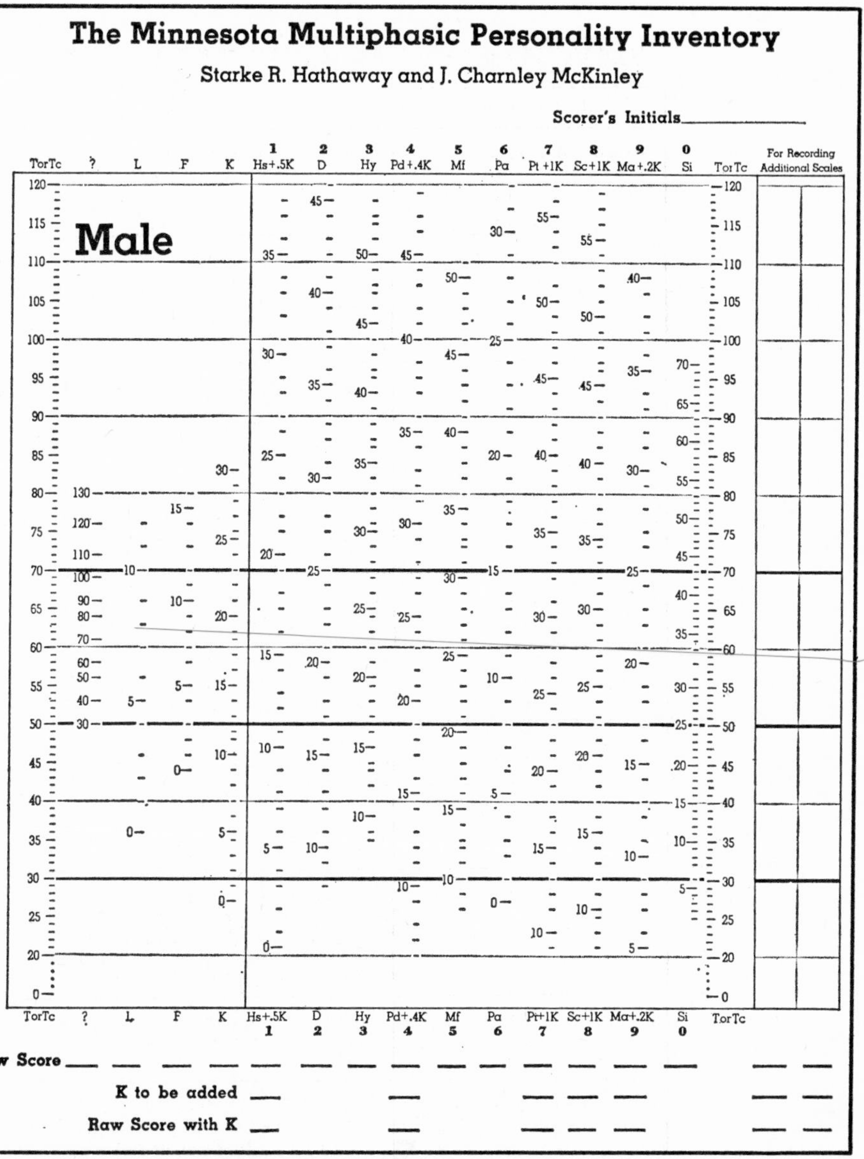

The Minnesota Multiphasic Personality Inventory

Starke R. Hathaway and J. Charnley McKinley

Scorer's Initials_____

Male

(MMPI profile sheet with validity scales ?, L, F, K on the left-hand side and clinical scales 1 through 0 across: Hs+.5K, D, Hy, Pd+.4K, Mf, Pa, Pt+1K, Sc+1K, Ma+.2K, Si; T-score scale from 0 to 120)

Raw Score ___ ___ ___ ___ ___   ___ ___ ___ ___ ___   ___ ___

K to be added ___   ___   ___ ___   ___

Raw Score with K ___   ___   ___ ___   ___

FIGURE 8–1. An MMPI profile sheet. The validity scales ?, L, F, and K are shown on the left-hand side; and clinical scales 1 to 0 are on the right-hand side. There are separate norms for males and females (compare with Figure 8–2). (Reproduced by permission. Copyright 1943 by the University of Minnesota. Published by the Psychological Corporation, New York, N.Y. All rights reserved.)

numbers rather than their psychiatric diagnostic labels, are as follows: Scale 1, Hypochondriasis (Hs); Scale 2, Depression (D);

TABLE 8-1

The Validity and Clinical Scales of the MMPI

Scale	Sample Item	Interpretation
?	No sample. It is merely the number of items marked in the "cannot say" category.	This is one of four validity scales, and a high score indicates evasiveness.
L	I get angry sometimes (FALSE).*	This is the second validity scale. Persons trying to present themselves in a favorable light (e.g., good, wholesome, honest) obtain high L Scale elevations.
F	Everything tastes the same (TRUE).	F is the third validity scale. High scores suggest carelessness, confusion, or "fake bad."
K	I have very few fears compared to my friends (FALSE).	An elevation on the last validity scale, K, suggests a defensive test taking attitude. Exceedingly low scores may indicate a lack of ability to deny symptomatology.
Hs	I wake up fresh and rested most mornings (FALSE).	High scorers have been described as cynical, defeatist, and crabbed.
D	At times I am full of energy (FALSE).	High scorers usually are shy, despondent, and distressed.
Hy	I have never had a fainting spell (FALSE).	High scorers tend to complain of multiple symptoms.
Pd	I liked school (FALSE).	Adjectives used to describe some high scorers are adventurous, courageous, and generous.
Mf	I like mechanics magazines (FALSE).	Among males, high scorers have been described as aesthetic and sensitive. High-scoring women have been described as rebellious, unrealistic, and indecisive.
Pa	I am happy most of the time (FALSE).	High scorers on this scale were characterized as shrewd, guarded, and worrisome.
Pt	I am certainly lacking in self-confidence (TRUE).	Fearful, rigid, anxious and worrisome are some of the adjectives used to describe high Pt scorers.
Sc	I believe I am a condemned person (TRUE).	Adjectives such as withdrawn and unusual describe Sc high scorers.
Ma	I am an important person (TRUE).	High scorers are called sociable, energetic, and impulsive.
Si	I enjoy social gatherings just to be with people (FALSE).	High scorers: modest, shy, and self-effacing. Low scorers: sociable, colorful, and ambitious.

* The True or False responses within parenthesis indicate the scored direction of each of the items.

Scale 3, Hysteria (Hy) ; Scale 4, Psychopathic deviate (Pd) ; Scale 5, Masculinity-Feminity (Mf) ; Scale 6, Paranoia (Pa) ; Scale 7, Psychasthenia (Pt) ; Scale 8, Schizophrenia (Sc) ; Scale 9, Hypomania (Ma) ; and Scale 0, Social Introversion (Si). Referring to the clinical keys by their numbers, according to their ordinal positions on the profile sheet, has simplified profile coding procedures (see later discussion, pp. 229–231), and has served to eliminate psychiatric labeling when referring to a person's score profile. The four validity keys are: Question Scale (?) ; Lie Scale (L) ; F Scale; and Correction Scale (K). The clinical and validity scales are discussed in detail in the following sections, and their characteristics are summarized in Table 8–1.

Clinical Scales

The reader should bear in mind throughout the following discussion of the clinical scales of the MMPI that although high scores on these scales are found among the various clinical groups, the converse is not necessarily true. That is to say, studies have repeatedly indicated that diagnosed depressed patients, for instance, score high on Scale 2 (depression), but it is not true that a high Scale 2 score necessarily indicates that a respondent can be diagnosed as a depressive disorder. High scores on many clinical scales are found among normal subjects, and rather than indicating gross psychiatric pathology, they suggest that these normals share certain symptoms and characteristics with the psychiatric patients who also score high on these scales. Thus a normal who scores high on Scale 2 may be somewhat depressed or dejected but need not necessarily qualify for hospitalization or even outpatient treatment. The research evidence regarding the meaning of low scores is less clear than that pertaining to high scores.

Scale 1 (Hs). The clinical group that served as a criterion reference sample for the construction of Scale 1 consisted of 50 persons diagnosed as hypochondriacs (McKinley and Hathaway, 1940). These persons characteristically display an unusual preoccupation with their bodily functions and worry constantly about physical ailments. No amount of evidence and reassurance to the contrary seem to convince them that they are indeed healthy.

Scale 1 is mostly composed of somatic items[3] such as, "I have a

---

[3] Readers are cautioned that the items included here as examples are an unrepresentative set of each of the clinical scales, and consequently interpretation of responses to these items are meaningless.

great deal of stomach trouble" (if answered "true," this item is counted toward the Hs scale), "The top of my head sometimes feels tender" (true), "I am very seldom troubled by constipation" (false), "My sleep is fitful and disturbed" (true), and "I wake up fresh and rested most mornings" (false).

There are a total of 33 items on this scale (Hathaway and McKinley, 1951) and the average normal male answers between 8 and 15 of these in the hypochondriacal direction (raw scores of 16 and 19 are equivalent to T-scores of 60 and 70, which are one and two standard deviations above the mean, respectively). Females in our society are expected to be somewhat more preoccupied with bodily functions and consequently the obtained mean for females is higher (their raw scores can be as high as 18 and 23 before exceeding one and two standard deviations above the mean). Normal persons who score high on Scale 1 have been described by their friends and acquaintances as sociable, enthusiastic, kind, responsive, modest, frank, courageous, and versatile (Hathaway and Meehl, 1952). Among psychiatric patients, high Hs scorers have been characterized as crabbed, dissatisfied, defeatist and cynical (Cuadra and Reed, 1954).

Scale 2 (D). Fifty persons were selected by Hathaway and McKinley to serve in the criterion group for the construction of the D scale. They were characterized by clinicians as depressed and preoccupied with suicidal thoughts and death. Depressed patients are often considerably slowed down in their activities and tend to describe themselves as worthless, hopeless, and desperate individuals.

Among the 60 items that appear on Scale 2, and the direction in which they are scored, are the following: "I usually feel that life is worth while" (false), "I am easily awakened by noise" (true), "At times I am full of energy" (false), and "Once in a while I laugh at a dirty joke" (false).

On the average, 20 (male) to 28 (female) items can be answered in the D direction before one is considered to be two or more standard deviations higher than the normal Minnesota reference group. College students whose highest MMPI profile score was on Scale 2 have been repeatedly described as shy (Black, 1953), physically distressed, and depressed (Guthrie, 1950).

Scale 3 (Hy). The criterion group (50 persons) selected for the third scale of the MMPI exhibited such symptoms as loss of voice, deafness, tingling sensations, or numbness, over various portions of the body. These symptoms are considered "hysterical" because frequently they have no physical basis of fact.

There are 60 items on this scale, and some typical ones are illustrated by the following four: "I have never had a fainting spell" (false), "I frequently notice my hand shakes when I try to do something" (true), "I am happy most of the time" (false), and "Once a week or oftener I feel suddenly hot all over, without apparent cause" (true).

College students who score high on Scale 3 have been described by their peers as flattering, irritable, and religious (Black, 1953). Medical patients often suffered from tachycardia, palpitation, and headaches (Guthrie, 1950).

Scale 4 (Pd). Most persons included in the criterion group (100 prisoners and 78 diagnosed clinic cases) for psychopathic deviancy were ill from the point of view of society. That is to say, their illness took the forms of stealing, lying, promiscuity, violence, forgery, and truancy. Many of these persons were referred to a psychiatric setting by the police or by court judges.

Some of the 50 items on this scale reflect the psychopathic deviate's antisocial and asocial behaviors, but many more items tap certain other and more subtle dimensions of personality within this diagnostic group. For example, answers on the following two items are clearly in accord with the stereotype: "I liked school" (false), and "In school I was sometimes sent to the principal for cutting up" (true). On the other hand, unless you accept the empirical point of view, it is difficult to understand on a rational basis why the next set of items are scored in the Pd direction: "I am against giving money to beggars" (false), "I have very few fears compared to my friends" (false), and "I am easily downed in an argument" (false). Each of these items is on the Pd scale simply because it is an empirically established fact that psychopathic deviates say this about themselves, and normals, on the average, do not.

Among normals, Hathaway and Meehl (1952) obtained some of the following adjectives to describe high Scale 4 scorers: adventurous, courageous, enthusiastic, verbal, individualistic, and generous. Medical patients (Guthrie, 1950) tended to be alcoholic and have histories of excessive gambling and poor work habits.

Scale 5 (Mf). There are a total of 60 items on Scale 5, the masculinity-feminity scale (Mf), and a group of 13 male sexual inverts were used as a criterion sample. An attempt to develop an Fm scale to identify female inverts was unsuccessful. Items were also selected for inclusion on this scale if they differentiated between the sexes. The item content on the Mf scale was drawn from the Strong Vocational Interest Blank (see pp. 219–221) and ranges over interests for various occupations, hobbies, avocations, social activities, and family relationships. Some of these items are illustrated here: "I would like to be a florist" (true), "I like mechanics magazines" (false), "I sometimes tease animals" (false), "I like to talk about sex" (true).

Although it has been reported (Renaud, 1950) that high scores on the Mf scale characterize overt male and female homosexuals, the dependability of Scale 5 for this kind of evaluation is seriously doubted (Dahlstrom and Welsh, 1960). These doubts have been raised because of the fakeability of the scale and due to the fact that elevated scores have been obtained by persons who evidently are not sexually deviant.

Among college women with high scores on Scale 5, Black's (1953) adjective study indicated that peers described them as indecisive, rebellious, and unrealistic. High Scale 5 scorers among males in the normal population were characterized by their peers as sensitive, idealistic, worrisome, peaceable, and aesthetic (Hathaway and Meehl, 1952).

Scale 6 (Pa). The Pa scale was designed to detect paranoid personalities. The criterion subjects—number not reported (Hathaway, 1956)—were defensive, suspicious, jealous, and litigious; and generally these persons tend to persist in this type of delusional thinking in the face of even the most convincing evidence that their beliefs are unfounded.

Some of the statements on this 40-item scale are as follows: "I have no enemies who really wish to harm me" (false), "Someone has it in for me" (true), "I am sure I am being talked about" (true), and "I am happy most of the time" (false).

Hathaway and Meehl have reported that males with Scale 6 elevations were rated by their peers as sensitive, emotional, and worrisome. College girls rated their high-point Pa scale peers as clever, high-strung, submissive, hardhearted, and shrewd. Medical patients with primary elevations on this scale tend to establish poor rapport with the physician and frequently do not return for a follow-up visit.

Scale 6 has often been referred to as the weakest of the MMPI keys. It seems that a large group of hospitalized, clinically paranoid patients consistently manage to evade being detected on Scale 6 (these persons are sometimes called "test misses," see pp. 210–212). Among MMPI users, this phenomenon has resulted in a certain amount of "clinical paranoia." For example, if a psychiatric patient in a hospital obtains a "normal" profile (all scores more or less within the normal range of plus or minus one standard deviation from the mean), the test interpreter becomes suspicious of such a profile and tends to regard it as the MMPI of a paranoid patient. Furthermore, MMPI interpreters tend to believe that paranoid persons are astute and therefore are able to "see through" the intent of the more obvious Pa scale items (Wiener, 1948). However, one study (Kleinmuntz, 1958, 1960c), in which patients were given the semantic differential[4] indicated that both "test hits" and "test misses" are sufficiently astute to detect the mentally ill flavor of these items. The difference between paranoid persons within these two groups, according to this study, was that persons who evade detection on the test tend to deny that the Pa items are self-descriptive, whereas test hits do not deny the items' relevance to themselves.

Scale 7 (Pt). Although psychasthenia (Pt) is no longer used as a diagnostic category today, the clinical types that were included in the criterion group (20 persons) for Scale 7 are still with us. Persons included in that criterion category were beset with obsessive thoughts, compulsive rituals, incessant fears, guilt, and a host of other anxiety-inducing conflicts.

The item composition on this 48-item scale covers such personality features as dread, lack of self-confidence, self-doubt, and moodiness. Here are some examples: "I am inclined to take things hard" (true), "I almost never dream" (false), "I usually have to stop and think before I act even in trifling matters" (true), "I am certainly lacking in self-confidence" (true), and "I certainly feel useless at times" (true). Scale 7, undoubtedly because of its heavy loading on the anxiety dimension, served as a prototype for Taylor's (1953) Manifest Anxiety Scale (see the discussion of this scale, pp. 241–242).

High scorers on Scale 7 have been described as sentimental,

---

[4] For a review of the semantic differential and the study referred to, see Chapter 7, pp. 208–213.

peaceable, verbal, individualistic, emotional, and high-strung. Self-descriptive adjectives that were used by college girls included gloomy, dreamy, sentimental, indecisive, absent-minded, and unpopular. Guthrie (1950) described high-scoring medical students as fearful, rigid, anxious, and worrisome.

Scale 8 (Sc). The 78 items of Scale 8 were derived from a larger pool of items administered to 50 schizophrenic patients. This diagnostic group included persons characterized by marked distortions of reality, and those whose symptoms included bizarre thinking, withdrawal from interpersonal contacts, ambivalence, and inappropriate affect. With its 78 items, Scale 8 is the longest of the original MMPI scales.

Perusal of several of the following items, reveals the nature of the dimension being tapped: "Peculiar odors come to me at times" (true), "Most of the time I wish I were dead" (true), "I often feel as if things were not real" (true), "I believe I am a condemned person" (true), and "Everything tastes the same" (true).

Persons with primary and substantial elevations on Scale 8 are almost always found among psychiatric samples. Some descriptive adjectives applied to high Sc scorers are apathetic, serious, seclusive, moody, stubborn, and opinionated (Black, 1953; Gough, McKee and Yandell, 1955). Generally, when persons with elevated Scale 8 scores are found among normal samples, they present a withdrawn, somewhat unusual and schizoid personality makeup.

Scale 9 (Ma). The 24 patients included in the hypomania criterion group were overactive, excited, and irritable persons. These persons are noted for their flurries of overactivity, in which they suddenly believe that their mission on earth is to resolve all problems simultaneously, do everything at once, and purchase every commodity wisely and quickly—and accomplish all these things in a single day.

The 46 items on Scale 9 cover a range of content that includes the grandiosity, as well as the overactivity and excitement, that suddenly seems to beset these individuals. Here are some examples: "I am important person" (true), "At times I feel that I can make up my mind with unusually great ease" (true), "I work under a great deal of tension" (true), and "At times my thoughts have raced ahead faster than I could speak them" (true).

The high-scoring males on this scale were described as sociable, energetic, open, impulsive, self-dissatisfied, and prone to alcoholism (Hathaway and Meehl, 1952). Girls with high scores were described as poised, self-confident, articulate, efficient, and responsible (Hovey, 1953). The self-ratings of these persons tend to characterize them as impulsive, talkative, and adventurous, and generally seem to concur with descriptions made by others.

Scale 0 (Si). The 10th and last scale of the MMPI was constructed by item analysis (Drake, 1946), contrasting the percentage of responses of two groups of students to the items. MMPI items retained were those which differentiated the students who scored above the 65th centile rank from those scoring below the 35th centile rank on the Minnesota T-S-E Inventory[5] (Evans and McConnell, 1942 to 1957). Thus scores on the T-S-E served as criteria for Scale 0.

There are 70 items on this scale; four samples are: "I am not unusually self-conscious" (false), "I enjoy social gatherings just to be with people" (false), "Whenever possible I avoid being in a crowd" (true), and "I enjoy gambling for small stakes" (false).

Men and women who score high on Scale 0 have been described as modest, shy, self-effacing, and sensitive (Hathaway and Meehl, 1952). Perhaps a more important consideration for this scale than the high-point descriptions are those which describe low scorers: versatile, sociable, colorful, exhibitionistic, active, ambitious, and articulate. Self-ratings of low scorers tend to corroborate the peer ratings, and they characterize themselves as sociable, enterprising, enthusiastic, talkative, and friendly (Black, 1953).

The Validity Scales

In addition to the clinical scales there are four validity scales.[6] The first of these is the *Question Scale (?)*, which consists of the number of items marked in the "cannot say" category. Excessive scores on this scale suggest evasiveness or indecisiveness and therefore any comparison with a normative group becomes spurious. If a respondent has answered 100 or more items in this direction his profile is usually considered invalid.

The second validity scale, the *Lie Scale (L)*, consists of 15 items worded in a way such that individuals who attempt to present

---

[5] This inventory yields three introversion-extroversion scores on thinking, social, and emotional categories.

[6] The term "validity" as used to describe the MMPI scales refers only to these scales' function to validate or invalidate the credibility of the clinical scales. This form of validity is unrelated to the psychometric validation procedures discussed in Chap. 2.

themselves in an ultragood light will endorse them. For example, "I get angry sometimes" is a statement that most people would answer in the "true" direction. However, a person who is trying to "fake good," that is to say, a person who does not want to put himself in a socially unfavorable light, would not endorse this item. The assumption is that if an examinee answers many of the L Scale items in a statistically infrequent direction, then most of his other test responses may be equally untrustworthy. A weakness of this scale has been its visibility. Most sophisticated subjects, especially college students, tend to "see through" these items and consequently are not easily baited by them. Therefore, the L scale detects some faking in the "good" direction but is far from an entirely dependable validity key.

The third validity scale, *F*, consists of 64 items that were endorsed infrequently by the normative samples. A high score on the F scale suggests either carelessness, misunderstanding, confusion, a "fake bad" test taking attitude, or any combination of these factors. Sometimes, chance or random test responding, obtained by answering true or false on the basis of a coin flip, is also detected by exceedingly high F scores.

The last validity scale, *K*, sometimes also called the *Correction Scale* (Meehl and Hathaway, 1946), consists of 30 items which reflect the respondent's guardedness or defensiveness in admitting to certain symptoms and abnormalities. In order to correct for these persons' low test scores (if they are defensive, their clinical scales will show low scores but their K scale scores will be elevated), proportions of K are added to certain clinical scales. For example, scales 1, 4, 7, 8, and 9 have the proportions .5, .4, 1.0, 1.0, and .2 of K respectively added to their raw scores. The proportions of K to be added, and the specific K scale items, were empirically determined and were designed to optimize the MMPI's capability of detecting clinically ill persons. Additional information regarding K's construction and function is presented in a later section of this chapter under the heading of "test taking attitudes."

NEW MMPI SCALES

Since the MMPI originally came out in 1942, more than 200 scales have been developed. Most of the new scales have not been adopted for routine use, and they are often applied in personality research or as the practical occasion dictates. An exception to this has been the addition of Scale 0, the Social Introversion scale, which has been incorporated into the MMPI profile sheet as the 10th scale.

Other experimental MMPI scales vary widely in the types of traits they measure. More than 30 scales have been developed for use among normal college students. Most of these 30 scales are used for the purpose of measuring personality traits unrelated to psychiatric abnormalities (Kleinmuntz, 1962). Examples of some new scales that have come into popular but not routine use include measures of Ego Strength (Es), Manifest Anxiety (MAS), Dominance (Do), Prejudice (Pr), and Maladjustment (Mt) (Barron, 1953; Taylor, 1953; Gough et al., 1951; Gough, 1951; Kleinmuntz, 1960b, 1961).

CODING

With increasing experience in the clinical use of the MMPI in nonpsychiatric settings, it has become clear that evaluations based on single scale elevations, rather than patterns or profiles of scale scores, were inadequate. It has also become apparent to test users that the implications of the scales had to be extended beyond their original psychiatric intent. That is, instead of referring to the "hypochondriasis" scale, it seemed best to adopt the simple label "Hs." This helped remove the connotation that persons who score high on Hs necessarily belong to the group diagnosed as hypochondriacs. After all, as noted earlier, normal persons do score high on these scales. More recently, MMPI users have become accustomed to substituting numerals for the abbreviated scale names. This has served to remove further the scales' psychiatric connotations and has paved the way for a "profile language" for coding (Hathaway, 1947).

In coding the profile, each clinical scale is assigned a digit, depending on its serial position, from left to right, on the MMPI profile sheet (see Figure 8–2). Thus Hs becomes 1, D becomes 2, and so on, until the last scale, Si, is assigned the numeral 0. The next step is to write down the scale digits in the order of their T-score elevations, from highest to lowest. Thus in Figure 8–2, where a hypothetical profile is presented with the highest T-score elevation (95) on Scale 3, the digit 3 would be the first number in the code. The second highest scale is Mf (Scale 5) at 87; the code now is 35.

The third and fourth highest scales are 7 and 8—3578; and this continues until all the clinical scales are listed in descending order of T-scores. The digit sequence for the example in Figure 8–2 is 3578902164.

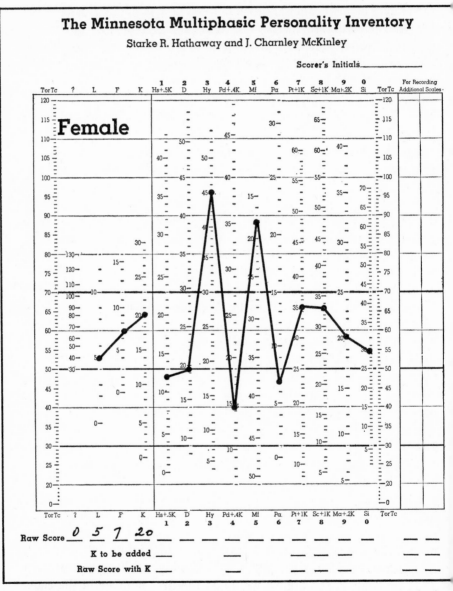

FIGURE 8–2.   A sample MMPI profile in which the Hathaway code is 35′789021–64.

After the digits have been recorded in this way, the appropriate elevation symbols, as shown in Figure 8–2, are notated. Thus in the Hathaway system, a prime (′) is inserted after the last number in the code which represents a T-score of 70 or above. All adjacent scale numbers for which the T-scores are within one point of each other are underlined; and a dash (–) separates those digits which represent T-score values greater than 54 from those that are less than that value. After the dash, the digits of the lowest scales are written, if they have T-score values less than 46. Finally, the raw scores for L, F, and K are recorded to the right of the code. If the raw score of L is equal to or greater than 10, or if the raw score of F is equal to or greater than 16, a capital X is placed after the clinical scale code. The X indicates that there is a possibility that the profile may be invalid. For the profile presented in Figure 8–2, the correct code for clinical scales is 35′789021–64; and for the validity scales, 5:7:20.

Several MMPI atlases are now in use (Hathaway and Meehl, 1951a; Hathaway and Monachesi, 1961; Marks and Seeman, 1963), and all of these notate profiles according to the Hathaway, or Welsh's (1948) modification of the Hathaway, coding system. These atlases are specifically compiled to provide descriptive information about coded profiles, and the first and still the most popular of these is: *An Atlas for the Clinical use of the MMPI* (Hathaway and Meehl, 1951a). This atlas provides short case histories of 968 patients, arranged according to similarity of profile pattern. Other such atlases deal with data from college counseling centers, juveniles, and hospital patients. The most thorough and by far the most comprehensive summary treatment of interpretive procedures on MMPI profiles can be found in Dahlstrom and Welsh's *An MMPI Handbook* (1960).

MMPI INTERPRETATION

Only some examples can be given here of interpretations associated with major configural profile patterns. Perhaps the most talked about profile pattern among normal and hospital populations is one called "neurotic triad." This profile consists of elevations of scales 1 and 3 (Hs and Hy), or 3 and 1, higher than that of Scale 2 (D). This configuration, which is depicted in Figure 8–3, is sometimes also called the "conversion V" code because of the V-shaped profile that is produced by such a combination of elevations, and because it is often found among persons diagnosed "conversion hysterics." In Black's study (1953), mentioned earlier in this chapter, in which college women rated their peers, persons with MMPI profiles with scales 1 and 3 elevated tended to earn the following descriptive adjectives: selfish, dependent, indecisive; and these women were described as having many somatic complaints. Within psychiatric hospital settings, the same profile patterns often present problems characterized by the presence of somatic complaints and pains. Hathaway and Meehl (1952) report that conversion hysteria is the most frequent diagnosis associated with this pattern.

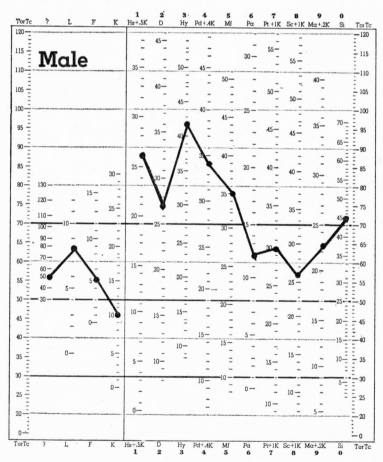

FIGURE 8-3.   Sample MMPI profile illustrating the "conversion V."

A closely related designation of patterns and relationships among the psychotic scales, in which scales 6, 7, 8, and 9 play a role, has been called the "paranoid valley" (Dahlstrom and Welsh, 1960). Figure 8–4 illustrates this pattern. The "valley" is formed by the elevations on scales 6 and 8, with scales 7 and 9 relatively lower. Either scale 6 or 8 may be the high-point score in this pattern. Of course, the rest of the profile must be taken into consideration also, but the paranoid valley pattern shown in Figure 8–4 is often found among paranoid schizophrenic patients.

Among themselves, experienced MMPI users have gotten into the habit of talking about profiles in terms of their code types. Rather than trying to remember the 10, 12, or sometimes even 15 digits

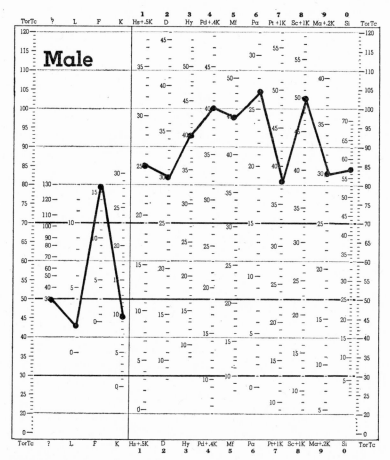

FIGURE 8–4.   Sample MMPI profile illustrating the "paranoid valley."

representing a profile, clinicians tend to talk about these in two-digit terms. Thus they talk about 85's or 26's, and these code types represent abbreviated versions of significant personality variables. For example, one of the most common two-digit high-point codes is 94 (a peak on Ma and a secondary peak on Pd), which is frequently found among normal males. Some other well-known code

TABLE 8–2

Descriptions of Some Typical MMPI Code Types

Code Types	Descriptions
12 and 21	Pain, depression, irritability, shyness, and seclusiveness.
23 and 32	Depression, weakness, apathy, agitation, and tenseness.
27 and 72	Depression, tenseness, anxiety, and undue sensitivity.
28 and 82	Depression, anxiety, agitation, and hysterical tendencies.
31 and 13	Pain, eating problems, sociable, and extraverted.
64 and 46	Depression, irritability, and suspiciousness.
68 and 86	Paranoid delusions, withdrawal, and apathy.
78 and 87	Depression, introversion, irritability, and tendency to worry.
49 and 94	Overactive, violent, talkative, and extroverted.

SOURCE: Hathaway and Meehl, 1951b.

types are presented in Table 8–2, and are notated in terms of their two-digit primary elevations.

EVALUATION OF THE MMPI

As mentioned at the outset of this chapter, the MMPI has had an impressive impact on personality measurement, but its acceptance, although widespread, has not always been uncritical. Such criticism as noted before has come largely from the popular press. However, informed criticism of this test is not uncommon; and in the evaluation which follows, some of the highlights of both the positive and negative comments about it are reviewed.

In its favor, much of the MMPI's popularity can be explained by its widespread use and the large number of situations in which it has been found to be valid. The MMPI, to mention only a few instances of what seems to be an infinitely large list of uses, has been found valid as a test to aid in screening and selection of emotional and adjustmental problems in the following settings: high school (Hathaway and Monachesi, 1951, 1952, 1953, 1957); college (Kleinmuntz, 1960b, 1963b, 1963c; Sloan and Pierce-Jones, 1958); military (Green, 1955); medical (Meehl and Dahlstrom, 1960); and industrial (Drasgow and Barnett, 1957).

Furthermore, the MMPI has been used successfully to appraise the severity of symptoms among psychiatric patients (Feldman, 1958); to assess their contact with reality (Meehl, 1946; Taulbee and Sisson, 1957); to measure the extent of patients' overt anxiety —i.e., the extent to which they openly manifest tension, nervousness, insecurity, or fears (Welsh, 1952; Taylor, 1953); and to assess ego strength or the degree to which patients might benefit from treatment (Barron, 1953). Cross-validation studies (repeating validity studies by using new samples of subjects), and evidence for the validity of specific individual MMPI scales for many of these uses, have often and admittedly fallen short of the test authors' expectations (Hathaway and McKinley, 1943). Their willingness to publicize their test's inadequacies, however, and hence their recognition of the need for continual work with this instrument, has in no small measure contributed to the test's current success.

On the debit side, the MMPI has been strongly criticized for the unreliability of some of its scales (Anastasi, 1961). The reliability of the individual scales, computed on the basis of test-retest procedures, ranges from the .50's to the low .90's. Retests lower than these have also been reported in a study with college students where intervals between tests were as short as one week. The mean of these reliabilities was only .61 (Gilliland and Colgin, 1951).

The MMPI test authors, when discussing some of the low reliabilities obtained with the clinical scales, have tended to suggest that traditional psychometric criteria of reliability cannot be applied to personality tests (McKinley and Hathaway, 1944). They point out that many traits of personality are highly variable, and that test-retest data on MMPI scales are more a measure of trait variance than of the test's reliability. Such trait variance is especially to be expected among psychiatric patients, where exacerbations and remissions of symptoms are frequent. This is probably true for scales affected by temporary fluctuations. However, split-half reliabilities, which are not subject to such trait fluctuations, have also been exceedingly low. Several studies among psychiatric groups have reported coefficients within the range of .11 (Welsh, 1952) to .96 (Winfield, 1952). In one study with normal college students, a coefficient as low as −.05 (Pa scale) has been reported (Gilliland and Colgin, 1951). Such low reliabilities cannot be so easily explained away. They do suggest that chance fluctuations influence scale scores.

The effectiveness of any profile interpretation is weakened if the separate scales are subject to chance fluctuations. When individual scales are unreliable, many of the profile patterns are unstable. It is important therefore, in future research with the MMPI, to select new items that may replace some of those which contribute to the low reliabilities. The three scales that have consistently yielded low reliability coefficients in a number of studies have been Hy, Pa, and Ma (see Table 2, Appendix K, p. 474, in Dahlstrom and Welsh, 1960); studies aimed at their reconstruction may well be worthwhile.

Another argument often heard—one not favorable to the MMPI—is that its construction was based on small numbers of subjects (Sarason, 1966). More generally, this argument holds that the procedure used was inadequate in terms both of the number and the kind of subjects used. For example, in the derivation of the depression scale (Scale 2), the criterion group consisted of 50 depressed patients who represented only a small and unusual segment of depressed patients generally (they were in the depressed phase of manic-depressive psychosis).[7]

In the first place, it is often argued, a larger group of patients, and a sample more representative of hospitalized depressed persons, should have been selected. Secondly, as these critics have correctly noted, diagnostic labeling tends to be dependent as much on semantics as on the behavior of the patients themselves. There is variability from one hospital to another, from one clinic to the next, and even among psychologists and psychiatrists, in the way diagnoses are made. A number of factors contribute to this, not the least of which are the differing theoretical orientations among clinicians. And by what criteria were the so-called "normal" comparison groups normal? Mainly by virtue of the fact that they were not hospitalized as psychiatric patients. The result of these inadequacies is that the scales which were based on these procedures are as

---

[7] The criterion clinical groups in the construction of scales 5, 8, and 9 were even smaller, consisting of 13, 20, and 24 persons respectively.

questionable as the procedures themselves. Many critics attribute the instability (temporal unreliability) of numerous MMPI scales to these deficient construction methods.

The greatest limitation of the MMPI, as critics have repeatedly indicated (Adcock, 1965; Lingoes, 1965), is its lack of sensitivity in discriminating within abnormal or normal groups themselves. Unquestionably, the MMPI's chief claim to prominence and uniqueness as a personality measuring instrument has always been, and still is, its power to discriminate between those persons coming from normal and those from abnormal populations. Thus it is valuable for making broad nosological distinctions, as Meehl and Dahlstrom (1960) have demonstrated, between neurotics and psychotics; but it is weak in drawing finer distinctions within any one of these groups.

But if the MMPI is not accepted unconditionally as the method of choice for personality measurement, tangible gains are still to be realized as a result of its existence. Sarason (1966, p. 158) has stated this matter well:

> The evaluation of the MMPI, or of any other test or procedure, should be based as much on what lessons have been learned from it as on how useful it has proven to be. . . . Were a new MMPI to be developed today this sort of criticism would be of value in shaping a better inventory, one of greater discriminatory validity than the present one.

To this need only be added, that self-report inventories could hardly have arrived at their present high level of sophistication if it had not been for the MMPI's appearance at the time it did. Prior approaches to inventory construction were naïve and uninspiring; and subsequent approaches have borrowed generously and extensively the format of the MMPI.

THREE SELF-REPORT INVENTORIES DERIVED FROM THE MMPI

California Psychological Inventory

A test which was devised by criterion keying and which in fact drew about half its items from the MMPI is Professor Harrison Gough's (1956 to 1960) California Psychological Inventory (CPI). Although the MMPI has been found useful by some testers with normal groups, the CPI was developed specifically for that population. The CPI provides a profile (see Figure 8–5) of 18 scales, of

238   Personality Measurement: An Introduction

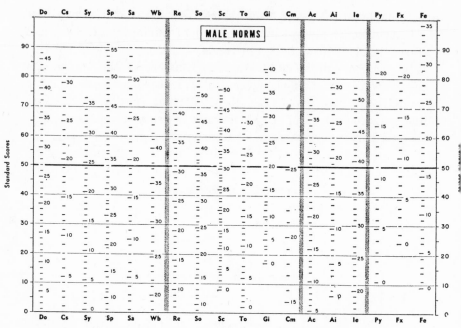

FIGURE 8–5. Profile sheet of the California Psychological Inventory. The male norms are displayed in this particular illustration. The CPI scales, from left to right, are dominance, capacity for status, sociability, social presence, self-acceptance, sense of well-being, responsibility, socialization, self-control, tolerance, good impression, communality, achievement via conformance, achievement via independence, intellectual efficiency, psychological mindedness, flexibility, and femininity. (Reproduced by special permission from The California Psychological Inventory by Harrison G. Gough. Copyright, 1956. Published by Consulting Psychologists Press, Inc.)

which 3 are validity scales. The other 15 scales include scores on such dimensions as dominance, socialization, tolerance, achievement via conformance, achievement via independence, intellectual efficiency, sense of well-being, self-control, and flexibility.

The CPI is composed of more than 480 true-false items which were selected and validated on the basis of such criteria as social class membership, course grades, participation in extracurricular activities, ratings for various traits, and upon college entrance groups with regard to each trait. Examples of some of these items are presented in Table 8–3.

In many respects the CPI is similar to the MMPI. The procedures for its administration, scoring, and profiling are like those of its parent test. However, the method of constructing its scales represents a considerable improvement over the MMPI. Many of these methodological advances result from lessons learned with the MMPI. Professor Gough, the test author, was among the earliest contributors to MMPI research, and he is intimately familiar with many of the earlier test's shortcomings. Thus in keying the various CPI scales, he used a much larger sample (6,000 males and 7,000 females) than Hathaway and McKinley. Moreover, Gough paid special attention to equating his samples on such important variables as age, social status, and geographical regions. His greatest

TABLE 8-3

Items from the California Psychological Inventory

Alternatives		Item
True	False	I enjoy social gatherings just to be with people.
True	False	I gossip a little at times.
True	False	I like poetry.
True	False	People often expect too much of me.
True	False	My home life was always happy.
True	False	Only a fool would ever vote to increase his own taxes.
True	False	I love to go to dances.
True	False	Sometimes I feel that I am about to go to pieces.
True	False	I have never deliberately told a lie.
True	False	My parents never really understood me.

SOURCE: Gough, 1956.

improvement consisted of using the peer nomination techniques for selecting and categorizing criterion subjects, rather than employing experts or psychiatrists. Peer nomination procedures, as the reader may recall from the earlier discussion, yield more reliable criterion categorizations than psychiatric labeling.

The CPI is already well on its way to becoming one of the best, if not the best, personality measuring instrument of its kind. It is designed, like the MMPI, on the principle that questionnaire items which correlate with socially significant criteria are important. Each scale consists of items that discriminate between members of groups on such nonpsychiatric variables as leadership, high and low introductory grades, and social class membership. Presumably there is some psychological similarity among persons within each of these criterion groups that accounts for their endorsement of similar items; and there seems to be sufficient dissimilarity between members of different groups to account for item discrimination between them.

The technical development of the CPI has been described as of the highest order (Cronbach, 1959). The reliabilities, which were carefully determined by the retest method, are generally high, in the upper .80's and lower .90's. The validity of each scale is adequate and was determined by comparing group scores of persons between whom the scale was designed to discriminate. The quality of the normative data, which as indicated was based on large samples, rounds out an impressive accomplishment in personality testing among normal people.

Although most test critics agree on the CPI's technical excellence, not all agree on its usefulness. The most severe critic has been R. L. Thorndike (1959). He maintains that the CPI's 18 dimensions provide a redundant, inefficient, and confused picture of a person. Thorndike points out that of the 18 scales, only 4 fail to correlate at least .50 with some other scale. Such intercorrelations, because they reflect the lack of independence between scales, are not desirable in a test designed for describing personality clearly and parsimoniously.

However, the most impressive feature of the CPI has been its adopters' and its publisher's relentless efforts at collecting pertinent research data and, as was true of the MMPI's authors, its developer's responsiveness to criticism. Between its inception and the publication of Buros' *Fifth Mental Measurements Yearbook* (1959), 33 studies were reported in the literature. The current *Yearbook* (1965) lists a total of 144 research reports, many of which reflect a readiness to repair rather than refute the test's shortcomings. By these criteria alone, one may conclude that the CPI's impact on personality research is impressive.

Minnesota Counseling Inventory

A second test derived from the MMPI is the MCI or Minnesota Counseling Inventory (Berdie and Layton, 1953 to 1957). Its use was intended to be at the high school level. This test consists of 355 true-false items, many of which are similar to those of the MMPI; and the categories on which it yields scores are: social relationship, emotional stability, conformity, adjustment to reality, mood, and leadership.

The norms are based on more than 20,000 high school students in 10 states. Two of its validity scales are similar to those of the

MMPI; and generally, there is a great deal of similarity between the MMPI scales and those of the MCI. For example, the category "conformity," both in terms of item content and number of items, is almost identical to the MMPI Pt scale. The MCI labels are psychiatrically less connotative than the scales of the MMPI, and this is appropriate and in its favor.

In comparison with the CPI, this test has stimulated little research since its inception in 1953 (10 papers), and has not had much impact on personality measurement. In some part this may be due to the fact that the test was intended for use among high school counselors, who have less time for research with personality tests and tend to be more interested in the applicability of tests for practical uses than in research. The test's technical excellence is adequate by most standards, but data on its validity or usefulness in counseling settings are sorely lacking.

Manifest Anxiety Scale

The third test derived from the MMPI was Professor Janet Taylor's (1953) Manifest Anxiety Scale (MAS). Actually, this test was not intended as a clinical instrument; but, surprisingly, it was adopted by many clinicians as an economical measure of anxiety. Taylor's main interest in developing the scale was as a research instrument to test a number of learning-theory implications about the "anxiety" construct.

The MAS consists of 225 items, of which 50 contribute to an anxiety dimension. The remainder of the items are not relevant, but are included as fillers or buffers to disguise the intent of the scale. In the construction of the MAS, a group of five clinicians selected items from the MMPI which corresponded to a textbook description of a chronic anxiety disorder (Cameron, 1947). Typical items are shown in Table 8–4.

While this scale was developed as an instrument for selecting subjects in conditioning and learning experiments, it became apparent that the MAS correlated with many other measures of anxiety and with clinical ratings of this dimension (see Franks, 1956; Korchin and Heath, 1961; Mandler et al., 1961).

Its use in conditioning experiments consisted mainly of demonstrations that high-scoring and low-scoring subjects (i.e., of high and low anxiety) performed differently in simple conditioning situations. Taylor's original study, comparing high- and low-anxiety subjects in conditioning experiments, postulated that high anxiety was comparable to a high drive state; and accordingly, she demonstrated that greater anxiety was related to greater ease and strength of conditioning (Taylor, 1951).

The concurrent validity of the MAS was investigated by correlating its scores with clinicians' ratings of anxiety of psychiatric patients (Lauterbach, 1958). A very substantial inverse correlation coefficient of −.67 between MAS and the MMPI K scale was obtained. This suggests that a K correction used with the MAS may enhance the scale's hit rate.

TABLE 8–4

Ten Items from Taylor's Manifest Anxiety Scale

I have very few headaches (FALSE).
I practically never blush (FALSE).
I have nightmares every few nights (TRUE).
I sweat very easily even on cool days (TRUE).
I feel hungry almost all the time (TRUE).
I have a great deal of stomach trouble (TRUE).
I am easily embarrassed (TRUE).
I am usually calm and not easily upset (FALSE).
I cry easily (TRUE).
I am happy most of the time (FALSE).

SOURCE: Taylor, 1953.

The major argument against the use of any single scale—MAS or any other self-report scale—for clinical prediction is that retest reliability coefficients and validity findings are not sufficiently high to warrant interpretation. It was recognition of this fact, as mentioned earlier, that led to the general shift in emphasis from MMPI interpretations based on single scales to a consideration of total profile patterns. All that is essential now is acknowledgement of this fact by clinicians.

SOME PROBLEMS OF SELF-REPORT INVENTORIES

In this chapter and in the preceding one, the discussion of self-report inventories has been critical only insofar as specific tests did not qualify as adequate psychological measuring instruments. The implication may have been imparted that future research designed to improve these tests need only aspire to obtain, for example, larger normative samples, more reliable scales, or increased evidence of these tests' validity in a variety of situations. Such an implication, however, would be misleading. There are some basic issues which concern all inventories of this type.

This method of personality testing—asking a respondent to answer questions about his behavior, habits, attitudes, or feelings in life situations—carries with it some problems that over the years have been the concern of persons working with these tests. Experience with self-report tests—especially with the MMPI—indicates that there are a number of factors that contribute to test score distortions. These factors, all of which must be taken into account in interpreting test responses, are discussed here.

Effects of Test Stimulus Properties on Responses

Items on self-report questionnaires are presumed to be more structured[8] than such ambiguous stimuli as abstract drawings or inkblots. Therefore a common misconception among testers is that these items convey similar meanings to many persons, and consequently are less subject to misinterpretation. Consider, however, the MMPI item, "I seldom worry about my health." Is this item unambiguous? No. Its meaning is far from clear. For example, does it refer to physical or mental health? And what do "seldom" and "worry" mean? The respondent may reflect upon his associates' health and worries, and conclude that the frequency of his concern (or worry) by comparison, is negligible (or considerable). Or he may compare the extent of his concern during the most recent period with a more distant time and may respond accordingly. Thus, not only are some of the words of the item open to varied interpretations, but the entire statement is ambiguous.

Similar language difficulties are encountered by the respondent who comes across an MMPI item such as "My father was a good man." Does this mean, he may wonder, that this statement can only be answered by persons whose fathers are deceased? Or perhaps the item is actually intended to convey the idea that the respondent's father was a good man when he was a child, but now that he is an adult he realizes that his father is not such a good man. Likewise,

---

[8] Because the items on self-report inventories are less ambiguous than test stimuli on projective techniques (with their inkblots or pictures), and because of the fixed alternative response categories of inventories, the latter are often called "structured tests."

on the *Personality Inventory* developed by Bernreuter (1931 to 1938) there is the item "Do you lack self-confidence?" Most people would like to answer "sometimes" or "under certain circumstances," but they must choose between "yes," "no," and "?." The difficulty here is twofold. First, the test constructor may have a "typical" situation in mind, but in the wording of the item he did not convey that meaning. The result is that the respondent's frame of reference may be different from the one which was the item's original intent. Allport and Allport (1928), in an early study using attitude scales, got around this difficulty by phrasing items so that they refer to actual or concrete situations in which respondents find themselves. For example, the Bernreuter item could read, "Do you lack self-confidence when you deal with your employer about a job matter?" or "Do you lack self-confidence when purchasing large commodities?"

The second difficulty with this item lies in the constraints provided by the answer sheet categories. The format of the fixed response alternatives ("yes," "no," or "maybe") does not allow for a description of the respondent's frame of reference. Moreover, as noted in the discussion on poll-type interviewing (Chapter 6) the limited choices offered may force the respondent to endorse items which are not true or descriptive of him. Many examinees actually elaborate their "yes" or "no" answers with lengthy explanations scrawled in the test booklet or on scrap paper. Many more refrain from filling the margins of test booklets in this way but express the desire to do so after they have completed the test.

Effects of Contextual Conditions on Responses

Many other features of the test situation besides the questionnaire items influence the way persons respond to tests. The ideal situation, of course, from the point of view of the tester, is to create a test situation in which the item is the main focus of the respondent's attention. However, this ideal is rarely encountered in actual practice. There are a number of contextual conditions—conditions that are an unavoidable part of the test setting—that are not entirely under the control of the tester or of the test constructor. Whereas the test stimulus can be controlled to the point where it is identical for all respondents, the context in which the test is taken cannot be thus controlled.

A number of external factors like lighting, timing, and test instructions can be standardized, but the ways in which individuals interpret the testing context are not subject to standardization. The person, for instance, who is hauled into juvenile court for stealing automobile hub caps probably responds differently under those conditions than to a set of identical items that may have been administered to him upon admission to high school. Or, to take another example, persons taking the MMPI as a condition of employment will perceive the test differently than those who volunteered to take the test as experimental subjects in a college research project. Therefore, there are different interpretations by the same person of the identical items under varying test conditions, and different interpretations by separate individuals under different conditions. The important thing to note about these differences is that they may be due to a complex interaction of factors within the context of testing, all of which may be unrelated to measurable personality dimensions.

There is the consideration also of the factors within any test setting that serve to differentiate it from many other settings. For example, it may reasonably be expected that from one setting to the next the physical and social environments will vary. Or the examiners themselves might be different, and therefore the manner of giving test instructions will vary. One examiner's manner might be courteous and thus encourage, perhaps unwittingly, questions from respondents; another tester might be brusque and thereby discourage any interchange between himself and examinees. Again, it is important to note that these conditions may be unrelated to personality. However, they do exert an important influence on test scores; and these considerations, taken together, emphasize the importance of knowing how a person takes a test as well as what test he took.

Effects of Self-Knowledge on Responses

A naïve view of self-report inventories is that respondents know about their own motives, or past and present behavior, because they are in a uniquely advantageous position to answer questions about themselves. However, a person is often unable to characterize himself. On theoretical grounds alone, one might predict that an individual's degree of self-knowledge is inversely related to the extent of his personality disturbance. That is to say, the more serious one's personality disorder, the less advantageous is his position to report accurately about himself. As Sigmund Freud made us aware, a large part of our actions and motivations is inaccessible to us (i.e., is unconscious). And by definition, these inaccessible aspects distort a person's views about himself, his personality, and his characteristic modes of behavior. The man with aggressive, hostile impulses frequently sees himself as a gentle and kind philanthropist; and the attractive woman with strong dependent needs may view herself as a homely and independent individualist.

Not all personality test items demand self-knowledge. For example, the following items require little insight: "I have diarrhea once a month or more," "I go to church almost every week," and "I like mechanics magazines." These statements seem to deal with facts easily observable about oneself. However, only the most naïve view of self-reporting on inventories would maintain that persons, in answering these items, tell the truth about themselves; or that they can be motivated (or trapped) into telling the truth about themselves. Experience with these tests suggested early in their history that certain test taking attitudes tend also to exert an important influence on test responding.

Effects of Test-Taking Attitudes on Responses

Even if items were constructed so carefully and unambiguously as not to invite misinterpretation, and in such a manner that they assessed only observable and factual aspects of a person's life, there still would remain the problem of falsification or faking of answers. The motivations underlying faking are well known and extensively documented (Gehman, 1957; Noll, 1951; Wesman, 1952; Wiggins, 1966).

A respondent may fake in a "good" direction because he would like to be released from (or not admitted to) a psychiatric hospital, or he may do so because he would like to convince his present or potential employer that he is the right man for the job (or that he is the right man for the job he has done well for the past 15 years!). Or he may fake "bad" because he wants to present himself in an unfavorable light. Among psychologists in military circles, stories abound of persons who, in order to obtain medical discharges from the Armed Forces, have claimed that they "faked" personality tests. More often than not, these respondents' convincing performances of faking required minimum effort on their parts because, as their acquaintances usually accede, no test was necessary to ascertain their personality disorders.

Some persons answer test items in a direction significant for abnormality because they would like to gain admission to a psychiatric hospital. Others have been known to "fake bad" because they would like to win the attention and sympathy of members of their family or even the tester. Hathaway's "Hello-Goodby" effect, in which the respondent admits to the most bizarre types of items, reflects a strategy some persons use to call the clinic's attention to their problem (Hathaway, 1957).

Not all faking is as willful and intentional as the preceding instances seem to indicate. Hathaway's post-therapy "Thanks Doc, I feel fine" type of response involves a different form of faking. The patient, for example, who had spent considerable time with a psychologist during his stay in a clinic or hospital displays his gratitude toward his therapist by assuring him that all his symptoms, even his minutest ones, have been cured by the doctor. Thus he tends to deny all symptoms on the post-therapy inventory. This form of faking is usually unconscious in the sense that the patient is not aware of his motivations to "fudge" the test.

Numerous other studies indicate that personality test scores can be modified, sometimes radically, when subjects are instructed to do so (Bird, 1948; Cofer *et al.*, 1949; Gough, 1947, 1950). In one of these (Bird, 1948), the MMPI was administered to a college class in abnormal psychology, first under normal conditions, and then with instructions to simulate various specific diagnostic syndromes. Following the completion of their course, these students again were requested to simulate abnormal syndromes. They were more successful in their second attempt at faking, and their improvement was reflected in lower validity scale scores (e.g., lower scores on F and K). In other words, the course in abnormal psychology provided them with a sufficient amount of information about psychiatric symptoms to allow them to assume the abnormal roles more expertly.

It was recognition of the fact that most self-report inventories fail to take into account unconscious role playing and self-deception that led Meehl and Hathaway (1946) to devise the K scale as a suppressor or correction variable for this form of dissimulation. The MMPI K scale was developed so that the conscious and unconscious tendencies of subjects to present a certain picture of themselves could be assessed and consequently neutralized. Moreover, its purpose was to increase the discrimination power of the test so that it differentiated between hundreds of normal persons, and persons hospitalized for psychiatric reasons, all of whom gave MMPI profiles in the borderline region. Profiles within this range are not distinguishable because both the normal and patient populations score at less than the critical psychopathological cutoff point (less than a T-score of 70). The chief source of error turned out to be a generalized tendency to describe oneself in socially desirable terms at one extreme, contrasted with a generalized self-criticism at the other extreme. Those MMPI scales that were most saturated with these generalized test taking tendencies, called the K factor by Meehl and Hathaway, were in turn corrected for those tendencies.

In one study designed to test the efficacy of MMPI's L, F, and K scales in detecting faking, the inventory was administered to three groups of college students (Cofer *et al.*, 1949). One group of subjects were given the test with the standard instructions on the first occasion, and then on the second testing were instructed to present themselves in an unfavorable light. A second group took the test with standard instructions and then were told to give the best possible impression of themselves. The third group took the test twice under normal conditions. For the "fake bad" group the F scale was best at identifying their intent. The "fake good" records were correctly classified by a combination of the scales K and L (74 percent of the faked profiles were identified in this way). Thus it was demonstrated that the K factor, in combination with the older L scale, can be applied successfully to identify certain forms of test dissembling.

Other forms of faking—first noted by Lorge (1937) and later reported by Cronbach (1946, 1950)—have been identified and are now called *response style*. This phenomenon, sometimes also called *response set*, is illustrated when individuals manifest a more or less consistent tendency to make a particular kind of response to a test. Fortunately, these response styles are common to many respondents and therefore are measurable.

Lorge (1937) noted that the use of fixed response categories such as "true," "false," "yes," "agree," and "like" makes self-ratings particularly vulnerable to response style biases. He counted how often persons answered "like" to Strong's Vocational Interest Blank items, and he observed that this response was subject to different interpretations by various respondents. Some persons use the word "like" for any activity that is not absolutely abhorrent to them, whereas others reserve the category only for exceptionally attractive activities.

Since the time of Lorge's observations, various response styles have been differentiated instead of being combined as one phenomenon. There is considerable controversy in personality testing at the present time about whether these response styles indeed are separate phenomena, and there is disagreement about their relative importance or contribution to test score distortion. Insofar as possible they are distinguished here, one from the other, in accordance with current thinking in psychology. Among these response styles are the tendency to endorse or agree with test items, or acquiescence; the tendency to endorse socially acceptable items, or social desirability; and the tendency to be different and take an extreme position on personality test items, or deviation.

Acquiescence. The tendency to accept an item or agree with it regardless of what it says has been called acquiescence. This tendency, more recently labeled with the catchy terms, "yeasaying" and "naysaying" (Couch and Keniston, 1960), was first identified by Lentz (1938) as "the tendency to agree rather than disagree . . . to propositions in general" (cited in Block, 1965, p. 6). According to Lentz, "acquiescence may be a very distorting factor in the measurement of various other continua which call for positive and negative reactions to propositions. . . ." It was in a series of papers by Cronbach (1941, 1942, 1946, 1950) that the importance of the acquiescent response bias for personality testing was emphasized.

The consequences of uncritical acceptance of item content, in effect, is to make it impossible to interpret self-reports as if their content were true (Block, 1965; Jackson and Messick, 1958, 1961). On the MMPI, for example, the effect of acquiescence on the content of items can be demonstrated by considering the following statement: "I like to study and read about things that I am working at." The statement is worded in a way that may make it difficult to ascertain whether persons who endorse it are "yea-saying" (acquiescent response style), or whether it reflects their feelings about the content of the item as descriptive of them. Moreover, the statement encourages lying. Who, in a society that esteems reading and scholarliness, would want to "nay-say" such an item? It is a loaded item that almost beckons endorsement or acquiescence from respondents. Such an item might perhaps best serve its measurement purpose if it were reworded.

Another possible reason for acquiescent responding is attributed to imbalance of a test's scoring key. For example, if the items are keyed predominantly "true" or predominantly "false," the result may be one-sided responding because the subject has become accustomed to acquiescing with (or to denying) all items. A simple way of avoiding this effect of response style is to construct a balanced scoring key in which half the items are tallied for the answer "true" and half for the answer "false" (Block, 1965; Couch and Keniston, 1960).

As a result of the confounding effects of the acquiescent response style, some psychologists (Jackson and Messick, 1958, 1961) have raised doubts about the MMPI's item format as the method of choice for assessing psychopathology. But the data, pro and con, that respondents react to the item format rather than its content are only beginning to be collected (Block, 1965; Rorer, 1963, 1965).

Social Desirability (SD). This tendency was first noted by Edwards (1953). As indicated in the previous discussion of the relation of this variable to the development of forced choice inventories (see Chapter 7), Edwards demonstrated that the endorsement of an item is more probable when that item is judged socially desirable. He found that the awareness of persons in our society of a "right" way of behaving and feeling is reflected in their tendency to give answers on personality inventories that are "good" and "wholesome." As a matter of fact, personality tests are said to reflect this tendency more than they reflect actual emotional characteristics.

According to the SD interpretation of test answers, a respondent presents himself in a favorable light by putting up a facade on an item such as "In school I was sometimes sent to the principal for cutting up." One response ("false") is socially desirable and the alternative is not. The great majority of persons will select the more desirable answer in order to "put up a good front." It is important to note that Edwards does not assert that deliberate lying is involved when respondents answer in a socially acceptable way (Edwards, 1957; Edwards *et al.*, 1962). He acknowledges that such deliberate faking is possible—and that a respondent's set to do so will enhance the social desirability response tendency—but he maintains that SD is a form of unconscious faking. The distinction between deliberate and unintentional distortion of test responding is important because in the former instance, the respondent is aware of assuming a facade, and therefore he recognizes it as ungenuine or sham. In unconscious dissimulation, the person is not aware of this tendency, and therefore it may be interpretable as an expression of his personality. An extreme position about the extent of the social desirability factor in the MMPI holds that once SD is extracted—that is, once the effect of social desirability is controlled in the MMPI—then not much beyond error variance will be found in the test responses (Edwards, 1959; Edwards and Walker, 1961; cited in Block, 1965).

A direct test of the notion that society's precepts and stereotypes affect test taking attitudes was made by Rosen (1956). He administered the MMPI to 200 college students under three conditions: (1) usual manner (self-appraisal); (2) instructions to endorse items as "true" if they personally considered the items desirable (personal desirability); and (3) instructions to endorse them as "true" if it was thought that society would consider it a desirable characteristic (social desirability). The results indicated that the social desirability of items clearly influenced personal choices, and that the probability of an item's endorsement is increased as a consequence of its desirability.

Some investigators (Crowne and Marlowe, 1964) have offered an interesting motivational conceptualization of social desirability. According to this view, respondents' tendencies to select socially desirable answers on self-report tests reflect their needs for self-protection, avoidance of criticism, and their strong concern to maintain a socially and personally acceptable image of themselves. Furthermore, these needs tend also to display themselves in a variety of contexts that are less conspicuous than the self-evaluation assignments of inventories. Individuals who answer items in a socially desirable way tend to be more conforming, cautious, and persuasible, and their behavior is less deviant than persons who depict themselves less favorably (Barthel and Crowne, 1962; Barthel, 1963; Conn and Crowne, 1964); and in their social interchange, these persons tend to emit more smiles than low-scoring respondents (Rosenfeld, 1966). Apparently, individuals who seek approval, and who are ingratiating, try to purchase such approval by conformity and with their smiles.

Psychologists agree that one way to minimize the contribution of the SD factor to test distortion is through the use of forced choice item arrangements (see Chapter 7). If the alternative choices are equally socially desirable (or undesirable) for the group under consideration, this form of unconscious faking can be attenuated. Typically, psychologists attempt to get around this type of faking by introducing the self-report inventory to the respondent with some such imploring and reassuring statement as, "We want your honest opinion; there are no right or wrong answers"; but it has been noted (Dahlstrom, 1962) that the examinee's complete cooperation is dependent on many more subtle factors than the tester's technique of persuasion.

Deviation. Still another response style studied extensively is deviation (Berg, 1957, 1959, 1961). This is the tendency to answer personality test items in an unusual or uncommon direction. The noting of this response style gave rise to Berg's "deviation hypothesis," which holds that the tendency to give atypical responses to items is associated with atypical or deviant behavior in other areas, and is related to the respondent's personality makeup. This point of view, which can be considered clinical in that it treats response deviation on tests as a valuable indicator of personality deviation, is radically different from the point of view of more psychometrically inclined psychologists (Jackson and Messick, 1962; Rorer, 1963, 1965; Wiggins, 1962) who consider deviation, along with acquiescence and social desirability, as sources of error in testing that need to be identified, and then eliminated or corrected.

According to the deviation hypothesis, the respondent's answers are not related to item content. As a matter of fact, Berg's (1961, p. 336) position has been that item content is unimportant and he has expressed this emphatically in the following way:

This is not saying . . . that any item is as good as any other for a particular purpose. Such an assertion would be absurd. But it is saying that for a given verbal item, for example, one would find a design or sound that would do as well. At least, all the evidence we have thus far garnered forces us to that conclusion.

The most intriguing idea expressed in this passage is that "contentless" or nonverbal tests will yield responses that might discriminate criterion groups. This is the extreme of the empirical approach and has been aptly described as "militantly atheoretical" (Norman, 1963).

And indeed, a series of studies have indicated that different groups show distinctive patterns of responding on nonverbal tests. The most widely cited example in support of Berg's position about the unimportance of item content comes from a study by Barnes (1955). Using the PRT or *Perceptual Reaction Test* (Berg *et al.*, 1949), which is composed of 60 geometrical drawings that are rated "like much," "like slightly," "dislike slightly," or "dislike much," Barnes has shown that different groups show distinctive patterns of responding on the test. With five scales, which he labeled Delta, Psy, Sigma, Chi, and Psi-chi, he demonstrated that he could distinguish the responses of patients from normals, psychotics from normals, character disorders from normals, and the responses of psychotics from character disorders, respectively. Subsequent investigations have largely failed to replicate Barnes' results (Harris, 1958; Norman, 1963), but the original study was so well designed in terms of the variables controlled and the sampling techniques used that further explorations along these paths are definitely in order.

At this point, the weary reader may well ask, "But what's the difference whether or not acquiescence, social desirability, or deviation influences test responding?" The difference is simply this: If scores on tests such as the MMPI, CPI, or EPPS are affected by the format of the item (the way it is written) rather than by its content, then the psychological meaning on these tests is overshadowed by factors possibly unrelated to the personality dimensions under investigation. Arguments on one side of the controversy contend that test taking attitudes play a dominant role in personality inventories, and arguments on the other side contend that these attitudes or response tendencies are not significant. The controversy is far from settled, and because of its importance for personality test interpretation it will probably continue to stimulate research for some time to come. Undoubtedly, a consequence of this research will be realized in the form of better self-report inventories.

SUMMARY

There are four major methods of personality test construction: (1) content validation, (2) criterion keying, (3) factor analysis, and (4) forced choice methods. The first of these involves item selection on an a priori basis, and item inclusion is determined by judgments about probable relevance to particular personality dimensions or psychiatric syndromes. Unless this method of inventory construction is accompanied by careful empirical validation procedures, it is the least satisfactory way to construct a personality test. It does serve to assure the "face validity" of an inventory because it samples from a universe of signs and symptoms, but tests constructed in this manner lack subtlety and tend not to be useful measures of personality dimensions.

A method that makes few theoretical assumptions is criterion keying. This is an empirical validation procedure. One self-report inventory that has been constructed by this method and has been most thoroughly researched is the Minnesota Multiphasic Personality Inventory. The scoring keys for this inventory were developed for the purpose of psychiatric classification, and accordingly, the MMPI profile is composed of 10 clinical scales which cover most of the neurotic and psychotic disorders. In addition, there are four validity scales to aid in the detection of test distortion. At least 200 scales have been developed for various other test situations and for personality research purposes, but these are not commonly used by the majority of psychologists.

Three self-report tests—the California Psychological Inventory, the Minnesota Counseling Inventory, and the Taylor Manifest Anxiety Scale—have been derived from the MMPI and are intended mainly for use with normal groups and for personality research purposes. Among these, the CPI has had the greatest impact on personality measurement. As with the MMPI, its author and his associates have made thorough and self-critical efforts for its improvement. The MCI has not stimulated much research, and evidence regarding its usefulness is inadequate. Taylor's MAS was not intended for use in clinical settings—although some clinicians use it, sometimes inappropriately, as an abbreviated test of anxiety—but rather as a research tool to test certain inferences about anxiety as an acquired drive.

Two other methods of test construction—in addition to content and empirical keying—consist of factor analytic and forced choice approaches. J. P. Guilford, R. B. Cattell and H. J. Eysenck are the major test constructors who use factor analytic techniques. The methods of these three psychologists vary somewhat, one from the other, but in the main they are essentially in agreement that personality traits are best extracted by factorial analyses.

Test development by the forced choice method was introduced to minimize the effects of the social desirability variable on item responses. Social desirability, and a number of related test taking attitudes that influence responding, have been the concern of numerous psychometrically oriented psychologists. Research revolving about this issue is actively being conducted and has resulted in lively controversies about the importance of response styles.

A number of special self-rating methods also exist, with promise for personality measurement. These are the Q-sort technique, the Semantic Differential, and the Role Construct Repertory Test. The authors of these self-rating techniques do not consider them psychometric instruments; and except for the *Rep* Test, they were developed for personality research purposes.

FOR FURTHER READING

1. BERG, I. A. The unimportance of test item content. In BASS, B. M. & BERG, I. A. (Eds.), *Objective approaches to personality assessment.* Princeton, N.J.: D. Van Nostrand Co., Inc., 1959.

   The literature on PRT (Perceptual Reaction Test) is reviewed in light of the hypothesis that test item content is unimportant (see also Berg, 1961).

2. BLOCK, J. *The challenge of response sets.* New York: Appleton-Century-Crofts, 1965.

   The recipient of the 1964 Appleton-Century-Crofts award for a distinguished manuscript in psychology, this monograph is certain to be required reading for graduate students for years to come. With special reference to the MMPI, the purpose of this tightly packed polemic is to challenge Messick and Jackson's (1961) interpretation that "acquiescence, as moderated by social desirability, plays a dominant role in personality inventories."

3. CROWNE, D. P. & MARLOWE, D. *The approval motive: Studies in evaluative dependence.* New York: John Wiley & Sons, Inc., 1964.

   In a construct validation approach to social desirability, these authors suggest that SD need not be seen simply as a set to present oneself in the most favorable light possible. Rather SD may be viewed as a constellation of attitudes reflecting dependence on the esteem of others.

4. DAHLSTROM, W. G. & WELSH, G. S. *An MMPI handbook: A guide to use in clinical practice and research.* Minneapolis: University of Minnesota Press, 1960.

   As indicated throughout portions of the present text, Dahlstrom and Welsh have written the basic handbook on the MMPI. Together with their earlier book of readings on the MMPI (Welsh & Dahlstrom, 1956), this volume supplies all the information up to 1959 pertaining to the inventory of inventories.

5. DEMPSEY, P. The dimensionality of the MMPI clinical scales among normal subjects. *Journal of consulting Psychology*, 1963, 27, 492–497.

A short report of research with the MMPI among normals, this article supported the generally held opinion that some MMPI scales (e.g., 1, 3, 7, 8, 9, K) are much better than others (e.g., 2, 4, 6) for use in this population.

6. EDWARDS, A. L. *The social desirability variable in personality assessment and research.* New York: The Dryden Press, 1957.

This short monograph contains an account of the author's and others' research leading up to and with the SD scale.

7. JACKSON, D. N. & MESSICK, S. Content and style in personality assessment. *Psychological Bulletin*, 1958, 55, 243–252.

Together with an earlier article by these authors (Jackson & Messick, 1957) and several later ones (Jackson & Messick, 1961, 1962; Messick & Jackson, 1961), this paper serves to acquaint readers with one set of studies designed to explore the role of acquiescence in personality inventories.

8. JONES, E. E., GERGEN, K. J., & DAVIS, K. E. Some determinants of reactions to being approved or disapproved as a person. *Psychological Monographs*, 1962, 76, No. 2 (Whole No. 521).

These authors set out to validate a test-taking attitude measure reported in the literature as Machiavellianism (e.g., tough-minded, cynical, detached), but failed to find any evidence for it. The study is significant for it illustrates the many difficulties encountered when trying to predict from individual difference measures to behavior in complex social situations.

9. MINARD, J. G. Response-bias interpretation of perceptual defense. *Psychological Review*, 1965, 72, 74–88.

This selective review of the recent relevant literature in the area musters evidence for and maintains that response bias interpretations of stimulus responding is spurious and does not take into account perceptual defense.

10. NORMAN, W. T. Relative importance of test item content. *Journal of consulting Psychology*, 1963, 27, 166–174.

Addressing himself to the question raised by Berg regarding the unimportance of test item content, the author musters an impressive array of evidence that the opposite is true. Also see Norman's (1959) critique of the semantic differential.

11. PERKINS, JULIA E. & GOLDBERG, L. Contexual effects on the MMPI. *Journal of consulting Psychology*, 1964, 28, 133–140.

This interesting little study was designed to determine in what ways and to what extent MMPI scores are influenced by the ordering of their items.

12. PITTELL, S. M. & MENDELSOHN, G. A.   Measurement of moral values: a review and critique. *Psychological Bulletin*, 1966, 66, 22–35.

Although the review deals explicitly with the relationship of measured moral values to moral behavior, this paper has important implications for the relationships of all measured dimensions to overt behavior.

13. RORER, L. G.   The great response style myth. *Psychological Bulletin*, 1965, 63, 129–156.

A distinction is made between response styles and response sets in this review of the literature in the area; and the evidence pro and con leads the author to the conclusion that the former are trivial in their contribution to responding on personality, interest, and attitude inventories.

14. SECHREST, L.   The psychology of personal constructs: George Kelly. In WEPMAN, J. M., & HEINE, R. W. (Eds.), *Concepts of personality*. Chicago: Aldine Publishing Co., 1963. Pp. 206–233.

Of course no substitute for reading Kelly's original two volumes on the subject (1955), this chapter nevertheless furnishes an adequate introduction to the theory and work surrounding Kelly's formulation.

15. TAYLOR, JANET A.   Drive theory and manifest anxiety. *Psychological Bulletin*, 1956, 53, 303–320.

Numerous experiments are discussed that compared performance of anxious and nonanxious subjects.

16. TELLEGEN, A.   Direction of measurement: A source of misinterpretation. *Psychological Bulletin*, 1965, 63, 233–243.

Failure to regulate direction of measurement, it is argued in this paper, produces misleading results by affecting the distribution and intercorrelations of test characteristics.

17. WEISS, R. L. & MOOS, R. H.   Response biases in the MMPI: A sequential analysis. *Psychological Bulletin*, 1965, 63, 403–409.

In this paper a general technique is presented for assessing sequential dependencies in MMPI responses.

18. WIGGINS, J. S.   Strategic, method and stylistic variance. *Psychological Bulletin*, 1962, 59, 224–242.

In contrast to Norman's and Rorer's positions regarding the importance of item content (see references above), Wiggins' careful analysis leads him to conclude that some of the variance of responding to psychiatric inventories is accounted for by stylistic consistencies among subjects to certain item formats. A more recent restatement of Wiggins' position in this controversy can be found in a current number of *Educational and Psychological Measurement* (1966).

CHAPTER 9

PROJECTIVE TECHNIQUES:

THE RORSCHACH

HAMLET: Do you see yonder cloud that's almost
in shape of a camel?
POLONIUS: By the mass, and 'tis like a camel, indeed.
HAMLET: Methinks it is like a weasel.
POLONIUS: It is backed like a weasel.
HAMLET: Or like a whale?
POLONIUS: Very like a whale.

Hamlet, III, ii.

Polonius may have been more politic than honest in agreeing so readily with Hamlet. Each of us, however, at one time or another has had an experience similar to that of Polonius when looking at cloud formations. We see such shapes as animals, landscapes, cotton candy, human figures, and even familiar faces. Obviously, since clouds do not really represent anything but themselves, the interpretations each person gives must come from within himself. These perceptions, or *projections* as they are sometimes called by psychologists, express something about the unique way in which each of us sees and organizes amorphous stimuli.

Projective tests consist of amorphous stimuli (like the clouds) and are used by psychologists for assessing personality. These stimuli are intentionally left ambiguous so that people can express themselves in any way they choose. Consider, for example, the inkblot depicted in Figure 9–1. Persons often respond to this picture by saying something to the effect of ". . . two persons talking to one another about a way in which . . ." or ". . . two persons trying to pull apart. . . ." Since the inkblot in Figure 9–1 does not make it altogether clear that there are two persons

258

involved, or that they are saying or doing anything, such responses as the preceding must originate from within the respondent—i.e., he must be projecting his own thoughts and feelings. This suggests the reason for the label of this type of test. The respondent is said to project his own attitudes and ideas onto the ambiguous stimulus.

In practical personality assessment situations, projective techniques are usually administered in conjunction with interviews, case history data, and self-report inventories. Some clinical practitioners prefer self-report inventories for obtaining descriptions of the more molecular aspects of personality (e.g., response tendencies, habits, traits, or behavioral dispositions) and reserve projective techniques for making inferences about the deeper facets of personality (e.g., needs, unconscious wishes, and fantasies). However, not all practitioners or test theorists would agree with this oversimplified division of labor. At one extreme there are those clinicians who consider projective techniques as the only tests of any value for supplementing clinical observation and interviewing; and at the other extreme there are those who consider them to be based on faulty theories of personality and who therefore would not consider using them under any circumstance. The underlying issues are far from settled, but most knowledgeable psychologists (Anastasi, 1961; Cronbach, 1960; Vernon, 1964), although critical of the shortcomings of projective tests, are reluctant to reject them as useless in view of their obvious value as exploratory procedures in clinical practice.

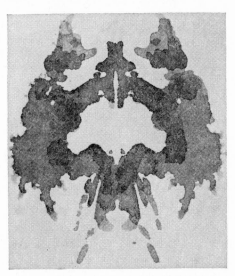

FIGURE 9–1. Inkblot similar to one used in the Rorschach test.

PROJECTION VERSUS PROJECTIVE TECHNIQUE

The concept of *projection* was introduced into the psychological literature by Freud. He defined it as a process of ascribing one's own drives, feelings, and sentiments to other people, or to objects in the outside world, as a defense against becoming aware of these threatening qualities in oneself. It was also clear from Freud's (1911) published analysis of the case of a paranoid psychotic patient that projection was intended to refer to a process in persons whereby perceptions of the outer world are influenced by inner states. According to Freud, the use of projection permits the individual to deny the presence within himself of obnoxious impulses. By projecting these impulses, they are no longer recognized as a part of himself but are now a part of others.

The term *projective technique* gained its popularity from an article by L. K. Frank (1939) in which he pointed out the importance of a "disguised" personality measuring device.[1] Such a method, he believed, would allow the tester a glimpse of a person's private world and the way he attributes meaning to, or projects onto, a relatively "plastic field." Textbook definitions of "projective techniques" variously categorize the term according to the text author's particular biases. Thus one author emphasizes the ambiguity of the *stimulus* materials; another calls attention to the *response* side, and the degree of freedom that subjects have in formulating answers; and a third author chooses to dwell on the projective techniques' relatively greater subtlety and the advantages that these tests have over the more structured ones in pointing to *latent* or *unconscious* aspects of personality.

One of the difficulties in differentiating between the term projection, as used by Freud, and as it has come to be used in the test situation, stems from the similarity in sound and the overlapping meaning of the two uses of the term. In Freudian projection—sometimes also called "abnormal" or "defensive" projection—the person really believes that the projected attributes are not his own. Moreover, the defensive projector's behavior is unconscious—he is not aware that he is projecting; and his purpose is to rid himself of undesirable or unacceptable wishes, thoughts, and impulses.

On the other hand, projection in the test context is a process whereby a person, when presented with a number of ambiguous stimuli, responds to these stimuli in an active and sometimes

---

[1] Until quite recently the origin of the term "projection," when used to denote a form of test, was attributed to Frank (1939). However the origin should be credited to H. A. Murray (1938), who, in his volume *Explorations in Personality*, used the label "projection" tests (Lindzey, 1961).

conscious manner. The test respondent may draw on a resevoir of his own feelings, needs, or emotions, but such behavior can never be considered defensive. In short, normal projection is broader than its abnormal manifestation, since the latter is reserved only for the Freudian defense mechanism. The best definition of a projective technique offered to date is the following one by Gardner Lindzey (1961, p. 45) :[2]

A projective technique is an instrument that is considered especially sensitive to covert or unconscious aspects of behavior, it permits or encourages a wide variety of subject responses, is highly multidimensional, and it evokes unusually rich or profuse response data with a minimum of subject awareness concerning the purpose of the test.

DEFINING CHARACTERISTICS OF PROJECTIVE TECHNIQUES

As noted in the preceding chapter, one of the problems of self-report inventories is that their purpose is too obvious, and consequently they are easily falsified. A common characteristic of projective techniques, in contrast to inventories, is that their purpose is disguised and the subject does not easily comprehend the way in which his responses will be utilized and interpreted. Such disguise is accomplished through the use of highly unstructured stimulus materials.[3]

The stimulus ambiguity of projective techniques varies with the different particular methods, but compared to self-report inventories, they are all unstructured. These techniques consist of the presentation of inkblots, pictures, incomplete sentences, or incomplete stories, and require that the subject structure, or organize, these stimuli. This stimulus ambiguity and the multiplicity of responses permitted the subject (e.g., versus the fixed alternatives of self-report tests) encourage the use of his imaginative processes and do not require that he be particularly knowledgable about his characteristic behavior, habits, or symptoms. As a matter of fact, most projective techniques are deceptively undemanding in this regard, and the subject is instructed explicitly that there are no right or wrong answers. These aspects of projective tech-

---

[2] Readers who would like to delve more deeply into the details of the concept of test projection are referred to Holzberg (1966), Lindzey (1961), and Zubin et al., (1965).

[3] See n. 8, Chapter 8.

niques—the lack of stimulus structure, the multiplicity of responses permitted, and the absence of right or wrong responses—were designed primarily to evoke fantasy responses from the subject and help the tester gain access to aspects of the person that are inaccessible even to himself. For the remainder of this chapter—the first of two on projective tests—the most widely used of these techniques, the Rorschach Inkblots are the main focus of attention.

THE RORSCHACH INKBLOTS

Projective methodology's greatest boost came in 1921 with a report by Hermann Rorschach, a Swiss psychiatrist, in which he described a technique for determining modes of behavior from an individual's verbal responses to a set of inkblots. His technique was intended as a clinical tool for the study of unconscious factors in behavior and personality, and his aim in developing his method was to help the psychiatrist obtain a better understanding of patients on a more standardized basis than routine clinical observation afforded.

Toward these ends, Rorschach devised a standard series of 10 inkblot pictures to serve as the stimulus material in his diagnostic procedure. Five of the inkblots are of various shades of gray, two are gray with one shade of red, and three are all in color. Each inkblot is bilaterally symmetrical (see Figure 9–1).

Background of the Rorschach Inkblots

Hermann Rorschach was not the first to use inkblots as psychological test materials. The earliest recorded use of them date back to 1857, when Justinus Kerner, a German physician, reported that he inadvertently discovered the possibilities in the use of inkblots by noting how, as he observed them, they assumed various shapes which conveyed different meanings to him. Kerner observed that it was difficult to create inkblots according to a preconceived plan; but he was even more impressed by the observation that inkblots tended to be perceived even by their producer in unpredictable ways. Although Kerner did not quite grasp the relationship between inkblot perceptions and personality diagnosis, he was credited with the discovery that there is an interplay between these stimuli and subjects' responses.

The first person to grasp the inkblots' possibilities for the purpose of personality assessment was Alfred Binet. In 1895, Binet, who is best known as the founder of modern intelligence testing, suggested the use of inkblots as stimulus material for free associations. He was mainly interested in the implications of visual imaginativeness for the study of personality traits (Binet and Henri, 1895–96).

Binet's work, and subsequent investigations with inkblots by psychologists were reviewed by Whipple in 1910. Whipple, an American psychologist interested in mental testing, also published the first series of standardized inkblots. From inspection of the inkblots' accompanying *Manual of Mental and Physical Tests* (Whipple, 1910), it is apparent that much of the early research with inkblots was largely concerned with the imaginative or cognitive processes of persons and the light they shed on personality characteristics.

It was not until Hermann Rorschach published his now famous *Psychodiagnostik* in 1921 that there was a shift of emphasis from the viewpoint that responses to inkblots reflect imaginativeness to the idea that the whole of personality structure is reflected in associations to these blots. His work with patients in psychiatric hospitals and his explorations with inkblots in that setting provided the basis for what Rorschach considered an objective method of total personality diagnosis.

Unfortunately, Rorschach's first published monograph was also his last. The year following the publication of the *Psychodiagnostik,* he died. He had been working on some amplifications and refinements of his inkblot administration and scoring techniques. Shortly after his death, the Rorschach technique was introduced into the United States as a result of an English translation of his work (Rorschach and Oberholzer, 1924).

During the early years of its introduction in this country, the pioneer Rorschach work met some stubborn resistance from psychiatrists and psychologists. The former mistrusted the seemingly mysterious numerical manipulations that the technique's scoring required and were even more suspicious of the psychodynamic interpretations (e.g., formulations about motivations that underly overt behavior) that were based on Rorschach scores. Psychologists, on the other hand, then as now, questioned the scientific value of a technique that relied so heavily on a subject's introspection and was conducted, in comparison to experimental methods, in a manner that was haphazard and uncontrolled. However, in the middle 1930's the Rorschach technique began to be accepted; an English version of the manual appeared in the form of *Psychodiagnostics* (Rorschach, 1942) ; and interest in it has grown since then to the point that, according to a recent national survey (Sundberg, 1961), it is by far the most frequently used of all tests for personality assessment.

The Rorschach technique has undergone several modifications and refinements, and its widest application is in the field of mental health. As a result of the growing popularity of this particular projective methodology among divergent groups, a wide variety of techniques of inkblot administration and scoring have arisen over the years, but the standardized series of 10 cards have not undergone any changes.

Rationale of Rorschach Testing

The fundamental assumption underlying this projective technique is that there exists a relationship between the way an individual organizes or "structures" the inkblots, and his personality. The blots are considered suitable stimulus materials because they are relatively ambiguous. So, when a subject is instructed to tell what he "sees" in the blots, he presumably reacts in a personal and unlearned manner. His perceptions are said to be selected and organized in terms of his projected needs, wishes, desires, characteristic patterns of response, and by the physical properties of the blots themselves.

The fact that the inkblots are not socially familiar objects or situations, to which a subject must give culturally prescribed responses, is the Rorschach procedure's greatest asset. This unfamiliar "plastic field"—in the form of blots that offer the subject an opportunity to reveal his "private world" without being aware of what he is telling about himself—led L. K. Frank (1939) to comment that the respondent "has no cultural norms behind which to hide himself."

Administration of the Rorschach

The administration, scoring, and interpretation of the Rorschach test vary from one school of users to another. Numerous systems have arisen, mainly because general agreement has not been attained among Rorschach followers about the optimal use and interpretation of this technique. However, as a result of the founding of the Rorschach Institute in 1939 (called the Society for Projective Techniques since 1948), and due to the publication of the *Journal of Projective Techniques,* there are sufficient similarities among all the methods so that when one system of administration and scoring is learned, most of the others are easy to understand. The description of procedures presented in this and following sections is based on the Klopfer system (Klopfer and Davidson, 1962), which is one of the two major commonly used systems of Rorschach administration and scoring (also see Klopfer and Kelley, 1942; Klopfer, Ainsworth, Klopfer, and Holt, 1958). The other major system is one developed by Samuel Beck (1944).

The Klopfer method suggests that the procedure for administration consist of four parts: performance proper, inquiry, analogy period, and testing-the-limits. The first part, the *performance proper,* is the phase during which the subject is given the 10 inkblots and instructed to examine each of the cards and to communicate what he sees in them. The tester merely acts as observer and recorder. There is as little interference as possible with the subject's spontaneous reactions to the cards, and the examiner does not pressure or guide the subject.

More specifically, each of 10 cards is placed on the examination table, face down, in its proper sequence, so that Card I is on top and Card X at the bottom. The examiner presents each of these cards to the subject and instructs him to relate what the blot looks like and what it might be. The subject's direct questions about procedure are usually evaded in order to leave the test situation as unstructured as possible. Some typical questions raised by subjects during the performance proper are: "May I turn the card?" "Should I tell you the first thing that comes to mind or should I think about the card?" All such questions are answered as noncommittally as possible (e.g., "That's entirely up to you"), throwing the responsibility for making the decision right back to the subject.

Responses to the cards, some of which are shown in Figure 9–2 along with the inkblots that elicited them, are recorded verbatim and descriptive remarks are made about the subject's general behavior and mode of responding. Additional notations are made of the subject's reaction time (the time between the presentation of the card and his first response to it), total response time per card, .

INKBLOT	TYPICAL RESPONSES
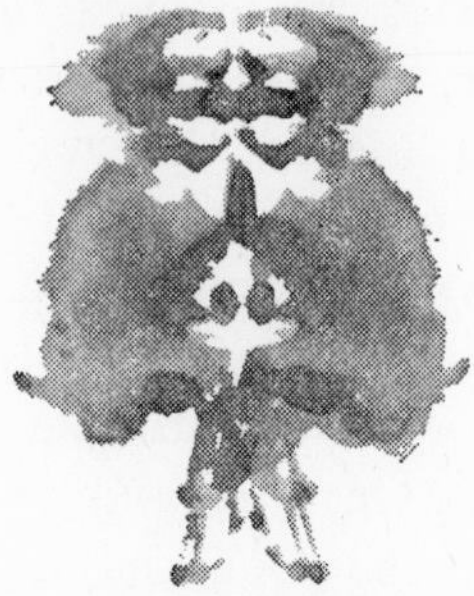	TWO BEARS KISSING TWO CLOWNS CLAPPING HANDS A SPINNING TOP
	A BEAR RUG A MONSTER SITTING ON A TREE STUMP
	ANIMALS CLIMBING THE INSIDES OF A PERSON
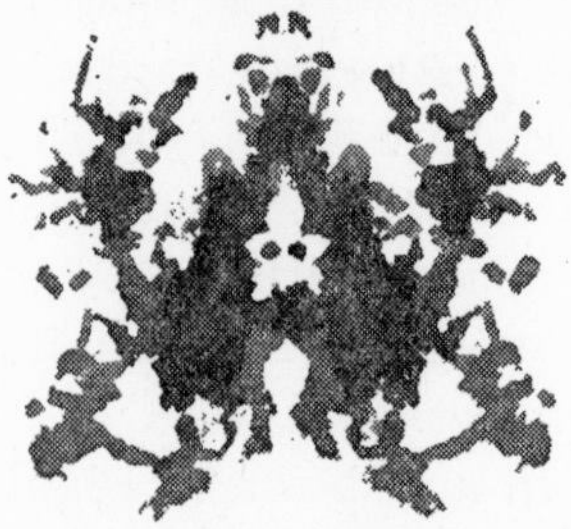	TWO BUGS BITING EACH OTHER POACHED EGGS

FIGURE 9–2.   Four inkblots and some typical responses to each.

and the length of time taken to complete the performance proper. The position in which the card is held by the subject when he gives his response is also noted (right side up is $\wedge$; top of the card facing the subject's right and left sides are $>$ and $<$ respectively, and facing down is recorded as $\vee$).

The second part of Rorschach administration, the *inquiry* period, is the phase designed to reveal how the subject arrived at his responses. In order to clarify certain aspects of the subject's responses, the examiner asks questions to determine what physical properties about a particular inkblot influenced the subject's spontaneous replies. Typically, the examiner asks such questions as, "Where on the card did you see the butterfly?" "Tell me more about the way you see two animals climbing up a hill," or "What is it in the card that makes it seem textured?"

Thus, during the inquiry period, the psychologist attempts to ascertain the precise way in which the subject arrived at responses made during the performance proper. Of course, there is always the danger of suggesting, or leading the subject during the inquiry to adopt certain fictitious reasons to explain his responses (or the examiner's preferred reasons). But experienced test administrators, like adept interviewers, have developed numerous skills that enable them to minimize the effects of their own presence to a considerable degree. Their questions also are worded in ways designed to attenuate undesirable test taking attitudes.

The *analogy* or follow-up period is an optional third phase used when the inquiry has not fully clarified certain scoring problems. In most cases, the appropriate procedure for conducting this follow-up inquiry is to use analogy questions for clarification purposes. Typical of these questions are the following: "Here you said that color contributed to your calling this an explosion; now can you select those responses in which color also helped?" or "You said here that you saw a bird in flight; are the birds you saw here also in flight?"

The fourth and final phase is called *testing-the-limits*. Its aim, especially in cases where subjects have given extremely few or no responses, is to find out whether or not a subject is capable of seeing certain kinds of concepts. Further, its purpose is to ascertain whether respondent is able to use specific portions of the blot, or organize particular properties of the card (e.g., color, shading, blacks, and whites), that he has not utilized in his spontaneous responses. During the testing-the-limits phase, the examiner may suggest definite concepts (e.g., "butterfly," "man in motion," "two people doing something"), and inquire whether the subject is capable of perceiving these concepts also.

Scoring of Rorschach Responses

The scoring of the Rorschach is complex and, all too often, highly individualized within any particular school of Rorschach methodology. However, as we noted earlier, there are sufficient similarities among all the scoring systems so that when one system is learned, most of the others are easy to understand.

The major scoring categories used in evaluating a subject's performance are: location, determinant, content, popularity-originality, and form level. Scoring for *location* consists of classifying a response according to five main categories. The score depends on how much of the inkblot the respondent used to arrive at his concept. The response may have used the whole blot (W), a large detail (D), a small detail (d), a rare detail (dr) of the blot, or the white space (S) between the blot and the test card. A location chart (see Figure 9–3) is sometimes used to score the subject's responses.

The *determinants* of the response refer to the quality of the blot that determined or is responsible for the subject's perception. Responses may be categorized according to movement (M, FM, or *m*), shading (*c*, K, or *k*), color (C or C') and form (F). Although there is, of course, no movement in the blot itself, the respondent's perception of the blot as a representation of an object "in movement" is scored in this determinant category. The shading of the blot can determine responses, and these are classified according to the extent to which darker or lighter shading, and the blacks, whites, and grays, influence the subject's perception. Color determinants are scored when the subject considers the chromatic aspects of the blot as important in shaping his response. A response is scored in the form category when the shape or contour of the blot—rather than movement, shading, or color—determines the concept. Several responses are scored according to their appropriate determinant categories in Table 9–1.

The *content* of responses are scored within three categories. Thus there are human (H), animal (A), and abstract (Abs) or inanimate content scores, depending on the subject matter of the

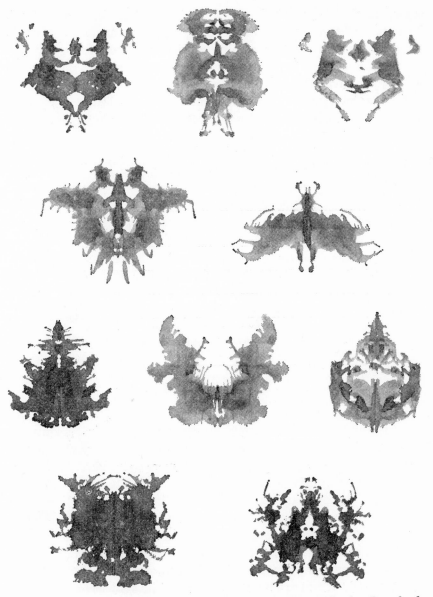

FIGURE 9-3.   A location chart similar to one used with the Rorschach inkblots.

concept seen. In addition, responses can be scored for the popularity (P) or originality (O) of the content of the subject's perception. For each of the ten inkblots, certain frequently occurring responses are designated as popular; and unusual or rare responses are scored as original. The most frequent content categories are animal, human, parts of animals or humans, anatomy, clouds, fire, landscape, and map responses naming continents or countries. Unusual or original content categories are scored in terms of their infrequency for particular portions of specific blots, and include responses that refer to literary or mythical characters (e.g., Falstaff or Mephistopheles) or concepts that relate to the subject's hobby, vocation,

TABLE 9–1

Rorschach Responses and Determinant Scores

Response	Score
This looks like a butterfly. (Q. What makes it like a butterfly?) Its Shape (Card III).	F
A couple of clowns clapping hands (Card II).	M
A bat in flight (Card I).	FM
Leaves falling down to earth	m
A bearskin rug (Q. What made it seem like a bearskin?) It has pile—a feeling that it would change form under your hand (Card IV).	Fc
This red part on top is blood (Card II).	C

SOURCE: Klopfer & Davidson, 1962.

or special interests (e.g., computer memory drum or transmission gears). If an original concept does not fit the blot in which it is presumably embedded, or if it is in other ways bizarre, the score given is an original minus (O −).

Finally, determinants are categorized into good *form level* and poor form level responses, depending on how well and accurately the subject tied together various parts of the inkblot into a meaningful concept. Form level ratings are based on an elaborate scoring procedure (each response is scored on a scale that ranges from − 2.0 to + 5.0), and are intended to reflect the subject's ability to fit the blots to his concepts and his capacity to communicate this information to another person (the examiner). Some examples of responses, their scoring categories, and some typical interpretations are presented in Table 9–2.

The scores for the categories discussed above, and the proportional interrelationships between categories, are expressed in a *psychogram* similar to the one presented in Figure 9–4. The psychogram is a bar graph representing the distribution of the determinant scores. On the horizontal axis, as indicated in Figure 9–4, spaces for the major determinant scoring categories are provided; on the vertical axis, spaces are provided for noting the number of responses. One of the most important features to observe in the psychogram is the shape of the distribution of the main determi-

TABLE 9–2

Examples of Interpretations of Rorschach Responses

Response	Location Category	Nature of Interpretation
This is a butterfly (pointing to the whole of Card V.) Here are the wings, feelers, and legs.	W	The use of many W (whole) responses is considered to reflect the subject's ability to organize and relate materials.
This is part of a chicken's leg (pointing to a large section of Card V).	D	Detail scores are usually interpreted as indicative of an interest in the concrete.
This could be a face (upper edge of "wings" on Card V).	dd	The use of unusual or tiny details (dd) may suggest pedantic trends.
Looks somewhat like a spinning top (center of Card II).	S	Persons who use S (reversing figure and ground) often are observed as oppositional, negative, and stubborn.

nant scores. For example, do most responses tend to cluster in the center, in the left half, or in the right half, or are they evenly distributed over the three main areas of the graph?

The psychogram summarizes at a glance the balance between the major determinants of inkblot perception. Some of the interpretations associated with these determinants, and their quantitative interrelationships, are discussed in the following section on Rorschach interpretation. It is convenient to note here, however, the interpretative significance of the three major portions of the psychogram.

If the subject's perception has been influenced largely by his own imagination, his own needs and drives, his responses pile up on the

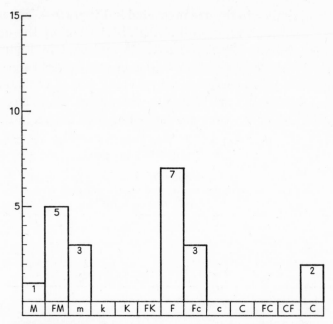

FIGURE 9–4.   The psychogram is a bar graph representing the distribution of the determinant scores. In this pycho-
gram, the distribution of the scores are mainly in the middle
and the left half of the area of the graph.

left side of the graph (indicating a preponderance of movement
responses) ; if his perception has been influenced largely by external stimuli, his responses pile up on the right-hand side of the
graph (indicating an abundance of color responses) ; and if the
perceptions are largely rational, impersonal, and unemotional, his
responses tend to concentrate in the center of the psychogram (an
overemphasis of form responses).

Interpretation of Rorschach Scores

Interpreting scored responses of the Rorschach record is an
elaborate process that has occupied many volumes of literature.
Here the presentation must be limited to highlighting only some of
the rudimentary aspects of the interpretive process.

Generally, it is agreed among Rorschach workers that the total
number of responses (R) given by the subject to all the test cards
indicates his productive capacity. The more intelligent the person,
the more productive is his overall Rorschach record. The average
number of R expected from normal adults ranges from 20 to 45.

The location categories—that is to say, the choice of areas upon which the subject projects his concepts—are said by some Rorschach testers to reflect the subject's intellectual manner of approach to any set of data. For example, the use of many whole responses, or W, presumably reflects the subject's abilities to organize material, to relate details to one another, and to be able to deal with the abstract and theoretical. Overemphasis of usual and unusual detail, or D and d responses in a record, is sometimes interpreted to indicate a subject's tendency toward pedantry or his need to be accurate, correct, and exact.

In general the determinant categories have been interpreted as related to the emotional aspects of personality. Thus responses determined exclusively by shape are said to reflect intellectual control; and movement responses, or the projection of action on the inkblots, are interpreted as reflecting inner emotional control and ability to accept oneself. Human movement responses are considered to be the most significant among the determinants and are interpreted to signify the ability to empathize with people.

Content scores generally are said to disclose the breadth of the respondent's interests. A wide range of content, where, for instance, responses are given that can be scored into human, animal, and inanimate categories, usually are associated with good intelligence. Preoccupation with particular parts of the anatomy may point to certain concerns and difficulties. For example, repeated perception of heads and faces may indicate a concern with one's intellectual abilities. Also, sexual significance is often attached to content responses. Thus problems in sexual identification are said to be revealed by an inability to determine whether the human figures seen are male or female.

The extent to which perceptions fit accurately the outline or form of the blot area, as mentioned earlier, is the response's form level. The form level rating for each response and for the overall Rorschach record are considered important in evaluating intellectual capacity. Poor form level responses, for example, are said to indicate limited intellectual capacity, as well as withdrawal from reality.

Finally, the popular-original responses are interpreted by many Rorschach workers to reveal ability to view one's world in the same way as most other people do, or in a manner different from that of most people. It is expected that subjects see about three of the popular responses (e.g., the inkblot shown in Figure 9–5 is usually seen as a bat). The occurrence of about three to eight popular responses in a record indicates an ability to see the world as others do; and an overabundance of populars (eight or more) is interpreted as a strong need in an individual to think as other people do. Good original responses (versus O −) mean superiority of intellect and originality. According to one system of interpretation (Klopfer and Davidson, 1962), a superior person tends to have twice as many originals as populars (provided there are at

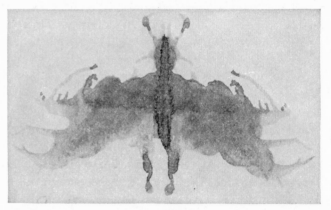

FIGURE 9–5.   This inkblot of the Rorschach is most popularly perceived as a bat.

least five P's). Too many O's may indicate that a person is excessively erratic in his thinking.

In addition to the various ways mentioned of interpreting responses according to the foregoing scoring categories, several systems of Rorschach interpretation perform a *sequence analysis* and a *content analysis*. The former consists of a card-by-card, and a response-by-response, search for characteristics of the subject's test behavior, his use of language, and certain special qualities of the blot material utilized by him that may confirm, modify, or discard hypotheses based on prior interpretations. Thus such variables are taken into account as the number of responses given to each card, or refusal to give responses to particular portions of a card; variations in reaction time from card to card; and the sequence of reactions to color or shading of cards. All of these factors are considered significant aspects of a subject's intellectual and emotional functioning.

In order to illustrate the way in which a sequence analysis is performed by a highly experienced Rorschach interpreter, the following short passage is reproduced. This is a portion on an interpretation of the sequence of responses to an inkblot similar to Card V of the Rorschach (see Figure 9–5) made by Klopfer and Davidson (1962):

> Card V is immediately interpreted as the popular concept of a bat flying. It is not surprising that this essentially intelligent and well-controlled subject makes immediate use of the popular connotation to Card V. However, her insecurity about this concept is rather puzzling. . . . the remark concerning the lower extension, seems to reveal a tendency on her part to be hypercritical of herself rather than putting the blame where it rightly belongs. . . .

Content analysis—that is, an analysis of what is perceived in the blot material rather than the sequence of perceptions—is usually considered valuable for the hypotheses it yields about motivational factors of personality. Thus the significance of human, animal, and inanimate content, already discussed, was seen as a reflection of certain facets of an individual's breadth of interest. Further, content analysis searches for such specific qualitative aspects of perceptions as sexual, anatomy, geography, or science responses. Such other miscellaneous content areas as emblems, spiders, numerals, letters of the alphabet, blood, food, or abstractions, depending on the particular theoretical orientation of the interpreter, take on differing interpretative significance. Psychologists subscribing to Freudian psychoanalytic theory, for example, might interpret certain content categories as follows:

> *Human Figures,* when seen as monsters, ghosts, clowns, or mythical characters, may indicate the subject's inability to identify closely with real people.
> *Animals,* especially if they are perceived as fierce or wild, may refer to aggressive tendencies that one is trying to control.
> *Sexual* responses must be interpreted in relation to the subject's other Rorschach scores and his life history. These responses could be expressed in their symbolic forms (e.g., train, purse, falling) or they may indicate concern with, or avoidance of, sexual problems.
> *Anatomy, geography,* or *science* content may reveal one's attempt to cover up real feelings by intellectualization of the blots. An extreme ex-

ample would be the person who responds to the card in Figure 9–5 by saying that it is a "mammal of the order Chiroptera" (a bat).

Masks may disclose an emphasis on role playing to avoid personal exposure.

Blood responses suggest strong, uncontrolled emotional reactions.

Food may indicate dependency needs—i.e., the wish to be nurtured by others.

Applications of Rorschach Testing

Generally, the uses to which Rorschach records have been put have been to assess persons' cognitive and affective (emotional) functioning. Accordingly, the Rorschach is used to assess level of intelligence, creative potential, spontaneity, degree of mood fluctuation, depression, euphoria, and the extent of anxiety. Inferences based on Rorschach records also include statements about passivity, introversion, assertiveness, reaction to emotional stress, and control of emotional impulses.

Furthermore, the Rorschach technique has been used as a method applicable for a large variety of personality assessment situations. One psychologist (Piotrowski, 1965) lists more than 250 studies in which the diagnostic capacity of this test was demonstrated. Most of these studies demonstrated the clinical usefulness of particular scoring elements and response characteristics as diagnostic signs of psychopathology. The list of studies included the following applications: diagnosis of psychosomatic, neurotic, and psychotic illness; more specific differentiation within the neurotic (e.g., hysteria v. depression) and psychotic (e.g., paranoia v. paranoid schizophrenic) groups; detection of suicidal tendencies; differential diagnosis between brain-damaged and nonbrain-damaged cases; prediction of overt behavior in various situations; and prognosis of favorable or unfavorable outcomes in the treatment of psychotic patients.

The claims made throughout the history of the technique by Rorschach workers for the wide applicability of their instrument led Holtzman (1959, p. 130) to write, "curiously enough, the same ten inkblots are used throughout!" It is beyond the purpose of this book to examine each of these claims, and the evaluative discussion below highlights only some of the complexities entailed in substantiating such claims. For a thorough review of many of the issues touched upon here, the reader is referred to Zubin, Eron, and

Schumer's recent and excellent volume (1965) on *An Experimental Approach to Projective Techniques,* and to recent articles by Shneidman (1965) and Holzberg (1960, 1966).

EVALUATION OF THE RORSCHACH

The appraisal of Rorschach reliability and validity has been a long-standing and perplexing problem which has invited clinicians and researchers (mostly clinicians) to publish voluminously. Perhaps one of the best reviews of the problems involved is one by Jules Holzberg (1960). He presents the attitudes of various divergent schools of psychology toward Rorschach reliability and validity. There are those psychologists, he points out, who insist that the Rorschach must meet the same criteria of psychometric excellence as all other methods of personality assessment; and then there are the less hardheaded—and these seem to make up the largest bulk of Rorschach workers—who argue that this test is not like others and that its purpose is to describe personality "globally" and to aid the clinician in obtaining insight into that personality.[4] And since it is not a measuring instrument in the usual psychometric sense, the latter argue, the demonstration of the Rorschach's reliability and validity is of no concern.

That the nonpsychometric assumption is not a valid one has also been clearly indicated by Holtzman (1959, p. 121), who has the following to say about the Rorschach user's scoring procedure:

When he classifies and enumerates any of S's responses to a projective technique, he is adopting, even if crudely, a psychometric frame of reference. When he counts such responses, he is implying a crude ordinal scale by which 10 M means more of something than 1 M.

The attitude adopted in this book is that the Rorschach must meet certain essential criteria of psychometric tools and procedures. It is also recognized, however, that this technique is different in its origin and rationale from self-report inventories, and as such, the methods for establishing its reliability and validity must be adapted accordingly. With this in mind, and with attention to the special character of the Rorschach, we embark on the following discussion

---

[4] The term "global," when used by psychologists in reference to the test itself, is intended to suggest that interpretations should be made in terms of large patterns of categories (in terms of wholes), rather than "atomistically", in terms of single response categories or even responses to single cards.

of some reliability and validity evidence presented in support of this procedure.

Reliability of Scoring

Most techniques for establishing the reliability of psychometric devices have been developed for tests of a more quantitative nature than the Rorschach. In ability testing, for example, and even in self-report personality inventories, scores are obtained which lend themselves to rather straightforward computational procedures. On a projective test like the Rorschach, however, scoring categories cannot be read directly from a table of norms as in usual psychometric techniques, but rather necessitate an intervening interpretative stage. Therefore, one form of reliability consists of determining the extent of agreement among judges in scoring the same protocols. Such studies, however, are not popular, probably because there are so many different schools of Rorschach scoring. These scoring systems often are diverse and follow their own ideological and methodological lines. What is necessary, then, in studies of inter-scorer reliability, is to provide scorers with a manual in which fixed and explicit rules are presented for scoring Rorschachs.[5]

It is evident from one major study (Hertz, 1934) that similarity of training in a system of scoring influences the extent of agreement between scorers. Using the Hertz system of scoring, two judges achieved 93 percent agreement in scoring 11,000 responses. Prior to scoring the responses, the judges had agreed among themselves on the use of score categories, and they trained by scoring a number of sample responses. Several later studies (Ramzy and Pickard, 1949; Baughman, 1951) also indicated that disagreement between scorers on a system of categorization is responsible for the oft-obtained unreliabilities; but that pretraining and agreement about categories of scores can enhance interscorer reliabilities.

Retest Reliability. A number of special problems present themselves in demonstrating Rorschach test-retest reliability. For one thing, the nature of the scoring system used in the Rorschach differs radically from other type tests. The number of responses within a single record scored in terms of percept categories (e.g., movement, plus or minus form level, color, shading, popular or

---

[5] Since different schools of scoring use different categories, scorers must not be expected to agree with each other unless their systems of scoring correspond closely and they have been thoroughly trained in the use of the new scoring scheme.

original) are few. The result is inadequate sampling of responses within these categories, which in turn results in temporal instability.

Furthermore, it is difficult to determine whether obtained differences on retest occasions are due to the instability of the method of measurement or to changes in a subject's temporary disposition. This problem is not unique to the Rorschach method, but it is magnified in the Rorschach because of the special nature of the test setting. The examiner, due to his active role both as tester and interviewer during the administration of the inkblots, could exert considerable influence on test taking attitudes. Unfortunately, the vast majority of retest studies do not take into account this possible influence on retest scores. Thus examiners are interchanged freely from one study to the next, and if their level of experience is dissimilar, then the results are equally dissimilar. A novice can hardly be expected to elicit the same number or kinds of responses as the highly experienced Rorschach worker. Likewise, the latter, as noted earlier, becomes adept at minimizing examiner effects during numerous phases of the administration procedure, and the less experienced worker probably has not developed these skills adequately.

Then there is the problem that retest scores tend to be more stable for some persons than for others, because of the differential effects on some persons of memory factors and contextual test conditions, as well as individual differences among them in terms of the amounts of their personality or mood fluctuations. The question to be asked, therefore, about retest reliability is: "Reliable for whom and under what conditions?" (Freeman, 1962, p. 628). In this connection one psychologist (Fiske, 1959) has advised that a distinction is appropriate between temporary dispositions and stable components of personality and has suggested one index of reliability might be to use a measure of successive interpretations of a single person's Rorschach. By the use of this measure, reliability would be established by demonstrating that Rorschach protocols of one person obtained at different times are less divergent than protocols elicited from different persons.[6]

---

[6] The reliability of interpretations (versus reliability of scoring) raises issues such as: How many interpreters agree on a particular personality description or diagnosis? Would two or more experts base similar predictions on this Rorschach record? These questions are treated in the validity section of this chapter, but it should be apparent that they could be discussed under reliability also (see Zubin et al., 1965, p. 186 ff.).

Equivalent Forms Reliability. Although it is difficult to develop a set of cards comparable but not identical to the Rorschach, several studies (Zulliger, 1941, 1952, 1956) have reported the use of a series of seemingly parallel blots devised by Behn-Eschenberg (called the Behn-Rorschach). Not only were the average coefficients obtained with the Behn-Rorschach discouragingly low (.56 to .65 with 20- or 21-day interval between retests of two groups) in these studies, but there is some evidence to indicate that the Rorschach and its parallel form, the Behn-Rorschach, are not at all equivalent (Holzberg, 1960). The utility of this particular parallel series, then, for testing equivalent forms reliability is questionable.

Other sets of equivalent forms for an inkblot series have been developed (Howard, 1953), but these were not designed as alternates for the Rorschach and must be evaluated in terms of their own reliability and validity.

Split-Half Reliability. When it is unfeasible or impractical to establish the reliability of a test by the retest or equivalent forms method, a split-half procedure is sometimes used. This method calls for only one administration of a test and requires scoring of two halves of the test. The most common way to accomplish this is to score all of the even-numbered items and then to score separately all of the odd-numbered items. The two halves of the test are then correlated to obtain an estimate of reliability.

The Rorschach cards, however, are not items whose equivalence can be easily established. Therefore the task of creating equal halves is difficult. In the first place, responses to the blots vary in number from one card to the next, and this creates unequal halves. Second, the cards themselves are heterogeneous in terms of the stimulus structure each presents and therefore cannot be considered equivalent. And finally, the small number of responses (or no responses at all) given to any single card, makes the split-half method unsuitable because of the inadequate sampling of responses in one half or the other, or both. Nevertheless, split-half studies have been conducted, but not surprisingly, the results have been contradictory.

In one study (Vernon, 1933) a high split-half coefficient (.91) was reported for the number of responses elicited from subjects for the two halves (i.e., R was as high for one half of the blots as for the other half), but other scoring categories in the two halves fell far short of adequate reliability coefficients. Another study (Hertz,

1934), on the other hand, reported high average split-half coefficients for all scoring categories. It has been suggested (Cronbach, 1949; Vernon, 1933; Zubin *et al.*, 1965) that the number of responses (R) in the record should be controlled when testing for this form of reliability, since variations in this number tend to distort the results. However, many Rorschachers find this solution unacceptable because it proposes to impede the subject's freedom of responding. And this freedom, in the last analysis, is among the technique's greatest achievements.

The trend generally among Rorschach investigators has been to stay away from split-half methods. In this regard, one of the leading Rorschach workers, Marguerite Hertz (1951, p. 316), has said, "Because of the global nature of the test, it is not possible to split and work with isolated variables."

In concluding this section on reliability, it may be said that while Rorschach workers have generally denied the applicability of traditional psychometric criteria, the fact remains that the rationale underlying the use of responses to inkblots is psychometric insofar as they are often scored and summated. Furthermore, since responses produced on these tests play a crucial part in personality description and assessment, and since reliability studies indicate that Rorschach responses are highly unstable, it is reasonable to conclude that interpretations based on them must continue to be considered highly speculative.

Validity of the Rorschach

The validity of the Rorschach, as with more structured self-report inventories, can be established by demonstrating that it is useful for its intended purposes. The purposes and settings in which the Rorschach are used are numerous, and accordingly they are considered separately under the headings of predictive, concurrent, and construct validities.

Predictive Validity. The Rorschach is used most often for the information it contributes toward understanding the individual, rather than as a mass screening device. It is therefore essential and entirely appropriate to insist that this technique excel in the prediction of the individual case. Unfortunately, however, clinical predictions based on Rorschach protocols are not sufficiently precise to allow follow-up; or when they do attain precision, they often are not followed up. A clinician predicts, for example, that a particular hospital patient will "recover quickly," "return to society," and find "gainful employment." If he takes the trouble to confirm or disconfirm his predictions—and one assertion here is that he does not take the necessary time—there are questions still to be answered: What constitutes a quick recovery? Is his return home, perhaps to a psychotic family, a return to society? and, How do you determine whether his employment is gainful?

Several studies report attempts to predict clear-cut, confirmable criteria. Ruth Munroe (1942) conducted a study in which, on the basis of Rorschach scores (her own method of scoring), she predicted the college grades of 100 women. Her predictions were more successful than those based on either the Bernreuter Personality Inventory or a standard objective college aptitude test (ACE examination). However, the use of these Munroe scores several years later (McCandless, 1949), in predicting achievement in the different setting of an officers candidate school, did not fare so well. No significant validity correlations were obtained in the latter study.

Much more encouraging results demonstrating the predictive validity of the Rorschach were recently obtained by a psychologist (Seidel, 1960) who applied two prognostic scales to a clinical sample in order to determine the interrelationship between these scales and their predictive potential. Of special importance in that study was the finding of substantial correlations between the criterion of recovery ("in less than three years") with an "ego-strength scale" (.40), and with Rorschach form level scores (.44). These validity coefficients, in the .40's, are about as high as one could reasonably expect; and this study, in terms of methodology and in terms of the criteria used, should encourage further investigation with the same Rorschach scales and score categories.

Concurrent Validity. Studies of the concurrent validity of the Rorschach abound. Within the scope of this book, the discussion must be limited to a brief presentation of the following three methodologies: *group comparisons; diagnostic screening studies;* and *matching.*

Studies comparing the characteristics of the test performance of groups are a popular type of research with the Rorschach, and even the founder of the test himself used 288 psychiatric subjects who represented extremes of certain personality traits. Hermann

Rorschach (1921) studied more than 100 artists, scholars, mentally defective individuals, and persons of average accomplishments. Among some of his findings, although they are questionable from a statistical viewpoint, were that neurotics' test protocols were distinguished by few movement responses, few or no form-color responses, and small numbers of responses to the cards as a whole.

More recent studies have rarely met with any noteworthy success. For example, in one study (Wittenborn and Holzberg, 1951), zero correlations were found between 36 independent Rorschach factors and clinicians' diagnoses of nearly 200 hospital admission cases. Even less encouraging findings were reported among nonpsychiatric groups. In one series of such studies (Roe, 1946a, b, c), expected differences between groups did not emerge; thus, although the presence of human movement (M) responses are presumably linked interpretatively with creativity, no preponderance of these responses were found among several groups of eminent artists. Similarly in another study (Schachtel, 1951), a preponderance of white space responses (S),[7] which are presumed to signify antisocial tendencies, were not found significantly more frequently among juvenile delinquents than nondelinquents.

Even among studies (Dorken and Kral, 1952; Fisher et al., 1955) where initial reports indicate the success of specific Rorschach indices in differentiating one group from another, cross-validation of these indices often meets with failure. That is to say, although success is sometimes achieved in using a set of Rorschach signs, rules, or indices, these results become insignificant when the indices are applied to a new sample. Even more discouraging, however, is the fact that many studies do not subject their findings to such cross-validation procedures.

A number of additional shortcomings of group comparison studies may be noted. For one thing, contrasted groups are not matched in terms of such relevant variables as intelligence, education, and socioeconomic status. Second, a common practice among investigators is comparing institutional respondents with noninstitutionalized persons. It should be apparent, for example, that persons in old-age homes differ in many respects from aged persons who are not institutionalized. Likewise, it should be even more apparent that

---

[7] White space responses are scored when there is complete reversal of figure and ground, and the white space rather than the inkblot itself is used by the subject in arriving at a concept. The use of the inkblot in this unusual manner is often interpreted to indicate negativism or deviance.

Rorschach findings with hospitalized psychiatric patients are not comparable to those with persons functioning in society. Unfortunately, however, such comparisons are made, and the results of these studies are offered as evidence of concurrent validity.

Finally, a shortcoming of comparison studies—one that would be easily surmounted if results were subjected to more careful controls and cross-validation procedures—is that clinicians tend to approach interpretation of Rorschach records of persons who belong to distinct groups with the belief that there should be significant differences in the two groups' protocols. Thus, perhaps after having themselves administered and scored Rorschachs of subjects belonging to different groups (e.g., neurotic v. psychotic patients), clinicians go back to the protocol and "find" signs which "unquestionably" predict the behavior under consideration. Even if they are not themselves involved in the test administration and scoring procedures, knowledge about a subject's group membership may have the same effect. These effects can be controlled by withholding identifying data from the interpreter and by conducting cross-validation studies.

Diagnostic screening studies often use the method of blind analysis. Blind analysis refers to basing diagnostic judgments on the Rorschach record without even a glimpse of the person to whom the inkblots have been administered. If used properly, this method could enhance the validity of group comparison studies. Typically, a Rorschach expert performs a blind analysis when he neither administered nor scored a respondent's test, but renders a personality description of that respondent on the basis of responses on test protocol. The accuracy of his description, interpretation, or diagnosis is judged either by the expert himself, which of course is a questionable practice, or by clinicians who have had lengthy contacts with the respondent under investigation.

In one such study (Siegel, 1948), Rorschach inkblots were administered to 26 children. Diagnoses of these childrens' psychopathologies were made independently by the test administrator, who was familiar with the child, and by another staff member, who performed a blind analysis. A comparison of the correctness of the two diagnoses indicated agreement between the two judges in more than 60 percent of the cases. This is an impressive achievement and speaks well for the expert's skill. After psychotherapy of about one year's duration, the two sets of diagnoses agreed in 89 percent of the cases. The higher degree of concurrence after therapy than before suggests even greater expertness in blind analysis. It indicates that when the criterion was made more reliable—i.e., when the therapist became more familiar with the children—agreement between the expert and the criterion was enhanced. Interestingly, this also suggests the possibility that the faulty criterion, rather than the fallible expert, may account for much of the error variance that contributed to the lower agreement percentage achieved on the first comparison occasion.

In another blind analysis study, in which diagnoses were based on Rorschach protocols, the criterion predicted consisted of diagnostic classifications arrived at by a psychiatric conference and by the use of standard clinical procedures (Piotrowski, 1965). The results reported were that in 39 out of 46 cases, the two diagnoses were in complete agreement, and that there were no serious discrepancies in the other seven cases.

Numerous psychologists (Zubin *et al.*, 1965) have suggested that the method of blind analysis is not as spectacular in its success as some experts would lead others to believe. In this method, the terms and labels used in the personality descriptions are sufficiently vague and general that most persons, if asked whether the descriptions apply to them, would tend to agree that there is some element of accuracy in them.[8] Moreover, as indicated earlier, many practitioners of the method of blind analysis are thoroughly familiar with the personality characteristics of the average or typical person of a particular setting, so that their descriptions often consist of a listing of statements that tend to be true of persons in that setting. For example, in describing the Rorschach protocol of a patient admitted to a hospital ward which only houses psychotics, the expert need only include in his description such factors as "bizarreness of thinking," "tendency to withdraw," "occasional lucid periods," "frequent verbal attacks on members of his family," and similar

---

[8] The late Professor Donald G. Paterson called the art of writing personality descriptions that are generalized the "Barnum Effect" (see Dunnette, 1957). Most individuals confronted with generalized descriptions of themselves, readily believe that it sizes them up pretty well. Example: "You have a tendency to worry at times, but not to excess. You do get depressed at times, but you couldn't be called moody because you are generally cheerful and optimistic." Using statements similar to these, several psychologists (Evans, 1962; Forer, 1949; Stagner, 1958; Sundberg, 1955) have demonstrated that persons tend overwhelmingly to rate these descriptions as accurate sketches of their own personalities.

phrases that may be accurate but could be made even without referring to the Rorschach record.

The use of blind analysis to arrive at diagnoses, although an interesting exercise for research demonstrations, and for competence training in Rorschach interpretation, is a dubious procedure when applied in clinical settings. Zubin *et al.* (1965, p. 198) have the following to say about it:

One would wish that the method of blind analysis could be made more explicit and more public, and that the enthusiastic proponents of this method were as ready to report their failures as their successes. Until this method becomes more open to public scrutiny, it has to be placed in the doubtful category, as far as validity is concerned.

In the method of *matching*, a number of judges are instructed to match personality sketches drawn from an analysis of the Rorschach protocol with personality descriptions written on the basis of either psychotherapy or close contact of some sort. Two studies frequently cited to exemplify this method are those of Vernon (1936) and Krugman (1942). The former reports a correlation of .83 in matches of written descriptions of personality and inkblot records. Krugman, in a more extensive study, instructed five judges to match the Rorschach records of 25 problem children with their clinical case reports. An average correlation coefficient of .83 was found for 125 pairings of this type. The average of correct matchings for the five judges was 84 percent.

In order to meet a common criticism of matching techniques, which is that they do not indicate the degree of rightness and wrongness of each prediction, Krugman also compared Rorschach interpretations with case records in terms of the following specific factors: intellectual level, emotional facets, diagnostic category, and total personality description. The findings were generally favorable in that almost perfect agreement was found in about 75 percent of the comparisons, and reasonably fair agreement in about 25 percent of the remaining cases.

Although most matching studies (Chambers and Hamlin, 1957; Glueck and Glueck, 1950; Palmer, 1951) have not met with success equal to that of the preceding ones, the method of matching has been criticized on several grounds (see especially Cronbach, 1948; Meehl, 1959c). For one, the method depends too heavily on the perceptive ability of particular judges. Second, its success is often based on cues or factors other than those appearing in the test record (e.g., age, health, education, or number of previous admissions to the hospital). And finally, matching techniques treat the Rorschach record in its totality, therefore making it difficult to identify which specific components contributed to particular aspects of the correct matchings. Failure to identify these signs or components makes the method a highly individualized one (e.g., in which each expert uses his favorite signs), and precludes any form of quantification.

Construct Validity. Studies conducted with the Rorschach usually are not intentionally designed to demonstrate its construct validity.[9] But indirect evidence of such validity (or lack of it) can be inferred from research in which the inkblots were administered before and after subjects underwent certain *physical manipulations,* such as surgical removal of portions of the brain, or before and after *experimental procedures* in a laboratory.

Certain psychological changes are expected as a consequence of the neurosurgical operative procedure of prefrontal lobotomy. Presumably this specialized surgical technique, which partially removes or ablates a portion of the frontal cortex, serves to lower the anxiety of patients. Studies measuring the effects of these operative procedures on Rorschach scores are contradictory. In one of these, reported by the Columbia Greystone Associates (Mettler, 1949), no changes in Rorschach performance were found among these patients. In another study, however, evidence of changes was reflected in the Rorschach protocols of operated patients (Allison and Allison, 1954). Generally, before-and-after-surgery studies have reported inconsistent findings (Helman, 1953; Zubin, 1949), and no particular trend is apparent.

Experimentally induced manipulations, which are preceded and followed by Rorschach testing, include states of induced tension, hypnosis, drugs, or even electroshock treatment. The purpose of inducing these experimental modifications, again, is to assess whether they result in changed Rorschach protocols. In one such study, using the Hertz scoring system, Eichler (1951) attempted to demonstrate that under conditions of experimental stress, Rorschach performance would be affected. An experimental group was first given arithmetic problems, with intermittent electric shocks introduced to harrass them, and then were given the Rorschach under the threat of further and more intense electric

---

[9] See Chapter 2, for a review of the meaning of construct validity.

shocks. Some of the Rorschach signs and indices of anxiety were reportedly increased, and differentiated significantly between the stress group and the control group. Specifically, the number of shading responses increased, and the total number of R's decreased. Eichler concluded that experimentally induced anxiety lent evidence to the validity of certain anxiety indices.

A second method utilized to artificially alter the state of the subject is hypnotic induction. One of the most interesting studies along these lines was an early one in which investigators administered the Rorschach to one subject nine times (Levine, Grassi and Gerson, 1943). The first administration was under standard conditions, then with a variety of seven different hypnotically suggested moods, and finally under hypnosis suggesting a normal and composed mood. As predicted by these psychologists, the first and last Rorschach protocols were quite similar. This similarity was interpreted by them as evidence for the negligible effect on the Rorschach of the hypnotic state by itself. There were a number of identifiable effects that occured because of the hypnotically induced mood changes; and all of these shifts were in keeping with accepted Rorschach theory. Under the hypnotic suggestion of depression, for example, there was considerable decrease in movement and color responses. Similarly, decreased human and animal movement scores, and many anatomy responses, accompanied a suggestion of hypochondriachal fears. And a somewhat euphoric mood occasioned a more mediocre record than that secured under normal conditions. All in all, the investigators concluded that changing moods, varying attitudes, and divers emotional states are systematically reflected in Rorschach performance.

Improvement after some form of somatic treatment or psychotherapy is predicted by most theories of personality, and Rorschach protocols secured after treatment should reflect the change for the better. Two studies conducted to test the hypothesis of improvement after treatment were those of Rioch (1949) and Windle (1952). Rioch's study reported the before and after protocols of 36 patients who had submitted themselves to psychoanalysis. All of these patients' Rorschach records reflected significant changes in the predicted direction, and these changes corresponded to the trends reported by the therapist. In the second study, insulin treatment had been administered to a group of schizophrenic patients; and in instances where patients had been judged to have improved on the hospital ward, this improvement was reflected in certain response categories of their Rorschach performance.

Generally, the validity studies cited so far have been sometimes encouraging but most often negative. These only begin to touch the surface of an enormous volume of Rorschach studies with similarly inconsistent results. More than 3,000 references are listed in Buros' *Sixth Mental Measurements Yearbook* (1965), and the overwhelming majority of them, especially the most recent ones (see the separate reviews by Dana, Eron, and Jensen in Buros, 1965, pp. 492–509), reach the same overall conclusion that has been heard for the past 45 years: There is very little convincing evidence to support the validity claims made for the technique by its proponents.

GENERAL EVALUATION AND CONCLUDING COMMENTS

The Rorschach is not a test in the usual psychometric sense of the term. Its structure differs notably from any of the devices of the self-report type. Whereas a test such as the MMPI, for example, is administered in an impersonal way in which the subject is required to give some 550 responses, the Rorschach is administered in an interpersonal situation and the respondent is free to give any kind or any number of different responses. These differences raise the question of whether or not the inkblots should be considered a traditional psychometric procedure. Perhaps it may be best to consider the Rorschach a variant of the interview, an approach that would be more compatible with considering the qualitative aspects of the test situation than the scores obtained.

This nonpsychometric view of the Rorschach is becoming increasingly popular with psychologists, and one author (Sarason, 1966, p. 187) writes that the responses observed during the inkblot procedure might consist of "such characteristics as the fluency of the subject's speech, the amounts of emotional expression with which the subject communicates his responses, his gestures and idiosyncracies, and the nature of the social interaction between the tester and testee."

If this view is rejected, however, and students of the Rorschach continue to base descriptions and predictions on responses elicited to inkblots, then the following weaknesses of the technique must be remedied. In the first place its administration is time consuming;

perhaps this process can be speeded up by having the subject record his own responses as the inblots are projected on a screen. Of course, this would also facilitate group administration of the blots. Second, the scoring of the protocols is complex and diverse. It is about time, considering the Rorschach's long history, for manuals to be published containing explicit scoring instructions. Simplicity of scoring could be accomplished by the introduction of fixed sets of scoring categories under which most responses could be included. Such scoring systems now exist for most individually administered intelligence tests (e.g., the Stanford-Binet and the Wechsler Adult Intelligence Scale), and although the problems are different in Rorschach scoring, they are not insurmountable. The third weakness, one which was repeatedly emphasized in the preceding sections, is that the test's relationship to observable behavior has not been adequately demonstrated. This last matter, by far the most important criterion of any psychometric procedure, is the test's most serious shortcoming.

The only aspect that has remained solidly in the test's favor is its unstructuredness and the concommitant subtlety and resistance to fakeability. Undoubtedly the ambiguity of the inkblots presents a formidable challenge to subjects who want to fake this test. This subtlety of the Rorschach stimulus materials, however, was designed to operate only against the respondent who may be motivated, consciously or otherwise, to distort his test results; it seems to be operating equally well against Rorschach scorers and interpreters whose scoring and interpreting are every bit as subtle as the inkblots themselves.

In view of the voluminous negative evidence that continues to be presented against the Rorschach's use as a psychometric device in clinical settings, it is surprising that the technique's popularity has not abated. Unquestionably, many clinicians have "faith" in the Rorschach's validity, and this serves to perpetuate its use. These clinicians are satisfied that Rorschach records help to provide insights into their patients' personalities which seem to fit in well with information from other sources, such as clinical interviewing. But at best, this form of evidence can only be considered in favor of the test's clinical usefulness, and does not constitute a demonstration of its psychometric validity—i.e., that it really measures what it purports to. In this regard, Cronbach (1960, p. 604) has wisely recommended that the Rorschach and other "impressionistic procedures" be used in clinical settings for hypothesis formation within the context of other psychometric and nonpsychometric data; but he cautions the prospective users that in other situations, above all

. . . where the decision is irreversible, as when surgery is prescribed or where the patient once classified is forever left in the same pigeonhole, is this use of impressions and imperfectly valid scores dangerous.

The real danger in the use of such "imperfectly valid" tests as the Rorschach—and this is related to some Rorschach users' unbounded faith in their instrument—is the claim that such a method can be used as the major or sole instrument to help make irreversible decisions. Difficulties arise when the clinician refuses to accept a legitimate but restricted role for any of his favorite procedures and consequently uses them in instances where their demonstrated validity is less than satisfactory.

About the only hopeful sign that has emerged in recent years of bringing the Rorschach into the arena of psychometric respectability has been the work done on the *Holtzman Inkblot Technique* (Herron, 1963; Holtzman, 1958, 1959; Holtzman *et al.*, 1961, 1963; Swartz and Holtzman, 1963). However, it should be noted that Holtzman's solution to some of the Rorschach inkblots' problems has been to construct a new technique and an entirely different set of stimuli.

Holtzman's inkblot test was devised by the method of empirical keying. On the basis of the test's power to discriminate between normal and psychiatric criterion groups, and by retaining inkblots that yielded high split-half reliability coefficients, Holtzman and his associates prepared two parallel forms of 45 cards each. Further, they developed 22 scales that can be scored to encompass most of the information commonly obtained from the Rorschach. The result has been a procedure that is clearly more reliable than the Rorschach. However, this increased reliability was purchased at a price that most "projectivists" would rather not pay: The wide latitude of responding that is possible on the Rorschach is almost completely curtailed on the Holtzman technique. The subject can make only one response to each of the 45 blots. The advantage of restricted responding, on the other hand, is the wider assortment of stimuli that can be administered (45 v. 10). From the standpoint of sampling subjects' reactions to stimuli, this increase expands the item data pool. It guarantees the number of R (45), and thus, has the advantage of increasing the R for reliability and validity studies.

In short, what these researchers have accomplished has been to translate the Rorschach into acceptable psychometric terms without losing too much of the essence of the original test. Although not all test critics (Eysenck, 1965) agree that its validity is or will be any more convincing than that of the Rorschach, most psychologists, and some projectivists among them, gladly welcome this new approach as a promising endeavor worthy of serious consideration. (Summary appears at end of Chapter 10.)

FOR FURTHER READING

1. EBEL, R. L.   Must all tests be valid? *American Psychologist*, 1961, 16, 640–647.

   This critical evaluation of the concept of validity leads the author to argue for interpreting test scores in terms of their meaningfulness.

2. EPSTEIN, S.   Some theoretical considerations on the nature of ambiguity and the use of stimulus dimensions in projective techniques. *Journal of consulting Psychology*, 1966, 30, 183–192.

   In this paper the author attempts to extinguish the enthusiasm for the exaggerated claims made for the value of ambiguous stimuli as essential for obtaining a "global" personality picture.

3. FRANK, L. K.   Projective methods for the study of personality. *Journal of Psychology*, 1939, 8, 349–413.

   More than any other paper, this influential article led to the popularization of the term *projective technique*. Almost 30 years later, it is still important reading matter.

4. GLESER, GOLDINE C.   Projective methodologies. In FARNSWORTH, P. R., MCNEMAR, OLGA, & MCNEMAR, Q. (Eds.), *Annual review of psychology*, Volume 14. Palo Alto: Annual Reviews, Inc., 1963. Pp. 391–422.

   This article is the first such review of this area. Dr. Gleser sees a number of hopeful signs that projectivists are accepting evidence that there are limitations of existing projective techniques.

5. HARROWER, MOLLY.   Differential diagnosis. In WOLMAN, B. B. (Ed.), *Handbook of clinical psychology*. New York: McGraw-Hill Book Co., 1965. Pp. 381–402.

   A short review of the uses of a number of projective tests and a prescription for the general conduct of diagnosticians is presented. More detailed information on these and related topics can be obtained from her book on *Appraising Personality: An Introduction to the Projective Techniques* (1964).

6. HOLZBERG, J. D.   Projective techniques. In BERG, I. A. & PENNING-

TON, L. A. (Eds.), *An introduction to clinical psychology.* New York: Ronald Press, 1966. Pp. 106–153.

An excellent and recent review of the place of projective techniques in psychometrics. For a similar review, with emphasis on different aspects of the research literature, the reader is referred to Shneidman's chapter (see reference below).

7. KINSLINGER, H. J. Applications of projective techniques in personnel psychology since 1940. *Psychological Bulletin,* 1966, 66, 134–139.

A review of such projective tests as the Rorschach, TAT, the Worthington Personal-History, and other tests have been applied in studies relating to various personnel problems.

8. KLOPFER, B. & DAVIDSON, HELEN H. *The Rorschach technique: An introductory manual.* New York: Harcourt, Brace & World, Inc., 1962.

Most of the parts of this manual are more useful to users than students, but the two leading chapters (pp. 3–25) serve to introduce the uninitiated to the background, theory, and method of the Rorschach technique.

9. LINDZEY, G. *Projective techniques and cross-cultural research.* New York: Appleton-Century-Crofts, 1961.

Delightful reading throughout, this book deals also with the definition, varieties, theoretical foundations, and interpretations of projective methods (Pp. 25–176).

10. SAUGSTAD, P. Effect of food deprivation on perception cognition. *Psychological Bulletin,* 1966, 65, 80–90.

Nine experiments, designed to investigate the effect of food deprivation on perceptual cognitive processes, are examined in detail. The author reached the conclusion that the projective material presented to the subject must be meaningfully related to the motivational state under which he is operating.

11. SCHAFER, R. *Psychoanalytic interpretation in Rorschach testing:* theory and application. New York: Grune & Stratton, Inc., 1954.

In addition to its applicability to Rorschach method and theory, this book by a gifted clinician is relevant to all aspects of developing sensitivity in interpersonal contacts.

12. SHNEIDMAN, E. S. Projective techniques. In WOLMAN, B. B. (Ed.), *Handbook of clinical psychology.* New York: McGraw-Hill Book Co., 1965. Pp. 498–521.

This chapter complements Holzberg's, above, and is especially valuable for its conveniently categorized references (e.g. "General References," and "References to Specific Projective Techniques").

13. STAGNER, R. The gullibility of personnel managers. *Personnel Psychology,* 1958, 11, 347–352.

Invoking the Roman saying, *caveat emptor*—let the buyer beware —the author applies this principle to personality tests.

14. ZUBIN, J., ERON, L. D., & SCHUMER, FLORENCE. *An experimental*

approach to projective techniques. New York: John Wiley & Sons, Inc., 1965.

Anyone interested in obtaining a perspective of the place of projective techniques within the mainstream of experimental and psychometric psychology must read at least the first five chapters of this extensive and singularly exhaustive tome. The remainder of the book is of greater interest to the expert than neophyte.

CHAPTER 10

PROJECTIVE TECHNIQUES
(Continued): THE TAT AND OTHER
TESTS

The only other projective technique that has approached the Rorschach method in amount of use and volume of research is the *Thematic Apperception Test* (TAT). The TAT materials consist of drawings and photographs, taken mostly from magazine illustrations but including some paintings and drawings from other art sources.

In contrast to the amorphous blots of the Rorschach, the identity of most objects in the TAT pictures is obvious. Some ambiguity is retained in the pictures, so that persons can "read into" them something from their own experience or fantasy, but almost everyone can agree that they depict familiar objects or scenes. For example, there is little question that the drawing shown in Figure 10–1 represents a woman standing on the threshold of a half-opened door, looking into a room. However, there is sufficient ambiguity in this scene to allow the subject to *apperceive*—i.e., to perceive according to his own experience and background, and interpret the stimulus card in various ways. Thus the woman shown in Figure 10–1 may be frowning or cheerful, she may be coming into the room or leaving it, and as she views the inside of the room she may see any one of an infinite number of things.

The TAT, which is the main focus of attention for much of this chapter, has occasioned numerous modifications and adaptations which have become personality measuring devices in their own

FIGURE 10–1.   A picture similar to one in the TAT. Although this picture is more structured than any of the Rorschach inkblots, there is still opportunity to "read into" various aspects of the stimulus task.

right. These are discussed briefly toward the end of the chapter. Concluding this chapter and the discussion of projective techniques is a listing of a series of procedures often used in conjunction with the Rorschach or TAT.

BACKGROUND OF THE THEMATIC APPERCEPTION TEST

The Thematic Apperception Test or TAT, was introduced by Christiana D. Morgan and Henry A. Murray (1935) as a method to explore unconscious thoughts and fantasies. They described a test that required subjects to tell stories associated with pictures, and they intended it as a device to speed up the progress of psychotherapy for patients who either could not afford or did not need complete psychoanalysis. Later Professor Murray (1938, 1943), who is chiefly credited as the founder of the test, expanded its scope by emphasizing that the TAT enables trained interpreters to reconstruct, on the basis of a subject's stories, his dominant drives, emotions, sentiments, complexes, and conflicts.

The idea of producing stories in response to pictures, as noted at the outset of the preceding chapter, was first reported in the psychological literature by Binet (Binet and Henri, 1896), the founder of modern intelligence tests, and was later described extensively in studies by a number of others (Brittain, 1907; Clark, 1926; Libby, 1908; Schwartz, 1932) who collected stories for psychological experimentation. However, the idea of such a test was not widely understood, or adopted, until H. A. Murray began to report his research at the Harvard Psychological Clinic on the application of the TAT for appraisal of college students.

Although the TAT was at first slow in gaining wide acceptance, it is now a test that approximates the Rorschach in popularity and in the amount of research it has stimulated (Sundberg, 1961; Buros, 1965). At first it gained popularity only among clinical psychologists, but gradually it became a research tool in developmental psychology, social psychology, personality, and cross-cultural studies in anthropology. It is also used for personality assessment in the fields of counseling and industrial psychology. Paralleling the widespread uses of the test, the TAT has given rise to vast literature describing its many practical applications and theoretical underpinnings.[1]

RATIONALE OF THE TAT

The principal assumption underlying TAT interpretation is that fantasies, experiences, desires, inner tendencies, attitudes, and conflicts have been projected onto the stimulus cards and the characters or objects depicted on them. However, this assumption has been seriously questioned by a number of TAT theorists. It has been noted (Tomkins, 1949), for example, that important fantasies and experiences often are actually withheld from TAT stories. In this connection, Abt and Bellak (1950), who have made extensive contributions to the theory of projective tests, contrast the projection which is elicited by the TAT with that which is utilized by a person as a defense against unacceptable forces. They note that the latter is an unconscious process that cannot be made conscious except through prolonged psychotherapy, whereas projection found

---

[1] The reader might consult more basic sources than the present one for a broader view of the field (Abt and Bellak, 1950; Harrison, 1965; Murstein, 1963; Stein, 1955; Symonds, 1949; Tomkins, 1947).

in TAT stories, or "apperception," as they prefer to call it, although it has unconscious determinants, involves recognition by the subject, at least partially, that he was speaking of himself in the stories recently produced. This difference has also been noted by another psychologist (Holt, 1961), who distinguishes between TAT stories and fantasies. He calls attention to the following facts: TAT storytelling is an active, rather than spontaneous, response to an external stimulus; TAT responses involve verbalizations, and fantasy does not; the TAT story is remembered by the subject who related it, but fantasy usually is not accessible to recall; and the subject relating a story only occasionally gets emotionally involved in its details, whereas fantasies always arouse affective responses.

Further, it has been assumed by TAT users that the wishes, needs, personality style, and motivational components revealed in TAT stories constitute material that cannot be secured without the test. This assumption holds that respondents are either unwilling or unable to talk about them in the ordinary psychodiagnostic or therapy setting. Whereas Murray (1943) only hoped that the subject would become "so involved in the task that he forgets his sensitive self and the necessity of defending it against the probings of the examiner," most TAT investigators have readily assumed that these unconscious components of personality cannot be obtained in another fashion. However, there is good evidence (Lebo, 1960) to suggest that there are other methods available that are equally effective in evoking various "private" responses. A mere verbal description of the scene depicted in a TAT card, for example, elicits responses similar to those given in association to the cards themselves. There are probably a host of other ways available that are equally effective.

Many TAT scoring schemes assume that the central character of the story, or the "hero," as he is commonly called, reflects the subject's needs, wishes, and personality style. In studies testing this assumption (Lindzey, 1958; Lindzey and Kalnins, 1958), it was aptly demonstrated that the hero does reflect many aspects of the storyteller's personality style. These investigators further ascertained that not all the characters in the narrative resemble the storyteller. The function of some of the "supporting cast" of characters is clearly to provide background for the central character(s).

Finally, two important assumptions are made in interpreting

TATs. It is assumed by some that test scores are related to overt behavior; and that it is sensitive to varying motivational states. These are topics that deserve detailed discussion, and they are taken up in later sections of the chapter. It is sufficient here to call attention to the fact that the evidence to support either of these assumptions is indeed scanty.

DESCRIPTION OF MATERIALS

The test material administered to any one subject consists of a set of 20 cards. Of these, 19 have pictures printed on them, and 1 is a blank card. There are actually 31 cards available, but a selection is made of especially pertinent ones for boys, girls, men, and women. The pictures include such diverse content areas as a young boy contemplating a violin, a country scene, a young woman staring off into space, science fiction mirages, apparent bedroom scenes, and a blank card. Several of the pictures on TAT cards are presented in Figure 10–2.

TEST ADMINISTRATION

Murray (1943), in his *TAT Manual*, recommends that the examiner establish a sympathetic and permissive environment to ensure the examinee every opportunity to yield the highest possible quality of creative story. The testing process is divided into two sessions, and for each of these it is suggested that no more than 10 TAT cards be administered, with at least one day intervening between the two sessions. More recent practical considerations have led to a reduction in the number of cards administered. Most testers now present the subject with 8 to 12 cards, and use only a single session.

The cards are presented individually, and the respondent is instructed to produce a story about the picture that describes the depicted scene, what led up to it, what the characters in the picture are thinking, and what the outcome will be. He is encouraged to spend about five minutes in creating and telling each story; and the examiner records the story verbatim, occasionally reminding the subject to clarify or expand some portion of his narrative.

Recording the stories is generally accomplished either by having the tester write the response, by means of a tape recorder, or through the use of a stenographer. The presence of a third person in the test

FIGURE 10–2. Several illustrations
of scenes such as appear on
the TAT cards.

session, such as a secretary or clerk, is considered awkward and disturbing to the subject, and therefore arrangements are often made to conceal this person's presence. It is less time consuming for the test administrator, and certainly less laborious, to give the selected cards to the subject with instructions to write his stories on paper. This form of self-administration can take place in the office, at home, or even as a member of a group to which the TAT pictures can be shown on a screen.[2]

FIGURE 10-3.   A card similar to the one which elicited the story reproduced in the text.

As an illustration of the type of responses elicited by the TAT, the following story, told in response to the picture presented in Figure 10-3, was related by a 12-year-old boy whose parents brought him to a child guidance center. The boy had difficulties in school, having just been retained in fifth grade for the second time.

---

[2] The traditional method of administering the TAT encourages "free responding"—that is to say, it encourages storytelling. Procedures are also available that restrict subjects to forced or multiple choice responses. However, much of the spontaneity is lost in the latter approach, and most projective testers assert that the evidence to date does not justify its adoption.

The parents reported that their son's teachers agreed that the boy was more than bright enough to pass all his subjects, but that something else seems to be impeding his progress. Here is his story:

Line 1: This boy was supposed to be practicing his violin but he really doesn't feel like it.

Line 2: If his mother catches him goofing off from practicing, he is going to get into a lot of trouble.

Line 3: She does a lot of yelling and screaming about these types of things and the boy has learned not to excite her.

Line 4: She really doesn't care whether he learns to play the thing or not, and as long as she doesn't catch him goofing off, she's satisfied.

Line 5: Right now the boy is trying to figure out how to fool his mother and he thinks maybe he'll tape-record his practice session and then in the future play back the tape recordings while he sneaks out the window and plays with his friends.

Line 6: Wait till he tells his friends about the tape recordings and the way he fooled his mother. They'll find out again how smart he *really* is.

In this boy's story there are numerous valuable clues regarding his personality makeup, which were corroborated by his psychologist in subsequent therapy sessions. Without borrowing from any particular personality theory, the following examination of each line of the narrative should illustrate a number of these clues. Of course, in actual practice, interpretation of the story would only proceed in conjunction with consideration of all his other narratives and within the context of all other assessment procedures conducted with the youngster and his parents.

Line 1: The opening comment indicates that the subject perceives the violin accurately (most but not all subjects do), that he has been instructed to practice his lessons, and that he does not enjoy the thought of playing the instrument.

Line 2: Here the boy suggests that his behavior may make mother unhappy, and she may punish him.

Line 3: There is some cynicism expressed in this remark, and the subject indicates that mother, as he perceives her, is to be placated.

Line 4: Mother is perceived here as uninterested in his progress with the violin; she will not reprove him so long as she is not confronted with his defiance of her instructions. This remark probably reveals the boy's opinion of her attitudes toward such things as lessons and seems to be an area of his personality functioning worth exploring.

Line 5: This boy's plan reflects some degree of ingenuity for a 12-year-old and suggests that he is capable of considerably risky be-havior.

Line 6: The final sentence of the story indicates that some of his be-havior is exhibitionistic, that he is interested in the opinions of others, and that he may be concerned about being stigmatized as ignorant or mentally slow. It also suggests that the subject has planned similar deceptions prior to the one described.

It should be apparent even from examination of such a brief narrative as the preceding that enough evidence can be gleaned from TAT stories to permit formulation of a number of working hypotheses.

SCORING THE TAT

In contrast to the Rorschach, with its two or three popularly accepted scoring systems, plus several others which have not gained general usage, the TAT has spawned a large number of scoring methods. Murray's lack of detailed scoring instructions, his thin manual (1943), and the relative ease with which the TAT can be administered, have been cited as factors contributing to the multi-plicity of scoring systems (Murstein, 1963). Furthermore, the nontechnical nature of the TAT, and the simple verbal content of stories, have encouraged clinicians to invent their own systems of analysis.

For these reasons, in addition to the fact that the TAT has been used for both clinical assessment and personality research, it has been difficult to formulate one widely acceptable system of TAT analysis. Although the TAT is used for studying the dynamics of personality in either the applied or research setting, the differences in the needs of the two settings are considerable. Clinicians must make immediate practical decisions on the basis of their findings with many tests, and therefore feel that they must use a scoring system that is minimally time consuming. Research psychologists, on the other hand, place little or no premium on ease of administra-tion, scoring, or interpretation of the test because time, in contrast to yield, is unimportant to them.

The discussion of scoring systems which follows reflects some of the differences that have arisen because of the test's various uses. The major division between these systems can be delineated along their quantitative versus nonquantitative orientations. Thus, following the division suggested in a recent book on TAT theory and research (Murstein, 1963), the distinction between quantitative or nonquantitative lies in whether or not the TAT scoring results in assigning numerical values to certain aspects of the stories. Each of these systems, of course, is accompanied by slightly different test administration procedures.

Murray's Scoring System (Nonquantitative)

Although amenable to quantification—and he did suggest an elementary scaling procedure for weighting some of scoring categories—Murray's (1943) recommended system of analysis is highly content-oriented and relies heavily on the qualitative characteristics of the stories. It proceeds by careful attention to the forces emanating from the "hero," and the forces emanating from the environment (called *press*). In turn these two forces are analyzed under six categories or tasks. The following outline of the analysis of the TAT includes Morgan and Murray's (1935) original description of the procedure, Murray's (1938, 1943) later suggestions and modifications of that procedure, and the process plus some variations, as it is most commonly used today by TAT workers.

1. *The Hero:* The first step in the analysis of a story is to distinguish the hero, or the character with whom the subject seems to have identified. In principle, this would be the character in whom the storyteller is most interested, and the individual who most resembles him. The tester must be alert to the fact that the hero of the story may shift from one story character to another, or that there may be two or three discernible heroes, or none at all. The interpreter should direct his attention to the following aspects of the heroes' traits: superiority, intelligence, leadership, belongingness, solitariness, and quarrelsomeness.

2. *Needs of the Hero:* After the scorer has identified the hero or heroes, he must formulate the reactions of the heroes to various forces. These formulations usually are made within the theoretical framework the tester happens to prefer; but Murray (1938) recommends that this be accomplished within a classification of the needs (abbreviated by n) of the hero. These needs are either primary ("viscerogenic") or secondary ("psychogenic"). Some of the primary needs include: n-Air, n-Water, and n-Food; and the secondary needs are: n-Acquisition, n-Order, n-Achievement,

n-Dominance, n-Aggression, n-Abasement, and n-Nurturance. Each of these needs can be scored on an intensity scale from one to five, depending on their strength as expressed by duration, frequency, and importance in the plot.

3. *Environmental Forces:* The environmental forces are categorized according to their effect on the hero. Murray's system consists of a comprehensive list of environmental forces, or press. These press could be real or imaginary, and include (p is the abbreviation of press): p-Aggression, in which the hero's property or possessions are destroyed; p-Dominance, where the hero is exposed to commands, orders, or forceful argument; and p-Rejection, in which persons reject, repudiate, are indifferent to, or leave the hero.

4. *Outcomes:* The relative strengths of the forces emanating from the hero and the strengths of those from the environment, the amount of hardship and frustration experienced, and the relative degree of success and failure of the hero, must be assessed. They can usually be inferred from the stories' outcomes—that is, the way in which respondents wind up their stories.

5. *Themas:* The interplay within a story of the hero's needs, press, and successful or unsuccessful resolution of his conflicts, constitutes a simple thema. Combinations of simple themas, interlocked or forming a sequence, are called complex themas. Essentially themas, simple or complex, are abstracts of the dynamic patterns and the outcome of each story; and they represent need-press combinations. The question the scorer should ask himself, when reviewing the totality of a subject's themas, is: "What issues, conflicts, or dilemmas are of the greatest concern to the respondent?"

6. *Interests, Sentiments, and Relationships:* The respondent apparently displays his own interests and sentiments by his choice of particular topics and in the selection of particular types of heroes.

There are numerous other nonquantitative scoring systems available (Bellak, 1954; Henry, 1956; Piotrowski, 1950),[3] but it is generally agreed that none of these will replace Murray's needs-press approach. For use of the TAT in research settings, where it is essential to ensure standard administration and scoring procedures, systems of analysis more quantitative than Murray's have been developed. Two of these systems—one developed by David C.

---

[3] The interested reader may wish to consult Wyatt's journal article (1947) and Murstein's book (1963) for more extensive summaries of these systems.

McClelland, and the other by Leonard Eron—have been described extensively and exceptionally well in the literature and are considered briefly here.

McClelland's System (Quantitative)

A scoring system second only to Murray's in terms of popularity among researchers is the one developed by David C. McClelland and co-workers (Atkinson, 1958b; McClelland, 1958a; McClelland *et al.*, 1953). This system's major application has been in research with the *achievement* motive (*n*-Ach), but has been extended to include the *power* and *affiliation* motives as well. For these research purposes, McClelland selected four pictures, only two of which were originally in the TAT. The pictures portray men working at a machine, a boy at a desk with a book, a father and son scene, and a boy who is evidently daydreaming. The stories are written around the following questions: "What's happening?" "What has led up to the situation?" "What is being thought?" "What will happen?"

The achievement motive is said to express a need for accomplishment. Here is an illustration of *n*-Ach in a story told by a college student in response to the scene depicting men working at a machine.

These men were assigned to this work detail. The one man who is looking intently at the machine wishes really to display his competence in being able to handle this job. Although he feels the nature of the work is not sufficiently challenging for a person of his training, he nevertheless believes that a job, no matter how trivial, should be well done.

Another college student made up this story:

This fellow's heart is just not in the work he is supposed to be doing. He would just as soon be out of it, and perhaps read a book or go to a movie. I don't know, he just doesn't look interested. Maybe he has some other problems occupying his mind at the moment.

The difference between these stories should be apparent. The first theme expresses the desire to accomplish and to excel over one's fellow man. If it can be assumed that his story represents the way he sees himself, one could speculate that this student has a strong desire to succeed at school and at other endeavors also. In contrast, the second story expresses nonchalance and lack of desire to concentrate on the task at hand. It might be suspected that this subject's motivation to achieve is considerably less intense than that of the first storyteller.

According to McClelland's scoring system, every story can be categorized into either unrelated imagery (UI), doubtful achievement imagery (TI), and achievement imagery (AI), depending on relevance to the achievement variable. Each of these categories is assigned one of three weighted scores (i.e., − 1, 0, and + 1 for UI, TI, and AI) ; and if a story receives + 1 (AI),—i.e., if it is related to achievement—then it is possible to score it for ten additional subcategories. The latter include scores for themes that express anticipation of success (or failure) ; scores for obstacles, imagined or real, to the attainment of success; and scores to credit some evidence that the central character of a story actively pursues his goals. More will be said about McClelland's system of scoring in the section on TAT interpretive procedures.

Eron's System (Quantitative)

Finally, the feasibility of a quantitative approach to TAT scoring has been demonstrated also by Eron and his co-workers (Eron, Terry *et al.*, 1950; Auld, Eron *et al.*, 1955). These investigators, using Guttman's scaling method, developed a set of scales that enabled them to tabulate the elements they considered essential in a TAT protocol.

Each story is evaluated in terms of *emotional tone* in the following way (Zubin *et al.*, 1965, pp. 578–579) :

General Rating Scale for Emotional Tone
?: Subject cannot make up a story.
0: Complete failure, submission to fate, death, murder, suicide, illicit sex with violence, revenge, aggressive hostility, severe guilt, complete hopelessness.
1: Conflict with attempt at adjustment, rebellion, fear, worry, departure, regret, illness, physical exhaustion, resignation toward death, loneliness.
2: Description, lack of affect, balance of positive and negative feelings, routine activities, impersonal reflection.
3: Aspiration, desire for success and doubt about outcome, compensation for limited endowment, description with cheerful feeling, reunion with friends, contentment with world, feeling of security.
4: Justifiably high aspiration, complete satisfaction and happiness, reunion with loved ones.

In addition to these ratings the *outcomes* of stories are rated (e.g., failure, frustration, or success at end of the story) and scores are provided for responses to each specific card (versus general ratings of all stories). Furthermore, stories are scored according to an elaborate checklist of more than 100 themes classified as interpersonal, intrapersonal, and impersonal.

This scoring sytem's usefulness has been demonstrated in research settings and in numerous studies. Adequate reliability coefficients were reported for most of these uses (Eron, 1950; Eron et al., 1950). Although its clinical usefulness still remains to be demonstrated, Eron's system of TAT protocol analysis permits the collection of normative data and allows intraperson and interperson comparisons. Therefore it brings the TAT closer to the mainstream of traditional psychometric research.

TAT INTERPRETATION

The task confronting the interpreter of TAT protocols is to relate the small segment of behavior reflected in a subject's story to some facet of his personality or to some future behavioral outcome. To provide these relationships, at least 10 major interpretive schemes are available, and this does not include the multitude of home brewed interpretive systems developed by clinicians in their daily practices. The scope of this book does not warrant a review of these, however interesting and useful they may be, and only the two most widely known systematic points of view can be presented here: one is the psychoanalytic method of interpretation, used most often by practicing clinical psychologists in mental health settings; and the other is David C. McClelland's system, which is related to his theory of motivation, and is used more often in personality research rather than in applied measurement situations.

Psychoanalytic Interpretation

Historically, the first TAT interpretations were rooted in Freudian psychoanalytic theory and technique. The founder of the TAT, Henry A. Murray, discussed depth interpretations in connection with patients under psychoanalysis and compared the interpretation of stories with dream analysis. Typically these interpretations focus on TAT protocol content rather than on its formal organizational characteristics. A theme such as running away from home, for example, may signify the desire for a new father, mother, or spouse. Bravado in the theme of a story may be interpreted as a denial of passivity; and passivity in a theme may be an expression of *reaction formation* (behaving in a manner opposite to the intent of an unconscious need). An unsuccessful outcome in a story is fequently related to sexual impotence. Furthermore, since psychoanalysts attach special significance to certain symbols in a patient's dreams or free associations, TAT stories are thoroughly scoured for symbolism.

Special attention is paid also to significant sequences in TAT materials. Occasionally these sequences are found within a particular story, but more often they are noted from one story to the next, so that it becomes necessary to consider a series of stories together in order to understand the dynamics, or the motivating forces at work. For instance, when a particular story contains evidence of a repressed wish (a wish that has been relegated to the unconscious), it may be followed, either within the same story or in response to the next card, by sterile, evasive, and noncommittal thematic material. Thus a number of patterns of sequences are commonly recognized by psychoanalysts as occurring together—crime and aggression followed by stories of a harmless and innocuous nature; hostility followed by punishment; guilt and self-punishment followed by expressions of superiority; and lack of achievement followed by success (Symonds, 1949).

The major weakness of the psychoanalytic approach does not lie in the TAT itself but reflects the common criticism of psychoanalysis. For example, the lack of quantification, so characteristic of psychoanalytic theory, leaves undefined the issue of how much of something must be present before it is labeled as such. Further, without measurement it is not possible to confirm or deny the presence of certain concepts or symbols in the TAT protocol. This leaves the clinician free to reconcile verbal behavior he finds on the TAT with any notions he may have about the respondent. If he believes, let us say, that the subject is paranoid, he can confirm his hypothesis by noting the number of scenes included in the subject's projections where suspicion is the motive. On the other hand, if the subject's stories are fraught with characters whose actions and deeds convey behavior that is just the opposite of paranoia, an interpretation of reaction formation could be made. Thus the psychoanalytic approach, by introducing its lack of preciseness into the interpretation of TAT stories, avoids negative research findings, and consistently ensures confirmation of its hypotheses.

McClelland's Interpretive Method

The work of McClelland and Atkinson has focused mainly on a general theory of motivation as it is related to TAT responses (see especially, Atkinson, 1958a). By assuming that the TAT pictures arouse motives in much the same manner as do the cues of real-life situations, and that these motives come out of the subject's past experiences, they maintain that the investigator is able to look upon differences in subjects' imaginative productions as reflections of motivational differences. In their early studies (Atkinson and McClelland, 1948; McClelland and Atkinson, 1948), they used the hunger drive as a motivating force and were able to demonstrate that increasing periods of food deprivation were accompanied by consistent changes in subjects' responses to pictures. In further experiments, they extended this procedure to the point where the intensity of the motive was controlled experimentally, and they observed the accompanying changes reflected in TAT stories. Their recent work (Atkinson, 1958a, b) has consisted mainly of manipulating the intensity of the achievement motive (e.g., by inducing feelings of success or failure in subjects), and observing corresponding changes in TAT performance.

In a typical laboratory experiment, McClelland and associates use a standard set of their pictures to divide their subjects into high achievers (HA) and low achievers (LA) on the basis of themes elicited. Then they select subjects from the upper and lower one third of the achievement distribution and attempt to discover whether the HA and LA differ with respect to a number of performance criteria. In one study (Lowell, 1952), for example, it turned out that HA learned a scrambled-words test more rapidly than LA subjects. In another study (McClelland and Lieberman, 1949), using briefly exposed words, high achievers recognized positive achievement words more rapidly than low achievers.

A variation of the preceding study consists of measuring the effects of TAT administration under different contextual conditions. Thus it has been observed (McClelland et al., 1949) that n-Ach, as measured by the TAT, increased in progressive order for the following contextual test conditions: relaxed, neutral, failure, and success followed by failure. Not all their laboratory studies support all of the foregoing findings. For example, in one study (Lazarus and Baker, 1957) it turned out that HA do not necessarily persist longer on a given task. In another study (Reitman, 1960), the TAT was administered to men under achievement-, neutral-, and affiliation-oriented conditions. Nonsignificant correlations were found between n-Ach and performance on arithmetic, spatial relations, and matching problems for all conditions.

More recently (McClelland, 1961), the motivational approach to personality assessment has been extended to studies of various societies, contemporary and ancient. The thesis guiding this work has been that achievement orientation, identified indirectly by studying the artifacts of the culture, is associated with that society's economic growth.

One criticism launched against McClelland's approach asserts that factors in addition to achievement motivation contribute significantly to n-Ach as measured on the TAT. It has been demonstrated (Lindzey and Silverman, 1959), for example, that verbal fluency, I.Q., and aptitude influence the n-Ach score. In addition, it has been shown (Turek and Howell, 1959) that n-Ach is also influenced by the number and kinds of cards administered to the subject and by his immediately preceding experiences (success or failure). These findings have led some critics to suggest viewing n-Ach as a highly unstable variable and to question McClelland's assumption that there is a simple relationship between n-Ach and overt behavior (see Murstein, 1963).

EVALUATION OF THE TAT

The major criticisms lodged against the TAT over the past two decades concern the scanty evidence that has been provided for its reliability and validity (Buros, 1965). In part, the inadequacy of evidence supporting its reliability and validity is due to the clinician's unfailing confidence in the "clinical usefulness" of the TAT; but in the main it is a consequence of the large numbers of schools or systems that have developed over the years, each with its own administration, scoring, and interpretation schemes. Within each of these schools or systems, the crucial question from a psychometric point of view, and the criterion against which the TAT will continue to be judged for sometime to come, is still whether or not it is a reliable and valid measure of personality.

Reliability

One method for establishing a projective technique's reliability has been to demonstrate that scorers or judges can agree in their separate analyses of TAT protocols. This agreement among scorers, also called interscorer or interjudge reliability, should be quite high if the test is to be of any value. Several psychologists (Gulliksen, 1950; Murstein, 1963) have recommended that interscorer reliability coefficients of less than .90 are inadequate, since such low correlations indicate that test scores are influenced by the subjective effects of scorers. Concern with this particular form of reliability is, of course, more relevant to projective methods than to various paper-and-pencil tests, because they lack the latter's fixed alternative (e.g., yes or no, true or false) response categories. A test such as the MMPI, for example, invites machine or clerical scoring that yields perfect scorer reliabilities.[4] As a matter of fact, the use of the term "objective" tests to designate self-report inventories originates in the high degree of agreement among scorers achieved on such tests. Developers of nonprojective tests do not even bother to report this form of reliability because it is taken for granted. Unfortunately such is not the case with the TAT, and concern with interscorer agreement is highly relevant.

Generally speaking, reliability among scorers is high when judges thoroughly familiar with a scoring system are used and when scoring categories are carefully defined in advance (Feld and Smith, 1958). Thus agreement among scorers for the categories n-Achievement, n-Affiliation, and n-Power is quite high when there is familiarity with this system among the scorers. When a manual is made available, which gives detailed instructions on how to score for each of these categories, reliability coefficients invariably approximate or surpass the .90's (Atkinson, 1950; Kagan and Moss, 1959; Lindzey and Herman, 1955; McClelland et al., 1949). The use of less refined scoring systems, on the other hand, where global or content-oriented approaches to TAT protocal analysis are made,

---

[4] This assumes that the clerks or machines do not commit copying or mechanical errors.

yields interscorer reliability indexes that are discouragingly low (Clark, 1944; Sanford *et al.*, 1943; Veroff *et al.*, 1960).

Another form of reliability, one that the TAT shares with all nonprojective devices, comes from demonstration of the test's temporal stability as measured by the test-retest correlation coefficient. Low retest reliability suggests that the TAT is strongly influenced by extraneous situational factors that may be minimally related to personality dimensions. Typically, retest reliabilities have been moderate to low. Of course, the longer the time interval between test and retest, the less stable are the coefficients.

This relationship was demonstrated clearly in one study (Tomkins, 1947) in which each of three groups of 15 women were tested at different intervals varying from two months to one year. Using H. A. Murray's needs-press scoring system, the following average reliability coefficients were obtained: .80 after a 2-month interval, .60 after 6 months, .50 after 10 months, and .46 after a 1-year interval. The same investigator suggests that these reliability estimates are influenced as much by the instability of the personalities tested as by the instrument itself; and he draws the analogy between the test situation and the reliability of a response to a joke (Tomkins, cited in Kagan and Lesser, 1961, p. 279): "Assuming that we can estimate accurately the test-retest reliability of fantasy responses is like assuming we can measure the reliability of a response to a joke. If I tell it to you twice in a row, or even separated by two days, and you don't laugh as much the second time, I say this is no measure of the reliability of that first response."

Many users of the TAT have argued also that retest reliability studies are not appropriate with this technique because subjects cannot be expected to relate the same narratives over a period of time. Thus, Harrison (1965) asserts that if retesting is done after a considerable interval, the psychological state of the subject is likely to have changed, and what comes out in the form of stories should reflect these changes without being considered unreliable. In this regard, we would suggest—as did Fiske (1959) with respect to Rorschach response fluctuations—that there should be less divergence of scores made by an individual in successive test protocols collected over a period of time, than between individuals.

Moreover, it is not necessary that the same story be related on test and retest any more than identical responses must be given on two administrations of the Rorschach. In computing retest coefficients, comparisons of scoring categories should be made for the two occasions, rather than a comparison of stories. Therefore, although the stories themselves may change, the consistency (or inconsistency) of response categories would be reflected in the retest coefficients.

Of all methods of testing reliability, the split-half or odd-even reliability is probably the least appropriate index of the TAT's stability. The pictures simply do not fall into equivalent or equal halves. It is not surprising, therefore, that in one such study (Child *et al.*, 1956), in which 10 scoring categories were used (10 Murray needs), extremely low coefficients were obtained (within the range −.07 to +.34). In other studies (McClelland, 1949; Tomkins, 1947) in which the number of scoring categories were reduced to less than ten, more substantial split-half estimates were reported. But these were not sufficiently high to be used as convincing evidence of the appropriateness of this technique for demonstrating reliability.[5]

When the method of split-half is used for estimating the stability of a projective device such as the TAT (or Rorschach), the correct procedure is to divide the cards in terms of the frequencies of specific response categories elicited by each card (or item). An arbitrary splitting of the cards into even and odd numbers is completely unacceptable because of the unequal "pull" of each of the stimuli.

Furthermore, TAT reliability studies often reflect errors of measurement due not only to the fallibility of the instrument but also to the variabilities arising from differences among test administrators and scorers. These measurement errors arise because test administration and scoring procedures are loosely standardized. For these reasons, the TAT is highly prone to examiner effects and is hypersensitive to extraneous influences (room temperature, conditions under which test is taken). Therefore it may be expected that the reliability of the TAT when administered and scored by carefully selected professional clinical psychologists, well trained in the use of a particular scoring system, may be quite different from the

---

[5] Even with the use of the Spearman-Brown formula (see Chapter 2), which is a somewhat questionable procedure because the items (cards) do not have equal pull (for certain scoring categories), numerous studies (Atkinson, 1950; Lindzey and Herman, 1955) reported unsatisfactory reliabilities (ranging from .41 to .78). The use of Kuder-Richardson estimates of internal consistency yielded equally low reliabilities (Auld *et al.*, 1955).

reliability of the same test administered and scored by students in training with little or no experience in a particular system. And since there is no such concept as *the* reliability of the TAT (or any other test, for that matter), it is all the more surprising that many studies of this test's reliability do not report the experience and training of the participating psychologists.[6]

Validity

The issue of the validity of the TAT can be summarized in the following way: How useful is this method for diagnostic differentiation, personality description, predicting behavioral outcomes, or for reflecting behavioral changes of persons? In other words, the question is whether or not the TAT is an efficient measure for the large number of its purported uses. In order to avoid the overwhelming and somewhat tedious and thankless task of describing the many studies conducted in behalf of the TAT's validity (or its invalidity), only a small sample of these are selected here to illustrate the test's various uses.

Differential Diagnosis. The TAT is not generally considered particularly well suited for differential psychiatric diagnosis, if diagnosis means the identification and classification of a patient's disorder within a particular taxonomic group. It has been suggested (Abt and Bellak, 1950), that the clinical interview or Rorschach could accomplish this more successfully. Therefore, leaving aside the issues of whether or not psychiatric diagnosis is important, and whether the effects of its unpopularity among psychologists influences differential diagnostic studies, it is not surprising to learn that the overwhelming majority of these studies with the TAT have generally led to discouraging results.

Occasionally, differential diagnostic studies suggest that particular characteristics of separate nosological groups can be identified in TAT stories, but most often these studies are anecdotal accounts based on the clinician's faith in the TAT. Well-designed studies where data are sought in support of these claims (e.g., Eron, 1950; Ritter and Eron, 1952) generally fail to find significant differences between nosological groups. There is one notable exception to this

---

[6] Murstein (1963, pp. 148–163) recommends numerous remedies for TAT reliability problems, and the interested reader may obtain this information by consulting that source.

trend, however, in the form of two studies recently reported by Lindzey (1965), in which a psychologist, on the basis of TAT protocols, was able to distinguish homosexuals from heterosexuals with 95 percent accuracy.[7] However, it should be noted that homo- and heterosexuality are not commonly considered separate psychiatric taxonomic groupings. This raises the question, of course, whether or not the present diagnostic system focuses on relevant dimensions of personality.

In another study (Little and Shneidman, 1959), where patients and normal persons were diagnosed on the basis of TAT protocols, there was little agreement between test judges and persons who had interviewed these subjects extensively. The subjects were three normals, three neurotics, three individuals with psychosomatic disorders, and three hospitalized psychotics. Of all the tests used in this study (the Rorschach, MAPS, and MMPI were also used) the TAT fared the least well. Agreement among judges about the subjects' diagnostic group membership did not differ from that expected by chance. Particularly embarrassing evidence attesting to the TAT's lack of usefulness was the consistent finding that the normal subjects were misclassified as seriously disturbed!

Generally, attempts at differentiation with the TAT have been unsatisfactory. In summing up this state of affairs, one psychologist (Murstein, 1963, pp. 286–287) notes that the current psychodiagnostic system is as much at fault as the test itself:

. . . perhaps the fault lies in the incessant search for an alchemist's stone which will turn the leaden data obtained via "shotgun approaches" to the gold of a clear, invariably differentiating TAT response. . . . Until we evolve a more refined classification system it is unlikely that a fair test of the TAT can be undertaken. At the same time, the use of more refined scoring procedures, as well as greater cognizance of the stimulus, background, and motivational factors impinging upon the subject, will accelerate the possibility of a fair test for the TAT.

Prediction of Personality Variables and Behavior. The studies most often cited in support of the TAT's usefulness in predicting personality dimensions are those of Harrison (1940a,b). Using 20 cards of the TAT, he administered the test to 40 patients in a mental hospital. He divided the patients into male and female groups and wrote personality descriptions on the basis of their TAT protocols. An independent judge (one having nothing to do

---

[7] These studies are discussed further in the next chapter (p. 348).

with the test administration) compared these descriptions to case history information available for each of the 40 patients and notated the congruencies and incongruencies. Validity was defined as the proportion of congruencies compared to the total number of predictions made. By this criterion, Harrison's evaluations were in agreement with biographical data in 83 percent of the cases, and his diagnostic inferences were correct in approximately 75 percent of the cases. He also predicted I.Q.s from the TAT protocols and these correlated .78 with obtained intelligence measures.

Most similar studies of the predictive validity of the TAT, however, have not been equally encouraging. Symonds (1949) actually obtained negative correlations between TAT predictors and a criterion; but in a follow-up study 13 years later, the adolescent themes of some of his respondents showed some relationship to adult behavior (Symonds and Jensen, 1961).

In another study (Hartman, 1949), predictive validity findings equally unfavorable to the TAT were reported. In this study the investigator correlated each of 56 specific TAT variables with 42 personality variables on 35 delinquent youths. Although he obtained several statistically significant correlations, their magnitudes were too low to be considered adequate for individual predictions (median r was .44).

Finally, in a study (Horowitz, 1962) in which experienced clinicians and naïve introductory psychology students predicted personality dimensions of individuals in therapy, the TAT contributed little to the accuracy of the predictions. Using, among other tests, the Rorschach and TAT, plus biographic data (age, sex, marital status, occupation, education), the clinicians' correlation between their judgments and therapists' criterion descriptions was lower than the correlation between an average description (e.g., base rate description) and the criterion description (r's of .35 versus .43). This means that the clinicians would have fared better if they had merely based their descriptions on what they believe to be an average patient in that clinic, rather than consulting the test results prior to writing descriptions. One other result of this study is that it indicated that clinicians are not significantly superior to naïve students in the use of information gained from biographical data (r's of .32 for clinicians versus .21 for students). This is all the more disturbing because the results of the study suggested that the addition of test information to biographical data did not appreciably improve the clinicians' predictions.

Personnel Selection. The TAT is often included as part of a battery of tests to aid in personnel selection, usually in conjunction with an interview, and has been used variously in the selection of combat officers, psychologists, psychiatrists, and middle and upper echelon managers in business and industry. Generally the usefulness of the TAT for these selection purposes has not been noteworthy. In predicting success in the professions of psychology and psychiatry, for example, the test's failures have been attributed to the familiarity of subjects with the test and their knowledge of its purpose. The TAT's failure in other professions, typically, has been

TABLE 10–1

Validity Coefficients of TAT and Selected Criterion Ratings

Activity	r	Activity	r
Academic performance	.08	Supervisory competence	.18
Clinical total	.10	Professional, interpersonal	
		relations	.10
General total	.08		
Diagnostic competence	.24		
Diagnostic prediction	.20	Integrity	−.01
Individual psychotherapy	.16	Clinical competence	.15
Research competence	.07	Preference for hiring	.12

Median Validity....................11
Number of significant variables........ 0

Source: Kelly and Fiske, 1951.

attributed to a combination of factors: inexperienced testers, the use of inappropriate scoring procedures, attempts to predict ambiguous criteria, and lack of information about the factors essential for success in the profession predicted.

In one particularly significant study (Kelly and Fiske, 1951), conducted for the purpose of selecting clinical psychology trainee candidates for graduate education (see also Chapters 5 and 6), the TAT's predictive validity was seriously questioned. Of special interest here are the correlations obtained between a 10-card group-administered TAT and numerous criterion ratings collected four years later. The correlation coefficients ranged from a low of −.01 to .24, with a median validity correlation of .11. These correlations are presented in Table 10–1.

The Construct Validity of the TAT. Although few investigators have deliberately set out to establish the construct validity of the

TAT, several studies bear direct relevance to this method of validation. Bellak's (1944) classic study on the experimental investigation of the concept of projection is an example in point. His procedure was to administer five TAT cards in the usual manner. After these cards were administered, the experimenter, having apparently contemplated the thematic content of the elicited stories, severely criticized them. Four more cards were administered, and after each of the accompanying stories was related, the experimenter criticized them in their turn. Prior to the experiment, Bellak had predicted that aggression would appear with greater frequency in the narratives after criticism of the subjects' stories than before. This prediction was confirmed when the TAT productions were analyzed in terms of the number of words in them connoting aggression. The credibility of the study is weakened somewhat by Bellak's failure to use control groups and by another investigator's (Matarazzo, 1954) inability to duplicate these results.

In summing up, it may be said that the evidence substantiating the general usefulness of the TAT is contradictory, and at best suggests minimal statistical validity. Such validity as does exist is too meager for individual prediction purposes. Routine diagnostic differentiation, descriptions of personality, and prediction of behavior by means of the TAT are therefore not feasible.

There are some hopeful indications, however, in the form of studies that indicate a relationship between TAT responses and aspects of experimentally manipulated behavior. A gradual collection of evidence from these and similar construct validity studies should increase the volume of knowledge of the TAT's relationship to overt behavior and to personality dimensions.

DERIVATIVES OF THE TAT

Numerous modifications of the TAT have gained popularity within recent years. Some of the most commonly used ones are mentioned briefly here. In the main, evidence for the reliability and validity of these techniques is no more encouraging than that of the parent test (Buros, 1959, 1965).

The Children's Apperception Test (CAT)

Bellak (1949 to 1961) developed a children's version of the TAT, called the Children's Apperception Test (CAT), which consists of

10 pictures of animals and animal scenes in humanoid situations. The test is intended for use with children between the ages of 3 and 10—although as you get to the upper ages of that range, considering the sophistication of television-wise children who have seen the Gemini capsules rendezvous in space, 7- to 10-year-old children are apt to find such scenes as "three little bears" ludicrous.

These 10 CAT pictures were designed to elicit stories that might reveal several critical stages of psychological development as postulated in Freud's psychoanalytic theory: feeding problems, attitude toward siblings and parents, aggression, and toilet behavior. In his manual (1961), Bellak provided some analyses of test results as well as samples of typical responses given to each of the cards. Although no quantitative norms are cited in the accompanying manual, several such studies have been reported in the literature (Boulanger-Balleyguier, 1957; Lehman, 1959; Simon, 1954).

A supplement to this test, consisting of 10 additional animal scenes, is available and was designed to probe for problems of a more transitory nature—fears in play situations, interpersonal problems in school, reactions to physical debilities, fears of physical illness, and fantasies about being an adult.

The rationale for the CAT is based on the assumption of its author that children identify more easily with animal figures than with humans, and therefore produce more projections with the animal test stimuli. There is little support for this assumption, and the contrary (human figures elicit more responses) is in fact true (Bills, 1950; Budoff, 1963; Furuya, 1957).

Most studies that have been conducted to compare the CAT and TAT demonstrated the superiority of the latter in eliciting the intended material. For this reason, plus those which follow, the CAT is urgently in need of additional research: there is a paucity of validity and reliability evidence for the CAT; the responses are interpreted completely in qualitative, subjective, and clinical ways; and the CAT's value is proportionate to the skill of its interpreter (Wirt, 1965).

Thompson Modification of the TAT (T–TAT)

Thompson's modification of the TAT consists of 21 cards in which Negro figures are portrayed rather than whites (see Figure 10–4). Thompson (1949) has reported that his modification, or the

T–TAT as it is called, is more productive in eliciting fantasy material from Negro college students than the TAT. Subsequent studies have not corroborated Thompson's findings (Cook, 1953; Light, 1955; Riess *et al.*, 1950), but did suggest possible uses of this test for exploring attitudes toward racial minority groups.

FIGURE 10–4.   A card similar to one appearing in the Thompson modification of the TAT.

The Auditory Apperception Test (AAT)

In many respects the Auditory Apperception Test, developed by Stone (1950) and published later (Western Psychological Service, 1953), is similar to the TAT, but with auditory rather than visual stimuli. The test consists of 10 sets of three sound situations. After listening to each set, the subject is instructed to create a story using as many of the sounds as he can, and to relate what led up to the sounds, what is happening, and how the story ends. No validity or reliability data have been reported, and the normative sample used to develop the test is inappropriate for its intended use with blind subjects and psychiatric patients.

Auditory apperceptive techniques still remain relatively unexplored as an area of projective testing, although they have been around for some time. For example, Shakow and Rosenzweig (1940), using a modified version of Skinner's (1936) Verbal Summator, have used the method. They presented a recording of a series of random vowel sounds to subjects and asked them to relate what different things the man on the record is saying.

More recently, an auditory apperceptive device was developed (Davids and Murray, 1955) in which incoherent recorded material is presented to a subject. He is presented with much more material than can possibly be retained and is instructed to recall, of this material, what he can. The subject has to indicate which of the recalled materials represent major ideas, and which ones are minor. Scores are then obtained for eight personality variables (e.g., distrust, anxiety, optimism) by computing the proportion of material relevant to each variable recalled. Again, as with other auditory techniques, additional research and conceptual clarification is urgently needed for this seemingly promising approach.

The Blacky Pictures: A Technique for the Exploration of Personality Dynamics.

The Blacky Pictures (Blum, 1950 to 1962) is a test that consists of a series of 12 cartoon drawings designed to study certain psychoanalytic concepts. The drawings depict a family of dogs whose activities are built around Blacky, the central character, who goes through a series of adventures. The cartoon situations are said to represent various stages and areas of psychosexual development. Following the administration of the test, the respondent is asked to answer a series of inquiries and to sort pictures into "liked" and "disliked" categories.

Reliability, validity, and normative data for the Blacky pictures are inadequate (Blum, 1956; Charen, 1956; Zubin et al., 1965), although clinicians occasionally offer testimonials as to its usefulness (see Sappenfield, cited in Buros, 1965). The test's author, Blum (1962), has been responsive to many aspects of the criticism launched at the Blacky pictures, and in an extensive research project designed to derive a new scoring system and collect additional normative data, he has engineered numerous refinements of the original test.

Michigan Picture Test

The Michigan Picture Test (Andrew *et al.*, 1953; Hartwell, 1951), consists of 16 TAT-like pictures. It was developed to investigate the emotional reactions of children who are between the ages of about 8 to 14. The scoring system is highly explicit and quantitative: responses are analyzed with regard to a "tension index" (love, extra- and intropunitiveness, superiority, submission), "direction of force" (hero acts or is acted upon), and "verb tense." The scoring procedure for this test is also highly standardized. Consequently such high interscorer reliability coefficients as .98 have been reported.

The Michigan Picture Test has been called the "most systematically and solidly constructed thematic apperception test" since the TAT (Freeman, 1962), and it has been especially commended (Zubin *et al.*, 1965) for its careful design, good standardization, adequate norms, and careful cross-validation. Yet from a strict psychometric point of view, evidence for its validity is still too meager to warrant its use.

The Make–A–Picture Story (MAPS)

The Make-A-Picture Story Test (Shneidman, 1947 to 1952) is a kind of do-it-yourself TAT, in which the subject makes up his own pictures and tells stories about them. The respondent is given the opportunity to construct his own picture situation from among 22 background settings and 67 cut out figures (65 human and 2 animal). The interjudge reliabilities are extremely low—in the range of .30 to .40 among experts—and the validity evidence is even less encouraging (Jensen, 1965). This device can hardly be recommended for research or practical assessment purposes and only loosely fits any criterion of a psychological test.

Iowa Picture Interpretation Test (IPIT)

The Iowa Picture Interpretation Test (IPIT) was introduced (Hurley, 1955) as a multiple choice modification of the TAT, in order to combine in one test "the objective and quantitative advantages of traditional paper and pencil personality measures with the so-called 'depth' of projective techniques." Accordingly the IPIT consists of the series of TAT cards with four alternate interpretations for each card. Subjects are asked to rank the four choices from 1 to 4. The choices are intended to represent anxiety, hostility, achievement, and blandness.

In devising these choices, clinical judges agreed almost unanimously on the categories into which the various alternative statements were placed. For example, the statement, "She is annoyed because she has to work while her friends go out," was unanimously placed in the hostility category.

Reliability coefficients, established by both test-retest and internal consistency measures, are moderately high. Validity studies, however, generally indicate minimal relationships to manifest behavior (Hurley, 1957). Normative data are scanty. As a result of these shortcomings, it may be said that while the IPIT is preferable to the TAT from the point of view of ease of scoring and amenability to group administration, its lack of demonstrated validity and dearth of normative data do not recommend it at this time. The possibility that it is more easily fakeable than the TAT, because of its use of obvious statements (the social desirability of the choices is apparent) presents a new set of problems that should stir up some research in the future.

A VARIETY OF OTHER NOTEWORTHY PROJECTIVE TESTS

A rather complete and up-to-date review of most available projective techniques has been made available recently by Shneidman (in Wolman, 1965), and here only the most popular ones will be mentioned briefly to illustrate the variety of methods currently in use.

Sentence Completions

The sentence completion procedure was first used by Tendler (1930). Such tests are easy to administer and consist of a series of sentence items, or stems as they sometimes are called, of one or more words which the respondent is instructed to complete. A few typical stems are presented below:

My father always . . .
He . . .
The way . . .
My health . . .
Suddenly I . . .
A voice . . .

There are several varieties of sentence completion tests. Among the best known of these is the Rotter Incomplete Sentence Blank (Rotter and Rafferty, 1950). Generally, test items for sentence completions are constructed to suit the needs of the particular population being tested. Although some attempts at quantification of responses have been made (Rohde, 1953, 1957), such scoring has not yet been found practical, and qualitative or "content" analysis is used instead.

Draw–A–Person Test (DAP)

In the Draw-A-Person Test (DAP), developed by Machover (1948, 1951), the examiner provides the subject with a blank sheet of paper and instructs him to "draw a person." Usually, after the first figure is drawn, the subject is asked to draw a person of the opposite sex. After the drawing session, the subject is asked to tell a story about each of the persons. A series of questions is used during this inquiry period in which the subject is asked about the age, education, ambition, fears, and other facets associated with the figures drawn (Machover, 1951; Urban, 1963).

Scoring of the DAP is qualitative and essentially consists of an analysis of the characteristics of the portrayed figures and the manner in which they were executed. Thus, the relative size of male and female figures, for example, is said to reveal facets of sex identification. Similarly, attention is focused on omission of specific parts of the body, disproportions of certain other parts, erasures, symmetry, or asymmetry

The DAP interpretive manual has been mainly criticized (Anastasi, 1961) for containing such sweeping generalizations as, "Disproportionately large heads will often be given by individuals suffering from organic brain disease," or, "The sex given the proportionately larger head is the sex that is accorded more intellectual and social authority." Evidence for these characterizations has been no more extensive than vague references to clinical experience and a few anecdotal accounts of selected cases.

There are several variations of the DAP, with equally unsatisfactory validity evidence. One of these is the *Draw-A-Person Quality Scale* (Wagner and Schubert, 1955), in which the drawing is assessed along an artistic scale running from zero to eight. Another is the *House-Tree-Person* (HTP) devised by Buck (1946 to 1956), in which a subject is instructed to draw a house, a tree, and then a person. Presumably, stories told in association with these objects should contain themes about the respondent's home, environment, and interpersonal relations, respectively. Numerous other drawing techniques and instructions for their use are available (see Anderson and Anderson, 1951, Chap. 14).

Bender Visual–Motor Gestalt Test

The Bender Visual–Motor Gestalt Test (1938 to 1964) was introduced by Lauretta Bender as a test of visual-motor coordination. The designs (see Figure 10–5) were selected by the author in order to illustrate certain principles of gestalt psychology in perception of form. The test consists of nine geometrical figures, each on a card, presented to the subject one at a time. The subject is instructed to copy each figure in turn; afterwards, he is asked to reproduce as many of the patterns as possible from memory.

Even though the technique was developed mainly to study visual-motor coordination, it has been used to test for the presence of central nervous system lesions (see Yates, 1954), as well as for differentiating between matched samples of normal and abnormal persons. For the latter purpose, a quantitative scoring key has been developed and normative data collected (Pascal and Suttell, 1951). This key has been cross-validated on samples of normals, neurotics, and psychotics, and these groups have been clearly and significantly differentiated on the basis of the scoring scheme.

The Bender–Gestalt has also been used as a projective device to reveal significant personality trends. It has been claimed, for example, that drawings in which the figures are in collision with one another reveal disorganization; that heavy lines indicate aggression and hostility; that figure reversals suggest negativism; and that exact reproduction indicates obsessive-complusive personality traits. Evidence for these claims is usually stored somewhere in the clinician's head and has not been made generally available (Billingslea, 1963; Blakemore, 1965).

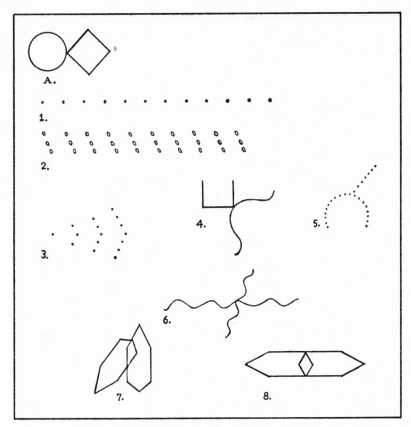

FIGURE 10–5. The figures for the Bender Visual–Motor Gestalt Test. (Reproduced by permission of Dr. Lauretta Bender and the American Orthopsychiatric Association. Copyright, 1946.)

The Picture–Frustration Study (P–F)

The Picture-Frustration Study (P-F) was designed in terms of Rosenzweig's (1944 to 1960) theoretical interest in the concepts of frustration and aggression. He considers the P-F study a controlled projective technique, and focuses on the subject's patterns of reactions to frustration.

The test consists of a series of cartoon-like drawings (see Figure 10–6), each of which portrays two principal characters. One of these persons is the victim of a somewhat frustrating set of circumstances, and the other character is either apologizing for the frustration he caused the victim, or calls attention to the frustrating circumstances in some other way. The respondent is instructed to

FIGURE 10–6. Examples from the Rosenzweig Picture-Frustration Study. (Reproduced by permission, from the Rosenzweig P-F Study, Adult form, copyright 1948.)

fill in, in the blank caption box, the answer he thinks the frustrated person would give. This test is available for children (4 to 13 years) and adults (14 years and older). A frame from the adult form is shown in Figure 10–6.

The P-F test is scored in terms of the direction of aggression in the response (intropunitive, extrapunitive, or impunitive),[8] and the specific type of reaction occurring. These categorizations, of course, are in terms of psychoanalytic theory. Combinations of direction and type of response yield nine different possible scores. There is also an overall group conformity rating which is an index of the extent of the responses' conventionality.

Generally, the P-F test, because of its highly structured stimulus materials and its relatively objective scoring procedures, has been considered one of the more thoroughly researched projective techniques. Norms have been gathered on many special groups, and a systematic collection of evidence for its reliability and validity are well documented. Most recently, a reviewer of the P-F test stated that it is still considered the most interesting and research-generating projective device available (Bjerstedt, 1965).

---

[8] These are terms used to characterize the response to frustration according to its tendency to blame oneself, others, or no one, respectively.

SUMMARY

Projective techniques are devices that encourage and permit a wide variety of subject responses. This is accomplished partially by constructing ambiguous test stimuli and partially by leaving the response situation loose or unstructured.

The most encouraging development in projective methodology's history occurred with the appearance in 1921 of Hermann Rorschach's inkblot technique. The Rorschach, as it has come to be called, consists of a set of 10 inkblot pictures that require subject responding. Scoring of the Rorschach record is complex and special problems in scoring and interpretation have arisen over the years. These problems, plus the fact that this method is more similar to the interview than to self-report inventories, have raised the question of whether or not it is appropriate to judge the technique by traditional psychometric criteria. By these criteria, the Rorschach has not fared well. It has been suggested by some of its proponents that its clinical usefulness rather than psychometric excellence is a more suitable criterion of its value.

A projective technique that has approached the Rorschach in the extent of its impact on personality testing has been the Thematic Apperception Test. In contrast to the ambiguous blots of the Rorschach, the identity of most objects in TAT pictures is evident. Also, subjects are required to create stories rather than just give opinions about what they imagine the test stimuli represent.

The scoring and analysis of TAT responses raise some of the same issues as the Rorschach about the technique's place in psychometrics. Moreover, evidence in support of the TAT's reliability and validity is equally as unsatisfactory as that presented in favor of the inkblots.

Several modifications and derivations of the TAT have gained some popularity among clinicians and research psychologists. Among these tests, the following are the more prominent: the Children's Apperception Test (CAT), the Blacky Pictures, the Michigan Picture Test, and the Iowa Picture Interpretation Test (IPIT).

Numerous other projective devices, with varying test administration methodologies and differing scoring procedures, exist also. Thus at one extreme of stimulus structuredness, there is the Sentence Completion Test, in which the subject is given stems to complete; and at the other extreme, there is the task that provides him with blank paper and requires that he draw pictures. Most of these procedures are analyzed qualitatively. However, there are some quantitative scoring schemes available also.

Generally, projective methodology's greatest shortcomings consist of its lack of standardized administration procedures and the dearth of information provided as evidence of its psychometric respectability. There are, of course, notable exceptions to this generalization, the most well known of these being the Holtzman inkblot technique. This test, in its conceptualization and development, however, seems to resemble personality inventories more closely than projective tests. Other exceptions exist also, the most recent example coming from the very promising Michigan Picture Test. The compromise that would seem to be the most acceptable, to both projectivists and psychometrically oriented psychologists, exists probably in the form of a test that is amenable to quantitative scoring schemes, while at the same time it retains its subtlety and open-endedness.

FOR FURTHER READING

1. ARNOLD, MAGDA B. *Story sequence analysis.* New York: Columbia University Press, 1962.

   Arnold's methods of TAT analysis have evolved gradually, from a 5-step procedure reported by her in 1949, to a technique that relies heavily on sequence analysis. This book also reports a number of successful predictive validity studies conducted by her and under her supervision within the last decade.

2. FESHBACH, S. The influence of drive arousal and conflict upon fantasy behavior. In KAGAN, J. & LESSER, G. S. (Eds.), *Contemporary issues in thematic apperceptive methods.* Springfield, Ill.: Charles C Thomas, 1961. Pp. 119–140.

   This chapter raises doubts concerning the use of the TAT as an instrument for predicting behavior in real-life situations. (Chapter 22 of the same volume includes a comprehensive discussion of the TAT).

3. FRIEDMAN, C. J., JOHNSON, C. A., & FODE, K. Subjects' descriptions of selected TAT cards via the semantic differential. *Journal of consulting Psychology,* 1964, 28, 317–325.

   A 30-scale form of the semantic differential was used to obtain data on the stimulus properties of 10 TAT cards.

4. HARRISON, R. Thematic apperceptive methods. In WOLMAN, B. B.

(Ed.), *Handbook of clinical psychology*. New York: McGraw-Hill Book Co., 1965. Pp. 562–620.

Shorter than Murstein's compendium (see below) on the TAT, this chapter is tightly packed with pertinent information on this projective test.

5. HOLT, R. R. The nature of TAT stories as cognitive products: A psychoanalytic approach. In KAGAN, J. & LESSER, G. S. (Eds.), *Contemporary issues in thematic apperceptive methods*. Springfield, Ill.: Charles C Thomas, 1961. Pp. 3–43.

The question raised by this psychoanalytically oriented psychologist concerns the relationship between TAT stories and private fantasies.

6. MURSTEIN, B. I. *Theory and research in projective techniques (emphasizing the TAT)*. New York: John Wiley & Sons, Inc., 1963.

Starting out to write a book that would deal extensively with many projective techniques, Murstein discovered that TAT-related matter in itself deserves an entire volume. The result is a thoroughly scholarly and readable production.

7. PINE, F. Thematic drive content and creativity. *Journal of Personality*, 1959, 27, 136–151. (Also reprinted in MEDNICK, MARTHA T. & MEDNICK, S. A. [Eds.], *Research in personality*. New York: Holt, Rinehart & Winston, Inc., 1963. Pp. 563–574).

This study described the relationships between creative quality of imaginative productions and drive content in these productions.

8. RAMSAY, R. W. Personality and speech. *Journal of Personality and social Psychology*, 1966, *4*, 116–118.

Following Eysenck's theory about the characteristics of extroverts and introverts, this brief report of a study found greater use of sounds and shorter silences in extroverts' speech patterns.

9. ROSENZWEIG, S. The Rosenzweig Picture-Frustration Study, Children's Form. In RUBIN, A. I. & HAWORTH, M. R. (Eds.), *Projective techniques with children*. New York: Grune & Stratton, 1960. Pp. 149–176.

This chapter is a summary of research with the children's form of the author's P-F Study.

PART IV

Overview and Preview

CHAPTER 11

THE PROCESSING OF PERSONALITY
MEASUREMENT DATA BY MAN AND
MACHINE

In this chapter, the main focus of attention is shifted from the consideration of specific measurement approaches and problems associated with their use to a discussion of the psychologist's role as decision maker and data processor in personality testing. The formulation of assessment goals, the selection of appropriate measurement procedures, and the analysis and interpretation of the resulting information involve a series of closely related data processing operations.

Many psychologists believe that they play a central role in the interpretation phase of data processing and that the preliminary and adjunct phases can be carried out by a trained clerk or computer. But there is no general agreement about this, because it is not altogether clear where the mechanical portions of information processing end and where the human element becomes essential. There has been considerable controversy in psychology over this issue, and lately some success has been reported by persons associated with the view that computers will someday supplant the clinician. The details of this controversy, known as the clinical versus statistical prediction issue, and a discussion of the use of computers for personality test interpretation, occupy the latter portions of this chapter. Before embarking on a discussion of these topics and a consideration of the data processing functions of man and machine, it may be well here to review briefly the broad purposes of personality measurement.

THE AIMS OF PERSONALITY MEASUREMENT

The measurement of personality serves two major purposes. One is theoretical, the other practical.[1] From the theoretical standpoint, personality measurement facilitates identification of personality variables and constructs; and it is through measurement that these constructs are related to observed behavioral patterns. The second major aim of personality measurement, the main focus of attention in this chapter, is practical in the sense that it is conducted in order to permit decisions and predictions about persons in applied settings.

Up to a point, the aims governing both testing procedures are indistinguishable; thereafter, additional problems arise in the practical situation. For example, in both instances, the psychologist may ask himself the question, "How do I make sense about this person from these observations and test results?" But it is only in the practical situation that he asks himself the additional question, "How can I best organize and integrate these findings to arrive at a diagnostic decision or prediction about this person?" Both questions relate to the way the psychologist must process personality test data; but in the first instance the concern may be a theoretical one, whereas the second question clearly reflects a practical concern about the use of personality test data. In personnel selection, or in the context of a psychiatric clinic or hospital setting, for example, it is not sufficient merely to arrive at a personality description or to postulate abstractly about attitudes, defenses, or motives; rather it is essential to relate the set of test scores and other data to decisions about a particular person's suitability for that job or a specific patient's probable responsiveness to such-and-such treatment plan.

Contributing in no small measure to the difficulty encountered when attempting to process personality test data is the fact that psychological theory in the field of personality is not in very satisfactory condition. A sound theoretical system of personality functioning would allow the practicing psychologist to relate

---

[1] For a review of several other more specific aims of personality testing, the reader is referred to Chapter 1.

observed facts to one another and to make deductions about interrelationships between observed behavioral patterns. But as matters now stand, there are many divergent theories of personality, and there exist as many ways to measure it. Freudian theory, for example, postulates one set of personality variables and accordingly uses units and tools of measurement relevant to it. The theories of Adler, Sullivan, and Rogers each formulate their own postulates and select the most appropriate ways for their measurement, and as noted in Chapter 3, communication between theorists and more psychometrically oriented psychologists is either nonexistent or highly unsatisfactory when it does exist. Fortunately, however, the guiding principles that govern personality measurement in practical decision-making situations are similar; therefore, existing tests and ideas about their use allow decisions about persons. We now turn our attention to the decision maker and to a discussion of some of the problems confronting him.

A DATA PROCESSING POINT OF VIEW

Taking a mechanistic viewpoint of the psychologist's role in data collection and interpretation, we may describe him as an information processor who has collected direct observations, interviews, and tests as "inputs" that he must process (analyze, organize, and integrate) prior to "outputting" his diagnosis, description, decision, or prediction. His data processing function can be depicted, as in Figure 11–1, after the fashion of the *flow chart* used by computer programmers. A flow chart traces the flow of information from the point at which it enters the computer until it emerges in its processed form. The chart shown in Figure 11–1 represents the several stages that lead to the decision of the human data processor in the applied setting.

These stages may be divided into three main parts: (1) the input stage, during which assessment goals are formulated, personality measurement procedures selected, and information collected and arranged in order to be "read in" to the human data processor; (2) the processing stage, when data are analyzed in terms of the assessment goals that were formulated; and (3) the output stage, during which time a prediction, diagnosis, personality description, recommendation for treatment, or decision to collect more data, is publicly communicated. The remainder of this chapter will concen-

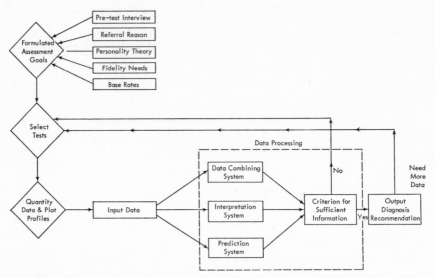

FIGURE 11-1.   Combination flow chart and block diagram to depict the flow of the assessment process.

trate on these separate components, and problems raised during each of these stages.

THE INPUT STAGE

Formulation of Assessment Goals

Unfortunately there is no simple one-to-one correspondence in personality testing between the formulation of measurement goals and the choice of an appropriate test. In most medical specialties and in some spheres of psychological testing, the relationship is a straightforward one between the purpose of evaluation and the instruments used. For example, in the medical specialty of clinical neurology, the diagnostician interested in ascertaining whether or not a patient is suffering from diabetic neuropathy may call for a highly discriminating laboratory test (nerve conduction time test), and depending on the outcome of that test, he determines whether his working hypothesis about the disease is reasonable. Likewise, the psychologist wishing to assess a student's scholastic aptitude administers one of several intelligence tests; and depending on the score he achieved, the probability of his success in a particular educational program can be stated. But the situation in personality testing is more complex. The specificity of purpose present in some laboratory tests and in intelligence testing is lacking in the measurement of personality. As noted in an earlier discussion (see pp. 60–62), this is partly due to the fact that the same personality test is used for a variety of purposes (for a majority of which it has no demonstrated validity); but mainly the problem seems to be that clinicians develop confidence in a test's clinical usefulness, and this confidence, rather than its demonstrated validity, often determines the choice of particular tests.

Yet the concept of validity, as already discussed at some length in Chapter 2, is basic to the whole purpose of testing. The demonstrated validity of an instrument for a particular assessment purpose must be the only criterion for the decision to use or not to use a specific test in a given situation. That is to say, before deciding to use a test, the psychologist must ask himself the questions, "What will the test result mean?" "Will it add anything to my understanding of the person?" "Can it help me in making a decision or recommendation in this particular situation?"

But the determination of the validity of personality measures encounters difficulties that are unique to this form of assessment. It has already been noted (see pp. 44–46, Chapter 2) that ordinary criterion-oriented methods of validation are not always entirely appropriate, and therefore construct validity procedures are adopted. However, even where empirical validity coefficients are appropriate, these must be evaluated in relation to the base rates of the characteristics being predicted.

The Base Rate Problem. What is a base rate? The concept of the base rate relates to the proportion of true incidence of a particular trait or behavior outcome in the population to be tested (Meehl and Rosen, 1955). From the clinician's viewpoint, the base rate consideration reduces to the question: "Can this test help me differentiate the characteristics of the patient I now have before me from those of the average patient who comes to this clinic?" And generally, another question to be asked is, "Does the test add anything to what we already know from past experience?" The wisest answer, from the point of view of time and cost, sometimes may be not to use a particular test. For example, if in the past 90 percent of college students admitted to a certain university have been classified "normal" according to some combination of criteria, the base rate of normalcy is 90 percent, and the probability is 9 out of 10 that an entering freshman will be "normal." A test purporting to differentiate college normals from others must improve upon this base rate to be of practical value for that setting.

The concept of the base rate is another way of saying that the validity of a test varies with the context in which it is used. Specifically, as Meehl and Rosen (1955) have shown by applying a mathematical formula known as "Bayes' theorem," some tests actually lead to more erroneous predictions than might occur without their use. Loosely stated, this formula asserts that for a test to be worthwhile, the ratio of the proportion of "false positives" to "true positives"—the ratio of the proportion of persons that a test incorrectly diagnoses as mentally ill (or as belonging to a particular category) to those that it correctly identifies as ill—must be less than the base rate.

As an illustration of this, consider the situation in which the base rate for psychiatric disorder X in a given clinic is known to be 2 percent of the intake population. Suppose there is a test available that correctly identifies the presence or absence of disorder X in 90 percent of the cases examined with it. That is to say, the number of persons correctly identified as belonging to category X plus the number of persons correctly identified as belonging to categories other than X is 90 out of 100. Under these conditions, classifying everyone as not belonging to X results in erroneous classifications in 2 percent of the cases. By using the test, however, errors would be made in 10 percent of the cases!

Bandwidth-Fidelity. That the advisability of selecting a particular test is not a simple all-or-none affair has been further illustrated by Cronbach and Gleser's (1957, 1965) use of the *bandwidth-fidelity* analogy. The bandwidth and fidelity notions were adopted from Shannon and Weaver's (1949) mathematical theory of communication (information theory). In any information communication system, according to this theory, there is a compromise between bandwidth and fidelity such that if there is a shift in the direction of greater fidelity, then bandwidth is reduced; and broader bandwidth reduces fidelity. Thus in home record playing systems, where the fidelity of a recording depends on the groove width, if grooves are crowded together to put more music within a given space on a record (greater bandwidth), then fidelity suffers.

The psychometric counterpart to the information theory model is demonstrated by validity studies that indicate that tests which attempt to get at many and complex types of information tend to have low fidelity. In other words, a test having broad bandwidth has predictive relevance to many criteria, but only moderate accuracy for any one of them; the test that tries to answer just one question (narrow bandwidth) usually is very accurate with respect to a specific criterion (high fidelity). While no rule can specify precisely the optimal bandwidth-to-fidelity ratio for testing, Cronbach (1960, p. 603) suggests a number of conditions favoring wider or narrower bandwidth. He suggests that except in instances of all-or-none selection decisions, or in predictions where radical treatments are prescribed (e.g., electroshock, surgery, radiation), decisions can be narrowed down progressively and sequentially. Thus relatively unstandardized and impressionistic procedures such as the Rorschach inkblots and interviews, which have low fidelity and large bandwidth, may be used to suggest hypotheses about possible treatment plans (these can be followed up without any great harm to the patient), but should not be used to help make all-or-none decisions.

The distinction between psychometric and impressionistic assessment, according to Cronbach and Gleser, cannot be made on the basis of test stimulus dimensions but should rather be based on the test's suitability for different prediction purposes. Thus narrow bandwidth instruments are highly focused and are therefore geared to predict specific criteria; and impressionistic or wideband techniques are flexible assessment procedures that may be used to shed light on idiosyncratic and perhaps dynamically significant test responses.

Generally, in selecting tests suitable for specific personality measurement goals, the decision has to be made whether the assessment task requires high fidelity or broad bandwidth or some combination of the two. Cronbach (1960, p. 604), in this regard, states:

Fallible tests can suggest assignments for an employee, treatments for a patient, teaching techniques for a student. Even if the test is little better than a guess, it has some value when there is no sounder basis for choice. Since trying out the hypothesis permits verification, and change when the hypothesis is wrong, little has been lost. We may say, in sum, that the fallibility of wideband procedures does no harm unless the hypotheses and suggestions they offer are regarded as verified conclusions about the individual.

Data Collection and Quantification

Having formulated particular assessment goals and having chosen to follow specific testing procedures, the psychologist must now reduce his observations to numerical values or scores. Fortunately, all assessment data are quantifiable. As noted throughout this book, direct observations and interview impressions can be ordered along a numerical scale; rating methods rely entirely on a measurement scheme; self-report inventories yield test scores; and projective technique responses can be expressed in the form of scores. Furthermore, even when a considerable degree of judgment is needed in arriving at a test score (e.g., scoring handwriting, quantifying expressive behavior, or analyzing personal documents), fairly objective scoring schemes can nevertheless be developed. Many of these data collection and quantification operations are currently being performed by electronic digital computers and can be considered to be a part of the data processing, rather than the input preparation, phase. However, regardless of whether quantification is performed by the human or the machine, the methods for accomplishing this remain the same.

After tabulating the number of responses or response categories according to a prescribed scoring scheme, these *raw scores* are expressed in the form of percentile ranks, z-scores, T-scores, stanines, or stens. The latter are sometimes called *standard* or *derived scores*. Comprehensive discussions of these scores can be found elsewhere (Cronbach, 1960; Lyman, 1963; Psychological Corporation, 1955), and it is sufficient here to mention that they are computed in terms of the arithmetic mean and standard deviation of the obtained distribution, and that they serve the twofold purpose of (1) rendering observations from different tests comparable; and/or (2) enabling the psychologist to make meaningful interpretations of raw test data.

Profiles. One of the most common ways of summarizing a series of derived scores obtained about the same individual is by means of the test profile. Test score profiles were discussed in connection with the MMPI (see Chapter 8). An individual's scores, as shown in Figure 11–2, are plotted graphically. In general, a profile is plotted by letting various points along the horizontal axis represent subtests or scales of the same test. Or a profile may include infor-

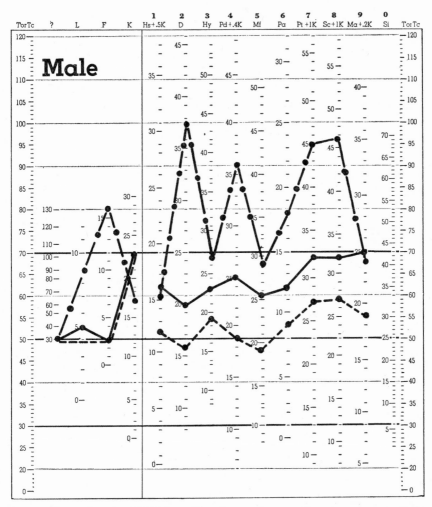

FIGURE 11–2. An MMPI profile of a student under no apparent strain (solid line), under strain (broken line), and after counseling (dotted line).

mation from a set of different tests entirely. In the latter instance, care must be exercised to ensure that the tests' raw scores are converted to the same standard score units. This renders them comparable to one another.

The MMPI profile presented in Figure 11–2 is of a case which Dahlstrom and Welsh (1960, pp. 229–233) describe in some detail, and it is reproduced here to illustrate how a profile is used in practice. It is the MMPI of a university student who was given the test at several different points in time. The important feature to note in the profile is the difference in scale elevations that were obtained when the student was under no particular strain (solid line), and when he presented himself at the university counseling center to seek help (broken line) about a number of problems centering around his marriage. The third profile depicted in Figure 11–2 (dotted line) was obtained two years after counseling and at a time when matters had settled somewhat (more favorably) for this student.

Not all assessment data can be presented in the form of a profile, but there are specific graphic procedures available for most of them. Thus the Rorschach can be plotted on a *psychogram*, and profile sheets are available for the California Psychological Inventory, and the Guilford-Zimmerman Temperament Survey (Figure 11–3)—to name just a few.

Profiles are usually interpreted on the basis of the configuration of scale elevations and according to the slope characteristics of a particular class of profile patterns. A number of mathematical and computer techniques have been devised to "capture" profile similarities and differences in order to simplify their interpretation (DuMas, 1955; Kleinmuntz, 1963d; Nunnally, 1959), and an excellent article on the pitfalls of such interpretations has been written by Cronbach and Gleser (1953).

THE PROCESSING OF INPUT DATA

During the second stage of the data processing procedure depicted at the outset of this chapter and in Figure 11–1, after the input information has been expressed in some quantitative form by means of which two or more persons can be compared, the psychologist asks himself a most important question: "How will I interpret these results?" That is to say, during the data processing stage of test interpretation, the psychologist must combine all his findings—impressionistic as well as psychometric—and give meaning to these in order to arrive at a diagnosis, decision, prediction, or recommendation.

Clinical Versus Statistical Prediction

Although psychologists are essentially in agreement about the usefulness of such aids as standard scores and test profiles, they are

PROFILE CHART FOR THE GUILFORD-ZIMMERMAN TEMPERAMENT SURVEY
For high-school, college, and adult ages

C SCORE	G General Activity / Energy	R Restraint / Seriousness	A Ascendance / Social Boldness (M F)	S Social Interest / Sociability	E Emotional Stability	O Objectivity	F Friendliness / Agreeableness (M F)	T Thoughtfulness / Reflectiveness	P Personal Relations / Cooperativeness	M Masculinity / Femininity (M F)	CENTILE RANK	NEAREST T SCORE
10	30 29 28	30 29 28 27	30 30 / 29 29 / 28 / 28 27	30	30 29	30 29	30 30 / 28 29 / 26 28	30 29 28	30 29 28	30 0 / 29 1	99	75
9	27 26	26 25	27 26 / 25 / 26 24	29	28 27	28 27	25 27 / 24 26	27 26	28 27	28 2 / 27 3		70
8	25 24	24 23	25 23 / 22 / 24 21	28 27	26 25	26 25	23 25 / 22 / 21 24	25 24	26 25	26 4 / 25 5	95 90	65
7	23 22	22 21	23 20 / 22 / 21 19	26 25	24 23	24 23	20 23 / 22 / 19 21	23 22	24 23	24 6 / 7	80	60
6	21 20	20 19 18	20 18 / 19 17 / 18 16	24 23 22	22 21 20	22 21 20	18 20 / 17 19 / 16 18	21 20	22 21 20	23 8 / 22 9	70 60	55
5	19 18 17	17 16 15	17 15 / 16 14 / 15 13	21 20 19	19 18 17	19 18 17	15 17 / 14 16 / 13 15	19 18 17	19 18 17	21 10 / 20 11	50 40	50
4	16 15 14	14 13 12	14 12 / 13 / 12 11	18 17 16 15	16 15 14 13	16 15 14	12 14 / 11 13 / 10 12	16 15 14	16 1'5 14	19 12 / 18 13	30	45
3	13 12 11	11 10	11 10 / 9 / 10 8	14 13 12 11	12 11 10 9	13 12 11 10	9 11 / 8 10 / 7 9	13 12 11	13 12	17 14 / 16 / 15 15	20	40
2	10 9 8	9 8 7	9 7 / 8 / 7 6	10 9 8 7	8 7 6	9 8 7	6 8 / 5 7	10 9 8	11 10 9	14 16 / 13 17 / 12 18	10 5	35
1	7 6	6 5	6 5 / 4 / 5 3	6 5 4	5 4	6 5	4 6 / 3 5	7 6 5	8 7 6	11 19 / 10 / 9 20		30
0	5 3 2 1	4 3 2 1	4 2 / 3 1 / 2 / 1 0	3 2 1 0	3 2 1	4 3 2 1	2 4 / 1 3 / 0 2 / 1	4 3 2 1	5 3 2 1	8 21 / 5 23 / 2 25	1	25

Bottom (M F) labels:
- G: Inactivity / Slowness
- R: Impulsiveness / Rhathymia
- A: Submissiveness
- S: Shyness / Seclusiveness
- E: Emotional Instability / Depression
- O: Subjectivity / Hypersensitiveness
- F: Hostility / Belligerence
- T: Unreflectiveness
- P: Criticalness / Intolerance
- M: Femininity / Masculinity

FIGURE 11-3. Profile sheet for the Guilford-Zimmerman Temperament Survey. (Reproduced by permission.)

not agreed about the best way to combine observations and test scores to arrive at decisions about patients or predictions of their future behavior. This lack of agreement has occasioned considerable controversy as to whether information processing is best accomplished by combining data in a subjective, intuitive, or clinical manner; or whether it would be more efficiently processed by formal, mechanical, or statistical means. This issue is basic to the question of how input data are to be processed.

The arguments over the merits of clinical versus statistical data processing are sometimes heated. Advocates of statistical methods refer to the clinical types as "mystical, vague, hazy, crude, sloppy, and muddleheaded," and view their own method as "verifiable, public, objective, reliable, precise, empirical, and sound." Critics of the statistical approach, on the other hand, label it as "pedantic, trivial, forced, rigid, and sterile," and tend to view their own method as "dynamic, holistic, real, concrete, and understanding."

Stripped of its pejorative and honorific adjectives, the clinical versus statistical prediction controversy revolves around the issue of whether more accurate predictions could be made by the use of a formula (e.g., statistical equation, set of rules, or reference to an actuarial table),[2] or by more subjective methods (e.g., formulating hypotheses, clinical impressions, or intuitive judgments). Addressing himself to this question, Paul E. Meehl (1954, p. 18), in his now classic *Clinical v. Statistical Prediction,* offered a useful distinction between types of data to be combined, and methods of data combination. Basically, there are two types of data and two modes of data combination: (1) psychometric data combined mechanically—e.g., MMPI profile elevations are interpreted according to a specified set of rules or are processed by some statistical formula; (2) psychometric data combined nonmechanically—e.g., MMPI profile elevations are inspected intuitively, and some guess is made about the possible significance of the patterns; (3) nonpsychometric data combined mechanically—e.g., biographical information, such as age, education, socioeconomic status, is combined by some formula and by a table-look-up procedure to arrive at a decision; and (4) nonpsychometric data combined nonmechanically—e.g., on the basis of biographical data, a guess is made about an individual's possible success in a particular treatment situation.

The issues surrounding the clinical versus statistical controversy may be best illustrated by the following example taken from

---

[2] An actuarial table is very similar to what insurance men call an experience table. These tables are a convenient way to store information about a particular setting's experience with the use and oucomes of specific tests and treatments. In principle, if large amounts of information are stored, probabilities can be stated of the success rates of specific tests and treatments.

Meehl's book (1954, pp. 90–92). In 1941, the first systematic investigation of the relative worth of the clinical and statistical methods was carried out by Sarbin (1941, 1943). The problem presented by Sarbin to psychologists consisted of predicting college grades of 162 freshmen (73 men and 89 women). In order to test the efficiency of the statistical approach, a clerk simply inserted each student's college aptitude test score and high school honor-point ratio rank into a regression equation developed from an earlier sample.[3] The clinical predictions were made by psychologists, using the same information as well as additional data, including other test results (Strong Vocational Interest Blank), another clinician's interview notes, an interview of their own with the student, and an eight-page record form filled out by each of the students. The task consisted of predicting the grades each student would receive at the end of the first quarter in college. The predictions made by the clerk using the statistical equation correlated with actual grades .45 for men and .70 for women For the psychologists, the respective correlations were .35 and .69. In other words, even though the clinician utilized all this additional information, there was essentially no difference between his forecasting and that of the clerk using a simple formula. The equation did fully as well as the psychologists.

Since Meehl's book appeared, clinicians have tended to align themselves on either one side of the clinical versus statistical controversy or the other.[4] Those psychologists who feel that they can bring reason to bear on the data—either in addition to or without the use of some statistical formula or mechanical rule— believe that they add to the richness and accuracy of the interpretive process. The more hardheaded interpreters take the position that clinical (nonmechanical) test interpretation is nothing more than an intuitive and relatively inaccurate approximation of statistical (mechanical) interpretation.

Persons on both sides of the controversy have collected evidence to substantiate their respective sides. Meehl (1965) claims that in his "box score" of some 50 studies, the statistical method has been demonstrated to have significantly superior predictive efficiency in

---

[3] A regression equation is a statistical formula obtained by correlating test scores with a criterion. When several tests are used, a multiple regression equation is developed, in which appropriate weights are assigned to each of its variables.

[4] The most recent reviews of the clinical versus statistical controversy may be found in Gough (1962), Sawyer (1966), and Sines (1966).

about two thirds of the investigations, and substantially equal efficiency in the rest. There is a notable exception in this box score, to which Meehl calls special attention. This is in the form of a recent study by Lindzey (1965), mentioned in the last chapter, in which evidence is provided for what Meehl (1965, p. 27) calls, "the first and *only* empirical comparison of the relative efficiency of the two methods showing clear superiority for the clinical judge."

Lindzey reported two studies in which TAT protocols from homosexual and normal college subjects, and homosexual and normal prisoners, were analyzed in terms of clinical versus actuarial methods. In the first of these studies, using the method of blind analysis, a clinician predicted the criterion from TAT protocols with 95 percent accuracy. The use of objective TAT indices, on the other hand, only worked nearly as well as the clinician. In the second study, which consisted of the prison population TAT's, two clinicians were more successful than actuarial methods in predicting the criterion. Lindzey refers to these studies as examples of "Seer versus Sign" to call attention to the seer's (clinician's) superiority over actuarial "signs." In granting the relevance of Lindzey's study for the clinical versus statistical controversy, Meehl titles his comments, "Seer over Sign: The First Good Example."

A recent counterexample, called "Sign and Seer: Another Example," using a computer program (see pp. 360–368) designed to interpret MMPI profiles, demonstrated the equivalence, and in some instances, the relative superiority of a set of formal rules (signs) over the clinician (Kleinmuntz, 1967). In that study a set of some 35 decision rules (developed by empirical means) were applied to the MMPI profiles of five college groups of adjusted and maladjusted students. Eight clinicians inspected scale elevation on MMPI profile sheets and Q-sorted these profiles into a distribution ranging from "least" to "most" adjusted. The clinicians were all highly experienced MMPI test users, and were free to use (or not use) any rules, formulas, or aids accessible to them. A comparison of the computer's and the clinicians' success in predicting maladjustment among these students indicated that the computer surpassed the average accuracy attained by the clinicians in all of the samples. An additional comparison of the computer rules with the best of these clinicians indicated the superiority of the former in about half the samples and the superiority of the clinicians in the other half.

The clinical versus statistical controversy is far from settled, and the evidence in support of either side has not been convincing to the proponents of the other side. One of the by-products of this controversy has been to call attention to the fact that the clinician must be able to give the bases for his judgments and that when asked for the evidence, he cannot hide behind such statements as, "My third ear tells me . . ." or "I don't know, but I feel very strongly about this patient. . . ."

What is often not remembered about Meehl's position in this controversy is that he does believe in the intuitive insights of the clinician but that he mistrusts the accuracy of these insights. In his volume, Meehl cited a rare bit of clinical intuition by a talented psychoanalyst (Reik, 1948) that he found convincing and which he considered beyond the cognizance of even the most informed clerical worker (Meehl, 1954, p. 51):

. . . After many minutes she complained about a toothache. She told me she had been to the dentist yesterday. He had given her an injection and then had pulled a wisdom tooth. The spot was hurting again. . . . She pointed to my bookcase . . . and said, "There's a book standing on its head." Without the slightest hesitation and in a reproachful voice I said, "But why did you not tell me that you had an abortion?"

Interpretations such as these, says Meehl, defy the actuarial table. Tooth extraction and birth may be symbolically equivalent, but how can an actuarial table (or computer) capture Reik's imagery that "book on its head" is similar to the fetus in the womb? Meehl (1954, p. 50) states that the interpretations are "psychologically *suggested* by these facts," and he thinks it is fair to say "it would not be suggested to a clerical worker . . . (because) we still would have to create in her a readiness to *invent particular hypotheses that exemplify the general principle in a specific instance.*"

It seems important, therefore, to clarify that the position of statistically or actuarially oriented psychologists is not that clinical judgment is inefficient and that the clinician's hypotheses regarding human behavior are invalid, but rather, as Meehl (1954, p. 67) put it so aptly, that the *"part* of the clinician's thinking which involves the use of empirical frequencies could not fail to be improved by having those frequencies objectively determined in a table rather than subjectively stored up in his skull."

Clinical And Statistical Methods

Regardless of whether one adopts a clinical or actuarial orientation toward processing input data, clinical inference and statistical aids to interpretation are nevertheless used. Essentially, in interpreting a test score or other behavioral data, the psychologist makes numerous inferences, even when consulting an actuarial table or "cookbook" (Meehl, 1956b). For example, the cookbook may specify that for a person whose MMPI profile contains two or more psychotic scales (e.g., Pa and Sc) above a T-score of 70, there is a .95 probability that he is schizophrenic. This probability value must still be interpreted and a decision must yet be made about the person in question. The interpretation and decision constitute inferences that go beyond the scores and the stated probability value.

Likewise, human judgment enters at many points in even the most mechanical data processing schemes. Thus judgments are made in the formulation of assessment goals, in selecting particular measurement tools, and in deciding who is to receive the assessment results. On the other hand, even the most intuitive clinician uses a number of statistical aids to arrive at his decisions. Thus he may convert raw scores to standard ones, consult a table of norms, plot a profile on a graph, or he may even rely on certain formal signs. He may use a regression equation, for example, to arrive at a decision. The main difference between his method and that of the more actuarially minded, however, as Goldman (1961, p. 162) has indicated, is that the latter rely exclusively on formulas, decision rules, and tables (e.g., there may be a computer rule that specifies when to enter specific tables and how much weight is to be given to the findings from these tables), whereas the clinician prefers to speculate beyond the formal aspects of his test and behavioral data.

Several useful distinctions have recently been made between levels of inference that occur during the data processing stage (Sundberg and Tyler, 1962, pp. 199–202). These levels are reproduced here to illustrate the extent to which both the statistical and the clinical data processor may utilize inferences. Figure 11–4 depicts the various levels.

The lowest level of inference occurring in personality assessment is exemplified in the screening situations where the psychologist is called upon to render adjusted versus maladjusted decisions. The psychologist's judgment may be based on whether scores on particular MMPI scales are above or below some critical point. A well-trained clerk or a computer can make such inferences.

At the second level of inference, the test scorer uses judgment about scoring categories. For example, the decision to classify certain observed interview behaviors as "psychomotor retardation" or as "hypermanic" involves inference. Similarly, the judgments

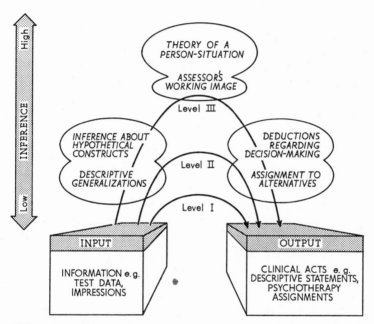

FIGURE 11-4.   Inference levels in personality assessment. (Adapted from Sundberg and Tyler, 1962, p. 200.)

made by a teacher in assigning school grades, the judgment of a rater in classifying someone as successful or competent, and the interpretation of Rorschach protocol responses according to specific scoring categories, all involve this level of inference.

The highest level of inference is characterized by the formulation of a "consistent overall *theory of the person-situation*" (Sundberg and Tyler, 1962, p. 201). This form of inference requires a self-consistent, sound theoretical system of hypotheses which permit deductions. Although good theories of this sort are not presently available in the field of personality, psychologists do seem to use "theory of a person" inferences in all personality assessment situations. The psychologist builds a working image or model of the person with whom he is dealing, and this model consists of a set of hypotheses about the person. His hypotheses about individuals generally arise from similarities he perceives among them in their responses to numerous situations. On the basis of these hypotheses, he formulates concepts to represent segments of behavior and attempts to relate these concepts to each other in some meaningful way. The problem in the field of personality study at this time is that there is disagreement among psychologists about which concepts are most useful. This disagreement, as already indicated earlier in this book, results in a situation in which psychologists from separate schools attend to different data about persons and consequently cannot use each other's concepts.

The Proper Use of Clinical and Statistical Methods

The question that still remains unanswered—and perhaps cannot be settled until more research is completed—is, as Meehl (1957) stated in the title of one of his papers, "When shall we use our heads instead of the formula?" In this regard, addressing himself to the use of tests in counseling, one psychologist (Goldman, 1961; pp. 202–204) offers a number of noteworthy recommendations. Drawing on some of these suggested guidelines to counselors, the following list includes the optimal uses of either one method or the other:

1. If experience tables or base rates are available, then these sources should be consulted rather than relying on the clinician's confidence in what he "feels" to be the significance of a set of scores.

2. Clinical predictions should not be made if a regression equation formula or other statistical method has demonstrated superiority.

3. For many occasions, however, where actuarial tables, prediction equations, or other formal methods are either not available or are obsolete, it is appropriate to use clinical methods. Such occasions arise most often when new or rare criteria are to be predicted and when new information about existing predictors has not yet been incorporated in the prediction formulas. For example, a personnel psychologist may have to wait several years to develop appropriate statistical prediction techniques that he could use routinely for selection or screening purposes. Likewise, when the

use of a particular set of predictors, which performed well over a number of years, no longer yields accurate predictions, then intuitive methods must be substituted until such time as optimal weighting can be achieved.

4. A fourth instance in which formal methods may not be suitable is in the prediction of low-probability events. Rosen (1954), and Meehl and Rosen (1955), discussed the problems of predicting such a rare event as suicide, and they demonstrated that even the most sophisticated statistical techniques may fail in such instances. This difficulty is also discussed by Meehl in another paper in which he illustrates the problems of predicting the "special case" of Professor X (1957, pp. 264–70) :

If a sociologist were predicting whether Professor X would go to the movies on a certain night, he might have an equation involving age, academic specialty, and introversion score. The equation might yield a probability of .90 that Professor X goes to the movies tonight. But if the family doctor announced that Professor X had just broken his leg, no sensible sociologist would stick with the equation. Why didn't the factor of a "broken leg" appear in the formula? Because broken legs are very rare, and in the sociologist's entire sample of 500 criterion cases plus 250 cross-validating cases, he did not come upon a single instance of it.

At such times Meehl would suggest the use of "our heads" instead of the formula.

5. Finally, the use of clinical judgment is necessary when personality descriptions are required rather than straightforward predictions of probable behaviors. Although in principle it is possible to devise a computer program that would process a large array of diverse data—interview impressions, attitudes toward tests and the interview, the effect of a particular set of circumstances on the respondent, and so forth—and organize this information into a meaningful description of the person, currently no such computer program is in existence.

THE OUTPUT STAGE

Reference to Figure 11–1 indicates that the psychologist's public communication resulting from his data processing can be in the form of a prediction, evaluation, description, diagnosis, or recommendation for treatment or for additional testing. Of course, all of these communications are not mutually exclusive, and each may include recommendations for specific courses of action or may call for particular treatments. However, each of these forms is distinguishable from the other in the following ways.

A *prediction* consists of a statement about the relationship of a person's scores to his probable behavior in a real-life situation. An *evaluation* may be based on this prediction but adds a value judgment to that prediction. For example, on the basis of an individual's MMPI scores, a psychologist may predict that this individual may encounter difficulty in social or employment situations that require frequent close contacts with other persons. An evaluation involves a judgment beyond that prediction and would include some statement of advice regarding a recommended course of action. In a sense, evaluation involves a higher level of inference than prediction, because the former is farther removed than prediction from test data.

A *description* is a collection of statements that are intended to convey a characterization that is unique to the person. A description may be in the form of a straightforward account of an individual's test scores and biographical data, or it may be an interpretation of this information. Depending on the psychologist's theoretical orientation, a description may be interpreted in terms of traits or may include statements about relationships of present dispositions to probable etiological factors. Again, varying levels of inference are reflected in different types of descriptions. For example, an answer to the question of how a person developed in a particular way, or what motivated him to behave in the manner observed, requires a higher level of inference than a comparison of his MMPI, GZTS, and Rorschach scores. The latter stays rather close to the data, whereas statements about motives require speculation about unobserved or hypothetical constructs.

Diagnosis consists of categorizing the individual into a disease class. Ideally, once a diagnostic label is attached, a host of other information about that person is conveyed. Thus the classification "schizophrenic reaction, paranoid type" is intended to convey information about the presence of a set of symptoms (on which the diagnosis is based), a prediction of probable behaviors in various settings, a prognostic statement about the possible course of the illness, and a recommendation for optimal treatments. Causative or etiologic factors are also implied by diagnostic labels but unfortunately are still unknown for this and many other diagnostic categories. Generally, psychodiagnostic classification has not been taken seriously by practicing clinicians. Cogent arguments in support of more widespread acceptance of a psychiatric classificatory system have been offered but will not be elaborated here (see Meehl, 1959b).

Finally, the psychologist may *recommend treatment* or he may indicate that present findings are inconclusive, and therefore no concrete proposals about a course of action can be made until further tests are conducted. In the first instance, the range of possible recommended treatments includes everything from straightforward advice about changing a specific mode of behaving, through more elaborate therapy plans that involve one or more outpatient visits per week, all the way to hospitalization and recommendations for intensive care. Of course, in the personnel setting, treatment in the usual sense of the word is not relevant.

In both settings decisions about additional tests occur throughout the data processing procedure. Thus at all stages of input preparation, and at points where feedback is obtained from tests already administered, the psychologist makes decisions about specific additional tests to be used. These decisions usually are not communicated publicly and remain an unverbalized part of the ongoing decision process. However, it is frequently necessary to communicate to a referring agency or to other interested sources that tests already administered must be repeated, or that other tests should be given after a certain period of treatment or waiting. Such recommendations then become part of the clinical data processor's output.

COMPUTER APPROACHES TO DATA PROCESSING

Thus far the discussion of data processing, although using such mechanistic terminology as flow of information, input, and output, has concentrated mainly on the human as the essential element of the procedure. There were implications throughout the chapter, and comments made in passing, about the possible changing role of the clinician as data processor. The discussion now turns to a consideration of the computer as an important element in the processing of personality measurement information.

Any scientific field that deals with large amounts of data to be analyzed, coordinated, and compiled at rapid rates, invites the application of high-speed data processing techniques. The area of personality measurement is just such a field. Accordingly, psychologists have applied electronic digital computer technology in this area for a number of years.

Perhaps the most extensive, and certainly the earliest, use of the computer for personality research occurred in R. B. Cattell's Institute for Personality and Ability Testing (IPAT) at the University of Illinois. Its use for factor analysis was readily recognized by these psychologists because they were faced with large numbers of intercorrelations to be computed, and discovered that with the aid of the computer, months of tedious calculations were reduced to hours or even minutes of computer time. To date, it has been fairly well documented that the computer has facilitated investigation of many factor analytic problems of theoretical interest that would otherwise have been prohibitive (Fruchter and Jennings, 1962; Vandenberg, 1960).

A related use of the computer in personality research has been demonstrated recently in a study (Williams, 1963; Williams and Kleinmuntz, 1966) in which the items of the MMPI were scored configurally. The method of scoring patterns or configurations of items rather than scoring them individually was first suggested by Meehl (1950) as a procedure for keying answers to an objective inventory, in order to enhance its subtlety. The motivation for considering configurations of items in scoring a personality test was sparked by the realization that some scales of the MMPI— especially the Pa scale—are relatively weak, in the sense that some psychiatric patients easily evade detection. By scoring items configurally, a considerably larger burden is placed on the person who wants to evade detection on this test. Now, instead of confronting him with the choice of earning a score in the direction of paranoia, let us say, on the basis of his "true" or "false" response to one item, the respondent is faced with the problem of answering certain combinations of items that are valid for the dimension in question. For example, by the method of configural scoring, this respondent may earn one point in the direction of paranoia if he answers certain specified items in TT ("true," "true") or FF pattern, and no points for the patterns TF or FT. Three-, four-, or five-item combinations can also be used to complicate the task of faking. The precise choice and combinations of items that are deemed significant when answered in certain ways are, of course, empirically established by prior statistical analysis of these items among particular patient or normal populations.

The patterns of responses, and the interitem correlations required to establish the joint validity of specific patterns of items, constitute an enormous computational task. For the MMPI, which consists of 550 items, this involves the computation of about 160,000 correlations prior to configural analysis. Even a large computer requires about three hours of running time for these computations. However, this formerly prohibitive data processing task is now possible because of advances in computer technology.

An entirely different use of computers in psychology has been in interpreting personality test data. This development can be traced to the influence of Professor Meehl's emphasis on the need for actuarial methods for making personality descriptions from MMPI profiles. In his 1954 book *Clinical versus Statistical Prediction,* and in his presidential address to the Midwestern Psychological Association entitled "Wanted—a Good Cookbook" (1956b), Meehl reached a large audience of clinical psychologists with the message, and its implications, that test results can be automated into standard descriptions by the use of a computer. Since the appearance of his book, and his address, a considerable amount of work has been completed in the area of computer interpretation of personality test data. Much of this work is still in its prepublication stages, and as indicated in Table 11–1, many of the studies use the MMPI as a basis of their computer studies. This is not surprising in view of the fact that Meehl, who has been associated with the University of Minnesota throughout his career, was the prime mover for many of these studies.

Before discussing the variety of ways in which the computer has been applied in test interpretation, it may be helpful here to include a description of the functional components of one of these machines. This description is necessary since some familiarity with computers is assumed in the ensuing discussion, and throughout the following chapter. For additional sources of information about digital computers and their use in the behavioral sciences, the reader is referred to books by Borko (1962), Green (1963), and Stacy and Waxman (1965).

Functional Components of the Computer

A computer is a machine that consists of four major sections, as shown in Figure 11–5. These sections, or functional components,

TABLE 11-1

Programs for Personality Test Processing by Digital Computer

Investigator	Title of Relevant Source
Borko (1962)	Computer applications in the behavioral sciences.
Cooley and Lohnes (1962)	Multivariate procedures for the behavioral sciences.
Eber and Cattell (1966)	Maximizing personality scale validities on the 16 PF by the computer.
Holtzman et al. (1961)	Inkblot perception and personality.
Institute for Personality and Ability Testing (IPAT News No. 20a, 1966).	Recent improvements in 16 PF computer analysis and reporting service.
Kleinmuntz and Alexander (1962)	A computer program for the Meehl-Dahlstrom rules.
Kleinmuntz (1963b)	Personality test interpretation by digital computer.
Kleinmuntz and McClean (1967)	Mental status interviewing by digital computer.
Rome et al. (1962; 1965)	The Mayo Clinic computer program for processing MMPIs.
Williams (1963)	A process for detecting correlations between dichotomous variables.

consist of *input-output* equipment for transferring information into and out of the machine; a *storage* unit, which is the machine's memory system where data and instructions are stored (and operated upon); an *arithmetic* or *processing* unit that performs various operations on stored data; and a *control* unit that directs and coordinates the timing and operation of the entire processing system.

The research psychologist communicates and receives communications from the machine via the input-output units. Input systems consist of a number of devices: punched cards, punched paper tape, magnetic tape, magnetic ink, or direct typewriter-to-computer hookups. Most commonly, processed data are transmitted in and out of the computer by some typewriting or printing device.

The storage or memory device consists of many cells, or regis-

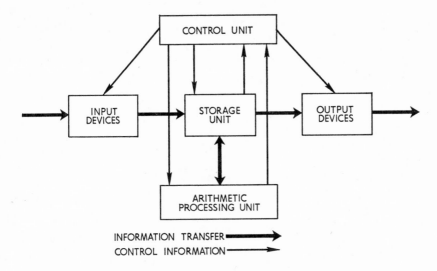

FIGURE 11-5. The functional components of a computer.

ters, which contain stored information. The location of each cell is indicated by an address. Storage can be internal or external to the computer, and only the internal storage unit is directly accessible to the arithmetic and control units for data processing. In order to perform operations on data stored in external memory, these data must first be transferred to internal storage.

The arithmetic or processing unit of the computer consists of electronic circuitry that performs the operations of addition, subtraction, multiplication, and division. This unit can also operate on coded nonnumerical data, transfer data from one register to another, and perform logical operations involving "branch" instructions. Characteristically, the computer performs it operations sequentially, but instructions can be written so that it deviates, or branches, from this sequence in accordance with the results of a prescribed test ("conditional branch"). This particular set of conditions, as will be demonstrated later, especially qualifies it for the task of conducting simultaneous "interviews" with a number of respondents.

The control unit has sometimes been referred to as the heart of the computer (Green, 1963) ; and in order to comprehend fully how its various parts function, a basic knowledge of computer programming is needed. It is sufficient here merely to point out that its major purpose is to select and interpret coded instructions and to control the movement of information from one part of the machine to another. It also integrates and coordinates the timing of the machines' circuitry and facilitates decoding of the complete computer programming system.

Profile Interpretations by Digital Computer

The use of the computer for interpreting personality test profiles (e.g., patterns such as are obtained with MMPI scores or the Rorschach psychogram) is exemplified by research conducted at the Mayo Clinic (Rome et al., 1962, 1965), and at Carnegie Institute of Technology (Kleinmuntz, 1963a, b, and c). There is an important difference in the way the computer is used for such tasks as factor analysis and item configural computations and its use in profile interpretation. In the former, the psychologist utilizes only the arithmetic or brute-force power of the computer to process data by certain prescribed formulas and methods; in profile interpretation procedures, however, the researcher is often forced to ask himself (or others) the question, "How is this task performed by humans?"[5] Two such programs are discussed in some detail here.

The Mayo Clinic Program. The computer program developed at the Mayo Clinic (Rome et al., 1965) consists of a series of coded statements that score the MMPI by scanning the items of a specially prepared answer sheet for true or false responses. These items are scored according to the validity and clinical scale categories of the MMPI (see Chapter 8). The elevations of these scales are examined in serial order, and depending on their height, specific descriptive statements are printed out by the computer. This procedure consists of retrieving from computer memory, statements specified by the program as associated with certain scale elevations. For example, if a person's raw score elevation on the Pa scale is between 11 and 14, the following statement is printed out: "Sensitive, alive to opinions of others." A slightly higher Pa scale score (15 to 19) calls for, "Touchy, overly responsive to opinions of others. Inclined to blame others for own difficulties." The statement for a Pa scale elevation of 20 or more reads, "Resentful and suspicious of others, perhaps to point of fixed false beliefs." Similarly, all

---

[5] Not everyone (See Nunnally, 1962) would agree that profile analysis requires human intervention, but the evidence to date seems to favor such a view (Helm and McKee, 1965; Kleinmuntz, 1963d; Meehl and Dahlstrom, 1960).

scales from L through Si have descriptions associated with specified elevations.

In addition to having prepared a series of 49 descriptive statements that characterize various types of elevations, the Mayo group developed a subset of statements that is retrieved from computer storage when a particular MMPI profile pattern appears. Thus, for a pattern in which the D scale is greater than 20, and Ma is within the range of 22 to 25, the computer program instruction reads, "Do not print Ma description. Instead, print D description plus "Somewhat tense and restless." Some of the computer's interpretive comments are illustrated in Table 11–2. These state-

TABLE 11–2

Samples from the Mayo Clinic Program for Configural Analysis

> 1. *Psychiatric referral*
> If 4 or more scales above T-score 70, print scale descriptions plus: "Consider psychiatric evaluation."
>
> 2. *Gerontic energy*
> If age > 69 and Ma < 15, do not print low Ma description. Print instead: "Low energy and motivation typical for age."
>
> 3. *Moderate K with normal profile*
> If T-scores on all clinical scales are > 70 and K = 15 to 20, print: "Patient views himself as well-adjusted and self-reliant."
>
> 4. *Invalid profile*
> F > 22. Print only high F description.

SOURCE: Rome *et al.*, 1962.

ments were intended by the Mayo group as aids to physicians in their overall understanding of their patients, and for this reason they have been kept relatively free of psychological jargon.

The Carnegie Tech Program. The Carnegie Tech computer program was developed to aid in the identification of emotional maladjustment among students who enter college each year. It consists of a set of sequential decision rules that process MMPI profiles one at a time, until that profile is labeled as either "adjusted," "maladjusted," or "unclassified." The rules of the program, based on an analysis of the "thinking-aloud" protocol of a single MMPI interpreter, are stored in the memory of the computer and are retrieved by a set of instructions that are "read into" the machine along with pertinent MMPI profile data.

Specifically, in the Carnegie Tech study (Kleinmuntz, 1963a, b, and c), several experienced MMPI interpreters were instructed to sort 126 MMPI profile sheets along a 14-step forced normal distribution (this procedure is called Q-sort; see pp. 205–208). The MMPI expert who achieved the highest valid positive (80 percent) and valid negative (67 percent)[6] success rates in predicting the criteria of "most" and "least" adjusted, was selected for intensive study. He was instructed to think aloud while performing his Q-sort task and was encouraged to elaborate his precise reasons for classifying each profile into one or the other category. His performance was tape-recorded. For illustrative purposes, the Q-sorter's verbalizations and each corresponding decision rule are presented in Table 11–3. The flow chart of the decision rules based on his protocol is presented in Figure 11–6.

The sequential rules (Figure 11–6) which render an adjusted, maladjusted, or unclassified decision were based on many hours of taped verbalizations. These rules were then coded into a set of programmed instructions for processing on the model CDC 20 electronic digital computer. The success rates of the programmed rules were surprisingly similar to those of the Q-sorter: The valid positive and valid negative hit percents of the computer program were 63 and 88, respectively, and this compares favorably with the expert's rates (80 and 67 percent). These programmed rules were then subjected to a trial-and-error process of statistical searching and shuttling back and forth between intuitive hunches about combinations of various scales and their possible effects on the hit percents in the student MMPI sample. On the basis of these statistical operations, an elaborate set of new rules was developed.

More specifically, the derivation of the new rules taxed to the utmost the computer's capabilities for storing and retrieving large quantities of information and its facility for high-speed arithmetical operations. For example, one of the techniques used consisted of letting the computer apply all the rules to a particular MMPI profile and instructing it to withhold its maladjusted or adjusted decision

---

[6] Valid positive and valid negative rates refer to the clinician's accuracy in classifying correctly the profiles of ill and well persons, respectively. Misclassifications into ill and well categories are called false positive and false negative rates.

TABLE 11–3

MMPI Decision Rules and Tape-Recorded Protocol

Rule	Protocol
1. If four or more clinical scales $\geq$ T-score 70, call maladjusted.	1. . . . Now I'm going to divide these into 2 piles . . . on the left (least adjusted) I'm throwing all Mults with at least 4 scales primed. . . .
2. If scales Hs, D, Hy, Pd, Mf, Pa, Pt, Sc, and Si are ≤ 60 and if Ma ≤ 80 and Mt $\leq 10_R$, then call adjusted.	2. . . . I'll throw all Mults to the right (most adjusted) if there's no clinical scale above a T-score of 60. . . . I'll let Ma go up as high as 80 . . . maybe a raw score of 10 on Mt would be playing it safe . . . so I'm looking at three things now and sorting according to these conditions. . . .
3. If the first two scales in the Hathaway code includes Pd, Pa, or Sc, and at least one of these is ≥ 70, then call maladjusted (if Mf is among the first two scales, then examine the first three scales in the Hathaway code).	3. If either Pd, Pa or Sc is primed I'm putting it on the left side (least adjusted) . . . it would also be nice to have all of these scales slightly more elevated than the others. . . .
4. If Pa or Sc ≥ 70 and Pa, Pt or Sc $\geq$ Hs, D, or Hy, call maladjusted.	4. . . . if the elevations are lopsided to the right with the left side of the profile fairly low, I'm throwing the Mults to the left (least adjusted).
5. Call maladjusted if Pa ≥ 70 unless Mt $\leq 6_R$ and K ≥ 65.	5. . . . here's a paranoid character. . . . I wish his K score were not quite so high . . . and he could use more Mt. . . . When that Mt score is less than 10, I figure something must be stabilizing him. . . . I like an inverted V with F high on the validity scales.
6. If Mt ≤ 6, call adjusted.	6. . . . Boy, I don't know that Mt is too low to call her maladjusted. . . . I'll settle for calling them adjusted if Mt is at a raw score of 6 or lower.
7. Call maladjusted if (Pa + Sc − 2· Pt) ≥ 20 and Pa or Sc ≥ 65.	7. . . . Here's a nice valley between scales 6 and 8, and both 6 and 8 are high. . . . I'll call this one maladjusted. . . .
8. If D or Pt are the primary elevations and Es $\geq 45_R$, call adjusted.	8. . . . these 27 profiles are giving me a pain. . . . If 2 or 7 is too elevated like, say, higher than a T-score of 80 and if the Es scale is approaching a raw score of 50 I'll call it adjusted. . . .
9. If Pd ≥ 70 and (a) Male: Mt $\geq$ 15 or (b) female: Mt $\geq 17_R$, call	9 . . . A primed Pd and an Mt raw score of 15 or more is going over

TABLE 11-3—*Continued*

Rule	Protocol
maladjusted.	to the left pile (least adjusted). . . . I guess on a male profile an Mt of 15 or more will do . . . and an Mt of 17 or more on a female profile. . . .
10. If Mt $\geq 23_R$ and Es $\leq 45_R$, call maladjusted.	10. . . . with Mt high and Es low, I'll call maladjusted at this stage of the game. . . .
11. If 5 or more clinical scales ≥ 65 and if either Pa or Sc ≥ 65, call maladjusted.	11. . . . Everything's up on this girl's MMPI. . . . I'm especially bothered by the high Pa. . . . Here's a high Sc . . . everything else is up too . . . over to the left (least adjusted). . . .
12. Call adjusted if at least 5 clinical scales are between 40 and 60 and Es $\geq 45_R$.	12. . . . Here are a couple of nice, normal-looking Mults . . . all scales hugging a T-score of 50, and Es is nice and high . . . over to the right (most adjusted). . . .
13. Call maladjusted if the profile is male and Mf ≥ 70 and Sc $\geq$ Pt and Sc ≥ 60.	13. . . . An elevated Mf is pretty common for boys around colleges, but when it's primed and when Sc is up and is higher than Pt, I'll throw it to the left (least adjusted). . . .
14. If Si ≥ 60 and Pa ≥ 60 or Sc $\geq$ 70, call maladjusted.	16. . . . That's a fairly high Si . . . and Pa is up, I'll call it maladjusted. . . . Here's one with a high Si, and Sc is also up; I'll call this maladjusted.
15. Call maladjusted if Es $\leq 35_R$.	15. . . . Here's a pretty good looking MMPI, but that low Es makes me think something might be wrong. . . . To the left (least adjusted).
16. Call adjusted if Mt $\leq 10_R$.	16. . . . these are all pretty bad looking Mults. . . . I'll call adjusted if the Mt is lower than 10. . . .

NOTE: The subscript R refers to raw scores.

until it computed a vote of the number of rules that favored one or the other of two classifications. Further, on the basis of an empirical determination (printed out by the machine) of the relative strength or weakness of particular decision rules, the computer was programmed to attend to specific patterns of rules (e.g., rules 2, 8, and 13 in combination with rule 5), rather than just to the number of votes that each profile received. The pattern analytic approach to

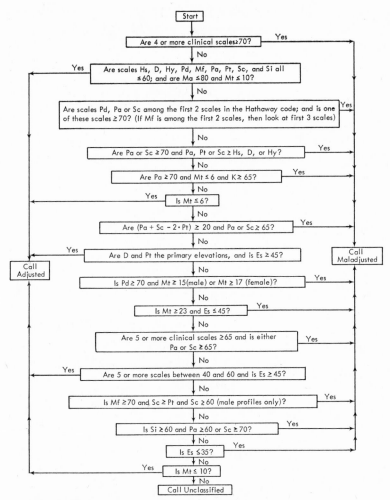

FIGURE 11-6. Flow chart of MMPI decision rules which appear in Table 11-3.

the rules themselves clearly removes this form of data processing from within the realm of human capabilities.

Finally, the completed set of MMPI pattern analytic rules included the original expert interpreter's information, a number of intraprofile slope characteristics that the expert failed to observe, and the optimal ordering of the various components that made up the whole. The success rates for the criterion sample indicated an improvement over the initial set of rules in that the valid positive

TABLE 11-4

College Maladjustment Rules for MMPI Interpretation

The MMPI should be scored on 16 scales, and these include: ?, L, F, K, Hs, D, Hy, Pd, Mf, Pa, Pt, Sc, Ma, Si, Es, and Mt. The latter two scales usually do not appear on the conventional MMPI profile sheet. They should be notated and are reported here as *raw scores*. K-correction is assumed for scales Hs, Pd, Pt, Sc, and Ma. All scores except for scales Es and Mt are reported here as *T-scores*.

Application of these rules without the aid of an electronic digital computer may be exceedingly cumbersome due to the pattern analytic approach to the decision rules themselves.

The following calculations will be needed:

1. Hathaway Code
2. Band location (Pt + Sc) − (D + Hs) = Beta

> Band 1: Beta = −31 and less
> Band 2: Beta = −31 thru −11
> Band 3: Beta = −10 thru +6
> Band 4: Beta = +7 thru +25
> Band 5: Beta = +26 and above

3. Delta = (Pd + Pa) − (Hs + Hy)

4. Anxiety index (A.I.) = $\dfrac{Hs + D + Hy}{3}$ + (D + Pt) − (Hs + Hy)

5. Internalization ratio (I.R.) = $\dfrac{Hs + D + Pt}{Hy + Pd + Ma}$

NOTE: Proceed to the next rule regardless of the maladjustment v. adjustment decision. Since a tally must be kept of the number of rules that apply to an MMPI profile, the rule number must be notated:

Call Maladjusted if:

1. Four or more clinical scales ≥ 70 (Mt and Es excluded).
2. The first two scales of the Hathaway code are among the scales Pd or Pa or Sc and one of these ≥ 70. If Mf is one of the first two scales in the Hathaway code, then examine the first three scales.
3. Pa or Sc ≥ 70 and Pa or Pt or Sc ≥ Hs or D or Hy.
4. Pa ≥ 70, unless Mt ≤ 6 and K ≥ 65.
5. (Pa + Sc − 2 · Pt) ≥ 20, if Pa or Sc ≥ 65 and if Pa and/or Sc ≥ Pt.
6. Pd ≥ 70 and

> *a)* Mt ≥ 15 (males)
> *b)* Mt ≥ 17 (females)

7. Pd ≥ 70 and

> *a)* Band 4 or 5 and Δ ≥ 0
> *or* *b)* Band 1 or 2 and Δ ≤ 0

8. Mt ≥ 23 and Es ≤ 50.
9. Mt ≥ 23 and Es ≤ 45.
10. Five or more scales ≥ 65 and Pa or Sc ≥ 65.
11. Male profile with Mf ≥ 70 and Sc ≥ 60 with Sc ≥ Pt.
12. Sc ≥ 70 and either Si or Pa ≥ 60.
13. Es ≤ 35.
14. IR ≥ .90 Δ ≤ −10.
15. Sc is primary elevation (first in Hathaway code) and is ≥ 65 and F ≥ L and (not plus) K.

TABLE 11–4—*Continued*

16. Band 2 profile.
17. Band 3 and I.R. ≥ 1.00.
18. K ≥ 50 and any scale except Es or Ma ≥ 70.
19. Male profile and

$$\text{Mf} \geq 65 \text{ and Pd} \geq 63$$

20. Sc ≥ 60 and Si ≥ 50 and A.I. ≥ 60, unless the Ma scale ≤ 65.
21. Sc ≥ 60 and Si ≥ 50 and Ma < 70 and AI ≥ 50.
22. Pd ≥ 63, and Hs ≤ 48 and AI ≥ 65.
23. Male profile and

$$\text{Pd} \leq 54, \text{ Hs} \geq 58, \text{ and Si} \geq 44$$

24. Hs ≥ 58, Hy ≤ 61.
25. Hy ≤ 61 and Pd ≥ 63; also hold for female profile if Pd is not the primary elevation.
26. Pa and Sc

$$>60 \text{ if male, or}$$
$$>65 \text{ if female}$$

27. $(\text{Hs} + \text{Hy} - 2 \cdot \text{D}) \geq 10$, Pa < 50, Pt ≥ 50, and Mt $\geq 10_R$.
28. $(\text{Mt} - \text{Es}) \geq 4_R$.
    Call Adjusted if:
29. Mt $\leq 6_R$.
30. All scales ≤ 60 except Ma ≤ 80 and Mt $\leq 10_R$.
31. D or Pt are primary elevations and D $\geq$ Hs and $\geq$ Hy; and Pt $\geq$ Pa and $\geq$ Sc; and Es ≥ 45.
32. Mt $< 10_R$.
33. Five scales between 40 and 60, and Es ≥ 45.
34. $(\text{Hs} + \text{Hy} - 2 \cdot \text{D}) \geq 20$; and Pt $<$ Pa ≤ 70 *or* Mt $\leq 10_R$.
35. $(\text{Mt} - \text{Es}) \leq 0_R$ if female; $\leq -20_R$ if male, unless Rule No. 5 calls profile maladjusted.

and valid negative percents were 91 and 84 (versus 63 and 88). The new set of rules, and the flow chart that describes the application of specific portions of these rules, are presented in Table 11–4 and in Figure 11–7.

The Carnegie Tech computer program has been cross-validated on the MMPIs of four new samples, and has not achieved the same success rate in the new studies. In one sample, the valid positive rate was as low as 68 percent, and this is particularly discouraging because the rules were developed for the specific purpose of identifying the MMPIs of maladjusted students. The overall hit percents, however, have been sufficiently high to encourage further work along these lines. Subsequent studies have indicated that when population base rates (incidence of adjustment and maladjustment within the population) are taken into account, the success rate of these rules is enhanced considerably.

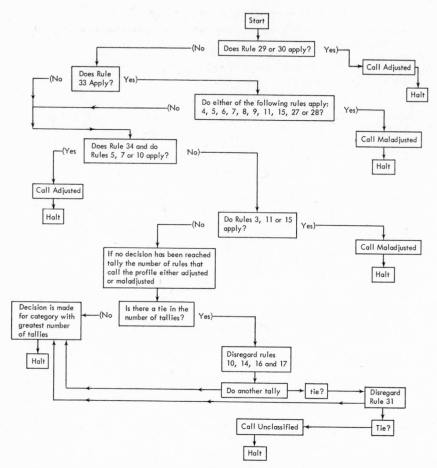

FIGURE 11–7. Flow chart describing the application of specific portions of the rules of Table 11–4.

Mental Status Interviewing by Computer

In yet another use of the computer, a second project at Carnegie Institute of Technology (Kleinmuntz and McLean, 1967) focuses on the design of a machine system to perform psychodiagnostic interviewing. From a technical standpoint, the programming of the computer consists of storing in it a set of questions relevant for psychodiagnostic interviewing, and writing a program of instructions to enable it to "ask" these questions, and receive and act upon the answers. The questions are stored in the computer so that they may be retrieved from memory in response to appropriate program cues. Once retrieved, the questions are printed out on a teletype or displayed on a cathode ray tube; similarly, the answers can be communicated from respondent to the computer by the same modes. Subjects' responses are then read into the machine, and these are "tested" for their significance as possible indicators of certain psychopathological diseases. Such testing is made possible by prior storing in the computer of a table of questions and answers significant for various diseases.

The rationale for using the computer for mass interviewing is provided by virtue of the imbalance between the large numbers of patients who need psychiatric attention and the meager number of trained professionals available for this job. Moreover, the computer is objective and conceptually neutral. It has no built-in biases other than those that are programmed for it and is, in fact, dependent on the explicit rules stored into it as its program. The machine, therefore, makes no "halo" errors nor does it have countertransference (emotional reactions to the interviewee) problems unless the computer program explicitly furnishes it with these appurtenances. Furthermore, the temperament of the computer is relatively stable from day to day, and its previous night's activities do not impede its functioning the morning after.

A computer is especially well equipped for psychodiagnostic interviewing. The three characteristics that highly recommend it for this task are flexibility, objectivity, and speed. As a matter of fact the computer excels in precisely those areas of a clinician's interview behavior in which he most prides himself. Holtzman (1960), in a hortative and somewhat reassuring article (for the clinician), predicted that the computer is not likely to supplant the clinician since the human is "viewed as a free floating processor with no hard and fast rules." In other words the chief advantage of the clinician over the computer, according to Holtzman, is the clinician's relatively greater flexibility.

The capability of the computer to alter its activity, however, as the result of the environment in which it is working, is its greatest strength. It has already been demonstrated in work with teaching machines (Silberman and Coulson, 1962) that a computer program can be written that instructs the control system of the machine to branch to one of several alternative content areas as a function of an individual's prior response. Similarly, in a mental status interview (see Chapter 6), the questions asked and areas probed with one type of patient are quite likely to be different from those of a patient with an entirely different set of symptoms. For example, an interviewer who is dealing with a paranoid patient might inquire about the patient's persecutors to help determine the extent of his delusional system. And when the interviewer believes he has exhausted that topic, he may select another but related area in which to concentrate his questioning. Generally, interviewers who find a particular line of questioning profitable, may dwell on it for a time. The point being made here is that computers, like interviewers, can be programmed to make conditional branches from one line of questioning to another, depending on the respondent's last reply to a specific item.

The clinical interview essentially is nothing more than a nonrandom sampling of the set of all possible questions that could be asked during a given period of time. How the subset of questions is selected often depends on the interviewer's master program (training) and his judgment of the relevance of certain items for the particular patient-problem combination. Given unlimited resources of time, patience, persistence, and money, one could ask a universal set of questions of all interviewees. Since in practice such resources are limited, the clinician uses a directed rather than an exhaustive search for questions relevant to the patient's problem. The facility of the computer to alter its line of questioning is limited only by its storage capacity and the programmer's ingenuity. The human interviewer is similarly restricted by his training, skill, an inventiveness.

It is tempting to claim that an entire mental status examination can be conducted by a computer—and ultimately this seems within reach—but there are a number of obstacles that must be surmounted before this becomes reality. Among the hardware problems that require attention and solution before an automated interview system becomes operationally practical are the large memory capacity needed, the speed of access necessary to such a memory, and the cumbersome input-output communication systems (between respondent and computer) currently available. These hardware problems, however, are relatively minor compared to the software (programming) considerations that need resolution. The largest of the software problems consists of the lack of knowledge about the clinician's processing of diagnostic information. His moment-to-moment differential responding to a patient's verbal cues, and the subsequent diagnostic and prognostic judgments based on these cues, are for the most part unknown and yet to be explored. Unfortunately, the results of the few systematic studies that have been conducted to date of the clinician's cognitive activities only begin to expose the enormous complexity of this form of data processing (see Bellman *et al.*, 1966; Hunt and Jones, 1962; Parker, 1958; Van Atta, 1966).

In the meantime the closest approximation to the psychiatric interview, and perhaps ultimately the method of choice, can be found to a large extent in the already developed techniques of psychometrics. Earlier in this book (see Chap. 7), the self-report inventory was shown to be nothing more than a standardized interview. The administration of this interview as a test in booklet format, at the time, was only intended as a convenience that enabled mass interviewing. It is time now, however, to modify this procedure. The development of computer technology no longer justifies the original format.

The advantage of the computer for the newer type of test administration (or standardized interviewing) lies in its greater facility for sampling intensively a specific set of personality dimensions. As an example of this advantage, consider the situation in which a psychiatric interview is conducted for the purpose of diagnostic classification. If the MMPI item pool is stored in the computer, a subset of these items, selected from each of several of its clinical scales, could be used as the starting point for the machine interview by having each subject answer these items. The number of subjects interviewed simultaneously is limited only by storage capacity and by the number of available input-output devices (teletypes or display tubes). On the basis of responses made by each subject to the items printed out to him, the computer branches to a set of additional items relevant to that subject's pattern of responding. The end result is that a shorter form of the test is administered, rather than the entire MMPI item pool. Moreover, the item responses are read directly into the machine and are immediately ready for computer quantification and interpretation.

In principle, this situation can be extended to the point where the computer is programmed with large numbers of items gleaned from many existing and to-be-developed personality inventories. Such a computer program could perform an exhaustive exploration of a few important psychiatric dimensions rather than conduct a superficial search of many dimensions, of which only a small subset may be relevant. In practice this means that rather than administering all 550 MMPI items—after it has become obvious from an initial set of items that, let us say, only the dimensions of schizophrenia and paranoia are relevant—the computer could branch to a set of highly discriminating items.

The feasibility of supervised test administration via the computer by using MMPI items was recently explored (Kleinmuntz and McLean, 1967). The computer program's goal was to evaluate respondents' replies to items from each of 15 scales (L, F, K, Hs, D, Hy, Pd, Mf, Pa, Pt, Sc, Ma, Si, Es, and Mt). At any point in the course of testing, the program assumed one of three states with respect to each of the scales: the subject was (1) assumed normal, (2) assumed abnormal, or (3) not yet classified. At the beginning of the computer run, all scales were in the third state.

A flow chart of the sample program is shown in Figure 11–8. The action of the program was as follows: first, the program presented a basic set of items consisting of five items for each of the 15 scales. This set provided data for the computer that served as a basis for its decision about what additional items were relevant. After the basic questions were asked, the computer calculated a T-score for each scale. All scales were then assigned to one of three states (normal, abnormal or not yet classified). The T-score was used for this purpose because it is the traditional manner of scoring the MMPI scales, and therefore is interpretable in terms of deviations from the typical response characteristics of the normative group of subjects. A scale was "assumed normal" if the T-score was within two standard deviations of the mean, i.e., 30 to 70, and it was "assumed abnormal" if its T-score deviated more than two standard deviations from the mean. The scale was marked "not yet classified" at the outset of the computer run. Each scale marked "not yet classified" was placed on a "critical" list.

The second phase of the computer program consisted of selecting a scale from those on the critical list and asking questions relevant to it. After each question, the T-score was again calculated for that scale. If the scale now qualified for one of the other states (normal or abnormal), questioning was discontinued, another scale was selected from the critical list, and the process was repeated. If the scale still remained in the "not yet classified" state, questioning from it continued until a classification was made.

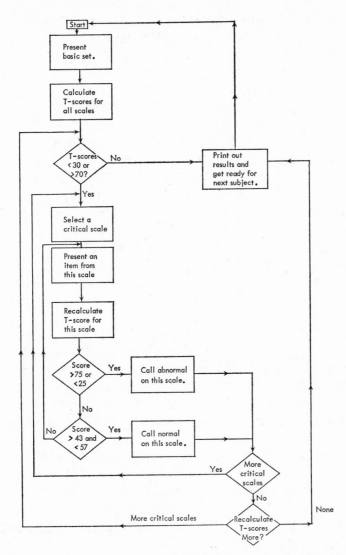

FIGURE 11–8. Flow chart of computer program simulated to interview respondent.

At some point all scales were removed from the critical list, and those that were not yet classified normal or abnormal were placed in an unclassifiable category, and the program was terminated. The computer then printed out its conclusions concerning the mental status of the person being tested with regard to each of the 15 scales.

This program was written in the computer language ALGOL–60.

and its feasibility as an interview technique was tested by using item responses of subjects (who took the entire MMPI) as data input to the machine. Thus instead of actually having respondents sit opposite a computer teletype—the manner in which the computer interview of the future would be conducted—MMPI answer sheets of several emotionally adjusted and maladjusted college students were read into the computer. The results indicated that the profiles of MMPIs administered by both methods, the computer and the conventional manner, were on the average remarkably similar. Even more important than the obtained profile similarities was the demonstration that such test administration by computer is feasible.

The technical aspects of constructing nontrivial computer interviewing methods, however, must play a secondary role to the consideration of the possible dehumanizing implications of this procedure. Although use of the computer in this way is intended as a diagnostic aid when demands for psychiatric screening are extraordinarily high—and in this sense its impersonal aspects should be considered in the same context as that of mass X-ray or innoculation procedures—the effects on the respondent may be considerable. After all, personal questions are posed during these sessions, and these may be sources of deep embarrassment. There is the additional consideration, also, that data read directly into a computer system becomes part of a permanent record unless erased or destroyed. This may be a source of concern for respondents, and aside from its influencing their interview behavior, they must be reassured of the privileged communication nature of their disclosures. It is urgent, therefore, in the planning of these procedures for the future, that the details be worked out with an interested and informed public. Undoubtedly a very special subset of ethical standards will be needed prior to using such an automated mass information gathering technique.

SUMMARY

The psychologist's data processing function consists of a number of operations that begin with his formulation of assessment goals and terminate in a decision or prediction about the person under investigation. These operations are broadly divided into input, processing, and output phases. Each of these divisions has its own characteristic problems; but the data processing phase has by far received the closest scrutiny.

A controversy that has been active in psychology over the past two decades concerns the relative merits of clinical versus statistical prediction. Proponents of the former approach believe that personality measurement data are best processed by human clinicians. Psychologists on the statistical side of the controversy, however, assert that clinicians are influenced by past experience and in this sense even their most "clinical" behavior is firmly grounded in actuarial methods of predicting. The controversy continues, and psychologists are busy collecting evidence to support their own points of view. In the meantime, there are numerous guidelines recommended for optimal use of both clinical and statistical methods for processing personality test data.

Most recently, the electronic digital computer has entered the clinical information processing picture. Its major contributions so far have been realized in the form of several programs designed as aids in mass statistical computational efforts and in the analysis of personality test profiles. In addition, work is currently under way which is designed to demonstrate the computer's use for diagnostic interviewing.

FOR FURTHER READING

1. BECHTOLD, H. P. Selection. In STEVENS, S. S. (Ed.). *Handbook of experimental psychology.* New York: John Wiley & Sons, Inc., 1951. Pp. 1237–1266.

    The basic principles and statistical procedures used in selecting individuals for jobs or treatment are summarized along with a number of theoretical considerations.

2. BORKO, H. (Ed.). *Computer applications in the behavorial sciences.* Englewood Cliffs, N.J.: Prentice-Hall, Inc., 1962.

    The first five or six chapters will serve to introduce the student to most aspects of elementary computing. Chapter 9 (pp. 172–203), by E. L. Kelly and J. C. Lingoes, concentrates on data processing of personality test data.

3. BROSS, I. D. J. *Design for decision.* New York: Macmillan Co., 1953.

    A delightful introduction to statistical decision theory, this book covers a lot of ground for the quantitatively uninitiated. The selected bibliography toward the end of the book (pp. 269–272) is exceptionally helpful in that it lists readings according to the amount of mathematical preparation necessary for their mastery.

4. CRONBACH, L. J. & GLESER, GOLDINE C. *Psychological tests and personnel decisions.* Urbana: University of Illinois Press, 1965.

   In its revised form, this latest edition of the authors continues to apply decision theory to personnel assessment problems.

5. DREGER, R. M. Objective personality tests and computer processing of personality test data. In BERG, I. A. & PENNINGTON, L. A. (Eds.), *An introduction to clinical psychology.* New York: Ronald Press, 1966. Pp. 154–190.

   Especially relevant here is the latter section of this chapter on computer processing approaches to personality test data (pp. 181–187).

6. EDWARDS, W., LINDMAN, H., & PHILLIPS, L. D. Emerging technologies for making decisions. In OLDS, J. & OLDS, MARIANNE (Eds.), *New directions in psychology II.* New York: Holt, Rinehart & Winston, 1965. Pp. 261–325.

   Topics discussed in this fascinating chapter include the concept of rationality, probability, and man-machine systems, all leading up to a Bayesian information-processing system.

7. EIDUSON, BERNICE T., BROOKS, S. H., & MOTTO, R. L. A generalized psychiatric information-processing system. *Behavioral Science,* 1966, 11, 133–142.

   An application of computer systems to institutional records is described. The generality of such a system for psychiatric facilities is explored.

8. FEIGENBAUM, E. A. & FELDMAN, J. (Eds.). *Computers and thought.* New York: McGraw-Hill Book Co., 1963.

   For information on the whole range of the computer's capabilities, this book is unexcelled. Many of the readings are equally relevant for the next chapter as well. Topics covered range from the chapter on "Can a Machine Think?" to one on "A Computer Model of Elementary Social Behavior."

9. FISHER, J. The twisted pear and the prediction of behavior. *Journal of consulting Psychology,* 1959, 5, 400–405.

   This paper raises the question of the appropriateness of statistical assumptions as they concern prediction problems.

10. GOLDBERG, L. R. Diagnosticians vs. diagnostic signs: The diagnosis of psychosis vs. neurosis from the MMPI. *Psychological Monographs,* 1965, 79 (Whole No. 602).

    Yet another study in which the diagnostic process is examined closely.

11. GREEN, B. F., JR. *Digital computers in research: An introduction for behavioral and social scientists.* New York: McGraw-Hill Book Co., 1963.

The chapters on programming computers (Part I), especially the first two (pp. 3–29), are particularly useful for introducing the history, hardware, and software of these machines.

12. HAMMOND, K. R., HURSCH, CAROLYN J., & TODD, F. J. Analyzing the components of clinical inference. *Psychological Review*, 1964, 71, 438–456.

Within the framework of a probabilistic statistical model, clinical inference is analyzed. This paper is an extension of an earlier formulation by the senior author (Hammond, 1955). Additional data to fit the model are provided in a later article (Hammond & Summers, 1965).

13. HATHAWAY, S. R. Clinical intuition and inferential accuracy. *Journal of Personality*, 1956, 24, 223–250.

A number of studies exploring clinical inference are examined. The author is led to the general conclusion that little evidence exists favoring the notion that intuition adds anything to the level of predictive accuracy attained by statistical procedures.

14. HOFFMAN, P. J. The paramorphic representation of clinical judgment. *Psychological Bulletin*, 1960, 57, 116–131.

In this paper, the author presents a configurational and a linear model of clinical judgment. He proposes also that digital computers are eminently reasonable ways to process such clinical assessment data. For a critique of some statistical oversights in this paper see Ward (1962), and also Hoffman's reply (1962).

15. HOLT, R. R. Clinical and statistical prediction: A reformulation and some new data. *Journal of abnormal and social Psychology*, 1958, 56, 1–12.

The controversy touched off by Meehl's polemic on clinical versus statistical prediction (see below) occasioned this article; it is critical of Meehl's point of view and calls attention to a number of studies that support his own stand: that clinical and statistical prediction are essential in assessment.

16. LEVY, L. H. *Psychological interpretation*. New York: Holt, Rinehart & Winston, Inc., 1963.

In a carefully reasoned presentation of the role of interpretation in testing, diagnosis, and therapy, the author offers a theory of interpretation. Of immediate relevance, however, to the student interested in supplementing his knowledge of the processing of personality test data, is Chapter 7 (pp. 197–241).

17. MEEHL, P. E. *Clinical versus statistical prediction*. Minneapolis: University of Minnesota Press, 1954.

Professor Meehl has stated (personal communication) that this book has cast him in the role of "the wicked actuary . . ." which he is not. Although he argues in this book that formulas are best for a certain class of prediction problems, he does examine the cases in which the special powers of the clinician excel. For further reading on Meehl's position in this controversy see Meehl, 1959a; Meehl and Dahlstrom, 1960; and Meehl, 1965.

18. SARBIN, T. R., TAFT, R., & BAILEY, D. E. *Clinical inference and cognitive theory.* New York: Holt, Rinehart & Winston, 1960.

Readers may recognize that the senior author of this book is among the early psychologists to propose the extreme actuarial position that clinical prediction is a special instance of statistical inference. In this volume, these three outstanding psychologists examine the clinician's conceptual activities in the light of a cognitive theory. The most surprising by-product of this book, in view of its high level of exposition, is the unfavorable critical comment it received from P. E. Meehl's review in *Contemporary Psychology* (1961).

19. STACY, R. W. & WAXMAN, B. (Eds.). *Computers in biomedical research.* Vol. I. New York: Academic Press, 1965.

Two chapters are of special interest: Chapter 13, by Lee B. Lusted, which deals with computer techniques in medical diagnosis; and Chapter 21, by the Mayo Clinic group, which is on automatic personality assessment. These two chapters provide a thorough summary of work in progress designed to automate the clinical decision process.

20. SUNDBERG, N. D. & TYLER, LEONA E. *Clinical psychology: An introduction to research and practice.* New York: Appleton-Century-Crofts, 1962.

Overall an excellent book on research and practice in clinical settings, Chapters 4 ("The Nature of Clinical Assessment"), 6 ("Clinical Use of Tests"), 7 ("Assessing Development in Life Situations"), and 8 ("Interpretation") are especially relevant to the present discussion.

CHAPTER 12

RETROSPECT AND PROSPECT OF PERSONALITY MEASUREMENT

Personality measurement has come a long way from the common-sense notions of sizing up people that prevailed until quite recently in the history of psychology; and from Woodworth's pioneer adjustment inventory of World War I, which naïvely asked persons such questions as, "Are you happy most of the time?" and even more naïvely expected truthful answers. In their stead there are today thousands of techniques and procedures available for measuring and diagnosing personality characteristics, entire books written on the interpretation of single tests such as the MMPI (Dahlstrom and Welsh, 1960), Rorschach (Klopfer and Davidson, 1962), and the TAT (Murstein, 1963), and large research institutes at major universities[1] which invest considerable time and effort in the development of personality tests.

At the same time that this proliferation of tests and their uses has taken place, there has been an ever increasing growth in the sophistication, technical knowledge, and theory about psychometric principles underlying the construction of these tests. Yet there are problems, as the evaluation of tests and procedures throughout this book has emphasized. Some of these problems concern the moral and ethical aspects of personality measurement and raise pertinent issues about the invasion of privacy and the civil liberties of persons exposed to these tests. Other problems are technical ones

---

[1] Two notable research organizations of this type are the Institute for Personality and Ability Testing (IPAT) at the University of Illinois, and the Institute of Personality Assessment Research (IPAR) at the University of California at Berkeley.

and concern the adequacy of available procedures. Wherever possible, psychologists have cooperated in efforts aimed at resolution of the moral issues and generally have not tried to evade these problems or to defend their personality measurement methods. Correspondingly, they have been responsive to one another's technical criticism of the tools they use, and therefore personality measurement has attained a high level of excellence.

Looking to the future of personality measurement, there are two avenues open for perfecting existing and yet to be developed techniques. One consists of continuing to refine available instruments

TABLE 12–1

Suggestions for Unconventional Methods for Personality Measurement

Technique	Advantage	Disadvantage
Content analysis of Personal documents	The person's own account of events. The analysis can be fully automated.	No early history. Distortions due to omissions, amplification and lying.
Biographical data	Can be treated like psychometric data.	Many items are not verifiable.
Computer simulation of personality	Computer is free of theoretical biases. Also it forces programmer to specify his variables.	Suggestion that personality structure can be reduced to mechanical processes.
Performance tests of personality	Subjects are unaware of purpose of tests.	Questionable generalizability of findings.
Physical indices of personality	Can add to the multivariate approach to personality measurement.	Not enough is presently known about relevant physical measures.

until they comply with psychometric standards. The other avenue is to develop entirely new methods of measuring personality. Some of the potentially promising new methods are discussed in the remainder of this chapter. It is important to emphasize, however, that the two approaches to personality testing are not mutually exclusive. Therefore, rather than looking toward these new methods as substitutes for more traditional personality tests, they should be considered as potential supplementary or adjunctive techniques. As an overview of these methods, Table 12–1 provides a summary of each technique, along with comments about the advantages, disadvantages, and problems associated with its use.

CONTENT ANALYSIS OF PERSONAL DOCUMENTS

The use of personal documents to study personality is not new. It has been most thoroughly explored by Allport and his students (1942, 1965), but it is only recently that the work involved in their analysis has been vastly simplified. This has been accomplished by the aid of electronic digital computers. Personal documents include such spontaneously written materials as autobiographies, diaries, letters, open-ended questionnaires (not standardized tests), verbatim recordings of interviews or confessions, and numerous other literary compositions. As personality measures, they can be used as one other source of information about the individual, in conjunction with data resulting from observations, interviews, and paper-and-pencil tests. And since this additional source for drawing inferences about personality is also amenable to computer processing, the same computer system that conducts interviews, and administers, scores, and interprets paper-and-pencil tests can be used for analyzing personal documents.

Spontaneous written productions differ from storytelling techniques such as the TAT in that the motivations for writing them differ. Allport (1961) lists some dozen possible reasons that persons have for writing autobiographical documents, including exhibitionism, literary appeal, securing personal perspective, catharsis, desire for immortality, and scientific interest. Recognition of these motives is important because it acknowledges a methodological problem: "Unless we know how and why the document came into being we cannot decide how much trust to place in it, nor can we evaluate its completeness of coverage." (Allport, 1961, pp. 402–3).

There are a number of disadvantages to the use of personal documents for personality assessment purposes. To begin with, since samples of such material are usually not representative of large portions of an individual's life, the interpreter of this material must speculate about the omitted or unwritten aspects of the life history. As far as the available material is concerned, it is impossible to distinguish between fact and fancy, and a checkup on the facts is often not possible.

Moreover, according to most depth theories, the early years of life are most important from the point of view of fixing certain personality patterns. Accounts of these early years are hardly ever available in personal documents. Some writers record their reminiscences about infancy and childhood, but such recollections are fraught with inaccuracies and confabulation. That is not to say that these highly select memories of events and people do not have their value—because like dreams and free associations, they may disclose valuable clues about present personality patterns—but as objective histories, they are grossly deficient.

Some persons, for any of a multitude of motives, actually write their autobiographical documents in order to deceive. Such deception may occur on the conscious as well as on the unconscious level, and the motives for so doing are not very different from those that operate in the case of faked responses on self-report questionnaires (see Chapter 8). Thus, crucial facts may be omitted or overelaborated, depending on the reasons for writing the personal accounts; and the topics selected by the author of the documents may have been carefully chosen to disclose as little or as much about certain facets of his life as he deems pertinent.

Fully aware of the interpretive pitfalls that are inherent in personal documents, Allport (1965, 1966) set out to interpret a set of some 300 letters written by a woman to two young friends. *Letters from Jenny* (Allport, 1965) is the resulting book, which consists of a collection of correspondence written by this middle-aged woman over an 11-year period. Most of these documents deal with Jenny's preoccupation with her relationship to her son. As a series of personal documents, Jenny's letters are fascinating reading; she is a highly literary correspondent beset by strong hatreds, fears, conflicts, and jealousies. Her correspondence clearly reflects these mental states and follows her through numerous stages of personality disintegration prior to her entry into, and following her final years in, a mental institution.

These letters were published originally in 1946 by Professor Allport, and he has used them in a didactic way from time to time in his classes for the light they shed on theories of personality. A familiar exercise for Allport's students has been to analyze the *Letters from Jenny* from the point of view of numerous theories, such as those of Freud, Adler, and Jung. Of immediate interest here, however, are the attempts that have been made at *content analysis* of these documents.

Content analysis has been defined by Berelson (1954; p. 489) as

". . . a research technique for the objective, systematic, and quantitative description of the manifest content of communication." As it is traditionally used in the analysis of personal documents, the method involves the selection of categories based on clinical inference or general theory, the counting of text units which fall in each category, and the quantitative expression of the results in terms of frequencies within each category.

The earliest report (Allport, 1942) on the content analysis of these letters describes a method which consisted of having 39 clinical judges list the essential characteristics of Jenny as they saw them. The results were expressed in the form of a series of 198 adjectives that clustered into several "commonsense" traits (e.g., quarrelsome, suspicious, aggressive, sentimental). This content analysis was extended (Baldwin, 1942) to include a more elaborate and quantitative scheme. Using a "personal structure analysis," Baldwin instructed raters to count the number of times particular categories occurred and to correlate the categories that clustered together. By this method, Jenny was described rather well in terms of the clusters of adjectives which tended to appear most often in the text. The important thing to note about personal structure analysis, when compared to content analysis of the same text by inspectional or clinical methods, is that the former, more quantitative approach, yielded greater amounts of information about the person under study.

Most recently, a still more quantified version of content analysis has been accomplished by means of the computer. Using a computer program that was designed specifically for content analysis of English text, called the "General Inquirer"[2] (Dunphy et al., 1965; Stone et al., 1962, 1966), a student in one of Allport's personality seminars at Harvard (Paige, 1964, 1966) performed an analysis of the Letters from Jenny. Based on this computer interpretation of the text, and a subsequent factor analysis of adjectives identified as descriptive of Jenny, eight highly stable factors were discovered. These factors were very similar to those which appeared in the earlier studies.

---

[2] The General Inquirer computer program essentially is a dictionary of adjectives (or "tags") stored in the machine. The program can be written so that it recognizes and tags certain designated adjectives as category members. The program also performs "tag tallies," which form the basis for a profile of scores that describe the document thus analyzed, and for factor analysis of these scores.

The critical point about the use of the machine for this task is that the relative amounts of time and energy expended in the analyses of identical documents by humans and by the computer are hardly comparable. While Baldwin (1942) estimated that his personal structure analysis of *Letters from Jenny* required between 100 and 150 hours of work by trained raters, the computer program performed considerably more work in 32 minutes (Paige, 1964, p. 19). Furthermore, the computer program allowed the investigator more scope and flexibility to explore additional facets of Jenny reflected in the documents, because he was free from much of the grinding routine normally associated with coding, recoding, counting, computing, and intercorrelating content analysis data.

With the rapid advances in computer technology, content analysis of personal documents can become a helpful adjunct to personality study. This method has recently also attained some popularity in studies conducted in conjunction with the police department of the city of Los Angeles, which have as their prime purpose the analysis of the text of suicide notes to identify traces of content that may aid in the prediction of suicide. Apparently police departments come into possession of large numbers of suicide notes, some of which belong to persons who have taken their lives, but many others of persons who merely threatened to do so. In cooperation with psychologists from a nearby suicide prevention center, some success has been reported for the computer's facility for differentiating between the two types of suicide notes (Stone, 1964).

THE USE OF BIOGRAPHICAL DATA IN PERSONALITY MEASUREMENT

The use of biographical data for personality measurement has been most thoroughly investigated in personnel selection settings. A number of psychologists (Guion, 1965; Nunnally, 1959) have argued for the predictive potential of biographical information, and they maintain that accuracy can be enhanced by systematizing data collection procedures and by treating these data like test scores. That is, administration and scoring procedures of biographical data sheets can be standardized, normative information collected, and scores can be validated by correlating them with empirical criteria, or by construct validation methods.

In his book on *Personnel Testing,* one psychologist (Guion, 1965) indicates that weighted application blanks and personal history inventories have been used over the years in applied settings for the purpose of selecting personnel for many occupational groups. Thus life insurance salesmen (Goldsmith, 1922), salesclerks (Mosel and Wade, 1951), aircrew personnel (Levine and Zachert, 1951), office employees (Kirchner and Dunnette, 1957), among others, have been selected on the basis of biographical data collected on their application blanks. These applications tend to include such demographic identifying data as age, sex, marital status, educational level, number of dependents, and location of home.

Personal history items that are less verifiable than demographic information have also been used (Albright and Glennon, 1961; Super, 1960; Walther, 1961). Thus respondents are asked specific questions about when they began to drive, how often they entertain guests, how many cocktails they have before meals, and so forth. In principle, such questions can be empirically validated and can become predictors of a number of personality dimensions. Personal history items that reveal attitudes, needs, and habits can be especially useful predictors. For example, it has been established that the amount of life insurance owned by insurance salesmen is related to the volume of policies they sell (Baier and Dugan, 1957), and convincing arguments have been offered that sales success is related to one's conviction of the value of life insurance rather than to better salesmanship or the fact that better salesmen have more money to spend. Therefore, items attempting to tap personality dimensions basic to successful insurance salesmanship might do well to explore how salesmen feel about the importance of life insurance ownership (see Hughes, 1956).

Elaborate statistical weighting schemes for prediction equations have been developed (see Guion, 1965, pp. 385–393), and some of these have demonstrated their worth for certain decisions. Research is continually being conducted to further test their effectiveness, and in the future it will probably concentrate on refining this method along the lines prescribed for traditional psychometric devices. A recent issue of *Science* (March 3, 1967) reports a summary of studies on "Biographical Predictors of Scientific Performance" in which C. W. Taylor and R. L. Ellison used empirically keyed biographical scores to predict successful scientific careers.

COMPUTER SIMULATION OF PERSONALITY

An entirely different approach to the measurement of personality has been presented at a conference on computer simulation of personality held at the Educational Testing Service at Princeton University in 1962 (Tomkins and Messick, 1963). The advantage of the computer over other methods of personality measurement has been succinctly and humorously expressed by Tomkins (pp. 7–8) :

The computer is not only neutral, it is deaf, dumb and inert, a *tabula rasa* whose passivity cries out for the activity of the programmer. Contrary to methods such as projective techniques and factor analysis, such inertness of the computer will serve to inhibit malignant data growth which is uninformed by prior ideation.

Two approaches presented at that conference are especially interesting for their implications in the measurement of personality.

Aldous

The first of these approaches described a computer program named *Aldous* by its author (Loehlin, 1963). It is a primitive, although not trivial, computer program written for a machine not much larger than a desk calculator. Aldous can be confronted with "situations," to each of which he "responds" by printing out a number. He is programmed to learn from certain of his experiences and not to learn from certain others. Aldous can "recognize" situations he has experienced (similar or identical situations have been stored in permanent or temporary computer memory), and he is capable of three "emotional reactions": attraction, anger, and fear. Aldous can react by approaching positively, attacking, or withdrawing, corresponding to which one of the three emotional states he may be in.

Loehlin has conducted experiments with his computer program by raising Aldous in benign and hostile environments, and checking up periodically on his attitudes by administering a personality inventory to him (a program of questions exploring how Aldous "feels" about what is happening to him). Also, he experimented with Aldous by shifting him from one environment to the other; and performed experiments in which personality trait changes were made involving different parts of his reaction system. The reaction patterns to various environments of a "decisive," "radical," "abstract," "standard," "hesitant," and "conservative" Aldous were then compared.

The importance of the Aldous experiments for personality measurement lies in the potential that such a computer program holds for formulating, on the basis of personality assessment data collected about a real person, "a more complex and comprehensive representation of his personality than any single human brain could comprehend."

One psychologist (Holtzman, 1963), in a discussion of Loehlin's paper, foresees a personality simulation model which eventually could be expanded to include Aldous's father, girl friend, or competitor. Such a program could deal with two-person interactions and problem-solving situations; but most important, such a program would necessitate sensitive personality measurement instruments that would allow its author to vary parameters of the model systematically and meaningfully.

Neurotic Personality

The second computer simulation study reported at the Princeton conference is one by Colby (1963, 1965), in which he attempts to simulate a neurotic process. A flow chart of Colby's computer system is presented in Figure 12–1. In addition to developing complexes, and coping with anxiety and conflict situations, Colby's neurotic personality is capable, among other things, of using mechanisms of defense such as displacement and projection.

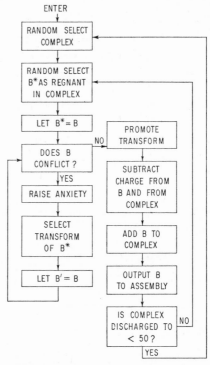

FIGURE 12–1. Flow chart of a neurotic process. (Reproduced by permission from *Computers in Biomedical Research.*)

The essential features of the programmed neurotic process are the adjustive mechanisms available to the simulated neurotic person so that he can handle conflict situations. Colby suggests that one test of the adequacy of his program might be to attempt predictions of what the simulated neurotic might select in an object-choice task. For example, given certain information about a patient, would the computer come to the same decision as the real patient in the same task environment? Such predictions must be confirmed or disconfirmed on the basis of a real patient's verbal reports of his behavior in a particular situation. Of course, the problems associated with such self-reports must be resolved before they are given any credibility.

The implications of Colby's program for personality measurement lie in the emphasis that computer programming places on quantifying the constructs of psychoanalytic (or any other) theory. As has been pointed out in the discussion of Colby's paper (Singer, 1963), the rigors of computer programming require careful specification and quantification of the relative power of defense mechanisms, drives, and anxiety states, and their reducers.

These novel uses of the computer, if pursued, will almost certainly make new demands on computer hardware accessories and software programming techniques. The large amounts of storage needed, and the quick access required between short- and long-term memory in order to stimulate interactive processes, are overly demanding for present-day machines. However, these hardware considerations will be dwarfed by the enormous problems associated with the large gaps that exist in personality theory. It is therefore too early to say whether or not this use of the computer will add anything to present knowledge about personality measurement that is not obtainable without its use.

PERFORMANCE TESTS OF PERSONALITY

In the study of personality, virtually no tests exist which measure traits directly by having subjects perform a number of assigned chores or tasks. Most procedures currently in use rely on the respondent's verbal reports about himself or about the character of amorphous stimuli. There are not many tests that resemble ability, aptitude, or "maximum performance" procedures in the sense of requiring persistence over a given set of tasks, demanding quick reactions to a variety of unusual circumstances, or testing perception of numerous visual or auditory cues. It is entirely possible, however, that personality characteristics are involved in what appear to be maximum performance type tests, and this presents another possible strategy for personality measurement. Some examples follow of work already under way in this aspect of personality testing.[3]

Dark Vision

One of the most interesting demonstrations relating perceptual functions to personality characteristics is Eysenck's work on dark vision. Eysenck (1947) compared the dark-vision ability of 96 neurotic patients with 6,000 nonneurotics. On a scale ranging from 0 to 32, the neurotics attained a mean score of 7.1 objects perceived compared to the normals' mean score of 19.3. These results showed that neurotics had substantially less ability to see in the dark than normals. Eysenck also demonstrated that the same measure can be used to differentiate between seriously ill, and less seriously ill, neurotic patients.

It has been known for sometime that dark vision is not necessarily related to day vision. Persons who see quite well in the daytime often express difficulty seeing well at night. The reverse of this has been reported also. The theory offered by Eysenck to explain the relationship between dark vision and neuroticism is less clear than the phenomenon itself, and its discussion here would serve no purpose. However, the really intriguing implication of Eysenck's work rests in the fact that this perceptual phenomenon has been applied as a measure to differentiate personality types. His most recent work relating dark vision to neuroticism is discussed in *The Causes and Cures of Neurosis* (Eysenck and Rachman, 1965).

Vigilance

Whenever attending to a continuous and monotonous visual or auditory task is demanded of subjects, it has been observed that vigilance at the beginning of the experiment is considerably higher than toward the end. The attention span displayed in this task has been associated with the personality dimensions of introversion-extroversion, and a number of studies indicate that introverts tend

---

[3] Fiske (1963) made the suggestion that another possible strategy for personality measurement might be to assess an individual's maximum tendency toward a particular kind of personality-relevant behavior under conditions designed to facilitate its appearance. For example, to explore "generosity," a number of situations could be concocted which are maximally favorable for eliciting generous (or ungenerous) responses.

to have a significantly higher vigilance capacity than extroverts (Bakan, 1957; Claridge, 1960). Again without going into the rationale or theory to explain these differences, the fact that they exist is important, and their implications as indices for personality measurement are apparent.

Conditioning

A more subtle index of performance than dark vision or vigilance is found in the phenomenon of conditioning. Eysenck's (1962) theory of personality predicts that introverts would form conditioned responses more quickly, more strongly, and more persistently than would extroverts.

Some studies using eyeblink conditioning to differentiate between introverts and extroverts have yielded results in favor of this theory (Brebner, 1957; Franks, 1956a; Symon, 1958), and some others have been unfavorable (Farber et al., 1957; Spence and Spence, 1964; Sweetbaum, 1963). Typically, in eyelid conditioning studies, a puff of air serves as the unconditioned stimulus (UCS) that elicits the conditioned or eyeblink response. (CR). After several pairings between the UCS and a conditioned stimulus (CS), which may be in the form of a light or buzzer, the latter alone elicits the CR. It is beyond the scope of this brief presentation to detail the considerable methodological and theoretical issues involved in the findings of differences between neurotics and normals; but it is important to emphasize the possibility that eyeblink conditioning may become a differentially diagnostic sign of some significance.

Another form of conditioning, in which the galvanic skin response (GSR) is the CR elicited by a buzzer or light (CS), has also been used as an index of certain personality disorders (Franks, 1956b; Lykken, 1957; Vogel, 1960, 1961). And although these studies are as fraught with methodological pitfalls as the eyeblink type, replications and corresponding refinements of these experiments may indicate their worth for the study of personality.

In the already established field of audiology, for example, GSR conditioning is a method that has been used for some time to test the hearing acuity of persons (usually children) who cannot or will not report hearing sounds. By pairing these sounds (CS) with electric shock (UCS), audiologists are able to observe the GSRs that are subsequently elicited by the sounds alone. The appearance of an elevated GSR as a reaction to sounds at various decibles is used as evidence of the person's ability to hear. This suggests that further research and thought may show that GSR can also be used as a personality test. Rather than relating GSR to incoming auditory stimuli, however, the use of this index in personality measurement would probably have to capitalize on its relationship to autonomic reactivity, and in turn, on the latter's relevance to personality (see pp. 393–394).

The number of additional performance phenomena related to personality variables is considerable, and concomitantly the number of methodological issues raised concerning their relative worth are also considerable. Discussion of the latter, although interesting, is not within the purpose of this book. It is sufficient here to summarize briefly some of these phenomena, and to call attention to the fact that many of them, when used in conjunction with psychometric devices, may prove in the future to be useful as measures of personality characteristics.

The relationship between *suggestibility* and neurosis has long been suspected in the history of psychology. One of the most widely used measures of suggestibility is the "body sway" test, in which the subject stands blindfolded, and the experimenter suggests that the subject is falling forward. Under these conditions some persons sway a great deal—almost to the point of falling—and others do not sway at all. A definite relationship between body sway and neuroticism has been reported in the psychological literature (Eysenck, 1947, 1952, 1957; Eysenck and Rachman, 1965).

Whenever a stimulus is presented to an organism, certain nonspecific reactions occur. These reactions are the organism's *adaptations*, and they include an orienting reflex (Berlyne, 1960; Razran, 1961), changes in electrical conductivity of the skin (Martin, 1960), and various other reactions, such as salivation and respiration, that are under autonomic nervous system control. As mentioned earlier, the relationships between the strength of these reactions and personality deserve further exploration (see Berlyne, 1960; Martin, 1960; Razran, 1961).

Many more similar laboratory-based performance tasks have been investigated by Eysenck and Rachman (1965, pp. 42–43), and were found relevant to the introversion-extroversion dimensions. Table 12–2 lists some of the phenomena and cites the names of

TABLE 12-2

Performance Studies and Their Relationships to
Introversion-Extroversion

Variable	Introversion	Extroversion	Reference
Intelligence	Low I.Q.	High I.Q.	Himmelweit (1945)
Sedation threshold	High	Low	Shagass (1956)
Time judgment	Longer	Shorter	Claridge (1960) Eysenck (1959c)
Time error	Small	Great	Claridge (1960)
Motor performance decrement	Little	Much	Ray (1959)
Problem solving; performance decrement	Little	Much	Eysenck (1959b)
Smoking	No	Yes	Eysenck, Tarrant, and England (1960)
Car driving constancy	High	Low	Venables (1955)
Cheating	No	Yes	Keehn (1956)

SOURCE: Eysenck and Rachman, 1965.

psychologists who reported the relationships between these and personality dimensions.

PHYSICAL AND PHYSIOLOGICAL INDICES OF PERSONALITY

There is little question in most persons' minds that a relationship exists between personality and physical states. Almost everyone has, at one time or another, experienced the discomforts of pain and illness and the disrupting influences that these have on their dispositions. Most persons have probably also experienced the effects of certain drugs and medicines. One drug may have a slightly exhilarating effect and cause euphoria, and another drug may have a depressing effect. The influence of alcoholic consumption on personality is also widely known, and it is apparent that the early stages of alcoholic intake are connected with hyperactive, elated, and generally pleasant behavior, whereas later behavior is best characterized as lethargic, glum, morose, and depressed.

More permanent physical states than temporary illness, occasional drug effects, or alcoholic intake also exert their influence on personality. An individual's height, weight, muscular build, facial features, resistance to illness, are a few of the physial factors which probably influence the shaping of his personality.

For a long time it was believed that different body types accompany different personalities (Kretschmer, 1925; Sheldon and Stevens, 1942). The popular notion, of course, is that tall, thin people are shy, serious, and suspicious ("Yond Cassius has a lean and hungry look; He thinks too much: such men are dangerous") and that short, fat people are friendly and jolly ("Let me have men about me that are fat"). Some of the research evidence in support of somato-typing, as it is called, has been severely criticized over the years.[4] But the point being made here is that insofar as relevant physical and physiological indices can be measured reliably, and their relationship to specific personality traits can be established, they can be used as measures of personality characteristics (Mandler *et al.*, 1961; Nunnally, 1959).

At the present time information about the most promising physiological measures of personality are obtained from studies that relate behavior to *autonomic nervous system* functioning. The latter regulates varying bodily states such as reaction to fear, alertness to danger, accomodation to heat, and most other reactions that require adjustment to an unusual set of internal or environmental circumstances. Some of the commonly known physiological measures currently used as indices of behavioral states include electrical conductivity of the skin or the GSR, level of blood pressure, rate of basal metabolism, tone of muscles, and rate of respiration. All of these indices are included in the polygraph procedure of measurement, popularly misnamed the "lie detector," which is routinely used to detect the presence of an emotional or aroused state. These and related indices are rarely used as methods of detecting or diagnosing emotional disorders, and work in this area is urgently needed and may prove useful for personality measurement.

---

[4] The interested reader is referred to sources by Sheldon *et al.* (1940, 1942, 1949) and Walker (1962, 1963) for reports that are favorable to somato-typing; and to reports by Allen (1958), O'Kelly and Muckler (1955), Tyler (1965), and Vernon (1964) for discussions that are somewhat more neutral. The stand that some of the latter psychologists have taken is simply that there is probably a relationship between body types and some personality variables, but that cultural factors as well as underlying physiological processes must be taken into account.

In the meantime several recent studies have reported positive results regarding relationships between physiological measures and personality. Most of these reports have come from research investigating the origins or etiology of schizophrenia; and these tend to link this severe psychotic disorder to various physiological components that are under the control of the autonomic nervous system. These studies tend to be highly specific in that they focus on very detailed *biochemical* agents as causative factors in the disease.

The possible use of biochemical indices to measure personality variables has received much encouragement from recent findings which relate specific chemical substances to schizophrenia. Much of this work had its origin in the discoveries that the blood chemistry of schizophrenics was different from that of normal persons (see Rubin, 1959, 1962); that schizophrenics are significantly different from normals in their rate of homeostatic[5] adjustments; and that the blood serum of psychotic persons is toxic to tadpoles (Fischer, 1953) as well as to other human cell tissues (Federhoff and Hoffer, 1956). These and similar, more technical, discoveries have led to close investigations of the relationships between many factors and psychotic behavior patterns. The phenomena being studied include the following: chemically mediated synapses (Wescoe, 1959); the role of the hypothalamus in synthesizing a chemical called serotonin (Himwich, 1960; Rubin, 1962); and the rate of metabolizing certain hallucinogenic[6] drugs (Osmond and Smythies, 1954).

The implication of these studies is apparent. Insofar as biochemical or metabolic differences can be shown to exist among individuals, these differences could be used to differentiate personality types. Just as, in medicine, a blood sample or a Shick test is used to detect mononucleosis or diphtheria, a number of biochemical tests could be administered as measures of the susceptibility to, or the presence of, certain personality disorders. It seems likely, moreover, that the most efficient use of physiological measures will consist of a multivariate approach (Sarason, 1966). Since the patterning of such physiological responses as heart rate, GSR, blood pressure, electrocardiogram (EKG), and even electroenceph-

---

[5] Homeostasis refers to the maintenance of steady physiological states of the body through self-regulating mechanisms. The most obvious example of this occurs in the form of sweating in order to maintain a steady body temperature.

[6] Hallucinogenic drugs produce temporary psychotic states in clinically "normal" persons. These states consist of hallucinations, delusions, and feelings of unreality. The most intensively studied and best known of these drugs is lysergic acid diethylamide (LSD-25).

alogram (EEG), seems to be more important than any one of these variables considered alone, the study of only one of the measures in isolation may complicate rather than clarify the empirical relationships discovered. Therefore, if progress is to be made in using physiological measures, the trend must be toward multidimensional studies of physiological responses. This trend should not come as a surprise to psychologists who have observed a similar movement in psychometrics from univariate to multivariate measurement.

The area of personality study particularly, and more generally, allied fields concerned with the problems of mental health and illness, stand to gain much from measurement breakthroughs resulting from work in the exploration of the etiology of schizophrenia. It is doubtful that physiological and physical measures alone, however, no matter how accurate or precise, could be used to make some of the complex predictions required in personality study. Unquestionably, the most efficient use of these tests will be in conjunction with some of the other measures proposed in this chapter as well as with the more traditional and currently available psychometric measures of personality.

SUMMARY AND CONCLUDING REMARKS

From its early forms, personality measurement has progressed considerably. This progress has resulted in a multiplication of tests and their applications, as well as a corresponding growth of technical knowledge about the theory underlying the use of these procedures. The standards by which personality tests are now judged are high, and this has resulted in strong criticism of currently available measuring procedures. Such criticism appropriately raises doubts about the efficacy of existing methods, but can be met by additional research designed to refine and improve these tests.

Furthermore, contributions toward improvement of personality measurement may come from the use of less conventional methods. The application of computers to the content analysis of personal documents and studies of computer simulation of normal and neurotic behavior are two such methods. In addition, the use of biographical data as a form of personality test also may contribute much to such improvements. Other hopeful signs which point in the direction of future developments in personality measurement come from studies of maximum performance tests and from investigations linking biochemical factors to the etiology of psychotic personality disorders.

FOR FURTHER READING

1. ALLPORT, G. W.   Traits revisited. *American Psychologist*, 1966, 21, 1–10.

   An excellent review of trait psychology over a period of four decades. The discussion of the content analysis of *Letters from Jenny* is placed in its proper historical perspective.

2. BELLMAN, R., FRIEND, M. B., & KURLAND, L.   Simulation of the initial psychiatric interview. *Behavioral Science*, 1966, 11, 389–399.

   A proposal is made to help the psychiatric trainee learn interviewing techniques by using a computer simulation device.

3. BERG, I. A. & ADAMS, H. E.   The experimental bases of personality assessment. In BACHRACH, A. J. (Ed.), *Experimental foundations of clinical psychology*. New York: Basic Books, 1962. Pp. 52–93.

   Topics covered in this research review include the traditional psychometric approaches as well as physiological measures, achievement indices, and experimentally induced personality change.

4. BLUM, G. S.   Programming people to simulate machines. In TOMKINS, S. S. & MESSICK, S. (Eds.), *Computer simulation of personality*. New York: John Wiley & Sons, Inc., 1963. Pp. 127–157.

   At a Princeton computer conference, Professor Blum exposes himself as an imposter and presents a noncomputer model for a theory of human thought, feeling, and action. He uses the systems approach to human thinking.

5. COLBY, K. M.   Computer simulation of neurotic processes. In STACY, R. W. & WAXMAN, B. (Eds.), *Computers in biomedical research*. Vol. I. New York: Academic Press, 1965. Pp. 491–503.

   A psychoanalyst by training and by choice, Professor Colby has been interested for several years in applying the rigors of computer programming to the therapeutic dialogue between patient and analyst. He believes that "writing and running a program . . . teaches a theorist a great deal about what he is really saying in his model . . . and gives him an opportunity to learn how to improve it." See also Colby's chapter in the Princeton conference volume (see Blum reference above).

6. COLEMAN, J. C.   *Abnormal psychology and modern life*. (3d ed.) Chicago: Scott, Foresman & Co., 1964.

   Reading Chapter 7, "Psychophysiologic Disorders," will equip students with information about some of the basic interrelationships between the autonomic nervous system and emotional reactivity.

8. DUNPHY, D. C., STONE, P. J., & SMITH, M. S. The general inquirer: Further developments in a computer system for content analysis of verbal data in the social sciences. *Behavioral Science,* 1965, 10, 468–480.

Progress in semiautomatic analysis of verbal material by computer is reported and comparisons made with the state of the art three years ago (Stone *et al.,* 1962).

9. ENDLER, N. S. & HUNT, J. McV. Sources of behavioral variance as measured by the S–R Inventory of anxiousness. *Psychological Bulletin,* 1966, 65, 336–346.

In the light of a reanalysis, the authors learn that behavior on the S–R Inventory is a function of a complex set of factors which include subjects, the test situations, modes of response, and their interactions.

7. ERIKSEN, C. W. Perception and personality. In WEPMAN, J. M. & HEINE, R. W. (Eds.), *Concepts of personality.* Chicago: Aldine Publishing Co., 1963. Pp. 31–62.

This chapter describes a line of research strategy that promises to combine the psychology of the laboratory and the psychology of applied settings.

10. EYSENCK, H. J. & RACHMAN, S. *The causes and cures of neurosis.* San Diego: Robert R. Knapp, Publisher, 1965.

This book, according to the authors, is an introduction to modern behavior therapy based on learning theory and the principles of conditioning. In addition, it provides a comprehensive summary of work of the last two decades coming out of Eysenck's laboratories at Maudsley Hospital, London.

11. GINSBURG, B. E. Genetics and personality. In WEPMAN, J. M. & HEINE, R. W. (Eds.), *Concepts of personality.* Chicago: Aldine Publishing Co., 1963. Pp. 63–78.

The author calls attention to the new research and discoveries in genetics and argues that certain aspects of personality, like other features of man, may be genetically determined.

12. HUNT, W. A. & JONES, N. F. The experimental investigation of clinical judgment. In BACHRACH, A. J. (Ed.), *Experimental foundations of clinical psychology.* New York: Basic Books, 1962. Pp. 26–51.

The psychophysical model used in experimental psychology is applied to the study of clinical judgment.

13. KLEIN, G. S. Cognitive control and motivation. In LINDZEY, G. (Ed.), *The assessment of human motives.* New York: Holt, Rinehart & Winston, 1958. Pp. 121–200.

The author and his associates have conducted a number of studies of the relationship of individual differences in perceptual style to task performance. Some recent evidence is cited which has indicated that the different perceptual styles may be related to personality pattern differences.

14. LACEY, J. I.   The evaluation of autonomic responses: Toward a general solution. *Annals of the N.Y. Academy of Science,* 1956, 67, 123–164.

This author reports that there appear to be characteristic patterns of physiological responses among persons, and that these are particularly clear when the physiological measures are obtained under stressful conditions.

15. MEEHL, P. E.   Schizotaxia, schizotypy, schizophrenia. *American Psychologist,* 1962, 17, 827–838.

In an entirely different mode, this versatile psychologist proposes a neurological model of schizophrenia. This interest is related to the author's conviction that eventually psychiatric diagnosis will become useful (see Meehl, 1959b). Most recently, Meehl (1966) has been engaged in formalizing a taxonomic system for categorizing psychotic disorders.

16. PRIBRAM, K. H.   Interrelationships of psychology and the neurological disciplines. In KOCH, S. (Ed.), *Psychology: A study of science.* Vol. IV. New York: McGraw-Hill Book Co., 1962. Pp. 119–157.

The author argues for a science of *neuropsychology* on which translations between psychological and neurological concepts can be based.

17. SCHACHTER, S.   *The psychology of affiliation: Experimental studies of the sources of gregariousness.* Stanford: Stanford University Press, 1959.

The author has taken into account, as a significant biographical variable, the subject's ordinal position in the family. His findings have stimulated considerable subsequent research about the significance of this variable.

18. TOMKINS, S. S.   Simulation of personality: The interrelationships between affect, memory, thinking, perception, and action. In TOMKINS, S. S. & MESSICK, S. (Eds.), *Computer simulation of personality.* New York: John Wiley & Sons, Inc., 1963. Pp. 3–57.

This introductory chapter by the senior author of an important book is thoroughly scholarly and enjoyable.

19. VANDENBERG, S. G.   The hereditary abilities study: Hereditary components in a psychological test battery. *American Journal of Human Genetics,* 1962, 14, 220–237.

Evidence is presented and arguments offered that hereditary factors interact with the environment to determine measured performance on psychological tests.

Bibliography

BIBLIOGRAPHY

ABT, L. E. & BELLAK, L. (Eds.). *Projective psychology.* New York: Alfred A. Knopf, Inc., 1950.

ADCOCK, C. J. Review of the sixteen personality factor questionnaire. In BUROS, O. K. (Ed.), *Fifth mental measurements yearbook.* Highland Park, N.J.: Gryphon Press, 1959. Pp. 196–199.

ADCOCK, C. J. Review of the MMPI. In BUROS, O. K. (Ed.), *Sixth mental measurements yearbook.* Highland Park, N.J.: Gryphon Press, 1965. Pp. 313–316.

ADORNO, T. W., FRENKEL-BRUNSWIK, ELSE, LEVINSON, D. J., & SANFORD, R. N. *The authoritarian personality.* New York: Harper & Row, 1950.

ALBRIGHT, L. E. & GLENNON, J. R. Personal history correlates of physical scientists' career aspirations. *Journal of applied Psychology,* 1961, 45, 281–284.

ALLEN, R. M. *Personality assessment procedures.* New York: Harper & Row, 1958.

ALLISON, H. W. & ALLISON, SARAH G. Personality changes following transorbital lobotomy. *Journal of abnormal and social Psychology,* 1954, 49, 219–223.

ALLPORT, G. W. *Personality: A psychological interpretation.* New York: Holt, Rinehart & Winston, 1937.

ALLPORT, G. W. *The use of personal documents in psychological science.* New York: Social Science Research Council, Bulletin 49, 1942.

ALLPORT, G. W. The trend in motivational theory. *American Journal of Orthopsychiatry,* 1953, 23, 107–119.

ALLPORT, G. W. *Pattern and growth in personality.* New York: Holt, Rinehart & Winston, 1961.

ALLPORT, G. W. (Ed.) *Letters from Jenny.* New York: Harcourt, Brace & World, Inc., 1965.

ALLPORT, G. W. Traits revisited. *American Psychologist,* 1966, 21, 1–10.

399

ALLPORT, G. W. & ALLPORT, F. H. *The A–S reaction study*. Boston: Houghton Mifflin Co., 1928.

ALLPORT, G. W. & ODBERT, H. S. Trait-names: A psycho-lexical study. *Psychological Monographs*, 1936, 47, No. 211, 1–171.

ALLPORT, G. W. & VERNON, P. E. *Studies in expressive movement*. New York: Macmillan Co., 1933.

AMERICAN PSYCHOLOGICAL ASSOCIATION. *Ethical standards: A summary of ethical principles*. Washington, D.C., 1953, 1–19.

AMERICAN PSYCHOLOGICAL ASSOCIATION. Technical recommendations for psychological tests and diagnostic techniques. Published as a supplement to the *Psychological Bulletin*, 1954, 51, No. 2, Part 2, 1–38.

AMERICAN PSYCHOLOGICAL ASSOCIATION. Ethical standards of psychologists. *American Psychologist*, 1959, 14, 279–282.

AMERICAN PSYCHOLOGICAL ASSOCIATION. Ethical standards of psychologists. *American Psychologist*, 1963, 18, 16–60.

AMERICAN PSYCHOLOGICAL ASSOCIATION. Special issue: Testing and public policy. *American Psychologist*, 1965, 20, 857–993.

AMERICAN PSYCHOLOGICAL ASSOCIATION. *Standards for educational and psychological tests and manuals*. Washington, D.C., 1966.

AMRINE, M. The 1965 Congressional inquiry into testing: A commentary. *American Psychologist*, 1965, 20, 859–870.

ANASTASI, ANNE. *Differential psychology*. (3d ed.) New York: Macmillan Co., 1958.

ANASTASI, ANNE. *Psychological testing*. (2d ed.) New York: Macmillan Co., 1961.

ANASTASI, ANNE & DRAKE J. An empirical comparison of certain techniques for estimating the reliability of speeded tests. *Educational and psychological Measurement*, 1954, 14, 529–540.

ANDERSON, H. H. & ANDERSON, GLADYS L. (Eds.). *An introduction to projective techniques*. Englewood Cliffs, N.J.: Prentice-Hall, Inc., 1951.

ANDREW, GWEN, HARTWELL, S. W., HUTT, M. L., & WALTON, R. E. *Michigan Picture Test*. Chicago: Science Research Associates, 1953.

ARNOLD, MAGDA B. *Story sequence analysis*. New York: Columbia University Press, 1962.

ARRINGTON, R. E. Time sampling in studies of social behavior. *Psychological Bulletin*, 1943, 40, 81–124.

ASCH, S. E. Opinions and social pressure. *Scientific American*, 1955 (November), 193, 31–35.

ASCH, S. E. Studies of independence and submission to group pressure: 1. A minority of one against a unanimous majority. *Psychological Monographs*, 1956, 70, (Whole No. 416).

ATKINSON, J. W. Studies in projective measurement of achievement motivation. Unpublished doctoral dissertation, University of Michigan, 1950.

ATKINSON, J. W. (Ed.). *Motives in fantasy, action, and society*. Princeton, N.J.: D. Van Nostrand Co., Inc., 1958 (a).

ATKINSON, J. W. Thematic apperceptive measurement of motives within the context of a theory of motivation. In ATKINSON, J. W. (Ed.), *Motives in fantasy, action, and society*. Princeton, N.J., D. Van Nostrand Co., Inc., 1958 (b), 596–616.

ATKINSON, J. W. & McCLELLAND, D. C. The projective expression of needs: I. The effect of different intensities of the hunger drive on thematic apperception. *Journal of experimental Psychology*, 1948, 38, 643–658.

AULD, F., JR., ERON, L. D. & LAFFAL, J. Application of Guttman's scaling method to the TAT. *Educational and psychological Measurement*, 1955, 15, 422–435.

BAIER, D. E. & DUGAN, R. E. Factors in sales success. *Journal of applied Psychology*, 1957, 41, 37–40.

BAKAN, P. Extraversion-introversion and improvement in an auditory vigilance task. *Medical Research Council*, 1957, A.P.U. 311/57.

BALDWIN, A. L. Personal structure analysis: A statistical method for investigating the single personality. *Journal of abnormal and social Psychology*, 1942, 37, 63–183.

BALDWIN, A. L., KALHORN, JOAN, & BREESE, FAY HOFFMAN. Patterns of parent behavior. *Psychological Monographs*, 1945, 58, No. 3.

BARKER, R. G. (Ed.). *The stream of behavior*. New York: Appleton-Century-Crofts, 1963.

BARKER, R. G., & WRIGHT, H. F. *One boy's day*. New York: Harper & Row, 1951.

BARKER, R. G., & WRIGHT, H. F. *Midwest and its children: The psychological ecology of an American town*. New York: Harper & Row, 1955.

BARNES, E. H. The relationship of biased test responses to psychopathology. *Journal of abnormal and social Psychology*, 1955, 51, 286–290.

BARNETT, W. L., JR. (Ed.). *Readings in psychological tests and measurements*. Homewood, Ill.: Dorsey Press, 1964.

BARRON, F. Some test correlates of responses to psychotherapy. *Journal of consulting Psychology*, 1953, 17, 234–241.

BARRON, F. The psychology of creativity. In OLDS, J. & OLDS, MARIANNE (Eds.), *New directions in psychology II*. New York: Holt, Rinehart & Winston, Inc., 1965. Pp. 3–134.

BARTHEL, C. E. The effects of the approval motive, generalized expectancy, and situational cues upon goal setting and social defensiveness. Unpublished doctoral dissertation, The Ohio State University, 1963.

BARTHEL, C. E., & CROWNE, D. P. The need for approval, task categorization, and perceptual defense. *Journal of consulting Psychology*, 1962, 26, 547–555.

BASS, B. M.   The leaderless group discussion. *Psychological Bulletin*, 1954, 51, 465–492.

BASS, B. M. & COATES, C. H.   Forecasting officer potential using the leaderless group discussion. *Journal of abnormal and social Psychology*, 1952, 47, 321–325.

BAUGHMAN, E. E.   Rorschach scores as a function of examiner difference. *Journal of projective Techniques*, 1951, 15, 243–249.

BAUGHMAN, E. E., & WELSH, G. S.   *Personality: A behavioral science.* Englewood Cliffs, N.J.: Prentice-Hall, Inc., 1962.

BEAVER, A. P.   Temperament and nursing. *Psychological Reports*, 1955, 9, 339–344.

BECHTOLD, H. P.   Selection. In STEVENS, S. S. (Ed.). *Handbook of experimental psychology.* New York: John Wiley & Sons, Inc., 1951. Pp. 1237–1266.

BECHTOLD, H. P.   Construct validity: A critique. *American Psychologist*, 1959, 14, 619–629.

BECK, S. J.   *Rorschach's test. I. Basic processes.* New York: Grune & Stratton, 1944.

BECK, S. J.   *Rorschach's test. II. A variety of personality pictures.* New York: Grune & Stratton, 1945.

BECKER, W. C.   The matching of behavior rating and questionnaire personality factors. *Psychological Bulletin*, 1960, 57, 201–212.

BECKER, W. C.   Comments on Cattell's paper on "perturbations" in personality structure research. *Psychological Bulletin*, 1961, 58, 175.

BELL, H. M.   *The adjustment inventory.* Palo Alto: Consulting Psychologists Press, 1934–1963.

BELL, J. E.   *Projective techniques.* New York: Longmans, Green & Co., 1948.

BELLAK, L.   The concept of projection. *Psychiatry*, 1944, 7, 353–370.

BELLAK, L.   *A guide to the interpretation of the Thematic Apperception Test.* New York: Psychological Corporation, 1951 (Revised).

BELLAK, L.   *The Thematic Apperception Test and the Children's Apperception Test in clinical use.* New York: Grune & Stratton, 1954.

BELLMAN, R., FRIEND, M. B., & KURLAND, L.   Simulation of the initial psychiatric interview. *Behavioral Science*, 1966, 11, 389–399.

BENDER, LAURETTA.   A visual motor gestalt test and its clinical use. *Research Monographs of the American Orthopsychiatric Association*, 1938, No. 3.

BENDER, LAURETTA.   *Visual Motor Gestalt Test.* Beverly Hills, Calif.: Western Psychological Services, 1938–1964.

BERDIE, R. F. & LAYTON, W. L.   *Minnesota Counseling Inventory.* New York: Psychological Corporation, 1953–1957.

BERELSON, B.   Content analysis. In LINDZEY, G. (Ed.), *Handbook of social psychology.* Vol. I. Cambridge, Mass: Addison-Wesley Publishing Co., Inc., 1954. Pp. 488–522.

BERELSON, B. & STEINER, G. A.   *Human behavior: An inventory of scientific findings.* New York: Harcourt, Brace & World, Inc., 1964.

BERG, I. A.   Response bias and personality: The deviation hypothesis. *Journal of Psychology,* 1955, 40, 61–72.

BERG, I. A.   Deviant responses and deviant people: The formulation of the deviation hypothesis. *Journal of counseling Psychology,* 1957, 4, 154–161.

BERG, I. A.   The unimportance of test item content. In BASS, B. M. & BERG, I. A. (Eds.), *Objective approaches to personality assessment.* Princeton, N.J.: D. Van Nostrand Co., Inc., 1959. Pp. 83–99.

BERG, I. A.   Measuring deviant behavior by means of deviant response sets. In BERG, I. A. & BASS, B. M., *Conformity and deviation.* New York: Harper & Row, 1961. Pp. 328–379.

BERG, I. A.   The clinical interview and the case record. In BERG, I. A. & PENNINGTON, L. A. (Eds.), *An introduction to clinical psychology.* New York: Ronald Press Co., 1966. Pp. 27–66.

BERG, I. A., & ADAMS, H. E.   The experimental bases of personality assessment. In BACHRACH, A. J. (Ed.), *Experimental Foundations of clinical psychology.* New York: Basic Books, 1962. Pp. 52–93.

BERG, I. A., HUNT, W. A., & BARNES, E. H.   *The Perceptual Reaction Test.* Evanston, Ill.: I. A. Berg, 1949.

BERLYNE, D. E.   *Conflict, arousal and curiosity.* New York: McGraw-Hill Book Co., 1960.

BERNREUTER, R. G.   *The Personality Inventory.* Palo Alto: Consulting Psychologists Press, 1931–1938.

BILLINGSLEA, F. Y.   The Bender-Gestalt: A review and a perspective. *Psychological Bulletin,* 1963, 60, 233–251.

BILLS, R. E.   Animal pictures for obtaining children's projections. *Journal of Clinical Psychology,* 1950, 6, 291–293.

BINET, A., & HENRI, V.   La psychologie individuelle. Annals de Psychologie, 1895–1896, 2, 411–465 (cited in Bell, 1948).

BINGHAM, W. V. D., MOORE, B. V., & GUSTAD, J. W.   *How to interview* (4th ed.) New York: Harper & Row, 1959.

BION, W. R.   The leaderless group project. *Bulletin of the Menninger Clinic,* 1946, 10, 77–81.

BIRD, C.   MMPI patterns under instructions to deliberately fake various psychiatric syndromes. Unpublished materials, University of Minnesota, 1948.

BIRDWHISTELL, R.   Kinesics and communication. In CARPENTER, E. (Ed.), *Exploration in communication.* Boston: Beacon Hill Press, 1960, Pp. 54–64.

BIRDWHISTELL, R.   The kinesic level in the investigations of emotions. In KNAPP, P. (Ed.), *The expressions of emotions in man.* New York: International Universities Press, 1963. Pp. 123–140.

BISCHOF, L. J.   *Interpreting personality theories.* New York: Harper & Row, 1964.

BJERSTEDT, A.   Review of the Rosenzweig P–F Study. In BUROS, O. K. (Ed.), *Sixth mental measurements yearbook.* Highland Park, N.J.: Gryphon Press, 1965. Pp. 511–516.

BLACK, J. D.   The interpretation of MMPI profiles of college women. Ph.D. dissertation, University of Minnesota, 1953 (reprinted in part in Welsh & Dahlstrom, 1956).

BLAKEMORE, C. B.   Review of Bender-Gestalt Test. In BUROS, O. K. (Ed.), *Sixth mental measurements yearbook.* Highland Park, N.J.: Gryphon Press, 1965. Pp. 414–415.

BLOCK, J.   *The challenge of response sets: Unconfounding meaning, acquiescence and social desirability in the MMPI.* New York: Appleton-Century-Crofts, 1965.

BLUM, G. S.   *The Blacky Pictures: Manual of instructions.* New York: Psychological Corporation, 1950–1962.

BLUM, G. S.   Defense preferences in four countries. *Journal of projective Techniques,* 1956, 20, 33–41.

BLUM, G. S.   A guide for the research use of the Blacky Pictures. *Journal of projective Techniques,* 1962, 26, 3–29.

BLUM, G. S.   Programming people to simulate machines. In TOMKINS, S. S. & MESSICK, S. (Eds.), *Computer simulation of personality.* New York: John Wiley & Sons, Inc., 1963. Pp. 127–157.

BONNER, H.   *Psychology of personality.* New York: Ronald Press, 1961.

BORDIN, E. S.   *Psychological counseling.* New York: Appleton-Century-Crofts, 1955.

BORDIN, E. S.   Review of the Edwards Personal Preference Schedule (1959 revision). *Journal of consulting Psychology,* 1959, 23, 471.

BORKO, H. (Ed.).   *Computer applications in the behavioral sciences.* Englewood Cliffs, N.J.: Prentice-Hall, Inc., 1962.

BOULANGER-BALLEYGUIER, G.   Étude sur le CAT: influence du stimulus sur les récits d'enfants de 3 à 8 ans. *Revue de Psychologie Applique,* 1957, 7, 1–28.

BREBNER, J. M. T.   An experimental investigation of the relationship between conditioning and introversion-extraversion in normal subjects. Aberdeen: Unpublished M.A. thesis, University of Aberdeen, 1957.

BRITTAIN, H. W.   A study of imagination. *Pedagogical Seminary,* 1907, 14, 137–207.

BROCK, T. C. & GUIDICE, C. D.   Stealing and temporal orientation. *Journal of abnormal and social Psychology,* 1963, 66, 91–94.

BROSS, I. D. J.   *Design for decision.* New York: Macmillan Co., 1953.

BRUNER, J. S., SHAPIRO, D., & TAGUIRI, R.   The meaning of traits in isolation and combination. In TAGUIRI, R. & PETRULLO, L. (Eds.), *Person perception and interpersonal behavior.* Stanford, Calif.: Stanford University Press, 1958. Pp. 277–288.

BRUNER, J. S. & TAGUIRI, R.   The perception of people. In LINDZEY, G. (Ed.), *Handbook of social psychology.* Cambridge, Mass.: Addison-Wesley Publishing Co., 1954. Pp. 634–654.

BRYAN, A. I.   *The public librarian.* New York: Columbia University Press, 1952.

BUCK, J. N. & JOLLES, I.   *H-T-P: House-Tree-Person projective technique.* Beverly Hills, Calif.: Western Psychological Services, 1946–1964.

BUDOFF, M.   Animal vs. human figures in a picture story test for young, mentally backward children. *American Journal of mental Deficiency,* 1963, 68, 245–250.

BUGELSKI, B. R.   *A first course in experimental psychology.* New York: Holt, Rinehart & Winston, 1951.

BURMA, J. H.   Self-tattooing among delinquents: A research note. *Sociology and Social Research,* 1959, 43, 341–345.

BUROS, O. K. (Ed.).   *The nineteen thirty-eight mental measurements yearbook of the School of Education, Rutgers University.* New Brunswick, N.J.: Rutgers University Press, 1938.

BUROS, O. K. (Ed.).   *The nineteen forty mental measurements yearbook.* Highland Park, N.J.: Gryphon Press, 1941.

BUROS, O. K. (Ed.).   *The third mental measurements yearbook.* Highland Park, N.J.: Gryphon Press, 1949.

BUROS, O. K. (Ed.).   *The fourth mental measurements yearbook.* Highland Park, N.J.: Gryphon Press, 1953.

BUROS, O. K. (Ed.).   *The fifth mental measurements yearbook.* Highland Park, N.J.: Gryphon Press, 1959.

BUROS, O. K. (Ed.).   *The sixth mental measurements yearbook.* Highland Park, N.J.: Gryphon Press, 1965.

BYRNE, D.   Assessing personality variables and their activation. In WORCHEL, P. & BYRNE, D. (Eds.), *Personality change.* New York: John Wiley & Sons, Inc., 1964. Pp. 38–68.

BYRNE, D.   *An introduction to personality: A research approach.* Englewood Cliffs, N.J.: Prentice-Hall, Inc., 1966.

CAMERON, N.   *The psychology of behavior disorders.* Boston: Houghton Mifflin Co., 1947.

CAMPBELL, D. T.   Recommendations for APA test standards regarding construct, trait, or discriminant validity. *American Psychologist,* 1960, 15, 546–553.

CAMPBELL, D. T. & FISKE, D. W.   Convergent and discriminant validation by the multitrait-multimethod matrix. *Psychological Bulletin,* 1959, 56, 81–105.

CANADY, H. G. The effect of "rapport" on the IQ: A new approach to the problem of racial psychology. *Journal of Negro Education*, 1936, 5, 209–219.

CATTELL, R. B. Psychological measurement: Normative, ipsative, interactive. *Psychological Review*, 1944, 51, 292–303.

CATTELL, R. B. *The description and measurement of personality.* Yonkers, N.Y.: World, 1946.

CATTELL, R. B. *Manual for forms A and B: Sixteen Personality Factor Questionnaire.* Champaign, Ill.: IPAT, 1949, 1954, 1956, 1957, 1961, 1962, 1963.

CATTELL, R. B. *Personality and motivation structure and measurement.* New York: Harcourt, Brace & World, 1957.

CATTELL, R. B. Theory of situational, instrument, second order, and refraction factors in personality structure research. *Psychological Bulletin*, 1961, 58, 160–174.

CATTELL, R. B. Cattell replies to Becker's "comments." *Psychological Bulletin*, 1961, 58, 176.

CATTELL, R. B. What is "objective" in "objective personality tests"? *Journal of counseling Psychology*, 1958, 5, 285–289. Also in BARNETTE, W. L. (Ed.), *Readings in psychological tests and measurements.* Homewood, Ill.: Dorsey Press, 1964. Pp. 260–265.

CATTELL, R. B. & EBER, H. W. *Manual for forms A and B of the Sixteen Personality Factor Questionnaire* (Young adults and adults). Champaign, Ill.: The Institute for Personality and Ability Testing, 1962.

CATTELL, R. B. & SCHEIER, I. H. *The meaning and measurement of neuroticism and anxiety.* New York: Ronald Press Co., 1961.

CHAMBERS, GUINVIERRE S. & HAMLIN, R. M. The validity of judgments based on "blind" Rorschach records. *Journal of consulting Psychology*, 1957, 21, 105–109.

CHAPPLE, E. D. "Personality" differences as described by invariant properties of individuals in interaction. *Proceedings of the National Academy of Sciences*, 1940, 26, 10–16.

CHAPPLE, E. D. The interaction chronograph; its evolution and present application. *Personnel*, 1949, 25, 295–307.

CHAREN, S. Reliability of the Blacky Test. *Journal of consulting Psychology*, 1956, 20, 16.

CHILD, I. L., FRANK, KITTY F., & STORM, T. Self-ratings and TAT: Their relations to each other and to childhood background. *Journal of Personality*, 1956, 25, 96–114.

CHURCHMAN, C. W. & RATOOSH, P. *Measurement: Definition and theories.* New York: John Wiley & Sons, Inc., 1959.

CLARIDGE, G. The excitation-inhibition balance in neurotics. In EYSENCK, H. J. (Ed.), *Experiments in personality.* London: Routledge & Kegan Paul, 1960.

CLARK, L. P.   The fantasy method of analyzing narcissistic neuroses. *Medical Journal Review*, 1926, 123, 154–158.

CLARK, RUTH M.   A method of administering and evaluating the Thematic Apperception Test. *Genetic Psychological Monographs*, 1944, 30, 3–55.

CLECKLEY, H.   *The mask of sanity.* (3d ed.) St. Louis: Mosby, 1955.

CLINE, V. B.   Interpersonal perception. In MAHER, B. A. (Ed.), *Progress in experimental personality research.* New York: Academic Press, 1964. Pp. 221–284.

CLOPTON, W.   If psychologists want understanding. *American Psychologist*, 1965, 20, 875–876.

COFER, C. N., CHANCE, JUNE E., & JUDSON, A. J.   A study of malingering on the MMPI. *Journal of Psychology*, 1949, 27, 491–499.

COLBY, K. M.   Computer simulation of a neurotic process. In TOMKINS, S. S. & S. J. MESSICK, (Eds.), *Computer simulation of personality.* New York: John Wiley & Sons, Inc., 1963. Pp. 165–179.

COLBY, K. M.   Computer simulation of neurotic processes. In STACY, R. W. & WAXMAN, B. (Eds.), *Computers in biomedical research.* Vol. I. New York: Academic Press, 1965. Pp. 491–503.

COLEMAN, J. C.   *Abnormal psychology and modern life* (3d ed.) Chicago: Scott, Foresman & Co., 1964.

COMREY, A. L.   Factored homogeneous item dimensions: A strategy for personality research. In MESSICK, S. & ROSS, J. (Eds.), *Measurement in personality and cognition.* New York: John Wiley & Sons, Inc., 1962. Pp. 11–26.

CONN, L. K. & CROWNE, D. P.   Instigation to aggression, emotional arousal, and defensive emulation. *Journal of Personality*, 1964, 32, 163–179.

Consumer Reports.   Home Video tape recorder. June, 1966, p. 280.

COOK, R. A.   Identification and ego defensiveness in thematic apperception. *Journal of projective Techniques*, 1953, 17, 312–319.

COOLEY, W. W. & LOHNES, P. R.   *Multivariate procedures for the behavioral sciences.* New York: John Wiley & Sons, Inc., 1962.

COUCH, A. & KENISTON, K.   Yea-sayers and nay-sayers: Agreeing response set as a personality variable. *Journal of abnormal and social Psychology*, 1960, 60, 151–174.

COUCH, A. & KENISTON, K.   Agreeing response set and social desirability. *Journal of abnormal and social Psychology*, 1961, 62, 175–179.

COVNER, B. J.   Studies in phonographic recordings of verbal material. I. The use of phonographic recordings in counseling practice and research. *Journal of consulting Psychology*, 1942, 6, 105–113.

CRONBACH, L. J.   An experimental comparison of the multiple true-false and multiple multiple-choice tests. *Journal of educational Psychology*, 1941, 32, 533–543.

CRONBACH, L. J. Studies of acquiescence as a factor in the true-false test. *Journal of educational Psychology*, 1942, 33, 401–415.

CRONBACH, L. J. Response sets and test validity. *Educational and psychological Measurement*, 1946, 6, 475–494.

CRONBACH, L. J. A validation design for qualitative studies of personality. *Journal of consulting Psychology*, 1948, 12, 363–374.

CRONBACH, L. J. Statistical methods applied to Rorschach scores: A review. *Psychological Bulletin*, 1949, 46, 393–429.

CRONBACH, L. J. Further evidence on response sets and test design. *Educational and psychological Measurement*, 1950, 10, 3–31.

CRONBACH, L. J. Coefficient alpha and the internal structure of tests. *Psychometrika*, 1951, 16, 297–334.

CRONBACH, L. J. Processes affecting scores on "understanding of others" and "assumed similarity." *Psychological Bulletin*, 1955, 52, 177–193.

CRONBACH, L. J. The two disciplines of scientific psychology. *American Psychologist*, 1957, 12, 671–684.

CRONBACH, L. J. Review of the California Psychological Inventory. In BUROS, O. K. (Ed.), *Fifth mental measurements yearbook.* Highland Park, N.J.: Gryphon Press, 1959. Pp. 97–99.

CRONBACH, L. J. *Essentials of psychological testing.* (2d ed.) New York: Harper & Row, 1960.

CRONBACH, L. J. & GLESER, GOLDINE C. Assessing similarity between profiles. *Psychological Bulletin*, 1953, 50, 456–473.

CRONBACH, L. J. & GLESER, GOLDINE. *Psychological tests and personnel decisions.* Urbana: University of Illinois Press, 1957.

CRONBACH, L. J. & GLESER, GOLDINE C. The signal/noise ratio in the comparison of reliability coefficients. *Educational and psychological Measurement*, 1964, 24, 467–480.

CRONBACH, L. J. & GLESER, GOLDINE C. *Psychological tests and personnel decisions.* Urbana: University of Illinois Press, 1965 (Revised).

CRONBACH, L. J. & MEEHL, P. E. Construct validity in psychological tests. *Psychological Bulletin*, 1955, 52, 281–302.

CRONBACH, L. J., RAJARATNAM, N., & GLESER, GOLDINE C. Theory of generalizability: A liberalization of reliability theory. *British Journal of statistical Psychology*, 1963, 16, 137–163.

CROWNE, D. P. & MARLOWE, D. *The approval motive: Studies in evaluative dependence.* New York: John Wiley & Sons, Inc., 1964.

CROWNE, D. P. & STEPHENS, M. W. Self-acceptance and self-evaluative behavior. *Psychological Bulletin*, 1961, 58, 104–121.

CUADRA, C. A. & REED, C. F. *An introduction to the MMPI.* Downey, Ill.: Veterans Administration Hospital, 1954.

CURETON, E. E. Recipe for a cookbook. *Psychological Bulletin*, 1957, 54, 494–497.

DAHLSTROM, W. G.   Commentary: The roles of social desirability and asquiescence in responses to the MMPI. In MESSICK, S. J. & ROSS, J. (Eds.), *Measurement in personality and cognition.* New York: John Wiley & Sons, Inc., 1962. Pp. 157–168.

DAHLSTROM, W. G. & WELSH, G. S.   *An MMPI handbook: A guide to use in clinical practice and research.* Minneapolis: University of Minnesota Press, 1960.

DAILEY, C. A.   The life history as a criterion of assessment. *Journal of counseling Psychology,* 7, 20–23.

DAVIDS, A. & MURRAY, H. A.   Preliminary appraisal of an auditory projective technique for studying personality and cognition. *American Journal of Orthopsychiatry,* 1955, 25, 543–554.

DAWES, R. M. & MEEHL, P. E.   Mixed group validation: A method for determining the validity of diagnostic signs without using criterion groups. *Psychological Bulletin,* 1966, 66, 63–67.

DEMPSEY, P.   The dimensionality of the MMPI clinical scales among normal subjects. *Journal of consulting Psychology,* 1963, 27, 492–497.

DINNEEN, G. P.   Programming pattern recognition. *Proceedings of the Western Joint Computer Conference,* 1955, 7, 94–100.

DITTMAN, A. T. & WYNNE, L. C.   Linguistic techniques and the analysis of emotionality in interviews. *Journal of abnormal and social Psychology,* 1961, 63, 201–204.

DIXON, G.   Cited in *The American Psychologist,* 1965, 20, 989.

DOERING, C. R. & RAYMOND, A. F.   Additional note on reliability. In *Schizophrenia: Statistical studies from the Boston Psychopathic Hospital,* Reprint No. 6, 1935.

DOHRENWEND, BARBARA SNELL & RICHARDSON, S. A.   Directiveness and nondirectiveness in research interviewing: A reformulation of the problem. *Psychological Bulletin,* 1963, 60, 475–485.

DÖRKEN, H., JR. & KRAL, V. A.   The psychological differentiation of organic brain lesions and their localization by means of Rorschach test. *American Journal of Psychiatry,* 1952, 108, 764–770.

DOYLE, W.   Recognition of sloppy, hand-printed characters. *Proceedings of the Western Joint Computer Conference,* 1960, 17, 133–142.

DRAKE, L. E.   A social I.E. scale for the MMPI. *Journal of applied Psychology,* 1946, 30, 51–54 (also reprinted in Welsh & Dahlstrom, 1956).

DRASGOW, J. & BARNETT, W. L.   F—K in a motivated group. *Journal of consulting Psychology,* 1957, 21, 399–401.

DREGER, R. M.   Fundamentals of personality: A functional psychology of personality. Philadelphia: J. B. Lippincott Co., 1962.

DREGER, R. M.   Objective personality tests and computer processing of personality test data. In BERG, I. A. & PENNINGTON, L. A. (Eds.), *An introduction to clinical psychology.* New York: Ronald Press Co., 1966. Pp. 154–190.

DRILLIS, R. Objective recording and biomechanics of pathological gait. *Annals of the New York Academy of Science*, 1958, 74, 86–109.

DUMAS, F. M. *Manifest structure analysis.* Missoula: Montana University Press, 1955.

DUNNETTE, M. D. Use of the sugar pill by industrial psychologists. *American Psychologist*, 1957, 12, 223–225.

DUNNETTE, M. D. Paper delivered at Carnegie Institute of Technology. Spring, 1966.

DUNPHY, D. C., STONE, P. J., & SMITH, M. S. The general inquirer: Further developments in a computer system for content analysis of verbal data in the social sciences. *Behavioral Science*, 1965, 10, 468–480.

EBEL, R. L. Must all tests be valid? *American Psychologist*, 1961, 16, 640–647.

EBER, H. W. & CATTELL, R. B. Maximizing personality scale validities on the 16PF by the computer synthesis service. *IPAT News*, September, 1966.

EDWARDS, A. L. The relationship between the judged desirability of a trait and the probability that the trait will be endorsed. *Journal of applied Psychology*, 1953, 37, 90–93.

EDWARDS, A. L. *The social desirability variable in personality assessment and research.* New York: Dryden Press, 1957.

EDWARDS, A. L. *Edwards Personal Preference Schedule.* New York: Psychological Corporation, 1959(a).

EDWARDS, A. L. Social desirability and personality test construction. In BASS, B. M. & BERG, I. A. (Eds.), *Objective approaches to personality assessment.* Princeton, N.J.: D. Van Nostrand Co., Inc., 1959(b).

EDWARDS, A. L. Social desirability and performance on the MMPI. *Psychometrika*, 1964, 29, 295–308.

EDWARDS, A. L. The assessment of human motives by means of personality scales. In JONES, M. L., *Nebraska Symposium on Motivation*, 1964, 12, 135–162.

EDWARDS, A. L. A comparison of 57 MMPI scales and 57 experimental scales matched with the MMPI scales in terms of item social desirability scale values and probabilities of endorsement. *Educational and psychological Measurement*, 1966, 26, 15–27.

EDWARDS, A. L., DIERS, CAROL J., & WALKER, J. N. Response sets and factor loadings on 61 personality scales. *Journal of applied Psychology*, 1962, 46, 220–225.

EDWARDS, A. L. & HORST, P. Social desirability as a variable in Q technique studies. *Educational and psychological Measurement*, 1953, 13, 620–625.

EDWARDS, A. L. & WALKER, J. N. Social desirability and agreement response set. *Journal of abnormal and social Psychology*, 1961, 62, 180–183.

EDWARDS, W., LINDMAN, W. H., & PHILLIPS, L. D. Emerging technologies for making decisions. In OLDS, J. & OLDS, MARIANNE (Eds.), *New directions in psychology II.* New York: Holt, Rinehart & Winston, 1965. Pp. 261–325.

EFRON, D. & FOLEY, J. P., JR. A comparative investigation of gestural behavior patterns in Italian and Jewish groups living under different as well as similar environmental conditions. *Zeitschrift der Sozialforschung,* 1937, 6, 151–159. Also reprinted in NEWCOMB, T. M. & HARTLEY, E. L. (Eds.), *Readings in social psychology.* New York: Holt, Rinehart & Winston, 1947. Pp. 33–40.

EICHLER, R. Experimental stress and alleged Rorschach indices of anxiety. *Journal of abnormal and social Psychology,* 1951, 46, 344–355.

EIDUSON, BERNICE T., BROOKS, S. H., & MOTTO, R. L. A generalized psychiatric information-processing system. *Behavioral Science,* 1966, 11, 133–142.

ELLIOTT, LOIS L. Effects of item construction and respondent aptitude on response acquiescence. *Educational and psychological Measurement,* 1961, 21, 405–415.

ENDLER, N. S. & HUNT, J. McV. Sources of behavioral variance as measured by the S–R Inventory of anxiousness. *Psychological Bulletin,* 1966, 65, 336–346.

EPSTEIN, S. Some theoretical considerations on the nature of ambiguity and the use of stimulus dimensions in projective techniques. *Journal of consulting Psychology,* 1966, 30, 183–192.

EPSTEIN, S. & LEVITT, H. The influence of hunger on the learning and recall of food related words. *Journal of abnormal and social Psychology,* 1962, 64, 130–135.

ERIKSEN, C. W. Perception and personality. In WEPMAN, J. M. & HEINE, R. W. (Eds.), *Concepts of personality.* Chicago: Aldine Publishing Co., 1963. Pp. 31–62.

ERON, L. D. A normative study of the Thematic Apperception Test. *Psychological Monographs,* 1950, 64, (Whole No. 315).

ERON, L. D. & CHERTKOFF, SHARON O. Psychological tests in clinical practice. In ABT, L. E. & RIESS, B. F. (Eds.), *Progress in clinical psychology.* Vol. VII. N.Y.: Grune & Stratton, 1966. Pp. 59–75.

ERON, L. D., TERRY, DOROTHY, & CALLAHAN, R. The use of rating scales for emotional tone of TAT stories. *Journal of consulting Psychology,* 1950, 14, 473–478.

EVANS, CATHERINE & McCONNELL, T. R. *Minnesota T–S–E Inventory.* Princeton, N.J.: Educational Testing Service, 1942–1957.

EVANS, C. C. Influence of "fake" personality evaluations on self-description. *Journal of Psychology,* 1962, 53, 457–463.

EYSENCK, H. J. *Dimensions of personality.* London: Routledge & Kegan Paul, 1947.

EYSENCK, H. J. *The scientific study of personality.* London: Routledge & Kegan Paul, 1952.

EYSENCK, H. J. The logical basis of factor analysis. *American Psychologist,* 1953, 8, 105–134.

EYSENCK, H. J. The inheritance of extraversion-introversion. *Acta Psychology,* 1956, 12, 95–110.

EYSENCK, H. J. *The dynamics of anxiety and hysteria.* New York: Frederick A. Praeger, Inc., 1957.

EYSENCK, H. J. *Maudsley Personality Inventory.* London: University of London Press, 1959 (a).

EYSENCK, H. J. Personality and problem-solving. *Psychological Reports,* 1959 (b), 5, 92.

EYSENCK, H. J. Personality and the estimation of time. *Perceptual and motor Skills,* 1959 (c), 9, 405–406.

EYSENCK, H. J. Personality and verbal conditioning. *Psychological Reports,* 1959 (d), 5, 520.

EYSENCK, H. J. *The structure of human personality.* London: Methuen, 1960.

EYSENCK, H. J. Conditioning and personality. *British Journal of Psychology,* 1962, 53, 299–305.

EYSENCK, H. J. Psychoticism or ten psychotic syndromes? *Journal of consulting Psychology,* 1963, 27, 179–180.

EYSENCK, H. J. Review of the Holtzman Inkblot Technique. In BUROS, O. K. (Ed.), *Sixth mental measurements yearbook.* Highland Park, N.J.: Gryphon Press, 1965. Pp. 440–441.

EYSENCK, H. J., & EYSENCK, SYBIL B. G. *Eysenck Personality Inventory.* Educational and Industrial Testing Service. London: University of London Press, 1963.

EYSENCK, H. J., & RACHMAN, S. *The causes and cures of neurosis.* San Diego: Robert R. Knapp, Publisher, 1965.

EYSENCK, H. J., TARRANT, M., & ENGLAND, L. Smoking and personality. *British Medical Journal,* 1960, 1, 1456–1460.

FAATZ, ANITA J. *The nature of choice in casework process.* Chapel Hill: University of North Carolina, 1953.

FARBER, I. E. A framework for the study of personality as a behavioral science. In WORCHEL, P. (Ed.), *Personality change.* New York: John Wiley & Sons, Inc., 1964. Pp. 3–37.

FARBER, I. E., SPENCE, K. W., & BECHTOLD, H. P. Emotionality, introversion-extraversion and conditioning. Paper presented at Midwestern Psychological Association, Chicago, Ill., 1957.

FEDERHOFF, S. & HOFFER, A. Toxicity of blood serum from schizphrenics and nonschizophrenic subjects. *Journal of mental and nervous Diseases,* 1956, 124, 396–398.

FEIGENBAUM, E. A. & FELDMAN, J. (Eds.). *Computers and thought.* New York: McGraw-Hill Book Co., 1963.

FELD, SHEILA & SMITH, C. P. An evaluation of the objectivity of the method of content analysis. In ATKINSON, J. W. (Ed.), *Motives in fantasy, action and society.* Princeton, N.J.: D. Van Nostrand Co., Inc., 1958. Pp. 234–241.

FELDMAN, M. J. An evaluation scale for shock therapy. *Journal of clinical Psychology,* 1958, 14, 41–45.

FERGUSON, J. T., McREYNOLDS, P., & BALLACHEY, E. L. *The Hospital Adjustment Scale.* Palo Alto: Consulting Psychologists Press, 1951–1953.

FESHBACH, S. The influence of drive arousal and conflict upon fantasy behavior. In KAGAN, J. & LESSER, G. S. (Eds.), *Contemporary issues in thematic apperceptive methods.* Springfield, Ill.: Charles C Thomas, 1961. Pp. 119–140.

FISCHER, R. Stress and toxicity of schizophrenic serum. *Science,* 1953, 118, 409–411.

FISHER, J. The twisted pear and the prediction of behavior. *Journal of consulting Psychology,* 1959, 5, 400–405.

FISHER, J., GONDA, T. A., & LITTLE, K. B. The Rorschach and central nervous system pathology: A cross-validation study. *American Journal of Psychiatry,* 1955, 111, 487–492.

FISKE, D. W. Variability of responses and the stability of scores and interpretations of projective protocols. *Journal of projective Techniques,* 1959, 23, 263–267.

FISKE, D. W. Effects of monotonous and restricted stimulation. In FISKE, D. W. & MADDI, S. R., *Functions of varied experience.* Homewood, Ill.: Dorsey Press, 1961. Pp. 106–144.

FISKE, D. W. The inherent variability of behavior. In FISKE, D. W. & MADDI, S. R., *Functions of varied experience.* Homewood, Ill.: Dorsey Press, 1961. Pp. 326–354.

FISKE, D. W. Problems in measuring personality. In WEPMAN, J. M. & HEINE, R. W. (Eds.), *Concepts of personality.* Chicago: Aldine Publishing Co., 1963. Pp. 449–473.

FISKE, D. W. Personal communication in a review of a preliminary version of this volume. 1966.

FISKE, D. W. & BUTLER, J. M. The experimental conditions for measuring individual differences. *Educational and psychological Measurement,* 1963, 23, 249–266.

FISKE, D. W. & MADDI, S. R. *Functions of varied experience.* Homewood, Ill.: Dorsey Press, 1961.

FLANAGAN, J. C. The critical incident technique. *Psychological Bulletin,* 1954, 51, 327–358.

FOREHAND, G. A. Comments on comments on testing. *Educational and psychological Measurement,* 1964, 24, 853–859.

FORER, B. R. The fallacy of personal validations: A classroom demonstration of gullibility. *Journal of abnormal and social Psychology*, 1949, 44, 118–123.

FRANK, L. K. Projective methods for the study of personality. *Journal of Psychology*, 1939, 8, 349–413.

FRANKS, C. M. Conditioning and personality; a study of normal and neurotic subjects. *Journal of abnormal and social Psychology*, 1956 (a), 52, 143–150.

FRANKS, C. M. L'echelle de Taylor et l'analyse dimensionelle de l'anxiété. *Revue de Psychologie Appliquee*, 1956 (b), 6, 35–44.

FREED, A., CHANDLER, P. J., MOUTON, J. S. & BLAKE, R. R. Stimulus and background factors in sign violation. *Journal of Personality*, 1955, 23, 499 (Abstract).

FREEDMAN, M. H. A plea to professional psychologists. *American Psychologist*, 1965, 20, 877–879.

FREEMAN, F. S. *Theory and practice of psychological testing* (3d ed.) New York: Holt, Rinehart & Winston, 1962.

FREUD, S. The psychopathology of everyday life. In *The basic writings of Sigmund Freud*. New York: Random House, 1938 (First German edition, 1904).

FREUD, S. Psycho-analytic notes upon an autobiographical account of a case of paranoia (dementia paranoides). In his *Collected papers*. Vol. III. London: Hogarth Press, 1933. Pp. 390–472 (First published in German, 1911).

FRICKE, B. G. A coded profile method for predicting achievement. *Educational and psychological Measurement*, 1957, 17, 98–104.

FRIEDMAN, C. J., JOHNSON, C. A., & FODE, K. Subjects' descriptions of selected TAT cards via the semantic differential. *Journal of consulting Psychology*, 1964, 28, 317–325.

FRUCHTER, B. *Introduction to factor analysis*. Princeton, N.J.: D. Van-Nostrand Co., Inc., 1954.

FRUCHTER, B. & JENNINGS, E. Factor analysis. In BORKO, H. (Ed.), *Computer applications in the behavioral sciences*. Englewood Cliffs, N.J.: Prentice-Hall, Inc., 1962. Pp. 238–265.

FULKERSON, S. C. & BARRY, J. R. Methodology and research on the prognostic use of psychological tests. *Psychological Bulletin*, 1961, 58, 177–204.

FURUYA, K. Responses of school children to human and animal pictures. *Journal of projective Techniques*, 1957, 21, 248–252.

GAGE, N. L. & CRONBACH, L. J. Conceptual and methodological problems in interpersonal perception. *Psychological Review*, 1955, 62, 411–422.

GEARING, F. The response to a cultural precept among migrants from Bronzeville to Hyde Park. Unpublished Master's thesis, University of Chicago, June 1952 (cited in Webb, *et al.*, 1966).

GEHMAN, W. S. A study of ability to fake scores on the Strong Vocational Interest Blank for men. *Educational and psychological Measurement,* 1957, 17, 65–70.

GESELL, A. & AMATRUDA, CATHERINE S. *Developmental diagnosis: Normal and abnormal child development* (2d ed.) New York: Harper & Row, 1949.

GESELL, A. & ILG, FRANCES L. *Child development: An introduction to the study of human growth.* New York: Harper & Row, 1949.

GHISELLI, E. E. Differentiation of individuals in terms of their predictability. *Journal of applied Psychology,* 1956, 40, 374–377.

GHISELLI, E. E. The prediction of preditability. *Educational and psychological Measurement,* 1960, 20, 3–8.

GHISELLI, E. E. *Theory of psychological measurement.* New York: McGraw-Hill Book Co., 1964.

GILLILAND, A. R. & COLGIN, R. Norms, reliability, and forms of the MMPI. *Journal of consulting Psychology,* 1951, 15, 435–438.

GINSBURG, B. E. Genetics and personality. In WEPMAN, J. M. & HEINE, R. W. (Eds.), *Concepts of personality.* Chicago: Aldine Publishing Co., 1963. Pp. 63–78.

GLESER, GOLDINE C. Projective methodologies. In FARNSWORTH, P. R., OLGA, McNEMAR, Q., McNEMAR, (Eds.), *Annual review of psychology,* volume 14. 1963 Palo Alto: Annual Reviews, Inc., 1963. Pp. 391–422.

GLESER, GOLDINE C., CRONBACH, L. J., & RAJARATNAM, N. Generalizability of scores influenced by multiple sources of variance. *Psychometrika,* 1965, 30, 395–418.

GLUECK, S. & GLUECK, E. *Unraveling juvenile delinquency.* New York: Commonwealth Fund, 1950.

GOEDINGHAUS, C. H. A study of the relationship between temperament and academic achievement. Unpublished master's thesis, Los Angeles: University of Southern California, 1954.

GOLDBERG, L. R. Diagnosticians vs. diagnostic signs: The diagnosis of psychosis vs. neurosis from the MMPI. *Psychological Monographs,* 1965, 79, No. 9 (Whole No. 602).

GOLDBERG, L. R. & WERTS, C. E. The reliability of clinicians' judgments: A multitrait-multimethod approach. *Journal of consulting Psychology,* 1966, 30, 199–206.

GOLDEN, M. Some effects of combining psychological tests on clinical inferences. *Journal of consulting Psychology,* 1964, 28, 440–446.

GOLDMAN, L. *Using tests in counseling.* New York: Appleton-Century-Crofts, 1961.

GOLDSMITH, DOROTHY B. The use of the personal history blank as a salesmanship test. *Journal of applied Psychology,* 1922, 6, 149–155.

GORDON, J. E. *Personality and behavior.* New York: Macmillan Co., 1963.

GOUGH, H. G.   Simulated patterns on the MMPI. *Journal of abnormal and social Psychology,* 1947, 42, 215–225.

GOUGH, H. G.   A new dimension of status: II. Relationship of the St scale to other variables. *American sociological Review,* 1948, 13, 534–537.

GOUGH, H. G.   The F minus K dissimulation index for the MMPI. *Journal of consulting Psychology,* 1950, 14, 408–413 (also reprinted in Welsh & Dahlstrom, 1956).

GOUGH, H. G.   Studies of social intolerance: II. A personality scale for anti-Semitism. *Journal of social Psychology,* 1951, 33, 247–255 (also reprinted in Welsh & Dahlstrom, 1956).

GOUGH, H. G.   *California Psychological Inventory.* Palo Alto: Consulting Psychologists Press, 1956–1960.

GOUGH, H. G.   Theory and measurement of socialization. *Journal of consulting Psychology,* 1960, 24, 23–30.

GOUGH, H. G.   Clinical versus statistical prediction in psychology. In POSTMAN, L. (Ed.), *Psychology in the making.* New York: Alfred A. Knopf, Inc., 1962. Pp. 526–584.

GOUGH, H. G., McCLOSKY, H., & MEEHL, P. E.   A personality scale for dominance. *Journal of abnormal and social Psychology,* 1951, 460, 360–366 (also reprinted in Welsh & Dahlstrom, 1956).

GOUGH, H. G., McCLOSKY, H. & MEEHL, P. E.   A personality scale for social responsibility. *Journal of abnormal and social Psychology,* 1952, 47, 73–80.

GOUGH, H. G., McKEE, M. G., & YANDELL, R. J.   Adjective check list analyses of a number of selected psychometric and assessment variables. Officer Education Research Laboratory, Technical Memorandum, OERL–TM–55–10, May, 1955.

GREEN, B. F., JR.   *Digital computers in research: An introduction for behavioral and social scientists.* New York: McGraw-Hill Book Co., 1963.

GREEN, G. A.   Personality correlates of enuresis in military trainees. Unpublished materials, 1955 (cited in Dahlstrom & Welsh, 1960).

GROSS, M.   *The brain watchers.* New York: Random House, 1962.

GROSS, M.   Testimony before House Special Subcommittee on Invasion of Privacy. *American Psychologist,* 1965, 20, 958–960.

GUETZKOW, H. S. & BOWMAN, P. H.   *Men and hunger: A psychological manual for relief workers.* Elgin, Ill.: Brethren Publishing House, 1946.

GUILFORD, J. P.   When not to factor analyze. *Psychological Bulletin,* 1952, 49, 26–37.

GUILFORD, J. P.   *Psychometric methods.* (2d ed.) New York: McGraw-Hill Book Co., 1954.

GUILFORD, J. P.   The structure of intellect. *Psychological Bulletin,* 1956, 53, 267–293.

GUILFORD, J. P.   *Personality.* New York: McGraw-Hill Book Co., 1959.

GUILFORD, J. P. & ZIMMERMAN, W. S.   *The Guilford Temperament survey: Manual of instructions and interpretations.* Beverly Hills, Calif.: Sheridan Supply Co., 1949.

GUILFORD, J. P. & ZIMMERMAN, W. S.   Fourteen dimensions of temperament. *Psychological Monographs,* 1956, Whole No. 417.

GUION, R. M.   *Personnel testing.* New York: McGraw-Hill Book Co., 1965.

GULLIKSEN, H.   *Theory of mental tests.* New York: John Wiley & Sons, Inc., 1950.

GUTHRIE, G. M.   Six MMPI diagnostic profile patterns. *Journal of Psychology,* 1950, 30, 317–323 (also reprinted in Welsh & Dahlstrom, 1956).

HADLEY, J. M.   *Clinical and counseling psychology.* New York: Alfred A. Knopf, Inc., 1958.

HALL, C. S. & LINDZEY, G.   *Theories of personality.* New York: John Wiley & Sons, Inc., 1957.

HAMMOND, K. R.   Probabilistic functioning and the clinical method. *Psychological Review,* 1955, 62, 255–262.

HAMMOND, K. R., HURSCH, CAROLYN J., & TODD, F. J.   Analyzing the components of clinical inference. *Psychological Review,* 1964, 71, 438–456.

HAMMOND, K. R. & SUMMERS, D. A.   Cognitive dependence on linear and nonlinear cues. *Psychological Reviews,* 1965, 72, 215–224.

HARRIS, J. L.   Deviant response frequency in relation to severity of schizophrenic reaction. Unpublished Master's thesis, Louisiana State University, 1958.

HARRISON, R.   Studies in the use and validity of the Thematic Apperception Test with mentally disordered patients. II. A quantitative validity study. *Character and Personality,* 1940 (a), 9, 122–133.

HARRISON, R.   Studies in the use and validity of the Thematic Apperception Test with mentally disordered patients. III. Validation by the method of blind analysis. *Character and Personality,* 1940 (b), 9, 134–138.

HARRISON, R.   Thematic apperceptive methods. In WOLMAN, B. B. (Ed.), *Handbook of clinical psychology.* New York: McGraw-Hill Book Co., 1965. Pp. 562–620.

HARROWER, MOLLY.   *Appraising personality: An introduction to the projective techniques.* (2d ed.) New York: Franklin Watts, Inc., 1964.

HARROWER, MOLLY.   Differential diagnosis. In WOLMAN, B. B. (Ed.), *Handbook of clinical psychology.* New York: McGraw-Hill Book Co., 1965. Pp. 381–402.

HARTMAN, A. A.   An experimental examination of the Thematic Apperception Technique in clinical diagnosis. *Psychological Monographs,* 1949, 63 (Whole No. 303).

HARTSHORNE, H. & MAY, M. A. *Studies in the nature of character*. Vol. 1. *Studies in deceit*. New York: Macmillan, 1928.

HARTSHORNE, H., MAY, M. A., & MALLER, J. B. *Studies in the nature of character*. Vol. 2, *Studies in service and self control*. New York: Macmillan, 1929.

HARTSHORNE, H., MAY, M. A., & SHUTTLEWORTH, F. K. *Studies in the nature of character*. Vol. 3. *Studies in the organization of character*. New York: Macmillan, 1930.

HARTWELL, S. W., HUTT, M. L., ANDREWS, GWEN, & WALTON, R. E. The Michigan Picture Test: Diagnostic and therapeutic possibilities of a new projective test in child guidance. *American Journal of Orthopsychiatry*, 1951, 21, 124–137.

HATHAWAY, S. R. A coding system for MMPI profile classification. *Journal of consulting Psychology*, 1947, 11, 334–337.

HATHAWAY, S. R. Clinical intuition and inferential accuracy. *Journal of Personality*, 1956, 24, 223–250.

HATHAWAY, S. R. Scales 5 (masculinity-femininity), 6 (paranoia), and 8 (schizophrenia). In WELSH, G. S. & DAHLSTROM, W. G. (Eds.), *Basic readings on the MMPI*. Minneapolis: University of Minnesota Press, 1956. Pp. 104–111.

HATHAWAY, S. R. Seminar to graduate clinical psychology trainees and residents in neuropsychiatry, 1957.

HATHAWAY, S. R. MMPI: Professional use by professional people. *American Psychologist*, 1964, 19, 204–210.

HATHAWAY, S. R. Personality inventories. In WOLMAN, B. B. (Ed.), *Handbook of clinical psychology*. New York: McGraw-Hill Book Co., 1965. Pp. 451–476.

HATHAWAY, S. R. & McKINLEY, J. C. *Minnesota Multiphasic Personality Inventory*. Minneapolis: University of Minnesota Press, 1942.

HATHAWAY, S. R. & McKINLEY, J. C. *Manual for the Minnesota Multiphasic Personality Inventory*. New York: Psychological Corporation, 1943.

HATHAWAY, S. R. & McKINLEY, J. C. *Minnesota Multiphasic Personality Inventory* (Revised Manual). New York: Psychological Corporation, 1951.

HATHAWAY, S. R. & MEEHL, P. E. *An atlas for the clinical use of the MMPI*. Minneapolis: University of Minnesota Press, 1951 (a).

HATHAWAY, S. R. & MEEHL, P. E. The Minnesota Multiphasic Personality Inventory. In *Military clinical Psychology*, TM 8–242, AFM 160–45, Departments of the Army and Air Force, July, 1951 (b).

HATHAWAY, S. R. & MEEHL, P. E. Adjective checklist correlates of MMPI scores. Unpublished materials, 1952.

HATHAWAY, S. R. & MONACHESI, E. D. The prediction of juvenile delinquency using the MMPI. *American Journal of Psychiatry*, 1951, 108, 469–473.

HATHAWAY, S. R. & MONACHESI, E. D.   The MMPI in the study of juvenile delinquents. *American sociological Review,* 1952, 17, 704–710.

HATHAWAY, S. R. & MONACHESI, E. D.   *Analyzing and predicting juvenile delinquency with the MMPI.* Minneapolis: University of Minnesota Press, 1953.

HATHAWAY, S. R. & MONACHESI, E. D.   The personalities of predelinquent boys. *Journal of criminal Law, Criminology and political Science,* 1957, 48, 149–163.

HATHAWAY, S. R. & MONACHESI, E. D.   *An atlas of juvenile MMPI profiles.* Minneapolis: University of Minnesota Press, 1961.

HEILBRUN, A. B., JR.   Evidence regarding the equivalence of ipsative and normative personality scales. *Journal of consulting Psychology,* 1963, 27, 152–156.

HELM, C. E.   Simulation models for psychometric theories. *Proceedings of the American Federation of Information Processing Societies,* 1965, 27, Part 1, Spartan Books, Inc.

HELM, C. E. & MCKEE, M.   Computer simulation of a system of interpretation for the California Personality Inventory, 1965. (Personal communication).

HELMAN, Z.   Rorschach et dessins dans un cas de lobotomie. *Bulletin Groups de Francaise Rorschach,* 1953, 3, 9–15.

HELMSTADTER, G. C.   An empirical comparison of methods for estimating profile similarity. *Educational and psychological Measurement,* 1957, 17, 71–82.

HELMSTADTER, G. C.   *Principles of psychological measurement.* New York: Appleton-Century-Crofts, 1964.

HELPER, M. M., WILCOTT, R. C., & GARFIELD, S. L.   Effects of chlorpromazine on learning and related processes in emotionally disturbed children. *Journal of consulting Psychology,* 1963, 27, 1–9.

HENRY, W. E.   *The analysis of fantasy: The Thematic Apperception Technique in the study of personality.* New York: John Wiley & Sons, Inc., 1956.

HERON, W.   The pathology of boredom. *Scientific American,* 1957, 196, 52–56.

HERON, W., BEXTON, W. H., & HEBB, D. O.   Cognitive effects of a decreased variation in the sensory environment. *American Psychologist,* 1953, 8, 366 (Abstract).

HERON, W., DOANE, B. K., & SCOTT, T. H.   Visual disturbances after prolonged perceptual isolation. *Canadian Journal of Psychology,* 1956, 10, 13–18.

HERRON, E. W.   Psychometric characteristics of a thirty-item version of the group method of the Holtzman Inkblot Technique. *Journal of clinical Psychology,* 1963, 19, 450–453.

HERTZ, MARGUERITE R.   Reliability of Rorschach Inkblot test. *Journal of applied Psychology,* 1934, 18, 461–477.

HERTZ, MARGUERITE R.   Current problems in Rorschach theory and technique. *Journal of projective Techniques*, 1951, 15, 307–338.

HEWES, G. W.   World distribution of certain postural habits. *American Anthropologist*, 1955, 57, 231–244.

HIGHLAND, R. W. & BERKSHIRE, J. R.   A methodological study of forced-choice performance ratings. *Research Bulletin*, San Antonio, Texas: Human Resources research center, 1951.

HIMMELWEIT, H. T.   The intelligence-vocabulary ratio as a measure of temperament. *Journal of Personality*, 1945, 14, 93–105.

HIMWICH, H. E.   Biochemical and neurophysiological action of psychoactive drugs. In UHR, L. & MILLER, J. G. (Eds.), *Drugs and behavior*. New York: John Wiley & Sons, Inc., 1960.

HOFFMAN, P. J.   The paramorphic representation of clinical judgment. *Psychological Bulletin*, 1960, 57, 116–131.

HOFFMAN, P. J.   Assessment of independent contributions of predictors. *Psychological Bulletin*, 1962, 59, 77–80.

HOLT, R. R.   Clinical and statistical prediction: A reformulation and some new data. *Journal of abnormal and social Psychology*, 1958, 56, 1–12.

HOLT, R. R.   The nature of TAT stories as cognitive products: A psychoanalytic approach. In KAGAN, J. & LESSER, G. S. (Eds.), *Contemporary issues in thematic apperceptive methods*. Springfield, Ill.: Charles C Thomas, 1961. Pp. 3–43.

HOLT, R. R.   Experimental methods in clinical psychology. In WOLMAN, B. B. (Ed.), *Handbook of clinical psychology*. New York: McGraw-Hill Book Co., 1965. Pp. 40–77.

HOLT, R. R. & LUBORSKY, L.   *Personality patterns of psychiatrists*. New York: Basic Books, 1958, 2 vols.

HOLTZMAN, W. H.   *The Inkblot Test—a provisional manual for research purposes only*. Austin: University of Texas, 1958.

HOLTZMAN, W. H.   Objective scoring of projective techniques. In BASS, B. M. & BERG, I. A. (Eds.), *Objective approaches to personality assessment*. Princeton, N.J.: D. Van Nostrand Co., Inc., 1959. Pp. 119–145.

HOLTZMAN, W. H.   Can the computer supplant the clinician? *Journal of Clinical Psychology*, 1960, 16, 119–122.

HOLTZMAN, W. H.   Discussion: The robot personality—static or dynamic. In TOMKINS, S. S. & MESSICK, S. J., *Computer simulation of personality*. New York: John Wiley & Sons, Inc. 1963. Pp. 213–220.

HOLTZMAN, W. H.   Personality structure. In FARNSWORTH, P. R., McNEMAR, OLGA, & McNEMAR, Q. (Eds.), *Annual review of psychology*, volume 16. Palo Alto: Annual Reviews, Inc., 1965. Pp. 119–156.

HOLTZMAN, W. H., MOSELEY, E. C., REINEHR, R. C., & ABBOTT, ELAINE. Comparison of the group method and the standard individual version of the Holtzman Inkblot Technique. *Journal of clinical Psychology*, 1963, 19, 441–449.

HOLTZMAN, W. H., THORPE, J. S., SWARTZ, J. D., & HERRON, E. W. *Ink-blot perception and personality—Holtzman Inkblot Technique*. Austin: University of Texas Press, 1961.

HOLZBERG, J. D. Reliability re-examined. In RICKERS-OSVIANKINA, MARIA A. (Ed.), *Rorschach psychology*. New York: John Wiley & Sons, Inc., 1960. Pp. 361–379.

HOLZBERG, J. D. Projective techniques. In BERG, I. A. & PENNINGTON, L. A. (Eds.), *An introduction to clinical psychology*. New York: Ronald Press Co., 1966. Pp. 106–153.

HORN, D. An experimental study of the diagnostic process in the clinical investigation of personality. Unpublished doctoral dissertation, Harvard, 1943.

HOROWITZ, MIRIAM J. A study of clinicians' judgments from projective test protocols. *Journal of consulting Psychology*, 1962, 26, 251–256.

HORST, P. (Ed.) The prediction of personal adjustment. *Bulletin 48*. New York: Social Science Research Council, 1941.

HORST, P. Pattern analysis and configural scoring. *Journal of clinical Psychology*, 1954, 10, 3–11.

HORST, P. Multiple classification by the method of least squares. *Journal of clinical Psychology*, 1956, 12, 3–16.

HORST, P. *Psychological measurement and prediction*. Belmont, Calif.: Wadsworth Pub. Co., 1966.

HOVEY, H. B. MMPI profiles and personality characteristics. *Journal of consulting Psychology*, 1953, 17, 142–146 (also reprinted in Welch & Dahlstrom, 1956).

HOVEY, H. B. The questionable validity of some assumed antecedents of mental illness. *Journal of clinical Psychology*, 1959, 15, 270–272.

HOWARD, J. W. The Howard-Inkblot test: A descriptive manual. *Journal of clinical Psychology, Monograph Supplement*, 1953, 9, 209–254.

HUGHES, J. L. Expressed personality needs as predictors of sales success. *Personnel Psychology*, 1956, 9, 347–357.

HUMM, D. G. & WADSWORTH, G. W. The Humm-Wadsworth Temperament Scale. *American Journal of Psychiatry*, 1935, 92, 163–200.

HUMPHREYS, L. Note on the multitrait-multimethod matrix. *Psychological Bulletin*, 1960, 57, 86–87.

HUNT, W. A. An actuarial approach to clinical judgment. In BASS, B. M. & BERG, I. A. (Eds.), *Objective approaches to personality assessment*. New York: D. Van Nostrand Co., Inc., 1959. Pp. 169–191.

HUNT, W. A. & JONES, N. F. The experimental investigation of clinical judgment. In BACHRACH, A. J. (Ed.), *Experimental foundations of clinical psychology*. New York: Basic Books, 1962. Pp. 26–51.

HURLEY, J. R. The Iowa Picture Interpretation Test: A multiple-choice variation of the TAT. *Journal of consulting Psychology*, 1955, 19, 372–376.

HURLEY, J. R.   Achievement imagery and motivational instructions as determinants of verbal learning. *Journal of Personality*, 1957, 25, 274–282.

HYMAN, R.   *The nature of psychological inquiry*. Englewood Cliffs, N.J.: Prentice-Hall, Inc., 1964.

INSTITUTE FOR PERSONALITY AND ABILITY TESTING.   Recent improvements in 16 PF computer analysis and reporting service. *IPAT News*, No. 20a, September, 1966.

JACKSON, D. N. & MESSICK, S. J.   A note on ethnocentricism and acquiescent response sets. *Journal of abnormal and social Psychology*, 1957, 54, 132–134.

JACKSON, D. N. & MESSICK, S. J.   Content and style in personality assessment. *Psychological Bulletin*, 1958, 55, 243–252.

JACKSON, D. N. & MESSICK, S. J.   Acquiescence and desirability as response determinants on the MMPI. *Educational and psychological Measurement*, 1961, 21, 771–790.

JACKSON, D. N. & MESSICK, S. J.   Response styles on the MMPI: Comparison of clinical and normal samples. *Journal of abnormal and social Psychology*, 1962, 65, 285–299.

JACKSON, J. M.   The stability of the Guilford-Zimmerman personality measures. *Journal of applied Psychology*, 1961, 45, 431–434.

JACOBS, A. & SCHLAFF, A.   *Falsification scales for the Guilford-Zimmerman Temperament Survey*. Beverly Hills, Calif.: Sheridan Supply Co., 1955.

JAHODA, MARIE, DEUTSCH, M., & COOK, S. W.   *Research methods in social relations*. New York: The Dryden Press, 1951.

JENSEN, A. R.   Review of Eysenck's Maudsley Personality Inventory. In BUROS, O. K. (Ed.), *Sixth mental measurements yearbook*. Highland Park, N.J.: Gryphon Press, 1965. Pp. 288–291.

JENSEN, A. R.   Review of the MAPS test. In BUROS, O. K. (Ed.), *Sixth mental measurements yearbook*. Highland Park, N.J.: Gryphon Press, 1965.

JOHNSON, R. C. & MEDINNUS, G. R.   *Child psychology: Behavior and development*. New York: John Wiley & Sons, Inc., 1965.

JONES, E. E., GERGEN, K. J., & DAVIS, K. E.   Some determinants of reactions to being approved or disapproved as a person. *Psychological Monographs*, 1962, 76, No. 2 (Whole No. 521).

JUNG, C. G.   *Contributions to analytical psychology*. New York: Harcourt, Brace & World, 1928.

KAGAN, J. & LESSER, G. S. (Eds.).   *Contemporary issues in thematic apperceptive methods*. Springfield, Ill.: Charles C Thomas, 1961.

KAGAN, J. & MOSS, H. A.   Stability and validity of achievement fantasy. *Journal of abnormal and social Psychology*, 1959, 58, 357–364.

KAHN, R. L. & CANNELL, C. F.   *The dynamics of interviewing: Theory, technique and cases*. New York: John Wiley & Sons, Inc., 1957.

KANE, F. Clothing worn by outpatients to interviews. *Psychiatric Communications*, 1958, 1 (2) (cited in Webb, *et al.*, 1966).

KANE, F. Clothing worn by an outpatient: A case study. *Psychiatric Communications*, 1959, 2 (cited in Webb, *et al.*, 1966).

KANE, F. The meaning of the form of clothing. *Psychiatric Communications*, 1962, 5 (1) (cited in Webb, *et al.*, 1966).

KAPLAN, A. *The conduct of inquiry: Methodology for behavioral science.* San Francisco: Chandler Publishing Co., 1964.

KEEHN, J. P. Unrealistic reporting as a function of extraverted neurosis. *Journal of clinical Psychology*, 1956, 12, 61–63.

KELLY, E. L. & FISKE, D. W. *The prediction of performance in clinical psychology.* Ann Arbor: University of Michigan Press, 1951.

KELLY, E. L. & GOLDBERG, L. R. Correlates of later performance and specialization in psychology. *Psychological Monographs*, 1959, 73, No. 12 (Whole No. 482).

KELLY, G. A. *The psychology of personal constructs.* New York: W. W. Norton & Co., Inc., 1955, 2 vols.

KERLINGER, F. N. *Foundations of behavioral research: Educational and psychological inquiry.* New York: Holt, Rinehart & Winston, 1964.

KERNER, J. *Klexographie.* Tübingen, Germany, 1857 (cited in Bell, 1948).

KHAN, LILIAN. Factor analysis of certain personality and aptitude variables. *Indian Journal of Psychology*, 1962, 37, 27–38.

KINSLINGER, H. J. Applications of projective techniques in personnel psychology since 1940. *Psychological Bulletin*, 1966, 66, 134–149.

KIRCHNER, W. K. & DUNNETTE, M. D. Applying the weighted application blank technique to a variety of office jobs. *Journal of applied Psychology*, 1957, 41, 206–208.

KIRKPATRICK, J. J. Validation of a test battery for the selection and placement of engineers. *Personnel Psychology*, 1956, 9, 211–227.

KLEIN, G. S. Cognitive control and motivation. In LINDZEY, G. (Ed.), *The assessment of human motives.* New York: Holt, Rinehart & Winston, 1958. Pp. 121–200.

KLEINMUNTZ, B. An investigation of the verbal behavior of paranoid psychotic patients and normals. Unpublished doctoral dissertation, University of Minnesota, 1958.

KLEINMUNTZ, B. An extension of the construct validity of the ego-strength scale. *Journal of consulting Psychology*, 1960 (a), 24, 463–464.

KLEINMUNTZ, B. Identification of maladjusted college students. *Journal of counseling Psychology*, 1960 (b), 7, 209–211.

KLEINMUNTZ, B. Two types of paranoid schizophrenia. *Journal of clinical Psychology*, 1960 (c), 16, 310–312.

KLEINMUNTZ, B.   The college maladjustment scale (Mt): Norms and predictive validity. *Educational and psychological Measurement*, 1961, 21, 1029–1033.

KLEINMUNTZ, B.   Annotated bibliography of MMPI research among college populations. *Journal of counseling Psychology*, 1962, 9, 373–396.

KLEINMUNTZ, B.   A portrait of the computer as a young clinician. *Behavioral Science*, 1963 (a), 8, 154–156.

KLEINMUNTZ, B.   MMPI decision rules for the identification of college maladjustment: A digital computer approach. *Psychological Monographs*, 1963 (b), 77, No. 14 (Whole No. 577).

KLEINMUNTZ, B.   Personality test interpretation by digital computer. *Science*, 1963 (c), 139, 416–418.

KLEINMUNTZ, B.   Profile analysis revisited: A heuristic approach. *Journal of counseling Psychology*, 1963, 10, 315–324. Abstract in *American Psychologist*, 1963 (d), 18, 353.

KLEINMUNTZ, B.   Review of the Jastak test of potential ability and behavior stability. In BUROS, O. K. (Ed.), *Sixth mental measurements yearbook*. Highland Park, N.J.: Gryphon Press, 1965. Pp. 1031–1034.

KLEINMUNTZ, B.   Sign and seer: Another example. *Journal of abnormal Psychology*, 1967, 72, (in press).

KLEINMUNTZ, B. & ALEXANDER, L. B.   Computer program for the Meehl-Dahlstrom MMPI profile rules. *Educational and psychological Measurement*, 1962, 22, 193–199.

KLEINMUNTZ, B. & McLEAN, R. S.   Diagnostic interviewing by digital computer. *Behavioral Science*, 1967, 12, (in press).

KLOPFER, B., AINSWORTH, MARY D., KLOPPER, W. G., & HOLT, R. R. *Developments in the Rorschach technique*. New York: Harcourt, Brace & World, Inc., 1954.

KLOPFER, B. & DAVIDSON, HELEN H.   *The Rorschach technique: An introductory manual*. New York: Harcourt, Brace & World, Inc., 1962.

KLOPFER, B. & KELLEY, D. M.   *The Rorschach technique*. New York: Harcourt, Brace & World, Inc., 1942.

KNOPF, I. J.   Rorschach summary scores in differential diagnosis. *Journal of consulting Psychology*, 1956, 20, 99–104.

KOGAN, KATE & KOGAN, W. S.   Social desirability scale values of items in the Interpersonal Check List (cited in Edwards, 1957).

KORCHIN, S. J. & HEATH, HELEN A.   Somatic experience in the anxiety state: Some sex and personality correlates of "autonomic feedback." *Journal of consulting Psychology*, 1961, 25, 398–404.

KOSTLAN, A.   A method for the empirical study of psychodiagnosis. *Journal of consulting Psychology*, 1954, 18, 83–88.

KRETSCHMER, E.   *Physique and character*. New York: Harcourt, Brace & World, 1925.

KRONHAUSEN, P. & KRONHAUSEN, E. *The sexually responsive woman.* New York: Grove Press, 1964.

KROUT, M. H. Autistic gestures: An experimental study in symbolic movement. *Psychological Monographs*, 1935, No. 208.

KROUT, M. H. An experimental attempt to determine the significance of unconscious manual symbolic movements. *Journal of general Psychology*, 1954, 51, 93–120.

KRUGMAN, JUDITH. A clinical validation of the Rorschach with problem children. *Rorschach Research Exchange*, 1942, 6, 61–70.

KUDER, G. F. & RICHARDSON, M. W. The theory of estimation of test reliability. *Psychometrika*, 1937, 2, 151–160.

LACEY, J. I. The evaluation of autonomic responses: Toward a general solution. *Annals of the New York Academy of Science*, 1956, 67, 123–164.

LA FORGE, R. Components of reliability. *Psychometrika*, 1965, 30, 187–195.

LANDRETH, C. Consistency of four methods of measuring one type of sporadic emotional behavior (crying) in nursery school children. *Journal of genetic Psychology*, 1940, 57, 101–118.

LAUTERBACH, C. G. The Taylor anxiety scale and other clinical measures of anxiety. *Journal of consulting Psychology*, 1958, 22, 314.

LAZARUS, R. S. *Adjustment and personality.* New York: McGraw-Hill Book Co., 1961.

LAZARUS, R. S. & BAKER, R. W. Motivation and personality in psychological stress. *Psychological News*, 1957, 8, 159–193.

LEBO, D. The development and employment of VTAT's or pictureless TAT's. *Journal of Psychology*, 1960, 50, 197–204.

LEEDS, C. H. Teacher attitudes and temperament as a measure of teacher-pupil rapport. *Journal of applied Psychology*, 1956, 40, 333–337.

LEHMAN, I. J. Responses of kindergarten children to the Children's Apperception Test. *Journal of clinical Psychology*, 1959, 15, 60–63.

LENTZ, T. F. Acquiescence as a factor in the measurement of personality. *Psychological Bulletin*, 1938, 35, 659 (Abstract).

LEVINE, A. S. & ZACHERT, VIRGINIA. Use of biographical inventory in the Air Force classification program. *Journal of applied Psychology*, 1951, 35, 241–244.

LEVINE, K. M., GRASSI, J. R., & GERSON, M. J. Hypnotically induced mood changes in the verbal and graphic Rorschach, a case study. *Rorschach Research Exchange*, 1943, 7, 130–144.

LEVY, L. H. *Psychological interpretation.* New York: Holt, Rinehart & Winston, Inc., 1963.

LIBBY, W. The imagination of adolescents. *American Journal of Psychology*, 1908, 19, 249–252.

LIEBERMAN, L. R. On "actuarial methods as appropriate strategy for the validation of diagnostic tests." *Psychological Review,* 1966, 73, 262–264.

LIGHT, B. H. A further test of the Thompson TAT rationale. *Journal of abnormal and social Psychology,* 1955, 51, 148–150.

LINDZEY, G. Thematic Apperception Test: The strategy of research. *Journal of projective Techniques,* 1958, 22, 173–180.

LINDZEY, G. On the classification of projective techniques. *Psychological Bulletin,* 1959, 56, 158–168.

LINDZEY, G. *Projective techniques and crosscultural research.* New York: Appleton-Century-Crofts, 1961.

LINDZEY, G. Seer versus sign. *Journal of experimental Research in Personality,* 1965, 1, 17–26.

LINDZEY, G. & HALL, C. S. (Eds.). *Theories of personality: Primary sources and research.* New York: John Wiley & Sons, Inc., 1965.

LINDZEY, G. & HERMAN, P. S. Thematic Apperception Test: A note on reliability and situational validity. *Journal of projective Techniques,* 1955, 19, 36–42.

LINDZEY, G. & KALNINS, D. Thematic Apperception Test: Some evidence bearing on the "hero assumption." *Journal of abnormal and social Psychology,* 1958, 57, 76–83.

LINDZEY, G. & SILVERMAN, M. Thematic Apperception Test: Techniques of group administration, sex differences, and the role of verbal productivity. *Journal of Personality,* 1959, 27, 311–323.

LINGOES, J. C. Review of the MMPI. In BUROS, O. K. (Ed.), *Sixth mental measurements yearbook.* Highland Park, N.J.: Gryphon Press, 1965. Pp. 316–317.

LIPKIN, S. The client evaluates nondirective psychotherapy. *Journal of consulting Psychology,* 1948, 12, 137–146.

LITTLE, K. B. & SHNEIDMAN, E. S. Congruencies among interpretations of psychological test and anamnestic data. *Psychological Monographs,* 1959, 73 (Whole No. 476).

LOEHLIN, J. C. Word meanings and self-descriptions. *Journal of abnormal and social Psychology,* 1961, 62, 28–34.

LOEHLIN, J. C. A computer program that simulates personality. In TOMKINS, S. S. & MESSICK, S. J. (Eds.), *Computer simulation of personality.* New York: John Wiley & Sons, Inc., 1963. Pp. 189–211.

LOEVINGER, JANE. Some principles of personality measurement. *Educational and psychological Measurement,* 1955, 15, 3–17.

LOEVINGER, JANE. Theory and techniques of assessment. In FARNSWORTH, P. R. & MCNEMAR, Q. (Eds.), *Annual review of psychology,* volume 10. Palo Alto: Annual Reviews, Inc., 1959. Pp. 287–316.

LOEVINGER, JANE. Person and population as psychometric concepts. *Psychological Review,* 1965, 72, 143–155.

LOEVINGER, JANE. The meaning and measurement of ego-development. *American Psychologist,* 1966, 21, 195–206.

LORD, F. M.   A strong true-score theory, with applications. *Psychometrika*, 1965, 30, 239–270.

LORGE, I.   Gen-like: Halo or reality? *Psychological Bulletin*, 1937, 34, 545–546.

LORR, M.   Rating scales and check lists for the evaluation of psychopathology. *Psychological Bulletin*, 1954, 51, 119–127.

LORR, M.   Classification of the behavior disorders. In FARNSWORTH, P. R., MCNEMAR, OLGA, & MCNEMAR, Q. (Eds.), *Annual review of psychology*, volume 12. Palo Alto: Annual Reviews, Inc., 1961. Pp. 195–216.

LORR, M.   Measurement of the major psychotic syndromes. *Annals of the New York Academy of Science*, 1962, 93, 851–856.

LORR, M.   Review of Cattell's 16PF Questionnaire. In BUROS, O. K. (Ed.), *Sixth mental measurements yearbook*. Highland Park, N.J.: Gryphon Press, 1965.

LORR, M., MCNAIR, D. M., KLETT, C. J., & LASKY, J. J.   Evidence of ten psychotic syndromes. *Journal of consulting Psychology*, 1962, 26, 185–189.

LORR, M., MCNAIR, D. M., KLETT, C. J., & LASKY, J. J.   Canonical variates and second-order variates: A reply. *Journal of consulting Psychology*, 1963, 27, 180–181.

LOWELL, E. L.   The effect of need for achievement on learning and speed of performance. *Journal of Psychology*, 1952, 33, 31–40.

LUTHE, W.   An apparatus for the analytical study of handwriting movements. *Canadian Journal of Psychology*, 1953, 7, 133–139.

LYKKEN, D. T.   A method of actuarial pattern analysis. *Psychological Bulletin*, 1956, 53, 102–107.

LYKKEN, D. T.   A study of anxiety in the sociopathic personality. *Journal of abnormal and social Psychology*, 1957, 55, 6–10.

LYKKEN, D. T. & ROSE, R.   Psychological prediction from actuarial tables. *Journal of clinical Psychology*, 1963, 19, 139–151.

LYMAN, H. B.   *Test scores and what they mean.* Englewood Cliffs, N.J.: Prentice-Hall, Inc., 1963.

MACHOVER, KAREN.   *Personality projection in the drawing of the human figure.* Springfield, Ill.: Charles C Thomas, 1948.

MACHOVER, KAREN.   Drawing of the human figure: A method of personality investigation. In ANDERSON, H. H. & ANDERSON, GLADYS L. (Eds.), *An introduction to projective techniques*. Englewood Cliffs, N.J.: Prentice-Hall, Inc., 1951. Pp. 341–369.

MACKINNON, D. W.   Fact and fancy in personality research. *American Psychologist*, 1953, 8, 138–146.

MACKINNON, D. W.   An assessment study of air force officers: Part V. Summary and applications. *WADC technical Report* 58–91 (V), Wright Air Development Center, 1958.

MACKINNON, D. W.   The nature and nurture of creative talent. *American Psychologist*, 1962, 17, 484–495.

MACRAE, D. & MACRAE, E. Legislators' social status and their votes. *American Journal of Sociology*, 1961, 66, 599–603.

MAHER, B. A. (Ed.). *Progress in experimental personality research*. Vol. I. New York: Academic Press Inc., 1964.

MAHER, B. A. (Ed.). *Progress in experimental personality research*. Vol. II. New York: Academic Press Inc., 1965.

MAHER, B. A. (Ed.). *Progress in experimental personality research*. Vol. III. New York: Academic Press Inc., 1967 (in press).

MALLER, J. B. Personality tests. In HUNT, J. McV. (Ed.), *Personality and the behavior disorders*. New York: Ronald Press Co., 1944. Vol. 1, pp. 170–213.

MANDLER, G., MANDLER, JEAN M., KREMEN, I., & SHOLITON, R. D. The response to threat: Relations among verbal and physiological indices. *Psychological Monographs*, 1961, 75, No. 9, (Whole No. 511).

MARKS, P. A. An assessment of the diagnostic process in a child guidance setting. *Psychological Monographs*, 1961, 75, No. 3 (Whole No. 507).

MARKS, P. A., & SEEMAN, W. *Actuarial description of abnormal personality: An atlas for use with the MMPI*. Baltimore: Williams & Wilkins Co., 1963.

MARSDEN, G. Content-analysis studies of therapeutic interviews: 1954 to 1964. *Psychological Bulletin*, 1965, 63, 298–321.

MARTIN, I. The effects of depressant drugs on palm or skin resistance and adaptation. In EYSENCK, H. J. (Ed.), *Experiments in personality*. London: Routledge & Kegan Paul, 1960.

MASLING, J. The influence of situational and interpersonal variables in projective testing. *Psychological Bulletin*, 1960, 57, 65–85.

MASLOW, A. H. *Motivation and personality*. New York: Harper & Row, 1954.

MASLOW, A. H. *Toward a psychology of being*. Princeton, N.J.: D. Van Nostrand Co., Inc. 1962.

MASTERS, W. H. & JOHNSON, VIRGINIA E. *The human sexual response*. Boston: Little, Brown & Co., 1966.

MATARAZZO, J. D. An experimental study of aggression in the hypersensitive patient. *Journal of Personality*, 1954, 22, 423–447.

MATARAZZO, J. D. The interview. In WOLMAN, B. B. (Ed.), *Handbook of clinical psychology*. New York: McGraw-Hill Book Co., 1965. Pp. 403–450.

MATARAZZO, J. D., SASLOW, G., & GUZE, S. B. Stability of interaction patterns during interviews: A replication. *Journal of consulting Psychology*, 1956, 20, 267–274.

MATARAZZO, J. D., WEITMAN, M., SASLOW, G., & WIENS, A. N. Interviewer influence on duration of interviewee speech. *Journal of verbal Learning and verbal Behavior*, 1963, 1, 451–458.

MATARAZZO, J. D., WIENS, A. N., SASLOW, G., DUNHAM, R. M., & VOAS, R. B. Speech durations of astronaut and ground communicator. *Science,* 1964, 143, 148–150.

MCCANDLESS, B. R. The Rorschach as a predictor of academic success. *Journal of applied Psychology,* 1949, 33, 43–50.

MCCLELLAND, D. C. *Personality.* New York: Dryden Press, Inc., 1951.

MCCLELLAND, D. C. Measuring motivation in fantasy: The achievement motive. In MCCLELLAND, D. C. (Ed.), *Studies in motivation.* New York: Appleton-Century-Crofts, 1955. Pp. 401–413.

MCCLELLAND, D. C. Personality. In FARNSWORTH, P. R., & MCNEMAR, Q. (Eds.), *Annual Review of Psychology,* volume 7. Palo Alto: Annual Reviews, Inc., 1956. Pp. 39–62.

MCCLELLAND, D. C. Methods of measuring human motivation. In ATKINSON, J. W. (Ed.), *Motives in fantasy, action, and society.* Princeton, N.J.: D. Van Nostrand Co., Inc., 1958 (a). Pp. 7–42.

MCCLELLAND, D. C. Risk taking in children into high and low need for achievement. In ATKINSON, J. W. (Ed.), *Motives in fantasy, action, and society.* Princeton, N.J.: D. Van Nostrand Co., Inc., 1958 (b). Pp. 306–321.

MCCLELLAND, D. C. *The achieving society.* Princeton, N.J.: D. Van Nostrand Co., Inc., 1961.

MCCLELLAND, D. C. & ATKINSON, J. W. The projective expression of needs: I. The effect of different intensities of the hunger drive on perception. *Journal of Psychology,* 1948, 25, 205–222.

MCCLELLAND, D. C., ATKINSON, J. W., CLARK, R. A., & LOWELL, E. L. *The achievement motive.* New York: Appleton-Century-Crofts, 1953.

MCCLELLAND, D. C., CLARK, R. A., ROBY, T., & ATKINSON, J. W. The projective expression of needs. IV. The effect of the need for achievement on thematic apperception. *Journal of experimental Psychology,* 1949, 39, 242–255.

MCCLELLAND, D. C. & LIEBERMAN, A. M. The effect of need for achievement on recognition of need-related words. *Journal of Personality,* 1949, 18, 236–251.

MCKEACHIE, W. J. Lipstick as a determiner of first impressions of personality: An experiment for the general psychology course. *Journal of social Psychology,* 1952, 36, 241–244.

MCKINLEY, J. C. & HATHAWAY, S. R. A multiphasic personality schedule (Minnesota): II. A differentiated study of hypochondriasis. *Journal of Psychology,* 1940, 10, 255–268 (also reprinted in Welsh & Dahlstrom, 1956).

MCKINLEY, J. C. & HATHAWAY, S. R. The MMPI: V. Hysteria, hypomania, and psychopathic deviate. *Journal of applied Psychology,* 1944, 28, 153–174 (also reprinted in Welsh & Dahlstrom, 1956).

MCNEMAR, Q. Review of the Kelly-Fiske study. *Journal of abnormal and social Psychology,* 1952, 47, 857–860.

McNemar, Q. *Psychological statistics.* (3d ed.) New York: John Wiley & Sons, Inc., 1962.

McReynolds, P., Ballachey, E., & Ferguson, J. T. Development and evaluation of hospitalized patients. *American Psychologist,* 1952, 7, 340–341 (Abstract).

Mednick, Martha T. & Mednick, S. A. (Eds.). *Research in personality.* New York: Holt, Rinehart & Winston, Inc., 1963.

Meehl, P. E. The dynamics of "structured" personality tests. *Journal of clinical Psychology,* 1945, 1, 296–303.

Meehl, P. E. Profile analysis of the MMPI in differential diagnosis. *Journal of applied Psychology,* 1946, 30, 517–524 (also reprinted in Welsh & Dahlstrom, 1956).

Meehl, P. E. Configural scoring. *Journal of consulting Psychology,* 1950, 14, 165–171.

Meehl, P. E. *Clinical versus statistical prediction.* Minneapolis: University of Minnesota Press, 1954.

Meehl, P. E. Clinical vs. actuarial prediction. *Proceedings, 1955 Invitational Conference on Testing Problems, ETS,* 1956 (a), 136–141.

Meehl, P. E. Wanted—A good cookbook. *American Psychologist,* 1956 (b), 11, 263–272.

Meehl, P. E. When shall we use our heads instead of the formula. *Journal of counseling Psychology,* 1957, 4, 268–273.

Meehl, P. E. A comparison of clinicians with five statistical methods of identifying psychotic MMPI profiles. *Journal of counseling Psychology,* 1959 (a), 2, 102–109.

Meehl, P. E. Some ruminations on the validation of clinical procedures. *Canadian Journal of Psychology,* 1959 (b), 13, 102–108.

Meehl, P. E. Structured and projective tests: Some common problems in validation. *Journal of projective Techniques,* 1959 (c), 23, 268–272.

Meehl, P. E. The cognitive activity of the clinician. *American Psychologist,* 1960, 15, 19–27.

Meehl, P. E. Logic for the clinician (Review of T. R. Sarbin, R. Taft, & D. E. Bailey. *Clinical inference and cognitive theory.* New York: Holt, Rinehart & Winston, 1960). *Contemporary Psychology,* 1961, 6, 389–391.

Meehl, P. E. Schizotaxia, schizotypy, schizophrenia. *American Psychologist,* 1962, 17, 827–838.

Meehl, P. E. Detecting latent clinical taxa by fallible quantitative indicators lacking an accepted criterion. Reports from *The Research Laboratories of the Department of Psychiatry, University of Minnesota,* Report No. PR–65–2, May 25, 1965.

Meehl, P. E. Seer over sign: The first good example. *Journal of experimental Research in Personality,* 1965, 1, 27–32.

MEEHL, P. E. & DAHLSTROM, W. G.   Objective configural rules for discriminating psychotic from neurotic MMPI profiles. *Journal of consulting Psychology,* 1960, 24, 375-387.

MEEHL, P. E. & HATHAWAY, S. R.   The K factor as a suppressor variable in the MMPI. *Journal of applied Psychology,* 1946, 30, 525-564 (also reprinted in Welsh & Dahlstrom, 1956).

MEEHL, P. E. & ROSEN, A.   Antecedent probability and the efficiency of psychometric signs, patterns, or cutting scores. *Psychological Bulletin,* 1955, 52, 194-216.

MENNINGER, K. A.   *A manual for psychiatric case study.* New York: Grune & Stratton, 1952.

MERRITT, C. B. & FOWLER, R. G.   The pecuniary honesty of the public at large. *Journal of abnormal and social Psychology,* 1948, 43, 90-93.

MESSICK, S. J.   Personality structure. In FARNSWORTH, P. R., MCNEMAR, OLGA, & MCNEMAR, Q. (Eds.), *Annual review of psychology,* volume 12. Palo Alto: Annual Reviews, Inc., 1961. Pp. 93-128.

MESSICK, S. J. & JACKSON, D. N.   Acquiescence and the factorial interpretation of the MMPI. *Psychological Bulletin,* 1961, 58, 299-304.

METTLER, F. A. (Ed.).   *Columbia Greystone Associates: Selective partial ablations of the frontal cortex.* New York: Harper & Row, 1949.

MINARD, J. G.   Response-bias interpretation of "perceptual defense." *Psychological Review,* 1965, 72, 74-88.

MOONEY, R. L. & GORDON, L. V.   *Mooney problem checklist: 1950 revision.* New York: Psychological Corporation, 1950.

MORENO, J. L.   *Who shall survive?* Washington, D.C.: Nervous and Mental Disorders Publishing Co., 1934.

MORGAN, CHRISTIANA D. & MURRAY, H. A.   A method for investigating fantasies: The Thematic Apperception Test. *Archives of Neurology and Psychiatry,* 1935, 34, 289-306.

MOSEL, J. N. & WADE, R. R.   A weighted application blank for reduction of turnover in department store sales clerks. *Personnel Psychology,* 1951, 4, 177-184.

MUNROE, RUTH L.   An experiment in large scale testing by a modification of the Rorschach method. *Journal of Psychology,* 1942, 13, 229-263.

MUNROE, RUTH L.   *Schools of psychoanalytic thought.* New York: Dryden Press, 1955.

MURRAY, E. J.   A case study in a behavioral analysis of psychotherapy. *Journal of abnormal and social Psychology,* 1954, 49, 305-310.

MURRAY, H. A. (and collaborators).   *Explorations in personality.* New York: Oxford University Press, 1938.

MURRAY, H. A.   *Thematic Apperception Test.* Cambridge, Mass.: Harvard University Press, 1943.

MURSTEIN, B. I.   *Theory and research in projective techniques (emphasizing the TAT).* New York: John Wiley & Sons, Inc., 1963.

NOLL, V. H. Simulation by college students of a prescribed pattern on a personality scale. *Educational and psychological Measurement,* 1951, 11, 478–488.

NORMAN, W. T. Stability-characteristics of the semantic differential. *American Journal of Psychology,* 1959, 72, 581–584.

NORMAN, W. T. Relative importance of test item content. *Journal of consulting Psychology,* 1963, 27, 166–174.

NUNNALLY, J. C. *Tests and measurements: Assessment and prediction.* New York: McGraw-Hill Book Co., 1959.

NUNNALLY, J. C. The analysis of profile data. *Psychological Bulletin,* 1962, 59, 311–319.

O'KELLY, L. I. & MUCKLER, F. A. *Introduction to psychopathology.* (2d ed.) Englewood Cliffs, N.J.: Prentice-Hall, Inc., 1955.

OLSON, W. F. *The measurement of nervous habits in children.* Minneapolis: University of Minnesota Press, 1929.

OSGOOD, C. E. The nature and measurement of meaning. *Psychological Bulletin,* 1952, 49, 197–237.

OSGOOD, C. E., SUCI, G. J., & TANNENBAUM, P. H. *The measurement of meaning.* Urbana: University of Illinois Press, 1957.

OSMOND, H. & SMYTHIES, M. B. Schizophrenia: A new approach. *Journal of mental Science,* 1954, 98, 309–315.

OSS ASSESSMENT STAFF. *Assessment of men.* New York: Rinehart, 1948.

PAIGE, J. M. Automated content analysis of "Letters from Jenny." Honors thesis, Department of Social Relations, Harvard University, 1964.

PAIGE, J. M. Summary of "Automated content analysis of 'Letters from Jenny.'" In STONE, P. J., DUNPHY, D. C., SMITH, M. S. & OGILVIE, D. M. *General inquirer: A computer approach to content analysis.* Cambridge, Mass.: MIT Press, 1966.

PALMER, J. O. A dual approach to Rorschach validation: A methodological study. *Psychological Monographs,* 1951, 65, No. 325.

PARKER, C. A. As a clinician thinks . . . *Journal of counseling Psychology,* 1958, 5, 253–261.

PASAMANICK, B. & KNOBLOCH, HILDA. Early language behavior in Negro children and the testing of intelligence. *Journal of abnormal and social Psychology,* 1955, 50, 401–402.

PASCAL, G. R. & SUTTELL, BARBARA J. *The Bender-Gestalt Test.* New York: Grune & Stratton, 1951.

PATTERSON, G. R. Personal communication, 1966.

PERKINS, JULIA E. & GOLDBERG, L. Contextual effects on the MMPI. *Journal of consulting Psychology,* 1964, 28, 133–140.

PHILLIPS, R. H. Miami goes Latin under Cuban tide. *New York Times,* March 18, 1962, 111, 85 (cited in Webb, *et al.,* 1966).

PINE, F.   Thematic drive content and creativity. *Journal of Personality,* 1959, 27, 136–151 (also reprinted in Mednick & Mednick, 1963).

PIOTROWSKI, Z. A.   A new evaluation of the Thematic Apperception Test. *Psychoanalytic Review,* 1950, 37, 101–127.

PIOTROWSKI, Z. A.   The Rorschach inkblot method. In WOLMAN, B. B. (Ed.), *Handbook of clinical psychology.* New York: McGraw-Hill Book Co., 1965.

PITTELL, S. M. & MENDELSOHN, G. A.   Measurement of moral values: A review and critique. *Psychological Bulletin,* 1966, 66, 22–35.

PORTER, E. H., JR.   The development and evaluation of a measure of counseling interview procedures. *Educational and psychological Measurement,* 1943, 3, 105–126, 215–238.

PRIBRAM, K. H.   Interrelationships of psychology and the neurological disciplines. In KOCH, S. (Ed.), *Psychology: A study of science.* Vol. IV. New York: McGraw-Hill Book Co., 1962. Pp. 119–157.

PSYCHOLOGICAL CORPORATION.   *Test Services.* Bulletins of the Psychological Corporation (H. G. SEASHORE, editor), 1955.

RADCLIFFE, J. A.   Review of the Edwards Personal Preference Schedule. In BUROS, O. K. (Ed.), *Sixth mental measurements yearbook.* Highland Park, N.J.: Gryphon Press, 1965. Pp. 195–200.

RAIMY, V. C.   Self-reference in counseling interviews. *Journal of consulting Psychology,* 1948, 12, 153–163.

RAJARATNAM, N., CRONBACH, L. J., & GLESER, GOLDINE C. Generalizability of stratified-parallel tests. *Psychometrika,* 1965, 30, 39–56.

RAMSAY, R. W.   Personality and speech. *Journal of Personality and social Psychology,* 1966, 4, 166–118.

RAMZY, I. & PICKARD, P. M.   A study in the reliability of scoring the Rorschach inkblot test. *Journal of general Psychology,* 1949, 40, 3–10.

RATHBONE, J. L.   *Corrective physical education.* (5th ed.) Philadelphia: W. B. Saunders Co., 1959.

RAUSH, H. L.   On the locus of behavior-observations in multiple settings within residential treatment. *American Journal of Orthopsychiatry,* 1959, 29, 235–243.

RAUSH, H. L., DITTMAN, A. T., & TAYLOR, T. J.   The interpersonal behavior of children in residential treatment. *Journal of abnormal and social Psychology,* 1959, 58, 9–27.

RAY, M. L. & WEBB, E. J.   Speech duration effects in the Kennedy news conference. *Science,* 1966, 153, 899–901.

RAY, O. S.   Personality factors in motor learning and reminiscence. *Journal of abnormal and social Psychology,* 1959, 59, 199–203.

RAZRAN, G.   The observable unconscious and the inferable conscious in current Soviet psychophysiology. *Psychological Review,* 1961, 68, 81-147.

REEVES, MARGARET P.   An application of the semantic differential to thematic apperception test material. Unpublished doctoral dissertation, University of Illinois, 1954.

REIK, T.   *Listening with the third ear.* New York: Farrar, Straus & Giroux, Inc., 1948.

REITMAN, W. R.   Motivational induction and the behavior correlates of the achievement and affiliation motives. *Journal of abnormal and social Psychology*, 1960, 60, 8–13.

RENAUD, H. R.   Clinical correlates of the masculinity-femininity scale of the MMPI. Unpublished doctoral dissertation, University of California, 1950.

RICHARDSON, S. A., DOHRENWEND, BARBARA SNELL, & KLEIN, D. *Interviewing: Its forms and functions.* New York: Basic Books, Inc., 1965.

RIESS, B. F., SCHWARTZ, E. K., & COTTINGHAM, ALICE.   An experimental critique of assumptions underlying the Negro version of the TAT. *Journal of abnormal and social Psychology*, 1950, 45, 700–709.

RIOCH, MARGARET J.   The use of the Rorschach test in the assessment of change in patients under psychotherapy. *Psychiatry*, 1949, 12, 427–434.

RITTER, ANNA M. & ERON, L. D.   The use of the Thematic Apperception Test to differentiate normal from abnormal groups. *Journal of abnormal and social Psychology*, 1952, 47, 147–158.

ROE, ANNE.   Alcohol and creative work. I. Painters. *Quarterly Journal in the Study of Alcohol*, 1946 (a), 6, 415–467.

ROE, ANNE.   Artists and their work. *Journal of Personality*, 1946 (b), 15, 1–40.

ROE, ANNE.   Painting and personality. *Rorschach Research Exchange*, 1946 (c), 10, 86–100.

ROGERS, C. R.   *Counseling and psychotherapy.* Boston: Houghton Mifflin Co., 1942.

ROGERS, C. R.   *Client-centered therapy.* Boston: Houghton Mifflin Co., 1951.

ROGERS, C. R.   *On becoming a person.* Boston: Houghton Mifflin Co., 1961.

ROGERS, C. R. & DYMOND, R. F. (Eds.).   *Psychotherapy and personality change.* Chicago: University of Chicago Press, 1954.

ROHDE, ARMANDA R.   *Sentence completion method: Its diagnostic and clinical application to mental disorders.* New York: Ronald Press Co., 1951; 1957.

ROME, H. P., SWENSON, W. M., MATAYA, P., MCCARTHY, C. E., PEARSON, J. S., & KEATING, R. F.   Symposium on automation techniques in personality assessment. *Proceedings of the Mayo Clinic*, 1962, 37, 61–82.

ROME, H. P., MATAYA, P., PEARSON, J. S., SWENSON, W. M., & BRANNICK, T. L.   Automatic personality assessment. In STACY, R. W. & WAXMAN, B. (Eds.), *Computers in biomedical research*. Vol. I. New York: Academic Press, 1965. Pp. 505–524.

RORER, L. G.   The function of item content in MMPI responses. Unpublished doctoral dissertation, University of Minnesota, 1963.

RORER, L. G.   The great response style myth. *Psychological Bulletin*, 1965, 63, 129–156.

RORER, L. G. & GOLDBERG, L. R.   Acquiescence in the MMPI? *Educational and psychological Measurement*, 1965 (a), 25, 801–817.

RORER, L. G. & GOLDBERG, L. R.   Acquiescence and the vanishing variance component. *Journal of applied Psychology*, 1965 (b), 49, 422–430.

RORSCHACH, H.   *Psychodiagnostik*. Leipzig: Ernst Bircher Verlag, 1921.

RORSCHACH, H.   *Psychodiagnostics* (translated by PAUL LEMKAU and BERNARD KRONENBERG). Berne, Switzerland: Huber Verlag, 1942.

RORSCHACH, H. & OBERHOLZER, E.   Zur Auswertung des Formdeuteversuchs für die Psychoanalyse, 1923 (in German). In English, The application of the interpretation of form to psychoanalysis. *Journal of nervous and mental Diseases*, 1924, 60, 225–248; 359–379.

ROSEN, A.   Detection of suicidal patients: An example of some limitations in the prediction of infrequent events. *Journal of consulting Psychology*, 1954, 18, 397–403.

ROSEN, E.   Self-appraisal, personality desirability and perceived social desirability of personality traits. *Journal of abnormal and social Psychology*, 1956, 52, 151–158.

ROSEN, E. & GREGORY, IAN.   *Abnormal psychology*. Philadelphia: W. B. Saunders Co., 1965.

ROSENFELD, H. M.   Instrumental affiliative functions of facial and gestural expressions. *Journal of Personality and social Psychology*, 1966, 4, 65–72.

ROSENTHAL, R.   The effect of the experimenter on the results of psychological research. In MAHER, B. A. (Ed.), *Progress in experimental personality research*. Vol. I. New York: Academic Press, 1964. Pp. 80–114.

ROSENZWEIG, S.   *Rosenzweig Picture-Frustration Study*. Rosenzweig, Inc., 1944–1960.

ROSENZWEIG, S.   The Rosenzweig Picture-Frustration Study, Children's Form. In RUBIN, A. I. & HAWORTH, M. R. (Eds.), *Projective techniques with children*. New York: Grune & Stratton, 1960. Pp. 149–176.

ROTTER, J. B. & RAFFERTY, JANET E.   *Manual for the Rotter incomplete sentences blank, college form*. New York: Psychological Corporation, 1950.

ROZEBOOM, W. W.   *Foundations of the theory of prediction*. Homewood, Ill.: Dorsey Press, 1966.

RUBIN, L. S.   Recent advances in the chemistry of psychotic disorders. *Psychological Bulletin*, 1959, 56, 375–383.

RUBIN, L. S.   Patterns of adrenergic-cholinergic imbalance in the functional psychoses. *Psychological Review*, 1962, 69, 501–519.

RUCH, F. L.   Review of the Humm-Wadsworth Temperament Scale. In BUROS, O. K. (Ed.), *Sixth mental measurements yearbook.* Highland Park, N.J.: Gryphon Press, 1965.

RUNDQUIST, E. A.   Item and response characteristics in attitude and personality measurement. A reaction to L. G. Rorer's "the great response-style myth." *Psychological Bulletin,* 1966, 66, 166–177.

SANFORD, R. N., *et al.*   Physique, personality and scholarship. *Monograph of social Research in Child Development,* 1943, 8, No. 1.

SARASON, I. G. (Ed.)   *Contemporary research in psychology.* Princeton, N.J.: D. Van Nostrand Co., Inc., 1962.

SARASON, I. G.   *Personality: An objective approach.* New York: John Wiley & Sons, Inc., 1966.

SARBIN, T. R.   The relative accuracy of clinical and statistical predictions of academic achievement. *Psychological Bulletin,* 1941, 38, 714 (Abstract).

SARBIN, T. R.   A contribution to the study of actuarial and individual methods of prediction. *American Journal of Sociology,* 1943, 48, 593–602.

SARBIN, T. R., TAFT, R., & BAILEY, D. E.   *Clinical inference and cognitive theory.* New York: Holt, Rinehart & Winston, 1960.

SASLOW, G., MATARAZZO, J. D., & GUZE, S. B.   The stability of interaction chronograph patterns in psychiatric interviews. *Journal of consulting Psychology,* 1955, 19, 417–430.

SAUGSTAD, P.   Effect of food deprivation on perception cognition. *Psychological Bulletin,* 1966, 65, 80–90.

SAWYER, J.   Measurement and prediction, clinical and statistical. *Psychological Bulletin,* 1966, 66, 178–200.

SCHACHTEL, E. G.   Notes on Rorschach tests of 500 juvenile delinquents and a control group of 500 non-delinquent adolescents. *Journal of projective Techniques,* 1951, 15, 144–172.

SCHACHTER, S.   *The psychology of affiliation: Experimental studies of the sources of gregariousness.* Stanford, Calif.: Stanford University Press, 1959.

SCHAFER, R.   *Psychoanalytic interpretation in Rorschach testing: Theory and application.* New York: Grune & Stratton, Inc., 1954.

SCHOFIELD, W. & BALIAN, LUCY.   A comparative study of the personal histories of schizophrenic and nonpsychiatric patients. *Journal of abnormal and social Psychology,* 1959, 59, 216–225.

SCHUTZ, R. E.   Patterns of personal problems of adolescent girls. *Journal of educational Psychology,* 1958, 49, 1–5.

SCHWARTZ, L. A.   Social-situation pictures in the psychiatric interview. *American Journal of Orthopsychiatry,* 1932, 2, 124–133.

SEASHORE, H. G. & RICKS, J. H., JR.   Norms must be relevant. *Test Service Bulletin of the Psychological Corporation,* 1950, 39, 16–19.

SECHREST, L.   The psychology of personal constructs: George Kelly. In WEPMAN, J. M. & HEINE, R. W. (Eds.), *Concepts of personality.* Chicago: Aldine Publishing Co., 1963. Pp. 206–233.

SECHREST, L.   Situational sampling and contrived situations in the assessment of behavior. Unpublished manuscript, Northwestern University, 1965 (cited in Webb, *et al.,* 1966).

SECORD, P. F.   Facial features and inference processes in interpersonal perception. In TAGUIRI, R., & PETRULLO, L. (Eds.), *Person perception and interpersonal behavior.* Stanford, Calif.: Stanford University Press, 1958. Pp. 300–315.

SEEMAN, J.   A study of the process of nondirective therapy. *Journal of consulting Psychology,* 1949, 13, 157–168.

SEEMAN, W. Subtlety in structured personality tests. *Journal of consulting Psychology,* 1952, 16, 278–283.

SEIDEL, CLAUDENE.   The relationship between Klopfer's Rorschach prognostic rating scale and Phillips' case-history prognostic rating scale. *Journal of consulting Psychology,* 1960, 24, 46–53.

SELFRIDGE, O. G.   Pandemonium: A paradigm for learning. *Proceedings of the Symposium on Mechanisation of Thought Processes.* London: H. M. Stationery Office, 1959.

SELLTIZ, CLAIRE, JAHODA, MARIE, DEUTSCH, M., & COOK, S. *Research methods in social relations.* New York: Holt, Rinehart & Winston, 1964.

SHAGASS, C.   Sedation threshold: A neurophysiological tool for psychosomatic research. *Psychosomatic Medicine,* 1956, 18, 410–419.

SHAKOW, D. & ROSENZWEIG, S.   The use of the tautophone ("verbal summator") as an auditory test for the study of personality. *Character and Personality,* 1940, 8, 216–226.

SHANNON, C. & WEAVER, W.   *The mathematical theory of communication.* Urbana: University of Illinois Press, 1949.

SHAW, M. E.   The effectiveness of Whyte's rules: "How to cheat on personality tests." *Journal of applied Psychology,* 1962, 46, 21–25.

SHELDON, W. H.   *Varieties of delinquent youth.* New York: Harper & Row, 1949.

SHELDON, W. H., STEVENS, S. S., & TUCKER, W. B. *The varieties of human physique.* New York: Harper & Row, 1940.

SHELDON, W. H. & STEVENS, S. S. *The varieties of temperament.* New York: Harper & Row, 1942.

SHNEIDMAN, E. S.   Schizophrenia and the MAPS Test. A study of certain formal psycho-social aspects of fantasy production in schizophrenia as revealed by performance on the Make-A-Picture story (MAPS) test. *Genetic psychological Monographs,* 1948, 38, 145–223.

SHNEIDMAN, E. S.   *The Make-A-Picture Story Test.* New York: Psychological Corporation, 1952.

SHNEIDMAN, E. S.   Projective techniques. In WOLMAN, B. B. (Ed.), *Handbook of clinical psychology.* New York: McGraw-Hill Book Co., 1965. Pp. 498–521.

SHOBEN, E. J., JR.   Toward a concept of the normal personality. *American Psychologist,* 1957, 12, 183–189.

SHONTZ, F. C.   *Research methods in personality.* New York: Appleton-Century-Crofts, 1965.

SHRAUGER, S. & ALTROCCHI, J.   The personality of the perceiver as a factor in person perception. *Psychological Bulletin,* 1964, 62, 289–308.

SIEGEL, M. G.   The diagnostic and prognostic validity of the Rorschach test in a child guidance clinic. *American Journal of Orthopsychiatry,* 1948, 18, 119–133.

SILBERMAN, H. F. & COULSON, J. E.   Automated teaching. In BORKO, H. (Ed.), *Computer applications in the behavioral sciences.* Englewood Cliffs, N.J.: Prentice-Hall, 1962. Pp. 308–335.

SIMON, MARIA D.   Der Children's Apperception Test bei gesunden und gestörten Kindern. *Zeitschrift Diagnostik Psychologie,* 1954, 2, 195–219.

SIMPSON, J. E.   A method of measuring the social weather of children. In BARKER, R. G. (Ed.), *The stream of behavior.* New York: Appleton-Century-Crofts, 1963. Pp. 219–225.

SINES, J. O.   Actuarial methods as appropriate strategy for the validation of diagnostic tests. *Psychological Review,* 1964, 71, 517–523.

SINES, J. O.   Actuarial methods in personality assessment. In MAHER, B. (Ed.), *Progress in experimental personality research.* New York: Academic Press, 1966.

SINES, L. K.   The relative contribution of four kinds of data to accuracy in personality assessment. *Journal of consulting Psychology,* 1959, 23, 483–492.

SINGER, J. L.   Discussion: Motivational models in the simulation of neurosis. In TOMKINS, S. S. & MESSICK, S. J. (Eds.), *Computer simulation of personality.* New York: John Wiley & Sons, Inc., 1963. Pp. 181–186.

SKINNER, B. F.   The verbal summator and a method for the study of latent speech. *Journal of Psychology,* 1936, 2, 71–107.

SLOAN, I. J. & PIERCE-JONES, J.   The Bordin-Pepinsky diagnostic categories. Counselor agreement and MMPI comparisons. *Journal of counseling Psychology,* 1958, 5, 189–193.

SMITH, H. C.   *Personality adjustment,* New York: McGraw-Hill Book Co., 1961.

SMITH, K. U.   Testimony before the Senate Subcommittee on Constitutional Rights. *American Psychologist,* 1965, 20, 907–915.

SMITH, K. U. & BLOOM, R.   The electronic handwriting analyzer and motion study of writing. *Journal of applied Psychology,* 1956, 40, 302–306.

SNYDER, W. U.   An investigation of the nature of nondirective psychotherapy. *Journal of general Psychology,* 1945, 33, 193–232.

SOSKIN, W. F.   Influence of four types of data on diagnostic conceptualization in psychological testing. *Journal of abnormal and social Psychology,* 1959, 58, 69–78.

SOSKIN, W. F. & JOHN, VERA P.   The study of spontaneous talk. In BARKER, R. G. (Ed.), *The stream of behavior.* New York: Appleton-Century-Crofts, 1963. Pp. 228–281.

SPENCE, K. W. & SPENCE, JANET T.   Relation of eyelid conditioning to manifest anxiety, extraversion and rigidity. *Journal of abnormal and social Psychology,* 1964, 68, 144–149.

STACY, R. W. & WAXMAN, B. (Eds.), *Computers in biomedical research.* Vol. I. New York: Academic Press, 1965.

STAGNER, R.   The gullibility of personnel managers. *Personnel Psychology,* 1958, 11, 347–352.

STAGNER, R.   *Psychology of personality.* (3d ed.) New York: McGraw-Hill Book Co., 1961.

STARKWEATHER, J. A.   Content-free speech as a source of information about the speaker. *Journal of abnormal and social Psychology,* 1956, 52, 394–402.

STEIN, M. I.   *The Thematic Apperception Test.* Reading, Mass.: Addison-Wesley Publishing Co., 1955.

STEPHENSON, W.   *The study of behavior: Q-Technique and its methodology.* Chicago: University of Chicago Press, 1953.

STERN, G. G., STEIN, M. I., & BLOOM, B. S.   *Methods in personality assessment.* New York: The Free Press, 1956.

STEVENS, S. S.   Mathematics, measurement and psychophysics. In STEVENS, S. S. (Ed.), *Handbook of experimental Psychology.* New York: John Wiley & Sons, Inc., 1951. Pp. 1–49.

STONE, D. R.   A recorded auditory apperception test as a new projection technique. *Journal of Psychology,* 1950, 29, 349–353.

STONE, P. J.   Colloquium delivered at the Carnegie Institute of Technology, 1964.

STONE, P. J., BALES, R. F., NAMENWIRTH, Z., & OGILVIE, D. M.   The general inquirer: A computer system for content analysis and retrieval based on the sentence as a unit of information. *Behavioral Science,* 1962, 7, 484–498.

STRICKER, L. J.   Review of the Edwards Personal Preference Schedule. In BUROS, O. K. (Ed.), *Sixth mental measurements yearbook,* Highland Park, N.J.: Gryphon Press, 1965. Pp. 200–207.

STRONG, E. K.   *Vocational interests of men and women.* Stanford: Stanford University Press, 1943.

STRONG, E. K.   Permanence of interest scores after 22 years. *Journal of applied Psychology,* 1951, 35, 89–92.

STRONG, E. K. *Vocational interests eighteen years after college.* Minneapolis: University of Minnesota Press, 1955.

STRONG, E. K., JR. Reworded versus new interest items. *Journal of applied Psychology*, 1963, 47, 111–116.

STRUPP, H. H. & WALLACH, M. S. A further study of psychiatrists' responses in quasi-therapy situations. *Behavioral Science*, 1965, 10, 113–134.

SULLIVAN, H. S. *The interpersonal theory of psychiatry.* New York: W. W. Norton & Co., Inc., 1953.

SULLIVAN, H. S. *The psychiatric interview.* New York: W. W. Norton & Co., Inc., 1954.

SUNDBERG, N. D. The acceptability of "fake" versus "bona fide" personality test interpretations. *Journal of abnormal and social Psychology*, 1955, 50, 145–147.

SUNDBERG, N. D. The practice of psychological testing in clinical services in the United States. *American Psychologist*, 1961, 16, 79–83.

SUNDBERG, N. D. & TYLER, LEONA E. *Clinical psychology: An introduction to research and practice.* New York: Appleton-Century-Crofts, 1962.

SUPER, D. E. The Biographical inventory as a method for describing adjustment and predicting success. *Bulletin of the International Association of applied Psychology*, 1960, 9, 18–39.

SWARTZ, J. D. & HOLTZMAN, W. H. Group method of administration for the Holtzman Inkblot Technique. *Journal of clinical Psychology*, 1963, 19, 433–441.

SWEETBAUM, H. A. Comparison of the effects of introversion-extraversion and anxiety on conditioning. *Journal of abnormal and social Psychology*, 1963, 66, 249–254.

SWENTZELL, R. & ROBERTS, A. H. On the interaction of the subject and the experiment in the matching model. *Psychometrika*, 1964, 29, 87–101.

SYMON, SHEENA M. An investigation of the relationship between conditioning and introversion-extraversion in normal students. Unpublished M.A. thesis, University of Aberdeen, 1958.

SYMONDS, P. M. *Adolescent fantasy.* New York: Columbia University Press, 1949.

SYMONDS, P. M. & JENSEN, A. R. *From adolescent to adult.* New York: Columbia University Press, 1961.

TAFT, JESSIE. The function of a mental hygienist in a children's agency. *Proceedings of the National Conference of Social Work, 1927.* Chicago; University of Chicago Press, 1927.

TAFT, R. The ability to judge people. *Psychological Bulletin*, 1955, 51, 1–23.

TAFT, R. Multiple methods of personality assessment. *Psychological Bulletin,* 1959, 56, 333–352.

TAULBEE, E. S. & SISSON, B. D. Configurational analysis of MMPI profiles of psychiatric groups. *Journal of consulting Psychology,* 1957, 21, 413–417.

TAYLOR, C. W. & ELLISON, R. L. Biographical predictors of specific performance. *Science,* 1967, 155, 1075–1080.

TAYLOR, H. C. & RUSSELL, J. T. The relationship of validity coefficients to the practical effectiveness of tests in selection. *Journal of applied Psychology,* 1939, 23, 565–578.

TAYLOR, JANET A. The relationship of anxiety to the conditioned eyelid response. *Journal of experimental Psychology,* 1951, 41, 81–92.

TAYLOR, JANET A. A personality scale of manifest anxiety. *Journal of abnormal and social Psychology,* 1953, 48, 285–290.

TAYLOR, JANET A. Drive theory and manifest anxiety. *Psychological Bulletin,* 1956, 53, 303–320.

TELLEGEN, A. The Minnesota Multiphasic Personality Inventory. In ABT, L. E. & RIESS, B. F. (Eds.), *Progress in clinical psychology.* Vol. VI. New York: Grune & Stratton, 1964. Pp. 30–48.

TELLEGEN, A. Direction of measurement: A source of misinterpretation. *Psychological Bulletin,* 1965, 63, 233–243.

TENDLER, A. D. A preliminary report on a test for emotional insight. *Journal of applied Psychology,* 1930, 14, 123–136.

THOMAS, H. Problems of character change. In DAVID, H. P., & VON BRACKEN, H., (Eds.), *Perspectives in personality theory.* New York: Basic Books, Inc., 1961.

THOMPSON, C. E. The Thompson modification of the Thematic Apperception Test. *Rorschach Research Exchange,* 1949, 13, 469–478.

THORNDIKE, R. L. *Personnel selection: Test and measurement technique.* New York: John Wiley & Sons, Inc., 1949.

THORNDIKE, R. L. Review of the California Psychological Inventory. In BUROS, O. K. (Ed.), *Fifth mental measurements yearbook.* Highland Park, N.J.: Gryphon Press, 1959. P. 99.

THORNDIKE, R. L. & HAGEN, ELIZABETH. *Measurement and evaluation in psychology and education.* New York: John Wiley & Sons, Inc., 1961.

THORNE, F. C. *Clinical judgment: A study of clinical errors.* Brandon, Vermont: Journal of Clinical Psychology, 1961.

THORNTON, G. R. The effect upon judgments of personality traits of varying a single factor in a photograph. *Journal of social Psychology,* 1943, 18, 127–148.

TOMKINS, S. S. *The Thematic Apperception Test.* New York: Grune & Stratton, 1947.

TOMKINS, S. S. The present status of the Thematic Apperception Test. *American Journal of Orthopsychiatry,* 1949, 19, 358–362.

TOMKINS, S. S.   Simulation of personality: The interrelationships between affect, memory, thinking, perception, and action. In TOMKINS, S. S. & MESSICK, S. J. (Eds.), *Computer simulation of personality*. New York: John Wiley & Sons, Inc., 1963. Pp. 3–57.

TOMKINS, S. S. & MESSICK, S. J. (Eds.).   *Computer simulation of personality: Frontier of psychological theory*. New York: John Wiley & Sons, Inc., 1963.

TORGERSON, W. S.   *Theory and methods of scaling*. New York: John Wiley & Sons, Inc., 1958.

TRIPP, C. A., FLUCKIGER, F. A., & WEINBERG, G. H.   Measurement of handwriting variables. *Perceptual and motor Skills*, 1957, 7, 279–294.

TUREK, E. V. & HOWELL, R. J.   The effect of variable success and failure situations on the intensity of need for achievement. *Journal of social Psychology*, 1959, 49, 267–273.

TYLER, LEONA E.   *Tests and measurements*. Englewood Cliffs, N.J.: Prentice-Hall, Inc., 1963.

TYLER, LEONA E.   *The psychology of human differences*. (3d ed.) New York: Appleton-Century-Crofts, 1965.

ULRICH, L. & TRUMBO, D.   The selection interview since 1949. *Psychological Bulletin*, 1965, 63, 110–116.

URBAN, W. H.   The Draw-A-Person. Beverly Hills, Calif.: Western Psychological Services, 1963.

VAN ATTA, R. E.   A method for the study of clinical thinking. *Journal of counseling Psychology*, 1966, 13, 259–266.

VANCE, F. L.   Review of Bell's Adjustment Inventory. In BUROS, O. K. (Ed.), *Sixth mental measurements yearbook*. Highland Park, N.J.: Gryphon Press, 1965. Pp. 148–149.

VANDENBERG, S. G.   Medical diagnosis by computer: Recent attempts and outlook for the future. *Behavioral Science*, 1960, 5, 170–174.

VANDENBERG, S. G.   The hereditary abilities study: Hereditary components in a psychological test battery. *American Journal of human Genetics*, 1962, 14, 220–237.

VENABLES, P. H.   Change in motor response with increase and decrease in task difficulty in normal industrial and psychiatric patient subjects. *British Journal of Psychology*, 1955, 46, 101–110.

VERNON, P. E.   The Rorschach inkblot test, II. *British Journal of medical Psychology*, 1933, 13, 179–205.

VERNON, P. E.   The matching method applied to investigations of personality. *Psychological Bulletin*, 1936 (a), 33, 149–177.

VERNON, P. E.   The evaluation of the matching method. *Journal of educational Psychology*, 1936 (b), 27, 1–17.

VERNON, P. E.   Mental faculties and factors, and landmarks in the development of factor analysis. *The structure of human abilities*. New York: John Wiley & Sons, Inc., 1950.

VERNON, P. E. *Personality tests and assessments.* London: Methuen, 1953.

VERNON, P. E. *Personality assessment: A critical survey.* London: Methuen & Co., Ltd.; New York: John Wiley & Sons, Inc., 1964.

VEROFF, J., ATKINSON, J. W., FELD, SHEILA, & GURIN, G. The use of thematic apperception to assess motivation in a nationwide interview study. *Psychological Monographs,* 1960, 94, No. 12 (Whole No. 499).

VOGEL, M. D. The relation of personality factors to GSR conditioning of alcoholics: An exploratory study. *Canadian Journal of Psychology,* 1960, 14, 275–280.

VOGEL, M. D. GSR conditioning and personality factors in alcoholics and normals. *Journal of abnormal and social Psychology,* 1961, 63, 417–421.

WAGNER, M. E. & SCHUBERT, H. J. P. Figure drawing norms: Reliability and validity indices for normal adolescents. II. Development of a pictoral scale of draw-a-person quality. *American Psychologist,* 1955, 30, 321.

WALKER, R. N. Body build and behavior in young children: I. Body build and nursery school teachers' ratings. *Monographs of social Research in child Development,* 1962, 27, No. 3 (Whole No. 84).

WALKER, R. N. Body build and behavior in young children: II: Body build and parents' ratings. *Child Development,* 1963, 34, 1–23.

WALTHER, R. H. Self-description as a predictor of success or failure in foreign service clerical jobs. *Journal of applied Psychology,* 1961, 45, 16–21.

WARD, J., JR. Comments on "the paramorphic representation of clinical judgment." *Psychological Bulletin,* 1962, 59, 74–76.

WATLEY, D. J. & MARTIN, H. T. Prediction of academic success in a college of business administration. *Personnel and Guidance Journal,* 1962, 41, 147–154.

WEBB, E. J., CAMPBELL, D. T., SCHWARTZ, R. D., & SECHREST, L. *Unobtrusive measures: Nonreactive research in the social sciences.* Chicago: Rand McNally & Co., 1966.

WEISS, R. L. & MOOS, R. H. Response biases in the MMPI: A sequential analysis. *Psychological Bulletin,* 1965, 63, 403–409.

WELLS, F. L. & REUSCH, J. *Mental examiner's handbook.* (2d ed.) New York: Psychological Corporation, 1945.

WELSH, G. S. An extension of Hathaway's MMPI profile coding system. *Journal of consulting Psychology,* 1948, 12, 343–344 (also reprinted in Welsh and Dahlstrom, 1956).

WELSH, G. S. An anxiety index and an internationalization ratio for the MMPI. *Journal of consulting Psychology,* 1952, 16, 65–72 (also reprinted in Welsh & Dahlstrom, 1956).

WELSH, G. S. & DAHLSTROM, W. G. (Eds.). *Basic readings on the MMPI in psychology and medicine.* Minneapolis: University of Minnesota Press, 1956.

WESCOE, W. C. The autonomic nervous system; general considerations. In DRILL, J. A. (Ed.), *Pharmacology in medicine.* New York: McGraw-Hill Book Co., 1959. Pp. 335–349.

WESMAN, A. G. Faking personality test scores in a simulated employment situation. *Journal of applied Psychology,* 1952, 36, 112–113.

WEXLER, D., MENDELSON, J., LEIDERMAN, P. H., & SOLOMON, P. Sensory deprivation, a technique for studying psychiatric aspects of stress. *Archives of Neurology and Psychiatry,* 1958, 79, 225–233.

WEYL, H. *Philosophy of mathematics and natural science.* Princeton, N.J.: Princeton University Press, 1949.

WHERRY, R. J. Test selection and suppressor variables. *Psychometrika,* 1946, 11, 239–247.

WHIPPLE, G. M. *Manual of mental and physical tests.* Baltimore: Warwick & York, 1910.

WHYTE, W. H. *The organization man.* New York: Doubleday & Co., Inc., 1956.

WIENER, D. N. Subtle and obvious keys for the MMPI. *Journal of consulting Psychology,* 1948, 12, 164–170.

WIGGINS, J. S. Strategic, method, and stylistic variance. *Psychological Bulletin,* 1962, 59, 224–242.

WIGGINS, J. S. Social desirability estimation and "faking good" well. *Educational and psychological Measurement,* 1966, 26, 329–341.

WIGGINS, NANCY. Individual viewpoints of social desirability. *Psychological Bulletin,* 1966, 66, 68–77.

WILLIAMS, J. G. A process for detecting correlations between dichotomous variables. Unpublished Master of Science dissertation, Carnegie Institute of Technology, 1963.

WILLIAMS, J. G. & KLEINMUNTZ, B. Configural scoring by digital computer. Unpublished materials, Carnegie Institute of Technology, 1966.

WINCH, R. F. & MORE, D. M. Does TAT add information to interviews? Statistical analysis of the increment. *Journal of clinical Psychology,* 1956, 12, 316–321.

WINDLE, C. Psychological tests in psychopath's logical prognosis. *Psychological Bulletin,* 1952, 49, 451–482.

WINFIELD, D. L. An investigation of the relationship between intelligence and the statistical reliability of the MMPI. *Journal of clinical Psychology,* 1952, 8, 146–148.

WIRT, R. D. Review of the CAT. In BUROS, O. K. (Ed.), *Sixth mental measurements yearbook.* Highland Park, N.J.: Gryphon Press, 1965. P. 425.

WITTENBORN, J. R. *Wittenborn psychiatric rating scales.* New York: Psychological Corporation, 1955. (Revised, 1964)

WITTENBORN, J. R. & HOLZBERG, J. D.   The Rorschach and descriptive diagnosis. *Journal of consulting Psychology*, 1951, 15, 460–463.

WITTSON, C. L. & HUNT, W. A.   The predictive value of the brief psychiatric interview. *American Journal of Psychiatry*, 1951, 107, 582–585.

WOODWORTH, R. S.   *Personal Data Sheet.* Chicago: Stoelting, 1920.

WORCHEL, P. & BYRNE, D. (Eds.).   *Personality change.* New York: John Wiley & Sons, Inc., 1964.

World almanac and book of facts.   New York: The *New York World Telegram*, 1966.

WYATT, F. A.   The scoring and analysis of the TAT. *Journal of Psychology*, 1947, 24, 319–330.

YATES, A. J.   The validity of some psychological tests of brain damage. *Psychological Bulletin*, 1954, 51, 359–379.

ZIGLER, E. & PHILLIPS, L.   Psychiatric diagnosis: a critique. *Journal of abnormal and social Psychology*, 1961, 3, 607–618.

ZUBIN, J.   Rorschach test. In Mettler, F. A. (Ed.), *Columbia Greystone Associates: Selective partial ablations of the frontal cortex.* New York, Harper & Row, 1949. Pp. 283–295.

ZUBIN, J., ERON, L. D., & SCHUMER, FLORENCE.   *An experimental approach to projective techniques.* New York: John Wiley & Sons, Inc., 1965.

ZULLIGER, H.   *Einführung in den Behn-Rorschach-Test.* Berne: Verlag Hans Huber, 1941.

ZULLIGER, H.   *Der Behn-Rorschach Test. I. Band: Text.* Berne: Verlag Hans Huber, 1952.

ZULLIGER, H.   *The Behn-Rorschach Test.* Berne: Verlag Hans Huber, 1956.

INDEXES

AUTHOR INDEX

This book has been set in 10 point Century Expanded, leaded 3 points, and 9 point Century Expanded, leaded 2 points. Part numbers are in 24 point Spartan Medium, and part titles are in 18 point Spartan Medium italics. Chapter numbers are in 24 point News Gothic, and chapter titles are in 18 point Spartan Medium. The size of the type page is 27 x 45½ picas.